fourteenthedition

YOUR COLLEGE EXPERIENCE

Strategies for Success

D0071914

John N. Gardner

Chair and Chief Executive Officer, John N. Gardner Institute for Excellence in Undergraduate Education
Brevard, North Carolina

Distinguished Professor Emeritus, Library and Information Science
Senior Fellow, National Resource Center for The First-Year Experience and Students in Transition
University of South Carolina, Columbia

Betsy O. Barefoot

Senior Scholar
John N. Gardner Institute for Excellence in Undergraduate Education
Brevard, North Carolina

bedford/st.martin's
Macmillan Learning
Boston | New York

For Bedford/St. Martin's

Vice President: Leasa Burton
Senior Program Director: Erika Gutierrez
Program Manager: Allen Cooper
Director of Content Development: Jane Knetzger
Development Editor: Melanie McFadyen
Associate Editor: Katherine McInerney
Director of Media Editorial: Adam Whitehurst
Media Editor: Nicole Erazo
Marketing Manager: Andrea Burgoa
Director, Content Management Enhancement: Tracey Kuehn
Senior Managing Editor: Lisa Kinne
Senior Content Project Manager: Peter Jacoby
Workflow Manager: Lisa McDowell
Production Supervisor: Robin Besofsky
Director of Design, Content Management: Diana Blume
Interior Design: Jerilyn DiCarlo/Cenveo Publisher Services
Cover Design: William Boardman
Text Permissions Manager: Allison Ziebka
Text Permissions Researcher: Udayakumar Kannadasan, Lumina Datamatics
Photo Permissions Editor: Angie Boehler
Photo Researcher: Krystyna Borgen, Lumina Datamatics
Director of Digital Production: Keri deManigold
Advanced Media Project Manager: Sarah O'Connor Kepes
Copyeditor: Julie Dock
Indexer: Sonya Dintaman
Composition: Lumina Datamatics, Inc.
Cover Image: Trendsetter Images/Shutterstock
Printing and Binding: LSC Communications

Copyright © 2021, 2018, 2016, 2014, 2012 by Bedford/St. Martin's

All rights reserved. No part of this book may be reproduced, stored in a retrieval system, or transmitted in any form or by any means, electronic, mechanical, photocopying, recording, or otherwise, except as may be expressly permitted by the applicable copyright statutes or in writing by the Publisher.

Manufactured in the United States of America.

1   2   3   4   5   6
25   24   23   22   21   20

For information, write: Bedford/St. Martin's, 75 Arlington Street, Boston, MA 02116

ISBN 978-1-319-20072-5   (Student Edition)
ISBN 978-1-319-35164-9   (Loose-leaf Edition)

Acknowledgments

Acknowledgments and copyrights appear on the same page as the text and art selections they cover; these acknowledgments and copyrights constitute an extension of the copyright page.

At the time of publication all Internet URLs published in this text were found to accurately link to their intended website.

Dear Student,

More than ever before, a college education is an essential step in preparing you for almost any career. With almost no exceptions, employers today require that job applicants have a college degree.

Higher education is becoming more expensive, and some people are questioning whether a college degree is worth the cost. Yes, college is expensive, but the benefits of a college education are well worth the price tag. According to current statistics, college-educated people receive better salaries and enjoy healthier lives, more confidence, and more promising futures for their children than those who do not attend college. Of course we can all name a few exceptions: Mark Zuckerberg of Facebook and Bill Gates of Microsoft were college dropouts who still managed to be highly successful. Such success stories are very rare, however.

While you might have many reasons for being in college, we hope your primary goals are to learn and ultimately to graduate, and you will be more likely to graduate if you have a successful first year. When we were in our first year of college, college success courses, with few exceptions, did not exist, and there was no "textbook" like *Your College Experience* that provided strategies for making the most of college. Most colleges and universities allowed new students to sink or swim. As a result, some students did well, some hardly survived, and some dropped out or flunked out.

Beyond graduation, some of you will want to continue your education in professional or graduate school, but others will want to begin a career. While it may be tough to land your ideal job immediately, your college education is an investment that will make you competitive in the marketplace.

You are likely reading *Your College Experience* because you are enrolled in a college success course—a special course designed to help you be successful. Although this book might seem different from your other textbooks, we believe that it could be the most important book you read this term because it's all about improving your chances for success in college and in your career. This book will help you identify your own strengths, as well as areas where you need to improve. We know that if you apply the ideas in this book to your everyday life, you are more likely to enjoy your time in college, graduate, and achieve your life goals.

As college professors, researchers, and administrators with many years of experience working with first-year students, we know that starting college can be challenging. But through your college success course, the faculty, staff, and academic resources on your campus will help you meet that challenge. Welcome to college!

John N. Gardner

Betsy O. Barefoot

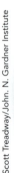

Scott Treadway/John. N. Gardner Institute

"As authors we especially wanted our book to be both timely and inclusive of the needs, strengths, hopes, dreams, and concerns of all of today's beginning college students. We thank Macmillan's editorial board for providing us with their wise feedback, counsel, and advocacy for what America's college students need the most."

John N. Gardner brings unparalleled experience to this authoritative text for first-year seminar courses. He is the recipient of the University of South Carolina's highest award for teaching excellence. He has twenty-five years of experience directing and teaching in the most respected and most widely emulated first-year seminar in the country: the University 101 course at the University of South Carolina. He is recognized as one of the country's leading educators for his role in initiating and orchestrating an international reform movement to improve students' transition to college. He is also the founding leader of two influential higher education centers that support campuses in their efforts to improve the learning and retention of first-year college students: the National Resource Center for The First-Year Experience and Students in Transition at the University of South Carolina (**sc.edu/fye**), and as the cofounder with his fellow author and wife, Betsy O. Barefoot, of the nonprofit John N. Gardner Institute for Excellence in Undergraduate Education (**jngi.org**), based in Brevard, North Carolina. The experiential basis for all of John Gardner's work is his own miserable first year of college, part of which he spent on academic probation—an experience that he hopes to prevent for this book's readers.

Scott Treadway/John. N. Gardner Institute

"We want to offer our sincere thanks to the members of the editorial board for helping keep us attuned to the diversity in our classrooms and how, within a college success framework, we can address the particular issues and diverse needs that first-year students bring with them to college."

Betsy O. Barefoot is a writer, researcher, and teacher whose special area of scholarship is the first year of college. During her tenure at the University of South Carolina from 1988 to 1999, she served as codirector for research and publications at the National Resource Center for The First-Year Experience and Students in Transition. She taught University 101, in addition to special-topics graduate courses on the first-year experience and the principles of college teaching. She conducts first-year seminar faculty training workshops around the United States and in other countries, and she is frequently called on to evaluate first-year seminar outcomes. She currently serves as cofounder and Senior Scholar in the Gardner Institute for Excellence in Undergraduate Education. In that role she works with both two- and four-year campuses to evaluate all components of the first year, especially first-year seminars.

oureditorialboard

"What we're doing is looking at the language, the content, the imagery, and the presentation in each chapter of the textbook to find out if we can do better with regard to diversity and inclusiveness. I think this should be at the forefront of what we do as educators: being mindful of the population that we serve. Our goal is for the textbook to represent the world that students live in."

Dorien Martin

Elizabeth Martin
Georgia State University, editorial board member

The Story

This revision of *Your College Experience* 14e was developed with the help of scholars in the fields of communication and college success, many of whom have held elected advocacy roles with the National Communication Association (NCA), with the John N. Gardner Institute for Excellence in Undergraduate Education, or with their own institutions. Together, this team of experts helped us revise photos and text examples throughout every chapter with the goal of creating a better, more inclusive experience for students and instructors. They are the Editorial Board for Diversity, Inclusion, and Culturally Responsive Pedagogy:

- **Dr. James Anderson,** Fayetteville State University
- **Tasha F. Davis,** Austin Community College
- **Bryan M. Dewsbury,** University of Rhode Island
- **Erin Doran,** Iowa State University
- **Danielle Harkins,** Germanna Community College
- **Tina Harris,** University of Georgia

- **Jill Kramer,** JRK Consulting LLC
- **Elizabeth Martin,** Georgia State University (pictured on this page)
- **Rody Randon,** Phoenix College
- **Dr. Molly J. Scanlon,** Nova Southeastern University
- **Myra Washington,** University of New Mexico

The Mission

To advance and evolve our understanding of diversity, inclusiveness, and culturally responsive pedagogy and to promote their fundamental, not ancillary, place in the development of learning materials.

What Does This Mean for Students?

Culturally responsive pedagogy promotes self-reflection and critical thinking among students and prepares them for global citizenship, a diverse workplace, and advocacy in various forms.

To learn more about our editorial board, their work, and their mission, visit macmillanlearning.com/college/us/.

David Schaffer/Getty Images

SDI Productions/Getty Images

nycshooter/Getty Images

Huntstock/Brand X Pictures/Getty Images

Phase4Studios/Shutterstock

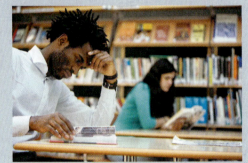

Track5/Getty Images

Hero Images/Media Bakery

Monkey Business Images/Shutterstock

Chris Ryan/Getty Images

Hill Street Studios/Getty Images

Hero Images/Getty Images

William Perugini/Shutterstock

Ariel Skelley/DigitalVision/Getty Images

PhotoAlto/Sandro Di Carlo Darsa/Getty Images

Image Source/Getty Images

brief contents

contents

PART ONE   FOUNDATIONS

David Schaffer/Getty Images

⌖ Indicates sections that refer to high-impact practices. See page 23 for more information.

SDI Productions/Getty Images

2 CULTIVATING MOTIVATION, RESILIENCE, AND EMOTIONAL INTELLIGENCE 29

nycshooter/Getty Images

3 TIME MANAGEMENT 49

Huntstock/Brand X
Pictures/Getty Images

PART TWO PREPARING TO LEARN

Phase4Studios/Shutterstock

🎯 Indicates sections that refer to high-impact practices. See page 23 for more information.

Monkey Business Images/
Shutterstock

Chris Ryan/Getty Images

⌖ Indicates sections that refer to high-impact practices. See page 23 for more information.

Hill Street Studios/Getty Images

PART THREE   PREPARING FOR LIFE

Hero Images/Getty Images

 Indicates sections that refer to high-impact practices. See page 23 for more information.

William Perugini/Shutterstock

Ariel Skelley/DigitalVision/
Getty Images

PhotoAlto/Sandro Di
Carlo Darsa/Getty Images

 Indicates sections that refer to high-impact practices. See page 23 for more information.

Image Source/Getty Images

yourturn features

⚙ Indicates Your Turn activities that involve high-impact practices. All Work Together and Write and Reflect activities involve high-impact practices.

Wellness Toolkit ✓

Wellness is a concept that encompasses the care of your mind, body, and spirit, and involves making healthy choices and achieving balance throughout your life. Below we have listed several key elements of physical and mental wellness, and we have pointed out where you can find more information on these elements throughout this textbook. Use this Toolkit as a reference whenever you feel that you could use more help on improving your physical and mental well-being.

In addition, you can find additional resources on each of these topics at the end of the chapters in which the topics are referenced (see p. 28 for an example). If you need immediate assistance in any of these areas, please reach out to the counseling center or other resource centers on your campus, a medical professional, or a licensed therapist.

for more on...	read this...

❶ Getting enough sleep

> **Getting Enough Sleep to Maintain Wellness** (Ch. 14, p. 316) for ways to establish better sleeping habits

> **TechTip: Turn Off Your Screens for Better Sleep** (Ch. 14, p. 324) for tips on preventing technology from disturbing your sleep

> **Connecting Memory to Deep Learning** (Ch. 8, p. 170) to understand the importance of getting enough sleep to retain information

> **Table 1.2: The Choices You Will Make** (Ch. 1, p. 23) to determine how you can make the choice to maintain a healthy sleep schedule

❷ Eating well and exercising

> **Managing Your Energy** (Ch. 3, p. 63) for an overview of how you can better manage your energy by establishing routines around your daily patterns of productivity

> **Prepare Physically** (Ch. 9, p. 188) for tips on how physical health can relieve stress and help you with studying for and taking exams

> **The Importance of Good Nutrition** (Ch. 14, p. 312) for an overview of the connection between what you eat and drink, your overall health and well-being, and stress

> **Exercising to Maintain Wellness** (Ch. 14, p. 315) to consider how regular exercise can help you manage stress, stay fit, and improve your overall health

❸ Managing stress

> **Managing Stress to Maintain Wellness** (Ch. 14, p. 311) to understand when your stress is out of control and how to seek help

> **Studying to Understand and Remember** (Ch. 8, p. 178) for tips on alleviating stress and developing a deeper understanding of your course information

❹ Managing anxiety

> **Anxiety** (Ch. 14, p. 318) for an overview of the impact of anxiety on college students and symptoms that it may cause

> **Overcoming Test Anxiety** (Ch. 9, p. 199) and **Strategies for Dealing with Test Anxiety** (Ch. 9, p. 202) for ways to identify and overcome test anxiety

> **Using Your Research in Presentations** (Ch. 10, p. 229) and **Guidelines for Successful Speaking** (Ch. 10, p. 229) for tips on how to manage presentation and speech anxiety

for more on...	read this...

⑤ Managing depression

> **Depression** (Ch. 14, p. 319) to recognize some of the symptoms of depression and understand the importance of reaching out to a health care professional before depression becomes serious

> **Suicide** (Ch. 14, p. 319) for some common indicators of suicidal thoughts, and for some information on contacting a professional for help

⑥ Dealing with loneliness

> **Loneliness** (Ch. 14, p. 318) for tips on how to develop meaningful relationships with people you can talk to, focusing on the quality, not quantity of those relationships

> **Get Involved** (Ch. 12, p. 280) for ways to get involved and make new friends on campus

⑦ Dealing with homesickness

> **Homesickness** (Ch. 12, p. 271) for tips on how to overcome homesickness by reaching out to others on campus

⑧ Using social media in a healthy way

> **TechTip: Maintain a Healthy Relationship with Social Media** (Ch. 12, p. 282) for tips on navigating social media in healthy, productive ways

> **Communicating in a Digital Age** (Ch. 12, p. 277) for advice on protecting yourself online, matching your messages to the digital channel you're using, and knowing when to move a conversation offline

> **Table 12.1: Best Practices for Online Communication** (Ch. 12, p. 278) for key points to remember when communicating online

> **Cyberbullying** (Ch. 12, p. 279) to understand the serious impacts and ways to get help if you have experienced online harassment

> See **Characteristics of Today's Economy** (Ch. 11, p. 240) and **Finding Career Resources on Your Campus** (Ch. 11, p. 247), for a discussion of how social media can be a tool for networking and job seeking

⑨ Maintaining your sexual health

> **Maintaining Sexual Health** (Ch. 12, p. 274) for information on communicating about safe sex, avoiding sexually transmitted infections (STIs), and using birth control

> **Protecting Yourself and Others against Sexual Assault and Violence** (Ch. 12, p. 276) for ways to help survivors of, and protect yourself and others against, sexual assault and violence

⑩ Avoiding harmful substances

> **Alcohol and Other Substances** (Ch. 14, p. 320) for an overview of the harmful effects of alcohol, tobacco, marijuana, and prescription drugs

> **Alcohol Use** (Ch. 14, p. 321) to learn about some of the risks of drinking alcohol, and some ways to reduce the harmful effects that alcohol can produce

> **Tobacco** (Ch. 14, p. 322) for information on the health hazards and financial costs associated with smoking tobacco and vaping

> **Marijuana** (Ch. 14, p. 322) for some information on the legalization of marijuana in a growing number of states in the United States

> **Prescription Drugs** (Ch. 14, p. 323) for a brief overview of the risks of becoming addicted to prescription medication

preface

Anyone who teaches beginning college students knows how much they have changed in recent years. Today's students are increasingly job focused, technologically adept, and concerned about the future. More than ever, students worry about how they will pay for college. Recently, popular media sources such as the *Washington Post* have reported that many people are asking whether the benefits of college are worth the cost.[1] While it is tempting to focus on the few individuals who succeed without finishing college, we know that for the overwhelming majority of individuals, a college degree is more essential than ever before.

Today, we see diverse students of all ages and backgrounds enrolling in two- and four-year public and private institutions, bringing with them the hopes and dreams that a college education can help fulfill—as well as expectations that may or may not be realistic. *Your College Experience* is designed specifically to give all students the practical help they need to gain self-knowledge, set goals, succeed, and stay in college so that those hopes and dreams have a better chance of becoming realities. To help with this, the revision of the Fourteenth Edition was supported with the help of our publisher's Editorial Board for Diversity, Inclusion, and Culturally Responsive Pedagogy, whose feedback helped inspire changes to ensure that our words, examples, and images are designed to foster diversity, inclusion, and cultural awareness throughout the text.

While maintaining its approach and emphasis on the importance of goal setting, *Your College Experience* teaches skills and strategies in areas where students often need the most help and that are critical for success in college and the workplace. These include time management, academic reading, test taking, research, and career preparation. At a time when institutions are moving to more online instruction, increasing class sizes, and mainstreaming developmental students, students will need more individual attention and the skills to ask for the help they need. They also have an increased need for resources to improve their mental health and physical wellness, particularly in relation to anxiety, loneliness, and depression. This Fourteenth Edition has increased coverage of mental health and wellness, with resources for students who feel that they are struggling and need help. Of course, concerns about student retention remain, as do pressures on college success educators to do more with less. These realities of college and university life mean that giving students strategies through excellent text material they can use immediately is more important than ever.

To help you meet the challenges of engaging and retaining today's students, we have created a complete package of support materials,

---

[1] www.washingtonpost.com/blogs/she-the-people/wp/2014/08/22/do-the-benefits-of-a-college-education-outweigh-the-cost

including an Instructor's Annotated Edition and an Instructor's Manual. In the Instructor's Annotated Edition, you will find clearly marked retention strategies and activities to help you engage and retain students. These activities, and all of the instructor support materials, are valuable for both new and experienced instructors as they prepare to teach the college success course.

What has not changed in the fifty years since the inception of the contemporary first-year college success course is our level of commitment to and deep understanding of our students. Although this edition of *Your College Experience* has been significantly revised, it is still based on our collective knowledge and experience in teaching new students and on the practices of hundreds of institutions and thousands of educators who offer college success courses. It is grounded in the significant and growing body of research on student success and retention and includes valuable contributions from leading experts in the field. Most of all, it is a text born from our career-long devotion to students and to their success. Simply put, we do not like to see students fail to achieve their potential. We are confident that if students both read and heed the information herein, they will become more successfully engaged in the college experience, learn, and persist to graduation.

We have written this text for students of any age in both residential and commuter institutions. Our writing style is intended to convey respect and admiration for students while recognizing their continued need for challenge and support. We have addressed topics that our experience, our research, and our reviewers tell us are concerns for students at any type of college or university and with any kind of educational background. We have also embedded various reading and writing strategies to support students' efforts to comprehend the material and apply the skills presented in each chapter, and we have included technology tools and tips that can enhance students' studying experience.

Your College Experience uses a simple and logical organization. Part 1, Foundations, begins with a chapter that covers strategies for thriving in college, in life, and opportunities for students to explore their purpose for attending college and to learn techniques to set goals. Next, in Chapter 2, students examine ways to cultivate motivation, resilience, and emotional intelligence. Students are armed with solid time-management strategies in Chapter 3, and then they explore learning preferences in Chapter 4. The chapters in Part 2, Preparing to Learn, enumerates essential learning skills like critical thinking, reading, note taking, studying, and test taking, and guides students in communicating and finding information. Part 3, Preparing for Life, includes chapters that emphasize practical and realistic considerations such as majors and careers, relationships, diversity, physical and mental health and wellness, and money management.

Whether you are considering this textbook for use in your college success course or have already made a decision to adopt it, we thank you for your interest, and we trust that you will find it to be a valuable teaching aid. We also hope that this book will guide you and your campus in understanding the broad range of issues that can affect student success.

A Revision Focused on Research-Based Strategies to Help Students Succeed

While retaining many of the hallmark features that characterize the Gardner/Barefoot text, new areas of emphasis introduced in the Thirteenth Edition have been further developed in the new edition and remain grounded in the latest research on student success.

1. **A focus on mental health coverage and wellness.** An exciting aspect of the Fourteenth Edition is the expanded coverage of mental health and wellness. Chapter 14, Wellness, has been thoroughly revised with the input of contributor **Warrenetta C. Mann**, the Director of Counseling and Psychiatry at the University of South Carolina, to include coverage of anxiety, loneliness, and body positivity. The section "Alcohol and Other Substances" has been updated with new information on tobacco and vaping products, marijuana, and prescription drugs. We have also expanded our coverage of mental health throughout other areas of the text. For example, we've added a "Homesickness" section to Chapter 12, Relationships, and two new TechTips in Chapters 12 and 14: "Maintain a Healthy Relationship with Social Media" (see page 282), and "Turn Off Your Screens for Better Sleep" (see page 324). For a reference on where to find mental health and wellness topics, we've also added a "Wellness Toolkit" to the beginning of this text (see page xix).

2. **An emphasis on the importance of diversity and inclusion on college campuses.** This book is made for all college students, regardless of race, age, gender, religion, ability, ethnicity, sexuality, or economic background. For the Fourteenth Edition, we have carefully revised Chapter 13, Diversity and Inclusion (formerly just "Diversity") with the guidance of our editorial board for Diversity, Inclusion, and Culturally Responsive Pedagogy (see page v). The "Sex, Gender, and Sexual Orientation" subsection (formerly "Sex and Gender," see page 290) has been revised to include more up-to-date coverage of gender identities and sexualities, with guidance on resources for LGBTQIA (lesbian, gay, bisexual, transgender, queer, intersex, and asexual) students and allies who may want to learn more. The revised Chapter 13 also offers more information on bias and microaggressions. This includes coverage of ableism and physical disability, as well as the addition of "The Pyramid of Hate" (see Figure 13.1, page 294), which illustrates the different forms of bias, from the more mild and insensitive remarks and stereotypes, to the severe and threatening forms of discrimination and bias-motivated violence. The theme of this revised chapter is encouraging students to embrace diversity and stand for inclusion on their college campus, in the workplace, and in life. We have also updated our photo program to include more diverse representations of all types of students throughout the text.

3. **The digital, modular format allows for flexible custom options.** The chapters in this text have been written as a set of fifteen modules—choose the ones you need, reorder them, add your own original content, and/or choose your format (print, digital) to build your

custom set of first-year experience materials at the price you want. For more information, reach out to a custom specialist through **macmillanlearning.com**.

4. **Attention to high-impact practices.** This edition continues the inclusion of strategies for using "high-impact practices"—eleven educational activities that have been shown to increase student learning, retention, and engagement throughout the undergraduate years.[2] The first chapter of the book introduces the concept of high-impact practices (HIPs) for students, lists and describes them, and discusses their benefits. Annotations in each chapter of the Instructor's Annotated Edition feature suggestions for utilizing one or more HIPs in the context of chapter content. This category of instructor's annotations is denoted with the heading "HIGH-IMPACT PRACTICE." Also, a special icon 🎯 identifies content in the features and narrative of the student edition that relates to HIPs. For instance, readers will see the HIP icon adjacent to the Your Turn: Work Together and Your Turn: Write and Reflect activities, and with content coverage related to writing, collaboration, diversity, global learning, or service learning. Furthermore, icons placed within the table of contents and the list of Your Turn features show you where to find HIP material.

5. **Updates across all chapters, with extensive revisions to fundamental coverage in several chapters.** A reconceived Chapter 4 features updated coverage on learning preferences rather than learning styles, reorganizing the chapter to focus on how students can adapt their learning preferences to their advantage. The TechTip has also been revised to help students navigate their college LMS. Chapter 12, "Relationships," has been reorganized to better reflect how students might navigate their relationships with their instructors, their families, their peers, and any romantic partners in college. The section "Maintaining Sexual Health," formerly located in Chapter 14, "Wellness," has been moved to this chapter so that students can consider sexual health as they reflect on romantic relationships. The subsection on "Cyberbullying" has also been moved to this chapter to reflect on its importance when "Communicating in a Digital Age." Finally, a new TechTip has also been added to focus more on communicating digitally and to encourage students to create and maintain a better relationship with social media. Your Turns, TechTips, "Reflect on Choices" prompts, and "Is This You?" boxes have been updated throughout the text. See more information about changes in each chapter on pages xxvii–xxix.

The Fourteenth Edition continues the Gardner and Barefoot tradition of helping students self assess their strengths, practice goal setting, focus on purpose and motivation, and maintain their engagement in this course. A section on goal setting in Chapter 1 gets students thinking immediately about this important skill. Assess Your Strengths and Set Goals boxes early in each chapter ask students to set goals, and Reflect on Choices and Apply What You Have Learned exercises at the end of each chapter ask

---

[2]George D. Kuh, *High-Impact Educational Practices: What They Are, Who Has Access to Them, and Why They Matter* (Washington, DC: Association of American Colleges and Universities, 2008). www.aacu.org/leap/hips

students to think back on how the chapter relates to choices they make and to apply what they have learned in the chapter to current and future academic work.

The following features return in the Fourteenth Edition, with many exciting enhancements:

Chapter-opening profiles help students see themselves in the text. Each chapter of the text opens with the story of a first-year student who has used the strategies presented in the chapter to succeed in college. The profiled students come from diverse backgrounds and attend diverse colleges and universities around the country.

Thought-provoking photographs and cartoons in every chapter—many of them new to this edition—with carefully written titles and captions reinforce concepts in the narrative and encourage critical thinking. For instance, in the diversity chapter, a captioned photo introduces students to the idea that through study-abroad programs, their college experience will help them expand their worldview. The chapter on reading includes an image of a textbook page that shows highlighting, underlining, and margin notes. The photo program in this chapter has been designed to illustrate the diversity that is found on college campuses throughout the country, thanks in part to the feedback from our Editorial Board for Diversity, Inclusion, and Culturally Responsive Pedagogy.

***Your Turn* collaborative learning activities foster peer-to-peer communication, collaboration, and critical thinking.** These activities can be used in class, as homework, or as group activities to strengthen the bond between students and their college communities. They are organized into four types based on what students are asked to do or to consider: Work Together, Write and Reflect, Making Decisions, and Setting Goals. A complete list of all Your Turn activities, organized by type and with page numbers included to make it easy for instructors to assign them, can be found on page xviii.

***Is This You?* boxes speak directly to students in circumstances that are commonly found among students taking first-year seminars.** Look for these special messages to first-generation college students, returning students, veterans, students with children, and student athletes. They also cover common first-year issues that many students encounter, such as being disappointed in a class, long-distance relationships, bouncing back from a bad grade, financial problems, and the clash of new ideas with old beliefs. The feature directs students to specific content within the chapter. Here is a list of these features:

> *Is This You?* I Don't Know What I'm Doing Here (Chapter 1)
> *Is This You?* Older than Average (Chapter 2)
> *Is This You?* Time Flies (Chapter 3)
> *Is This You?* Disappointed in My Classes (Chapter 4)
> *Is This You?* When New Knowledge and Old Beliefs Collide (Chapter 5)
> *Is This You?* The Challenge of Being "First" (Chapter 6)
> *Is This You?* Balancing Sports and Study (Chapter 7)

Is This You? Making A's without Studying (Chapter 8)
Is This You? Bouncing Back from a Bad Grade (Chapter 9)
Is This You? Dreading Writing Assignments (Chapter 10)
Is This You? No Plan for Life after College (Chapter 11)
Is This You? In a Long-Distance Relationship (Chapter 12)
Is This You? From Another Country (Chapter 13)
Is This You? Making Healthy Choices (Chapter 14)
Is This You? Too Much Month, Too Little Money (Chapter 15)

Coverage of technology and learning. The link between technology and learning is highlighted in every chapter of the Fourteenth Edition with a TechTip feature. These features introduce critical technology skills that span the classroom and real life. All TechTip features have been extensively revised for the new edition, with titles such as Build a Digital Persona (Chapter 2), Organize Your Time (Chapter 3), Navigate Online Learning with your College LMS (Chapter 4), Explore Note-Taking Programs and Apps (Chapter 7), Use the Cloud (Chapter 8), Conduct Effective Searches (Chapter 10), Join the Professional Community (Chapter 11), and two new TechTips, Maintain a Healthy Relationship with Social Media (Chapter 12), and Turn Off Your Screens for Better Sleep (Chapter 14). Models (including digital models) let students see principles in action. Because many students learn best by example, full-size models—more than in any competing book—show realistic examples of strategies for academic success such as working with time-management tools, annotating a textbook, using mind maps, and taking notes in various formats. Digital models are included to reflect the tools today's students use in their everyday lives.

Expanded examples from across the curriculum. The text includes concrete scenarios, pages, exercises, and problems from STEM, humanities, and social science courses.

Use Your Resources boxes connect students to their campus, faculty, and other students. To help students take more control of their own success, every chapter includes a quick overview of additional resources for support, including learning-assistance centers, books, websites, and fellow students—with a prompt for students to add their own ideas.

Skills-based practice exercises provide hands-on, point-of-use reinforcement of major concepts. Students use these exercises to practice skills that they can then apply to other academic courses. For instance, the Time Management chapter includes a tool for students to conduct a Procrastination Self-Assessment, and the test-taking chapter includes a Test Anxiety Quiz.

Retention strategies in every chapter of the Instructor's Annotated Edition offer best practices from John Gardner and Betsy Barefoot to help students persist in the first year. In addition, a sixteen-page insert at the beginning of the Instructor's Annotated Edition includes chapter-specific exercises and activities designed as retention strategies to support writing, critical thinking, working in groups, planning, reflecting, and taking action.

Key Chapter-by-Chapter Content

In addition to new features that appear across all chapters of the book, each chapter also features key new and updated content:

Chapter 1, Thriving in College and Life, introduces students to the concepts of purpose and goal setting and explores the value of higher education, including preparation for graduate school and opportunities to build professional networks.

Chapter 2, Cultivating Motivation, Resilience, and Emotional Intelligence, explores motivation, resilience, and grit. By presenting all these topics in the second chapter, students get the opportunity to explore them at a point early in the term, when this self-awareness is critical. They will also encounter these concepts throughout the book.

Chapter 3, Time Management, addresses the tools today's students use to stay organized. This chapter includes information about the relationship between locus of control and the ability to manage time. Students are guided in using time-management tools and understanding how to avoid procrastination. The chapter includes a procrastination self-assessment and a valuable tool for measuring the impact of distractions.

Chapter 4, How You Learn, introduces students to learning preferences. The chapter includes the VARK Inventory, which can be used in class. Also, three other learning-styles theories are described in the chapter: David Kolb's Experiential Learning Theory, the Myers-Briggs Type Indicator, and Howard Gardner's Theory of Multiple Intelligences. A brief version of the Multiple Intelligences Inventory is included. The chapter ends with an updated section on learning disabilities to help students know how and when to seek help for themselves or other students.

Chapter 5, Thinking in College, discusses what is involved in college-level thinking and includes both research-based information and practical strategies on how to achieve a high level of thinking. Students are clearly shown how concepts such as fast and slow thinking, problem solving, creativity, and collaboration all relate to critical thinking. The chapter includes a critical-thinking assessment as well as a new application of Bloom's taxonomy.

Chapter 6, Reading to Learn, helps students meet the particular challenges of reading college textbooks across the various disciplines. It introduces them to the steps involved in active reading and explains how to use strategies such as outlining and mapping to understand and retain important content for tests and exams. The chapter provides strategies for reading with concentration, reading improvement, and monitoring. Visuals include a sample organizer, several new photos, and sample textbook pages from economics and chemistry textbooks, which reflect the text's increased attention to the STEM fields.

Chapter 7, Getting the Most from Class, covers topics such as preparing for class, listening, taking notes, and participating. The chapter introduces students to various note-taking methods, particularly the Cornell method. The chapter's TechTip presents helpful note-taking apps. Students are encouraged to overcome any reluctance they might have about asking a question in class or actively participating in a group discussion.

Chapter 8, Studying, includes an essential focus on the basics—how to study and how to remember. Students are warned about the pitfalls of multitasking and the downsides of trying to study in an environment that is full of distractions. The chapter opens with an assessment that asks students to determine their willingness to make tough choices to improve their study habits and includes a figure showing a sample mind map.

Chapter 9, Test Taking, helps students learn how to prepare for tests and exams, understand and deal with test anxiety, and appreciate the value of maintaining academic integrity. The chapter covers different types of tests and different test environments, including online testing. A major theme in the chapter is the importance of being resilient—not allowing a poor grade on a test to negatively affect personal motivation. A visual showing a sample page from a math textbook reinforces the value of working practice problems as a great way to study for tests.

Chapter 10, Information Literacy and Communication, connects writing and speaking to the important topic of information literacy. The chapter clearly walks students through the steps of the writing process and emphasizes doing good research and getting comfortable using the resources at the campus library. Students are also introduced to ways to evaluate and cite sources and recognize bias.

Chapter 11, Majors and Careers, helps students understand how to consider different majors and to make a decision that sets them up for success and fulfillment. The chapter also provides a wealth of guidance on and tools for self-assessment and for career and industry exploration. This chapter offers a cutting-edge evaluation of the evolving new economy and guidance in developing the right mindset for creating a strong future, before moving on to discuss clear strategies for career planning, enhancing marketability—with a new section on branding yourself—conducting industry and company research, gaining experience while in college, and searching for jobs.

Chapter 12, Relationships, includes a major focus on the value of building positive student/instructor relationships. The chapter has been reorganized to better address the changing nature of interactions with instructors, family members, roommates, peers, and romantic partners. Coverage of sexual health has also been moved from Chapter 14, with updated information on the federal government's actions against sexual assault. The section on "Communicating in a Digital Age" now features a subsection on "Cyberbullying" (formerly located in Chapter 14) and a new TechTip on maintaining a better emotional relationship with social media. Finally, the chapter covers the value of involvement in campus life.

Chapter 13, Diversity and Inclusion, was extensively peer-reviewed for this edition with the guidance of Macmillan Learning's Editorial Board for Diversity, Inclusion, and Culturally Responsive Pedagogy. The chapter takes a broad view of diversity and considers the many advantages of a diverse campus environment that includes differences in race, ethnicity, gender and sexual identity, age, economic status, religion, and learning and physical abilities. This chapter offers new coverage of bias and microaggressions, including a new illustration of the Pyramid of Hate (see Figure 13.1). The chapter also features an updated discussion of sexual orientation and gender identity.

Chapter 14, Wellness, takes a holistic view of wellness, including mental, physical, and spiritual health with expanded coverage of health for all body sizes. A major focus of this chapter is stress and how to prevent and manage it through proper nutrition, sleep, and exercise. The chapter includes a stress self-assessment exercise and a new TechTip that provides suggestions on how to improve sleeping habits in the digital age. New wellness coverage has been added on prescription drugs, vaping, anxiety, loneliness, and body positivity.

Chapter 15, Money, emphasizes the importance of budgeting and gives students a template for designing their own budget. The chapter also explores responsible use of credit and debit cards, and ways for students to obtain and maintain financial aid.

Extensive Resources for Instructors

- **LaunchPad** macmillan learning **for *Your College Experience*, Fourteenth Edition.** LaunchPad combines an interactive e-book with high-quality multimedia content and ready-made assessment options, including LearningCurve adaptive quizzing. Pre-built units are easy to assign or adapt with your own material, such as readings, videos, quizzes, discussion groups, and more. LaunchPad also provides access to a gradebook that tracks performance for your whole class, for individual students, and for individual assignments.

  - **Unique to LaunchPad: LearningCurve for *Your College Experience,* Fourteenth Edition.** LearningCurve is an online, adaptive, self-quizzing program that quickly learns what students already know and helps them practice what they haven't yet mastered. LearningCurve motivates students to engage with key concepts before they come to class so that they are ready to participate; it also offers reporting tools to help you discern your students' needs.

  - Ordering information. LaunchPad for *Your College Experience*, Fourteenth Edition is available to package at a significant discount. To order LaunchPad as a standalone item, use ISBN 978-1-319-35186-1. To package the paper text with LaunchPad, use ISBN 978-1-319-38916-1. To package the loose-leaf edition with LaunchPad, use ISBN 978-1-319-38912-3.

  - **iClicker.** iClicker is the market-leading student engagement solution that enables instructors to pose questions during class time for real-time answers on student comprehension. With several question types, including multiple choice, open response, target, numeric, and exit polling, instructors can gather insight into student learning before they even get started on their first assignment. Visit **iclicker.com** for more information.

- **iClicker Questions.** Don't miss the brand-new suite of iClicker questions for *Your College Experience*, Fourteenth Edition. The questions come preloaded into LaunchPad.

- **Instructor's Annotated Edition.** A valuable tool for new and experienced instructors alike, the Instructor's Annotated Edition includes the full text of the student edition with abundant marginal annotations, chapter-specific exercises, and helpful suggestions for teaching that have been fully updated and revised by the authors. In this edition there are numerous retention strategies and high-impact practice tips and exercises to help your students succeed and stay in school.

- **Instructor's Manual.** The Instructor's Manual includes chapter objectives, teaching suggestions, an introduction to the first-year seminar course, a sample lesson plan for each chapter, sample syllabi, final projects for the end of the course, and various case studies that are relevant to the topics covered in the text. The Instructor's Manual is available online.

- **Computerized Test Bank.** The Computerized Test Bank contains more than 700 multiple-choice, true/false, short-answer, and essay questions designed to assess students' understanding of key concepts. An answer key is included.

- **Lecture Slides.** Available online for download, lecture slides accompany each chapter of the book and include key concepts and art from the text. Use the slides as provided to structure your lectures, or customize them as desired to fit your course's needs.

- **The Academic and Career Excellence System (ACES).** This instrument measures students' strengths in twelve critical areas and prompts students to reflect on their habits, behaviors, attitudes, and skills. Norm-referenced reports indicate whether students are at a high, moderate, or low skill level in particular areas. For more information on how to order the LaunchPad Solo for ACES, go to **launchpadworks .com**.

- **Curriculum Solutions.** Our new Curriculum Solutions group brings together the quality and reputation of Bedford/St. Martin's content with Hayden-McNeil's expertise in publishing original custom print and digital products. With our new capabilities, we are excited to deliver customized course solutions at an affordable price. Make *Your College Experience*, Fourteenth Edition, fit your course and goals by integrating your own institutional materials, by including only the parts of the text you intend to use in your course, or both. Please contact your local Macmillan Learning sales representative for more information and to see samples.

- **CS Select custom database.** The CS Select database allows you to create course materials that reflect your course objectives and uses just the content you need. Start with one of our core texts, and then rearrange chapters, delete chapters, and add additional content—including your own original content—to create just the book you're looking for. Get started by visiting **macmillanlearning.com/csSelect**.

- **TradeUp.** Bring more value and choice to your students' overall first-year experience by packaging *Your College Experience*, Fourteenth Edition, with one of a thousand titles from Macmillan publishers at a 50 percent discount from the regular price. Contact your local Bedford/St. Martin's sales representative for more information.

Student Resources

- **LaunchPad** macmillan learning **LaunchPad for *Your College Experience*, Fourteenth Edition.** LaunchPad is an online course solution that offers our acclaimed content, including e-book, videos, LearningCurve adaptive quizzes, and more. For more information, see the Instructors Resources section.

- **Unique to LaunchPad: LearningCurve for *Your College Experience*, Fourteenth Edition.** LearningCurve for *Your College Experience* is an online, adaptive, self-quizzing program that quickly learns what students already know and helps them practice what they haven't yet mastered.

  - **Ordering information.** LaunchPad for *Your College Experience*, Fourteenth Edition is available to package at a significant discount. To package the paper text with LaunchPad, use ISBN 978-1-319-38916-1. To package the loose-leaf edition with LaunchPad, use ISBN 978-1-319-38912-3. To order LaunchPad standalone, use ISBN 978-1-319-35186-1.

- **E-Book Options.** E-books offer an affordable alternative for students. You can find electronic versions of our books when you shop online at our publishing partners' sites. Learn more at **macmillanlearning.com/college/us/digital/ebooks**.

- **Macmillan Learning Student Store.** You want to give your students affordable rental, packaging, and e-book options. So do we. Learn more at **store.macmillanlearning.com**.

- ***Bedford/St. Martin's Insider's Guides.*** These concise and student-friendly booklets on topics that are critical to college success are a perfect complement to your textbook and course. One Insider's Guide can be packaged with *any* Bedford/St. Martin's textbook at no additional cost. Additional Insider's Guides can also be packaged for additional cost. Topics include academic planning, test anxiety, building confidence, career services, ethics and personal responsibility, credit cards, getting involved on campus, global citizenship, time management, and transferring. Insider's Guides are also available for specific types of learners, such as the *Insider's Guide for Adult Learners,* the *Insider's Guide for Returning Veterans,* and the *Insider's Guide to Community College.* For more information on ordering one of these guides with the text, go to **macmillanlearning.com/collegesuccess**.

Acknowledgments

Special thanks to the reviewers of this edition, whose wisdom and suggestions guided the creation of the Fourteenth Edition of the text: Josie Adamo, Buffalo State College; Amy Dolhay, Robert Morris College; Scott Feldman, Midwestern State University; Cathy Gann, Missouri Western State University; Cathryn Jeffers-Goodwine, St. Clair County Community College; Charlene Latimer, Daytona State College; Lisa Lavoie, University of Maine at Fort Kent; Krissy Leonard, Daytona State College; Melanie Marine, University of Wisconsin; Dr. Molly J. Scanlon, Nova Southeastern University; Alyssa Stephens, The University of Alabama; Kerry Tew, Arkansas State University; Dr. Buffy Stoll Turton, Miami University. We also thank Laura Rendon, The University of Texas, and James Reardon, who provided critical insight in their reviews of Chapters 13 and 14, Diversity and Inclusion and Wellness, respectively. We would also like to continue to thank our reviewers from previous editions, particularly the thirteenth, twelfth, eleventh, tenth, and ninth editions, as they helped to shape the text you see today.

As we look to the future, we are excited about the numerous improvements to this text that our creative Bedford/St. Martin's team has made and will continue to make. Special thanks to Leasa Burton, Vice President, Macmillan Learning Humanities; Erika Gutierrez, Senior Program Director; Allen Cooper, Program Manager; Melanie McFadyen, Development Editor; Peter Jacoby, Content Project Manager; Robin Besofsky, Production Supervisor; Lisa McDowell, Workflow Manager; Nicole Erazo, Media Editor; and Andrea Burgoa, Marketing Manager.

Most of all, we thank you, the users of our book, for you are the true inspirations for our work.

Contributors

Although this text speaks with the voices of its two authors, it represents contributions from many other people. We gratefully acknowledge those contributions and thank these individuals, whose special expertise has made it possible to introduce new students to their college experience through the holistic approach we value.

La Tasha Bellamy Photography

The content on mental and physical health and wellness in the Fourteenth Edition benefits from both a careful review as well as contributions from **Warrenetta Crawford Mann, Psy.D.**

After receiving degrees at Vanderbilt University, the University of Louisville, and Spalding University, she has worked with a wide range of diverse populations spanning age, income, educational, racial, ethnic, geographic and resource backgrounds. It was in this work that she became keenly aware of the juxtaposition of personal and institutional privilege and power. In her early career, she found herself focusing on both individual and organizational interventions aimed at strengthening multicultural competence and creating inclusive environments. Dr. Mann has spent the last fifteen years working in higher education as instructor, advisor, counselor and administrator. She currently serves as Director of Counseling and Psychiatry in Student Health Services at the University of South Carolina.

We would also like to acknowledge and thank the numerous colleagues who have contributed to this book in its previous editions:

Chapters 2, 6, 7, 8, 9: Jeanne L. Higbee, University of Minnesota

Chapters 2, 5, 14: Amber Manning-Oullette, Iowa State University

Chapter 2: Catherine Andersen, University of Baltimore

Chapter 3: Casey Reid, Lane Community College

Chapters 4, 12: Tom Carskadon, Mississippi State University

Chapter 7: Mary Ellen O'Leary, University of South Carolina

Chapter 10: Charles Curran, Distinguished Professor Emeritus, University of South Carolina at Columbia; and Lea Susan Engle, Texas A&M University

Chapter 11: Heather N. Maietta, Regis College

Chapter 11: Philip D. Gardner, Michigan State University

Chapter 13: Crystal J. Allen, Lone Star College-North Harris

Chapter 15: Natala Kleather (Tally) Hart, founding head of the Economic Access Initiative at The Ohio State University; and Kate Trombitas, Director of Development at The Ohio State University College of Nursing

YOUR
COLLEGE
EXPERIENCE

PART ONE

FOUNDATIONS

David Schaffer/Getty Images

1 THRIVING IN COLLEGE AND LIFE

Student Goals

- Gain strategies to thrive in college
- Learn what this course and this textbook are all about
- Appreciate the value of a college education
- Get to know the key people in your college experience
- Understand the importance of developing purpose and making good choices
- Practice setting SMART goals
- Learn about high-impact practices and how they can enrich your learning and heighten your success

SDI Productions/Getty Images

2 CULTIVATING MOTIVATION, RESILIENCE, AND EMOTIONAL INTELLIGENCE

Student Goals

- Understand the similarities and differences between motivation, attitude, and mindsets
- Explore resilience as a key to success in college and in life
- Learn strategies for understanding and evaluating your emotional intelligence
- Explore how your emotions affect your health and your outlook on life
- Explore high-impact practices 2 (writing), 3 (collaboration), and 5 (service-leaning)

nycshooter/Getty Images

3 TIME MANAGEMENT

Student Goals

- Gain strategies and tools to manage your time
- Learn how to combat procrastination and avoid distractions
- Understand how setting priorities leads to having more balance in your life
- Appreciate the value of time and energy and the importance of allocating these resources wisely
- Explore high-impact practices 2 (writing) and 3 (collaboration)

Huntstock/Brand X Pictures/
Getty Images

4 HOW YOU LEARN

Student Goals

- Become familiar with theories that explain how people learn
- Explore different tools for measuring your learning preferences
- Learn how to handle a mismatch between how you prefer to learn and how you are being taught
- Understand and recognize a learning disability
- Explore high-impact practices 2 (writing), 3 (collaboration), and 6 (learning communities)

David Schaffer/Getty Images

1

THRIVING IN COLLEGE AND LIFE

YOU WILL EXPLORE

How you can prepare to thrive in college

What this course and this textbook are all about

The value of a college education

The key people in your college experience

The importance of developing purpose and making good choices

How to practice setting SMART goals

⚹ High-impact practices 2 (writing) and 3 (collaboration)

> 66 **Prior to attending college, I never thought about my life purpose, and I took everything at face value. Now, I think more about my long-term goals and definitely feel that the price I pay for education is well worth it.** 99

michaeljung/Shutterstock

Setting both long- and short-term goals has always been important to Lewis. After high school, when he found himself living in Atlanta working at a dead-end job, he set his sights on going to college and enrolled at Georgia State University. Now that he's in college, he's majoring in economics with the goal of attending law school after graduation. He knows that getting good grades and staying involved on campus will help him achieve that ultimate goal.

Like many students, Lewis also needs to balance working with attending and participating in college activities, so many of his goals have involved small steps. "I am currently the president of the pre-law student association," he explains. "The group is small, but this semester I plan to attend a leadership seminar to get some extra skills in leading a successful student organization." He also gets involved on campus by working in student affairs to promote special events, which helps him stay connected with other students. He acknowledges, however, that working even on

campus does have its challenges that he is still trying to solve. "Working twenty hours while taking fifteen credits means that I rarely get enough sleep because I have to stay up late studying. My biggest goal for now is to find a better way to manage my time." Still, Lewis believes that the hard work will pay off. "Prior to attending college, I never thought about my life purpose, and I took everything at face value. Now, I think more about my long-term goals and definitely feel that the price I pay for education is well worth it," he says.

In the future, Lewis hopes to travel the world tackling issues such as poverty, cultural barriers, and the economic glass ceiling that many people face, and his favorite elective class so far, Psychology 1101, plays nicely into those goals. "That class pushes my life message that we should try to understand other people and not be so convinced we always know what's best for everyone else," he says. "I have been the subject of negative stereotypes, and I just love the way this class shows how this kind of thinking came about."

To access the LearningCurve study tool, video activities, and more, go to LaunchPad for *Your College Experience.*
Launchpadworks.com

WELCOME TO YOUR COLLEGE EXPERIENCE

Congratulations—you are going to college! You've joined about two million other students who are starting college this year. No matter your age, background, academic skills, or economic circumstances, you can succeed if you have the motivation, commitment, and willingness to take advantage of all that your college or university has to offer. You may find that the college experience is even transformative.

assess your strengths

Think about the topic of this chapter. What do you think it means to thrive in college? Do you have a clear sense of your own purpose? What personal and career goals do you want to pursue during and after college? Can you describe the experiences you have had with setting goals and reaching them? If you are not quite ready to answer these questions, think about them as you read through this chapter.

set goals

Think about a challenge you have had in making academic decisions or setting personal goals. As you read this chapter, set a goal that relates to some of the chapter material, and be prepared to talk with others in your class about why you selected this goal. For example, you might set a goal to understand the research on the value of a college degree and apply it to your own personal goals for your future.

What do we mean by "transformative"? For most college students, completing a degree will have a profound influence on their employment opportunities and income over a lifetime. But far beyond that, college can have an impact on how you think about and understand the world around you, whom you select as friends and associates, whom you may commit to or marry, how you raise children if you choose to have them, how you vote and worship, how you spend your spare time—and a long list of other lifetime outcomes. So what you have chosen to do right now is really exciting and holds enormous potential for you. It can be a lot of fun and very satisfying, but it can also be a lot of work. This course, this instructor, your fellow students, and this textbook are going to be your companions and partners in launching you toward success in your college experience. Who are we to be telling you all this? Well, if you Google us you will see that we have many years of experience in helping students be successful. But, as we wrote in the preface to this book, we were once just like you—first-year students trying to overcome our own challenges and struggles.

Thriving in College

As authors of this textbook, our overarching goal for you is that you not only be "successful" in college and life but that you *thrive* in both. Thriving is about achieving the goals you initially set for yourself and other goals you can't yet imagine. Thriving means going beyond minimum requirements to meet and exceed these goals, and it includes discovering talents and abilities you didn't know you had. Thriving is about achieving your highest possible level of performance and deriving a maximum amount of self-satisfaction, self-esteem, and pleasure. Thriving is about peak performance—it involves excitement, exhilaration, and even joy.

The college years are a unique period and set of experiences in life when you will be surrounded by some of the smartest and most supportive people you will ever meet. They will help you thrive so that you become the person you want to be! So hang on for the exciting ride that is beginning right now.

high-impact practice 1

Making the Most of the College Success Course and This Textbook

This course is known by several names, including not only college success but also University 101, College 101, first-year seminar, or first-year colloquium. No matter what your course is called, you've acquired a textbook—as you've done for most of the other courses you are taking this term. You will also have a syllabus that includes many components as described in Table 1.1. You are probably asking, "What is the point of this course, and why do I need a textbook?"

What all college success courses have in common is that they introduce you, a new, transferring, or returning college student, to a central topic: how to be a successful student in college and successful in life. Currently, the course and this text are based on extensive research in a field called "student success" that investigates what students need to know to thrive in college, why some students do a better job at making the most of their college experience, and the strategies and attitudes of the most successful students.

So what does the research tell us? Here are the most important takeaways:

- Students who complete a college success course are more likely to continue in college and finish their degrees.
- These students not only know about where to get help; they actually seek out and utilize such help.
- Students who complete a college success course are more involved in organizations and activities, and they interact more often with faculty outside class.
- And perhaps most important, these students make better choices overall while they're in college.

TABLE 1.1 > The Syllabus

The syllabus is the formal statement of course requirements. On the first day in all your courses, pay very close attention when your instructors review the syllabus. Each syllabus will be slightly different. Select a syllabus, either for this or another course. Then highlight or place a checkmark by these important components of the syllabus, and make some notes or add some details here about each area:

Components of the Syllabus	Your Notes
Course objectives or "learning outcomes"	
Class attendance policy	
Instructor's e-mail address, phone number, office location, and office hours	
Due dates for papers or projects (enter dates in your paper or electronic calendar)	
Midterm and final exam dates (enter dates in your paper or electronic calendar)	
Required textbook and other readings	
Rules and policies	
Other information	

And why *do* you have a textbook in this course? Because your college or university wants you to have, in writing, instructions on how to "do college," so to speak. As authors, we predict with great confidence that if you take the material in this book seriously, apply it to your own beginning college experience, and make your best good-faith effort to use its suggestions, then you will be successful in college—and in life.

While you attend class and when reading this textbook, you will get valuable advice that applies not only to your college success class but also to all your college courses this year and in the future. Think of this course as a kind of laboratory for what to do in all your college courses to be successful.

The First Day of This Course

You are probably reading this chapter in association with your first or second class meeting in this college success course. You are not in this alone. Look at your fellow students. Do they look like you? Do you think their thoughts and feelings are the same as yours? Surely many of them are excited and nervous. Maybe some are even scared. Some are overconfident; some are already bored. Some are confused or even clueless about why they are here, now, at this institution. Others are highly motivated and very goal-oriented. In sum, they are different from one another.

You will get to know these students much better than students in your lecture courses. Your college success course will include a great deal of discussion, conversation, and group work so you will have the opportunity to make friends and learn from your classmates. Help them when you can, and they will help you. Don't prejudge them, and don't prejudge yourself. You don't know yet what you are going to do in college and how it may transform you. This course will help you discover your own unique strengths and aptitudes, so make the most of it.

INTRODUCING VERY IMPORTANT PEOPLE (VIPS)

When you talk to college graduates and ask them what part of college was most memorable and most influential, they will often tell you that it was the people. To whom are they referring? There are all kinds of people in college. Some of them are truly memorable characters. Some of the characters will be fellow students, but many will be instructors. Colleges and universities give instructors a great deal of freedom in their interests, ideas, speech, and dress, and some of them you are never going to forget! Trust us on this. There will also be very special administrators, advisers, and other staff members who will give you support and assistance that you will remember for the rest of your life.

Let's consider the opportunities and challenges you will encounter in interacting with each group of people and how they can influence your college experience. With mutual understanding, it will be easier to support others and to know how they can support you.

Students

Of all the different types of people on campus, the ones who will likely have the most influence on you and the choices you make are your fellow students. They can be traditional-aged, older, veterans, part-time or full-time, roommates, or those who come from another country. But all of them can be tremendously important to your success.

Traditional Students. If you are a traditional student, meaning that you are around 18 years old and have just graduated from high school, the transition you are making will involve an adjustment to some significant differences between high school and college. For instance, in college you will probably be part of a more diverse student body, not just in terms of race and ethnicity but also in terms of age, religion, political opinions, sexual orientation, identity, and life experiences. If you attend a large college or university, you might feel like a "number" and not as special as you may have felt in high school. In college, you will have more potential friends, but you'll have to explore new ways of getting to know them. Familiar assumptions about what people are like based on where they live, where they go to church, or what high school they attended might not apply to the new people you're meeting.

It is easy to understand why traditional students feel more drawn to and comfortable with fellow traditional students. But we want to remind you that college is a perfect time and place to step outside your comfort zone and peer group. You will find your college experience significantly enriched by spending time with those who are older or younger than you or are, or different in some other way.

Nontraditional Students. If you are a nontraditional or adult student, you might have experience in the job market, and you might have a spouse or partner and children. You might be returning to college or beginning college for the first time. You will face a special set of challenges, such as trying to relate to younger students and finding enough time to juggle the important, competing responsibilities of work, caring for a family, and being in college. Remember, though, that nontraditional students have intrinsic motivation that comes with maturity and experience, and they appreciate the value of an education. You will have the advantage of approaching college work with a very clear purpose for why you are there, which your instructors will notice and appreciate. You may be intimidated by the advantages many younger students seem to enjoy by virtue of being in school more recently, and you may also be intimidated by technology. But your cohort also has many advantages as well, and you need to build your college success on those advantages.

Veterans. You might be one of hundreds of thousands of veterans who have come to campus after service during the Iraq and Afghanistan conflicts or in other areas of the nation and world. If you are a veteran, you may have traveled the world, met all kinds of people, and faced life-threatening experiences. You may have already started college while you were on active duty. You likely made sacrifices such as leaving your family behind, and you might have suffered either visible or invisible injuries. We believe that others on campus will find you and the stories you share about your time in military service very inspiring. Let your instructors know you are a vet. But also associate with students who have not had military experience. You may observe that some of them are less focused and serious than you are. But be patient; they are developing people just like you. Your knowledge and global experiences will enrich classroom discussion, and your perspectives will be appreciated. Speak up and join in as much of campus life as your time will permit. Finally, we urge you to take advantage of special support services on your campus for veterans. Your institution's Office of Veteran Services is there to help you maintain good grades and keep up with your veterans' benefits as Congress regularly revises benefits legislation.

First-Generation Students.

Are you the first person in your family to attend college? If so, both you and your family will be experiencing transitions such as navigating admissions and financial aid processes, adapting to the college schedule, and experiencing more independence from each other. Because you will also be setting an example for other family members who will follow in your path, you may feel some additional pressure to succeed. Many colleges and universities now offer special support for first-generation students; taking advantage of these kinds of services will help you experience a smoother transition into college life.

International Students.

If you are a student who has come to the United States from another country, the U.S. college campus may seem very different from what you expected. Perhaps you have immigrated with family members or on your own. You may be a refugee, or you may be undocumented. Whatever your particular situation, learning the unique language, culture, and what others expect at a U.S. college or university can be a challenge. Do instructors' expectations and students' behaviors seem different from what you experienced in your home country? Are you not

Navigating the U.S. Campus Culture

Are you a student who has recently come to the United States from another country? Perhaps you have immigrated with family members or on your own. Resources, described in this section, are available to help you meet your unique set of challenges!

kaz_c/Getty Images

a native English speaker? If you need help with your English skills, seek out English as a second language (ESL) courses or programs. Also, visit the international student center on your campus to find out how you can continue to increase your understanding of life in the United States, both on and off campus.

Part-Time Students. If you are a part-time student, you are part of a large cohort in U.S. higher education. At many colleges, part-time students are the majority, even though the campus may seem to be organized primarily for the interests of full-time students. One important distinction between being a part-time or full-time college student is eligibility for financial aid, a system that usually favors full-time students. This may surprise you, but we believe that borrowing money to enable full-time participation is often a good idea. Full-time students are more likely to complete their degrees, and they complete them in significantly less time, thus increasing their earning power faster. If you are attending college part-time, it would be a good idea for you to talk to a financial aid adviser and analyze what it would cost you to move from part-time to full-time status in terms of the debt you would acquire versus the time and money you would ultimately gain by completing college more quickly. If you decide to continue as a part-time student, know that college is just as much for you as it is for the full-time students. There are lots of part-time students on campus.

Online Learners. If you are taking courses online, your experience is going to be significantly different from that of students who attend classes in person at your college. Online courses offer some advantages—for instance, you can take a class from home without having to travel to a college or university campus. If you are shy or reluctant to speak in class, online courses will make participating in class discussions or chats easier than in a face-to-face environment. Some students even report that they find it easier to concentrate in online courses because they are not distracted by other students.[1]

Online learning, however, requires students to be more disciplined, to be better time managers, and to be able to study more independently. Without in-person class meetings, you might find it more challenging to make connections with other students, so you might need to make an extra effort to do so. However, your online course will surely provide you with electronic means to chat with other students and the instructor. To increase your engagement in such a course, it is important to use such means to communicate, especially with other students.

Peer Leaders. Many college success courses like yours utilize peer leaders—upper-level students who are also co-teachers for the course. If your college success course has a peer leader, get to know him or her. Peer leaders are selected because of their academic success, knowledge, experience, and willingness to help new students. A peer leader can serve

---

[1] Paul Fain, "Only Sometimes for Online," *Inside Higher Ed*, April 26, 2013, https://www.insidehighered.com/news/2013/04/26/online-courses-are-second-choice-community-college-students-some-subject-areas.

as an informal academic adviser, mentor, and friend. And it is very likely you will want to consider becoming a peer leader later in your undergraduate career. Peer leaders receive valuable leadership and communication experience and earn either college credits or financial compensation for their work in the college success course.

No matter what your age or particular characteristics, you will bring certain strengths to your college experiences that will help both you and others. Older students have a lot of determination and a set of real-life experiences that relate to what they're learning. Eighteen- and nineteen-year-olds are comfortable with technology and social media, and they are often pop-culture experts. Veterans have a unique set of life experiences to share, and international students bring an important view of the world to any U.S. campus. Part-time students are exemplars of time management, often juggling work, education, and home responsibilities. Online learners have to overcome the challenges of learning remotely to make their online learning experience as valuable as learning in a face-to-face setting. These kinds of strengths are all important to the learning process.

Need Help? Ask Another Student
Your peer leader or another upper-level student can give you the advice you need about how to navigate your first year of college.
skynesher/Getty Images

Instructors

Of all the people who work at a college or university, instructors have a major influence on students because they influence your thinking and understanding, and your choice of major and vocation. Depending on their position at your college or university, your instructor may carry the title "Professor," "Instructor," "Adjunct professor," or "Doctor." If they do not inform you of what they prefer to be called, ask before addressing them. Collectively, they are referred to as "the faculty."

Whether you're a nontraditional student adjusting to less freedom than you've been used to or a traditional student adjusting to more freedom, you will find that your instructors are not going to tell you what, how, or when to study. In addition, they will rarely monitor your progress. However, you will have more freedom to express views that are different from theirs. Many instructors have private offices and keep regular office hours when they can meet with you. Check with them to find out if you need to make an appointment before coming to their office. (Read the Tech Tip: E-Mail with Style, which shows you how to communicate with your instructors appropriately via e-mail.) You might be able to ask your instructors a quick question before or after class, but you will be able to get far more help by actually visiting their offices. By taking advantage of instructors' office hours, you will also let them know that you are serious about learning. You can ask your instructors for direct help with any question or misunderstanding that you have. You might also want to ask some questions about their educational careers and particular research interests. Many students develop close relationships with their instructors, relationships that can be important both now and in the future.

Depending on where you went to high school, you may find it similar to or completely different from college. One of the biggest differences will be the expectations of college faculty and staff that you will make your own decisions. Although college employees are there to help, they will expect you to take the lead in requesting what you need. Assuming you have the academic qualifications, decisions about your major will be up to you. You will also make daily decisions about what and when you eat, whether you get enough sleep, and whether or not you are engaged in out-of-class activities.

Another big difference between high school and college has to do with relationships between faculty members and students. In high school, you may have developed positive relationships with your teachers, especially if you worked hard in class or if you interacted with them in extracurricular activities like sports, drama, or yearbook. However, some high school students might have considered their teachers as "the enemy," or they might have lost status within their peer group if they were seen talking to or interacting with teachers. In high school going to the "office" was often viewed as some kind of punishment or disciplinary action.

College is completely different. You will seek out assistance from some instructors outside class or find some of them so interesting that you will want to spend time learning about how they developed their academic careers. Much research has been done on the importance of first-year students interacting with instructors outside class. We know that students who engage in such interaction report more learning and higher levels of course satisfaction and are more likely to come back for a second year. You should look forward to your experiences with many of your instructors. It will be up to you to choose whether or not to take advantage of their help and to develop a unique relationship with one or more of them.

Staff Members/Administrators/Advisers

Staff members, administrators, and advisers at your college are there to provide you with all kinds of assistance and support: advising, tutoring, counseling, career planning, and much, much more. Their job is to keep you and other students on track and your campus running smoothly.

These people make the most significant policy decisions; determine important financial allocations and priorities; and, with the faculty, help govern the institution. You will interact with some of these leaders, but because they are so busy, you may have to make the effort to do so. One way to meet important staff members and administrators is to get a job on campus. Another way is to be active in student government or other organizations that have a faculty adviser.

Another big difference between high school and college is the great variety of staff members and administrators. In high school the staff was pretty much limited to the principal and vice principal, coaches, librarians, technology specialists, and guidance counselors. In college you will also find learning support specialists, tutors, academic advisers, career planning counselors, financial aid officers, student activity coordinators, directors of diversity and inclusion, special needs counselors, personal counselors, international student advisers, veterans' advisers, campus security personnel, and many more. Your college success course will introduce you to many of these individuals, what they do, and how they can help you, if you let them.

In summary, a big part of success in college will come down to the types, frequency, and depth of relationships you develop with all these different kinds of key people: other students, instructors, and staff members. Make the most of these potential relationships; they are a major component of the value of the college experience.

---

yourturn   **Write and Reflect**

 *high-impact practice 2*

Then and Now: How College Is Different from High School

Depending on where and when you went to high school and your experience there, you may find college very different or only slightly different from your time in high school. Think back to your high school days and write a brief essay on the most significant differences between then and now. These might include your experience in class, how you are dealing with more—or less—freedom, your involvement in out-of-class activities, and your sense of "school spirit." You might want to add an image that evokes high school or college. Use your imagination.

THE VALUE OF COLLEGE

You are likely in college because you and/or your family members believe that it is an important and valuable experience now and for the future. The value of college can be measured in many different ways. As you read this section of the chapter, think about how and why college is important to you.

Accessing Better Jobs, Higher Salaries, a Better Life

Overall, people around the world value higher education and this is certainly true in the United States. The demand for a college degree from a U.S. college or university explains, in part, why there are more than 4,000 of them. Around the world, having a college degree is a major opportunity for people to achieve upward social mobility and a higher standard of living.

That accurately describes the primary purpose most students have for being in college: to attain a higher standard of living than they would have without a college credential.

In earlier centuries, one's standard of living was almost always a function of family background. Either you were born into power and money or you spent your life working for others who had power and money. While, sadly these factors still have some influence on upward mobility in the United States, receiving a college degree can help level the playing field for everyone. A college degree can minimize or eliminate the restrictions to achievement that stem from differences in background, race, ethnicity, family income, national origin, immigration status, family lineage, and personal connections. Simply put, college participation is about ensuring that more people have the opportunity to be evaluated on the basis of merit rather than family status, money, or other forms of privilege. It makes achieving the American dream more possible.

In 1900, fewer than 2 percent of Americans of traditional college age attended college. Today, new technologies and the information explosion are changing the workplace so drastically that to support themselves and their families adequately, most people need some education beyond high school. Although today more than 69 percent of high school graduates are attending college (approximately eighteen million students), we are seeing a wave of questions in the media about whether or not college is really worth it.

Lewis, the student profiled at the beginning of this chapter, likely would answer, "Yes, college is really worth it," but what do the data say? A *New York Times* analysis of data from the Economic Policy Institute (epi.org) also finds that the answer is "yes." Dramatic differences exist between the earning power of students with a high school diploma and those with a four-year college degree. In 2014, four-year college graduates earned, on average, about $50,000 per year, while high school graduates earned $30,000 per year.[2] While there are concerns about the cost of college today, the cost of not attending college is even more dramatic. David Autor, an economist from the Massachusetts Institute of Technology, reported that not going to college will, over your lifetime, cost you about half a million dollars.[3]

You can also look at Figure 1.1 to see how earning a college degree will improve your earning potential. This figure breaks down unemployment rates and weekly earnings according to education level. The more education you have, the more likely you are to be employed, and the higher your earnings will be.

Beyond the financial benefits that earning a college degree gives to an individual, college is an established process designed to further formal education so that students who attend and graduate will be

---

[2] National Center for Educational Statistics. Table 502.30. "Median Annual Earnings of Full-Time Year-Round Workers 25 to 34 Years Old and Full-Time Year-Round Workers as a Percentage of the Labor Force, by Sex, Race/Ethnicity, and Educational Attainment: Selected Years, 1995 through 2014." Accessed online at https://nces.ed.gov/programs/digest/d15/tables/dt15_502.30.asp

[3] David Leonhardt, "Is College Worth It? Clearly, New Data Say," *The New York Times*, May 27, 2014, www.nytimes.com/2014/05/27/upshot/is-college-worth-it-clearly-new-data-say.html, accessed May 15, 2016.

FIGURE 1.1 ❯ Education Pays

Earning a college degree will improve your earning potential. This figure breaks down unemployment rates and weekly earnings according to education level. Use this information as motivation to make the most of college. The more education you have, the more likely you are to be employed and the higher your earnings will be.

Note: Data are for persons age 25 and over. Earnings are for full-time wage and salary workers.
Source: U.S. Bureau of Labor Statistics, Current Population Survey.

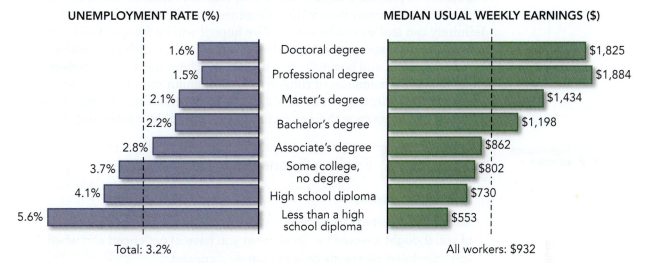

Unemployment Rates and Earnings by Educational Attainment, 2018

UNEMPLOYMENT RATE (%)		MEDIAN USUAL WEEKLY EARNINGS ($)
1.6%	Doctoral degree	$1,825
1.5%	Professional degree	$1,884
2.1%	Master's degree	$1,434
2.2%	Bachelor's degree	$1,198
2.8%	Associate's degree	$862
3.7%	Some college, no degree	$802
4.1%	High school diploma	$730
5.6%	Less than a high school diploma	$553

Total: 3.2%   All workers: $932

prepared for certain roles in society. Today, for many, those roles are found predominantly in what has become known as the information economy, which means that most college graduates will earn their living by creating, managing, and using information. For others, college is a crucial way to prepare for leadership roles in their communities, companies, professions, or military units. Every society throughout history has had proscribed routes for their members to achieve leadership status, and in our society it is most often by means of college degree attainment.

Preparing for Graduate or Professional Education

Another reason students get a four-year college degree is to prepare them to continue their education in a graduate or professional school. If you want to become a medical doctor, dentist, lawyer, or college professor, a four-year college degree is just the beginning, but it is a required step on the path to such professions. Let's say you aspire to be a physician and are planning to get a bachelor's degree in chemistry. Your primary purpose for your degree in chemistry is to gain admittance to medical school. Perhaps you have also considered that if your plans should change, having a degree in chemistry will get your foot in the door in several different industries, so another purpose for your degree is having an edge in the job market after graduation. If you have a long-term goal, work with your academic adviser to make sure you're meeting all the course requirements as you continue on your path.

Developing Lifelong Friendships and Professional Networks

College will provide you with numerous opportunities to develop a variety of formal and informal social networks. These networks will help you make friends and develop alliances with instructors and fellow students who share your interests and goals. Social networking sites such as Instagram, Twitter, and LinkedIn provide a way to enrich your real-life social networks in college. Whom you get to know during the college years really does matter. College definitely can and should be fun, and we hope it will be for you. You will meet new people, perhaps go to athletic events and parties, build camaraderie with new friends, and hopefully feel a sense of school spirit. Many college graduates relive memories of college days throughout their lives, continue to root for their institution's athletic teams, return for homecoming and class reunions, and encourage their own children to attend their alma mater.

 high-impact practice 3

---

yourturn **Feeling Connected**

Are You Surprised?

Talk with a classmate to discover whether college life so far is what each of you thought it would be. Share what you have experienced and when you have been pleasantly or unpleasantly surprised.

Building Academic Skills

In addition to being fun, college is about developing and practicing academic skills. First and foremost, college is about thinking, and it will help students understand how to become careful and critical thinkers who don't believe everything that they hear or read but instead look for evidence before forming opinions. Being a college student means spending many hours each week studying, staying up late at night, taking high-stakes exams, and probably working harder than you ever have before. For many students, college becomes much like a job, with defined duties, expectations, and obligations. Most important is that college will be a set of experiences that will help you to further define your goals and achieve your own purpose.

Considering Other Outcomes

Being a college graduate is linked to many other valuable outcomes. Which of the outcomes below interest you the most?

- College graduates are less likely to become unemployed in America's periodic economic downturns. And if they do become unemployed, they are more likely to become reemployed with less interruption of work and earnings.
- College graduates live longer! Now that's a biggee! They live longer because they eat differently, have different exercise habits, consume less alcohol, and are much less likely to use tobacco than people who do not complete college.

- College graduates stay married to the same person longer. They have fewer children, have them at older ages, and they raise their children differently.
- College graduates have more discretionary recreational time for fun and relaxation and more money to pursue such opportunities.
- College influences your choice of friends for the rest of your life. You will be more likely to have other college graduates as your close friends and social acquaintances.
- College graduates are more likely to be elected to public office. College also influences the political ideas and behaviors of citizens.
- College graduates are less likely to be swindled and taken advantage of as consumers.
- College graduates are less likely to be incarcerated.

In spite of all these positive outcomes, there is no evidence at all that college graduates are more or less honest than people who do not graduate from college, although many institutions do try to teach and influence integrity. College participation and completion do enhance self-respect, self-esteem, and feelings of self-worth and accomplishment. If these are outcomes you aspire to, college is the right place and experience for you.

EXPLORING PURPOSE AND SETTING GOALS

We have been discussing the overarching importance of college for students and for our society. Now it's time to focus more specifically on you and the unique purpose and goals that you can achieve in college.

Begin with the End in Mind

Imagine that you've arrived at your graduation day and you're looking back over your college experience. What can you do that will help you feel good about the time you've spent in college and prepare you for your life to come? We want to help you convert your ideas to reality through a plan to achieve the "end" you have in mind. In this section, we'll explore the most important driver of motivation and success in college: purpose.

Tom Wang/Shutterstock

Considering Purpose

Researchers on the college experience have concluded that the number one issue beginning college students have to grapple with is, in one word, purpose. Your sense of purpose will drive many outcomes. It will give you motivation for today, this week, this term, for college overall, and for life. It will shape many of the decisions you make. Purpose provides clarity, direction, commitment, meaning. People who have a clear sense of purpose know who they are, where they have come from, and where they are going. Purpose connects to motivation. And this connection plays out each day for college students in terms of the choices they make that either do or do not help them achieve their purpose.

To be both fair and realistic, most adults take quite a long time to develop a sense of purpose. For them college is one of the most important building blocks to leading a purpose-driven life. Think of the high performers you have either known or know about: athletes, politicians, artists, musicians, soldiers, preachers, parents, teachers. You are looking at individuals with a strong sense of purpose.

The majority of students enter college without a defining purpose but with some notions about what their major will be. But often these are not realistic choices. Students may find that the major and a connected occupation are not going to be a good fit for them. For instance, many students aspire to be physicians but can't seem to do well in the courses that are required for entry to medical school. College is designed to help you find an appropriate fit between your major, desired career, and ultimate purpose. You may be decided or undecided about your major and purpose. Unlike those in many other countries, U.S. colleges and universities allow students to change their minds about a major; however, when you do so these changes can add additional time and expense. But it is infinitely preferable to find a major that is a fit for your purpose than to be miserable in pursuing a major and then trying to work in a field that isn't right for you.

One very basic way to look at purpose is to reflect on these questions: Why am I going to college? Is this college a good fit for me now at this time in my life? Where am I on a scale for choosing purpose in college and life—very focused on one end of the scale and wide open and undecided, maybe even a bit indifferent, on the other end?

In this course you will probably be asked to write about such questions and to discuss them with other students. And you will learn about professionals on campus who can help you answer these questions in a comfortable and confidential environment. Your college will have academic advisers, career counselors, personal counselors, and faculty members who are at your service at no additional cost to you. This is part of the college experience and the tuition and fees you have already paid—so take advantage of it!

Getting Started with Goal Setting

Think about how you define success. Is success about money, friendship, love, sex, or power? Is it about achieving excellence in college and beyond, or is it about finding a sense of purpose in your life? For most people, success is a combination of all these factors and more. Although luck or "who you know" may play a role, first and foremost your success will be the result of intentional steps you take and your accomplishments. So in your quest for success, where do you start?

Identify Your Personal Strengths.

Do you like to talk, deal with conflict, and stand up for yourself and others? Are you a good reader? If your answers to these questions are "yes," you may want to consider a career in the legal profession. Are you a good science student, and do you enjoy working with your hands? If so, you might want to think about dentistry. Your campus career center can help you discover your unique strengths—and weaknesses—which can influence your direction as you explore career choices.

Ask Yourself Tough Questions.

Am I here to find out who I am and to study a subject that I am truly passionate about, regardless of whether it leads to a career? To engage in an academic program that provides an array of possibilities when I graduate? To prepare myself for a graduate program or for immediate employment? To obtain specific training in a field that I am committed to? To gain specific skills for a job I already have?

isthisyou?

I Don't Know What I'm Doing Here

Is everyone in your family excited about your being in college—except you? Are you wondering why you've made this major commitment of time, energy, and money? You will read in this chapter that finding a sense of purpose is important if you want to make the most of college. But identifying that purpose doesn't always happen for everyone at the same time or in the same way. Don't give up. It could be that you are a bit homesick, fearful of the unknown, or feeling lost in a new environment. Find a counselor, a chaplain, an academic adviser, an instructor, an older student, a peer leader, or a fellow first-year student you can talk to about the way you're feeling. It is very likely that others can relate to you because they either share these feelings or did in the past. Ask how they overcame these feelings to get ideas on how you can, too. Connecting with others who have overcome the same challenges that you are facing can make all the difference.

Establish Goals for Today, This Week, This Year, and Beyond.

Although some students prefer to go with the flow and let life happen to them, those students are more likely to flounder and less likely to achieve success in college or in a career. Instead of going with the flow and simply reacting to what college and life present, think instead about how you can take more control over the decisions and choices you make now because these decisions and choices will lay the foundation for the achievement of future life goals. It is easy to make vague plans for the future, but you must determine which short-term steps are necessary if those plans are to become a reality.

College is an ideal time to begin setting and fulfilling short- and long-term goals. A short-term goal might be to read twenty pages from your history text twice a week to prepare for an exam that will cover the first hundred pages of the book. A long-term goal might be to begin predicting which elective college courses you could choose that would help you attain your career goals.

Thinking about a career might seem unrelated to some of the general education courses you are required to take in your first year. Sometimes it's hard to see the connection between a history or literature course and what you want to do with the rest of your life. Lewis, whom we met at the beginning of the chapter, was majoring in economics and planning to go to law school. But his favorite elective course was psychology. Let's consider what Lewis could learn in psychology that would help him understand how to be a better attorney. For instance, psychology might help him understand why some people get into legal trouble. If you're open to learning, you will discover how different courses, even those that seem to have no connection, relate to each other.

Setting SMART Goals

Follow these guidelines to set some short-term goals and consider how they fall within the framework of setting goals that are *specific, measurable, attainable, relevant,* and *achievable* within a given *time* (SMART).[4] Figure 1.2 on the next page gives you a chance to practice.

1. Be specific about what you want to achieve and when.
2. State your goal in measurable terms.
3. Be sure that the goal is attainable. If you don't have the necessary skills, strengths, and resources to achieve your goal, change it to one that is more appropriate for you. Be sure that you really want to reach the goal. Don't set out to work toward something only because you want to please others.
4. Know how the goal is relevant to your life and why the goal matters. Be sure that your goal helps your larger life plan and gives you a sense of moving forward.
5. Consider the time frame and whether the goal is achievable within the period you desire. Allow yourself enough time to pursue it by considering any difficulties you might have. Plan for ways you might deal with problems. Decide which goal comes next. How will you begin? Create steps and a timeline for reaching your next goal.

For instance, let's assume that after you graduate, you are considering working in a developing country, perhaps spending some time in the Peace Corps or another volunteer organization abroad. What are some short-term goals that would help you reach this long-term objective? One goal might be to take courses focused on different countries or cultures, but that goal isn't very specific and doesn't state a particular time period. A much more specific goal would be to take one course each year that helps you build a body of knowledge about other countries and cultures. An even more specific goal would be to review the course catalog, identify the courses you want to take, and list them on a personal timeline.

Before working toward any long-term goal, it's important to be realistic and honest with yourself. Is it truly *your* goal—one that you yourself value and desire to pursue—or is it a goal that a parent or friend argued was right for you? Given your abilities and interests, is the goal realistic? Remember that dreaming up long-term goals is the easy part. To reach your goals, you need to be specific and systematic about the steps you will take today, this week, and throughout your college experience. To do well in college though, the most important goals are always short-term: What do I need to do today and this week to further my longer-term goals?

---

[4] George T. Doran, "There's a S.M.A.R.T. Way to Write Management's Goals and Objectives," *Management Review* 70, no. 11 (1981): 35–36.

FIGURE 1.2 ❯ Practice Setting SMART Goals

What are your goals for this term? Using the SMART goal-setting guide, try to set one goal in each of the four areas listed: academic, career, personal, and financial. Follow the goal through time, from immediate to long-term. An example is provided for you.

Type of Goal	S SPECIFIC goal	M How many MEASURABLE steps?	A Why can I ATTAIN the goal?	R How is this RELEVANT to me?	T What TIME FRAME do I desire? What potential difficulties will arise, and how will I deal with them to stay on track?
Academic	Complete my academic plan this term based on my chosen program of study.	1. In the next 2 weeks, review the college catalog to select a program of study that interests me and prepares me for my future career. 2. Select my required courses, and map out every term. 3. Choose my elective courses. 4. Meet with an academic adviser to make sure my academic map makes sense.	I am organized. I have a manageable range of interests.	I can't use my time in college well if I don't know where I am headed. An adviser can give me ideas for how I can apply my interests to a program of study.	• Meet with an academic and a career adviser by the middle of the term. • Obtain all the necessary signatures to finalize my academic plan before the end of the term. **Potential Difficulties:** • I do not know an academic or career adviser. • I haven't made a decision about what I want to study. **How to Deal with Difficulties:** • Visit the academic and career advising centers. • Discuss my academic and career goals with the advisers, and ask for their advice regarding the program of study I should select.
Academic					
Career					
Personal					
Financial					

yourturn | Making Decisions

The Decision to Become a College Student

Write five reasons that you chose to go to college at this time in your life. Share what you wrote with a classmate and see how many of your reasons are the same or different.

MAKING CHOICES

You will make choices every day of your college career, and some of them are far more important than others. Your choices may be consistent or inconsistent, but whatever they are, they will interact with each other and either support or sabotage the achievement of your larger goals and purposes in college and beyond. Sometimes, or frequently for some students, these choices, even small ones, can interfere with success and lead to negative outcomes, especially if students don't realize that they are the ones in charge.

Locus of Control

While no one has total and absolute control over what happens in life, one concept we want you to understand is what social scientists call locus of control. Basically, this means that healthy and successful people accept responsibility for their own lives, to the extent possible, by the choices they freely make. They decide what they are going to do. They don't see themselves as primarily ruled by fate or being made to do things by others. It's an active view rather than a passive view of self.

Here is an example: You can tell yourself that your roommate begged you to go out to a club when you should have been studying and that made you fail a test. Or you can take responsibility for your own actions, which in this case was not choosing to spend the evening in your room or the library preparing for the test. The idea is that, with few exceptions, you are a free agent. You actively choose to do certain things and choose not to do others.

Guided Pathways and the Downside of Poor Choices

Let's face it, students are like other human beings—they make good choices and they make some poor ones. And the poor ones can cost them a lot of time, money, and heartache. Some college and university educators believe that they have given students too much freedom to make choices in college and that students can't possibly understand all the options, particularly when it comes to course selections and majors. The result of this thinking has been to restrict students' choices. You may find yourself taking this course at a college or university that is recommending—or even requiring—that students take a "pathway" or a "guided pathway," a proscribed set of courses leading to certain majors and degrees.

These so-called pathways are based on the use of analytics, information about whether students like you will be more or less likely to complete

TABLE 1.2 › The Choices You Will Make

Being successful in college has a great deal to do with the choices you are making, will make, need to make, and should not make, often on a daily basis. Think about it. You are your own boss in college. Let's look at how this matter of making choices plays out for college students. Consider the following questions, and write in the choice you're likely to make about each one.

Questions	Your Choice
Are you going to get up in time for your first class or sleep in and skip it?	
Are you going to eat breakfast? We know that what you eat affects energy and ability to concentrate in class.	
How much time will you devote to homework today?	
Are you going to study alone for your next exam or with a study group? Research has long demonstrated the beneficial effects of study groups!	
Are you going to start preparing for the exam a week before or the night before? We know that procrastination has many negative academic effects.	
How much sleep are you going to get today? Sleep has a big impact on overall wellness, energy, and ability to concentrate—all needed for academic success.	
Are you going to get any exercise today? We know that exercise has a positive impact on overall health and energy.	
How much alcohol are you going to consume today? This choice can have a huge impact on your ability to function successfully in academic work the next day.	
Will you seek tutoring today or in the near future?	
Will you visit your instructor during office hours to get some questions answered? We know that students who seek academic support assistance perform better in college.	
Do you want to be like the friends you are choosing? Think about the kinds of friends you are choosing, and keep in mind that it is likely you will become like them.	

certain courses successfully. If your course choices are limited, you will be able to avoid courses where you would be unlikely to achieve success. You will save time, money, and energy by taking courses that are right for you.

BEING "HIP" IN COLLEGE: PARTICIPATING IN HIGH-IMPACT PRACTICES

high-impact practices 1–10

Those who run America's colleges and universities know a lot more now than in previous years about the kind of experiences students have in college that correlate with learning, satisfaction, and staying in college. A prominent higher education researcher at Indiana University, Professor George Kuh, has given a name to those experiences in college that seem to make the biggest positive differences for students in terms of their learning and success. He calls these experiences high-impact practices, or HIPs.

What Are High-Impact Practices?

Professor Kuh's work grew out of his studies of student engagement—how colleges and universities can intentionally engage students in educationally purposeful activities that yield high levels of learning and satisfaction. These activities require greater investments of time, energy, and commitment than more passive forms of learning. At some colleges some of these high-impact practices (HIPs) will be required and others will be voluntary. If they are voluntary, our advice would be that you try to be involved in them.

One of the high-impact practices is your college success course. Here is a comprehensive list of the eleven high-impact practices, listed in the order you are most likely to encounter them. (In this textbook, this icon ⌖ is used to alert you to these high-impact practices that will enrich your learning. You probably noticed some of these already in the chapter.)

1. **first-year seminars** The course in which you find yourself now, designed to help you be successful in your college experience by teaching you how to do college. We have already told you about this high-impact practice.

2. **writing-intensive courses** Courses across the curriculum that engage you in multiple forms of writing for different audiences. This textbook offers various writing activities that make your first-year seminar a writing-intensive course. Some colleges will list in their catalogs courses known as writing-intensive courses. We advise you to take as many of these as you can. Remember that college is really about making you a better thinker, and encouraging you to write intensively is one of the best ways to make you a clearer thinker and communicator.

3. **collaborative assignments** Learning activities in which you work and solve problems with your classmates in this and other courses. Employers want to hire college graduates who have had experience in collaboration, and research has found that collaborative experiences deepen the learning process. A good academic adviser can help you identify courses that will give you the opportunity to engage in collaborative assignments.

4. **global learning or diversity experiences** Courses and programs (such as study abroad) in which you explore cultures, life experiences, and worldviews different from your own. Your course catalogue may list diversity-enriched courses that fulfill a general education requirement called global learning. Here again, a good academic adviser can help you identify and select these opportunities. And financial aid is often available for students who have limited finances.

5. **service-learning** Programs or courses in which you engage in required field-based experiential learning and reflection while giving back to your community through service. Strictly defined, service-learning is mandatory, nonremunerative service (for no pay) that is embedded in a credit-bearing course. If you enjoy volunteering and community service, you will really love service-learning because not only do you have the opportunity to help others, you can also earn academic credit.

6. **learning communities** Programs in which you take two or more linked courses with the same small group of other students and work closely with one another and with your instructors. Learning communities are most commonly offered in the first year of college, but some institutions also offer them in the second year and beyond. Learning

communities are often linked to a common, shared academic theme so students can see how different disciplines approach a common issue.

7. **campuswide common intellectual experiences** Programs in which you take required common core courses, participate in a required learning community, or engage in other shared experiences such as a common reading. The essential characteristic is that these experiences are shared by all new students and have an intellectual component. Thus they become part of the shared traditions of the institution and are high-priority learning experiences.

8. **undergraduate research** A program that gives you the opportunity to participate in systematic investigation and research working one-on-one with a faculty member. This is more likely to be offered to sophomores, juniors, or seniors, but some institutions do make this opportunity available to first-year students. Ask your academic adviser if undergraduate research is available in any academic department. Frequently, undergraduate students participating in such research with their faculty actually produce joint publications or presentations, which are important additions to your résumé!

9. **internships** Direct experience in a work setting often related to your career interests. Usually, internships are offered after the first year. Some carry stipends; however, more commonly these are unpaid. Internships can be required in certain majors and can carry credit that applies to your degree. It is very common for students to be hired by companies or organizations where they were an intern.

10. **capstone courses and projects** Courses or experiences that require you in the senior year to reflect on what you have learned in all your courses. In a capstone experience you create a project, demonstration, thesis, original composition, or work of art that demonstrates and integrates your knowledge and applies it to a specific task or project.

11. **eportfolios** An eportfolio is an electronic collection of your work that shows your learning journey over time. At some institutions, you can begin your eportfolio in your college success course.

When, How, and Why Should I Be HIP?

We wanted you to know as you started college what HIPs are so that you can look forward to *and* plan for them. You should start talking about selecting HIPs with your academic adviser as early as your first-term academic advising session. We can assure you that you will experience deeper and more satisfying learning and success during college and more success after college in your vocation if you experience HIPs while in college.

You can engage in some of these HIPs immediately (such as taking this course or being part of a learning community). Others (such as internships, study abroad, or writing-intensive courses) will be offered throughout your undergraduate experience. Most HIP experiences can be obtained for no additional cost (except for travel expenses in study-abroad programs). An ambitious goal would be to enrich your college experience by participating in at least one HIP each term, but certainly try to experience at least one per year. It might help you to select a friend to join you for each of these. And you will certainly meet new friends through participating. The more HIPs you take advantage of, the more hip you are going to be in college as a learner and in your life and career after college.

E-MAIL WITH STYLE

As you planned for college, you probably heard about all the ways you'll use technology as a student. First, you need to activate your college e-mail as soon as possible to receive information regarding class cancellations, weather-related closings, student events, and other types of communication that your college or your instructors may send you. Many colleges require you to use your student e-mail account to send and receive official communications. Unfortunately, many students do not use the campus e-mail system, which is a mistake because they miss many important messages sent only to the student's official institutional address. It is a good idea to get in the habit of checking that account daily or at least every other day.

Whether your class meets online or face-to-face, at some point you will need to communicate with your instructor via e-mail. Although you may prefer to use Snapchat, Instagram, or Twitter, use e-mail to communicate with your instructors unless they tell you otherwise. Writing e-mails to your instructors is different from writing e-mails or sending texts to your friends.

The Problem

You need help with an assignment or you have a question about the syllabus. You need to send your instructor an e-mail, but you've never sent an e-mail to any kind of teacher before.

The Fix

Take a few minutes to figure out what exactly you need to ask, jot down your main points, and then construct a clear and concise e-mail.

How to Do It

Look at the example shown here and follow its format in your e-mail.

It's best to use your college e-mail address because it has your name and your college's e-mail address, which will help your instructor recognize immediately that your message has been sent by a student. If you have to use another e-mail address, use a professional, simple address that includes your name.

- Make the subject line informative. Your instructor might receive hundreds of e-mails every day, and a relevant subject like the name of the course or the assignment will help him or her respond to your e-mail promptly. A subject line like "Class" or "Question" isn't helpful; a blank subject line usually goes to the instructor's spam folder.
- Address your instructor with respect. Think about how you address your instructor in class, or look at your syllabus to see his or her proper title. If an instructor uses Doctor (Dr.), then you should use Doctor. If you don't know your instructor's title, you can never go wrong with Dear Professor, plus the last name.

- Sign every e-mail with your full name and course and section number.
- When attaching files to your e-mail, use widely accepted file formats like .doc, .docx, or .pdf. Also, include your last name as part of the file name. See the example shown above.

EXTRA STYLE POINTS: Set your college e-mail to feed into your phone, tablet, or regular online account. Tie it into your regular e-mail, like Google or Outlook. Most of these services can be configured so that you can receive e-mail from multiple accounts. This way, you will have all of your e-mail in one place that you're sure to check, and you won't lose your messages when your account is deleted from your college's network after graduation.

Note: If you want to cut back on e-mails from websites that you visit, use a free service like UnRollMe (https://unroll.me) that condenses the blanket e-mails you get but allows you to read them when you have time. You can list your instructors as "favorites" so you don't miss their e-mails.

checklist for success

Thriving in College and Life

■ **Understand what it means to thrive.** Appreciate how doing well in your college success course and mastering the material in your textbook will help you thrive in college and life—the research proves it.

■ **Get to know your campus VIPs.** Remember that these "very important people" include other students, instructors, staff members, and administrators. You may find that your relationships with these individuals are among the primary benefits of college.

■ **Know and appreciate the value of a college education, your college success course, and this textbook.** College is a major investment of both time and money, an investment that will pay rich dividends both now and in the future. This course and this textbook can help you make the right choices and increase your chances for success. Read the table of contents, skim the entire book, and access the information that you need now.

■ **Take charge of your choices.** You will make choices every day of your college career, and some of them are far more important than others. Learn to take an active approach to these choices rather than a passive one. Consider whether a guided pathway determined by your college makes sense for you.

■ **Explore your purpose for being in college and learn how to set SMART goals.** You are far more likely to succeed in college if your purpose is clear and your goals for today, tomorrow, and four years from now are well thought out. For instance, if you plan to graduate from college in four years, what goals could you set for this week or this term that would help you reach this important long-term goal?

■ **Pursue high-impact practices.** Throughout this textbook, we have highlighted high-impact practices. These practices will begin in the first year and continue throughout your college experience. By taking every opportunity to participate in high-impact practices, you will increase your learning and overall success in college.

REFLECT ON CHOICES

high-impact practice 2 Reflect and write about what you have learned about college success in this chapter and how you are going to apply this information to the choices that you need to make this term. Select a few choices such as when to meet with an academic adviser and when to visit instructors during their office hours.

APPLY WHAT YOU'VE LEARNED

Now that you have read and discussed this chapter, consider how you can apply what you have learned to your academic and personal life. The following prompts will help you reflect on chapter material and its relevance to you, both now and in the future.

1. Why are you in college? Reflect on your decision to enter this college at this time in your life. Be honest about who or what influenced you to make this decision. What challenges do you face, and what strategies for success can you use to overcome those challenges?

2. College students often feel the stress of trying to balance their personal and academic lives. How can you include time to engage in at least one high-impact practice each year?

USE YOUR RESOURCES

> **Academic Skills Center.** Whether you need help or not, explore this facility. Its services can include tutoring, help with study and memory skills, and help with studying for exams.

> **Adult Student Center.** If you are an adult or returning student, visit this center to learn about special programs, make contacts with other adult students, and gather information about services such as child care.

> **Career Center.** You may visit the career center as part of your college success course. If you do not, put it on your list of important campus services. Career centers usually feature a career library, interest assessments, counseling, and help in finding a major.

> **Commuter Services.** Commuter students are the new majority. If you are a commuter student, find the campus office that provides lists of special services for you.

> **Counseling Center.** Find out about your institution's counseling center and the services it offers, which will probably include stress-management programs and confidential counseling.

> **Diversity/Inclusion/Multicultural Center.** A diversity center can serve as a resource for information about special activities on campus highlighting diversity, and can also provide support for international students or for U.S. students who are underrepresented on campus.

> **Financial Aid and Scholarship Office.** Meet with someone in this office to learn about financial aid programs, scholarships, and grants.

> **Health Center.** Don't wait until you need a doctor or a nurse. Locate your campus health center and learn about its services.

> **Math Center.** If your math instructor hasn't already told you about help from the math center, ask whether your college or university has such a center. It may not be named separately and may be part of the Learning Center or Academic Support Center.

> **Student Affairs.** The student affairs division oversees out-of-class activities and opportunities such as Greek life, intramural sports, student clubs and organizations, campus leadership activities, and student academic support.

> **Veterans Affairs Office.** If you are a veteran, be sure to learn about the services of this office, including special financial aid and opportunities to meet other students who are vets.

> **Writing Center.** As you write your first research paper, ask an expert in the writing center to read a first draft to give you help with proper grammar, syntax, and punctuation, as well as the appropriate method for citing and listing references.

LaunchPad
macmillan learning

LaunchPad for *Your College Experience* is a great resource. Go online to master concepts using the LearningCurve study tool and much more. **Launchpadworks.com**

SDI Productions/Getty Images

2

CULTIVATING MOTIVATION, RESILIENCE, AND EMOTIONAL INTELLIGENCE

YOU WILL EXPLORE

The similarities and differences between motivation, attitude, and mindsets

How resilience is a key to success in college and in life

Strategies for understanding and evaluating your emotional intelligence

How your emotions affect your health and your outlook on life

⚙ High-impact practices 2 (writing), 3 (collaboration), and 5 (service-learning)

AJR_photo/Shutterstock

> ❝ **I'm doing better now. I'm still really busy and usually broke, but I'm so glad I didn't drop out.** ❞

Tiffany's first year at Wright State University got off to a great start. She was happy with all her courses, and she pledged a sorority. But her excitement was short lived. During the last week of October, Tiffany's father called and told her that he had lost his job and probably would not be able to pay her tuition for the spring term, much less her upcoming sorority dues. "I was so disappointed; I thought my life was over," recalls Tiffany. "For three weeks, I moped around campus. I totally lost my motivation to keep up in my courses. I dropped out of the sorority, but the girls didn't seem to care. I realized that they weren't really close friends. No one seemed to be concerned about what was going on in my life."

Tiffany's college success instructor noticed that Tiffany seemed unusually quiet and depressed. "It was interesting." Tiffany said. "I didn't think she knew me that well, but she asked me to stay after class just to talk about what was happening in my life. I told her that things had really changed at home because of my father's situation and that I probably would need to drop out of college. She didn't waste any time; she made an appointment for me the very next day with a financial aid counselor."

The financial aid counselor let Tiffany know that she was not alone and that many other students had serious financial challenges. She talked to Tiffany about loans and part-time employment. Tiffany made the decision to take out a student loan and to apply for a job either on or off campus. Immediately, she found an off-campus job with good pay, but it was about 10 miles from campus. "Initially, I thought I could handle the travel time and work demands, but the stress of trying to do everything was overwhelming," Tiffany remembered. "I was never really ready for class, and because of my class schedule and the bus schedule, I was often late for work." After a particularly bad week when her supervisor had given her a warning about being late and she had failed an exam, Tiffany once again came close to dropping out. She went back to the financial aid counselor's office. "The counselor asked me how I was doing, and I burst into tears," Tiffany said. "It was clear to her that I needed another game plan. Talking to her really helped me feel better."

The counselor told Tiffany not to give up. They talked about other options, including a job on campus that had just become available in the English Department. The new on-campus job gave Tiffany the chance to interact with other students and with faculty members, and she regained her optimism and determination to stay in college. "I'm doing better now. I'm still really busy and usually broke, but I'm so glad I didn't drop out."

With everything that was happening to Tiffany and her family, it is no wonder she was stressed; however, in accepting help from her college success instructor and a financial aid counselor, she got a new lease on college life. The rest of her college experience won't be easy, but now she knows she'll never have to face this kind of stress alone.

assess your strengths

How well do you understand the ways that your attitude and motivation will affect your success in college? As you read this chapter, think about your current strengths in maintaining your motivation, managing you emotional reactions, being resilient, and keeping a positive attitude.

set goals

Think about past challenges you have had in understanding and managing your emotions. Perhaps you are still sorry about an unnecessary argument you had with a friend or family member, or perhaps your disappointment about a test grade or performance has caused you to give up on yourself. How could you set goals to change your reactions to tough situations like these so that you would be more likely to experience a positive outcome?

THE IMPORTANCE OF MOTIVATION, ATTITUDE, AND MINDSETS

To access the LearningCurve study tool, video activities, and more, go to LaunchPad for *Your College Experience.*
Launchpadworks.com

Although your academic skills are very important in college, much of college success will also relate to your noncognitive characteristics—your patterns of thought, feelings, and behavior that will affect how well you do in your academic work. If you're like most students, you will face big challenges every day, and at some point in your college career, things *will* go wrong no matter how much you plan ahead, set goals, and work hard. When you're facing such challenges, how you *think, feel,* and *behave* will have a huge effect on your ability to keep going.

What if you have to work this afternoon, you have a test tomorrow, and you haven't studied enough? What if your computer crashes and you have a paper due tomorrow? In these tough moments, how you think and feel will make all the difference. If you feel powerless and overwhelmed, you're more likely to give up—to skip studying, be late for work, or turn in a late paper. But if you *believe* you can overcome these challenges, you'll feel energized to keep going and figure out solutions.

The good news is that everyone faces tough moments like these and that you can learn the skills you need to handle them. And remember, you're not alone. Although your classmates might not admit it, many of them share your challenges and fears. In this section, we'll go over habits of mind, and we will give you strategies that will help you achieve your goals. These strategies include staying motivated, keeping a good attitude, and developing a growth mindset, all of which we'll explain below.

Motivation

Motivation, the desire to get things done, is an essential ingredient of success, whether it is success in the classroom, on the playing field, or in life. The reasons that some of us are motivated or unmotivated represent a complex mix of our internal characteristics, attitudes, desires, and views on external rewards and punishments. When you are motivated, you have a high level of commitment and energy that you can use to set goals and then stay focused on them. You are determined to follow a course of action, and you do your best. When you hit obstacles, you make adjustments and work around them, or you deal with them head on.

In general, there are two kinds of motivation. **Intrinsic motivation** comes from a desire inside yourself to achieve something, and the reward is the feeling of satisfaction you get from your achievement. **Extrinsic motivation** comes from the expectation of an external reward or the fear of an undesirable outcome or a punishment.

Although intrinsic and extrinsic motivation are often described separately, in real life, these two types of motivation frequently work together. Think about the college degree you are working toward. It will be a source of personal satisfaction for you, and it will also be a ticket to a better career and a better life. Think about your choice of academic major. Is it one that you picked by yourself, or were you influenced by outside pressure? Hopefully it's an area of study that gives you pleasure but can also prepare you to find a career. Do you have a desire to study abroad? There are both intrinsic and extrinsic benefits to this high-impact practice. You may be enrolled in a course that includes a service project that becomes part of your grade. While the extrinsic motivation for participating will be the grade you receive, you will probably get a real feeling of personal satisfaction from serving others.

 high-impact practice 4, 5

If your source of motivation is only extrinsic, you may have a tough time persisting to reach a goal. For instance, if you want to be a lawyer only because you want money and status, you may find that these things become less and less important as the years go by. You might also find that the profession itself changes in ways that make it more difficult for you to enjoy. Your legal career will be far more rewarding if you are also intrinsically motivated by your personal interactions with clients and colleagues.

Attitude

Attitude is the way you are thinking and feeling in relation to the events around you. Attitude has a lot to do with how well you can maintain your motivation, whether it's being motivated to land a better-paying job, do well in your college courses, participate in extracurricular activities,

Components of Motivation

Think about how the words used in the word cloud relate to motivation.

Rob Wilson/Shutterstock

your turn   Setting Goals

What's Behind Your Current Motivations?

Think about the goals—academic, personal, professional—that you are working toward now. Using the table below, select one goal in each category and write it down. What is motivating you to work toward each goal? Name one or more factors, and circle whether each is an intrinsic or extrinsic factor. You can expand on this exercise in a journal entry or in a group discussion.

My Goals	My Motivation	Intrinsic, Extrinsic, or Both?		
Academic goal:	What motivates me to achieve this goal is _____.	intrinsic	extrinsic	both
Personal goal:	What motivates me to achieve this goal is _____.	intrinsic	extrinsic	both
Career goal:	What motivates me to achieve this goal is _____.	intrinsic	extrinsic	both

work out, or take advantage of all that college has to offer. If you have a bad attitude about writing, you might try to avoid the kinds of writing-intensive course experiences that are important to your success during and after college. If you have had negative experiences with group work in the past, those memories could cause you to avoid collaborating with other students, which is another important strategy for success.

Whether positive or negative, attitudes often come from our previous environments and experiences with others. For instance, if you "hate" math because you've had trouble with math in the past, you will be likely to give up on your math courses before you even give yourself a chance to do well. If sometime in the past a family member, friend, or teacher told you that you weren't college material, a comment like that could have negatively affected your attitude about starting college.

A good starting place to developing a more positive attitude is to think honestly about the attitude you're likely to have in certain situations. How would you handle stressful or surprising situations such as these?

- You ask for time off from work to study for a final exam, and your boss refuses your request.
- You break up with your romantic partner.
- Your financial aid check doesn't arrive in time for you to purchase your books.
- You lose a major paper or report because your computer crashes.
- You need to finish a paper the evening before the due date, and you get sick.
- Your mom wants you to visit but you have too much going on to make a trip home.
- As a non-native English speaker, you're struggling in many of your classes.

high-impact practice 2, 3

- Your commute to campus is taking twice as long due to major construction on the route.
- You fail a pop quiz that caught you entirely by surprise.
- You lose your psychology notebook, and the final exam is next week.
- A group project isn't going well because other members of the group aren't doing their share of the work.
- Your roommate keeps you up all night before an important exam.

Any of these things can and do happen to students just like you. Most college students have many responsibilities, which can make it hard to maintain a good attitude and stay motivated. When you face these kinds of frustrations, do you get really stressed or mad? Do you expect the worst, or do you stay relaxed, do your best, and keep going?

If you've been told by people who know you well that you're negative or pessimistic or you realize that you always expect the worst, try to discover the reason why. Is it a general feeling or one that relates to different aspects of your college experience? Here are some strategies you can use to make an attitude adjustment:

- Spend time thinking about what you can learn from difficult situations you faced and overcame.
- Give yourself credit for good choices that you made, and think about how you can build on these successes.
- Recall experiences when things did not work out, and try to think through the mistakes that you made and how you could have done better.
- Seek out individuals, both on and off campus, who are positive. Ask them where their optimism comes from.
- Identify a group on campus that has the reputation of being positive and successful. Is this a study group, a group that engages in community service, or something else? In your opinion what accounts for this group's actual or perceived success?
- Take advantage of the opportunities you will get in your college success course to explore the effect your attitude has on the outcomes you want.
- Be mindful of your attitude as you move through the weeks of this term.

Mindsets

Another way to look at motivation is to examine what are called mindsets. **Mindsets** refer to what you believe about yourself and about your most basic qualities such as your personality, intelligence, or talents. If you have a fixed mindset, you are likely to believe that your characteristics and abilities—either positive or negative—*are not going to change* through any adjustments to your behavior or effort. A growth mindset, however, means that you are willing to try new approaches and that you believe that *you can change*.[1]

People with a fixed mindset are often trying to prove themselves, and they're very sensitive about being wrong or making mistakes. They also think that having to make an effort means they are not smart or

---

[1] Based on Carol S. Dweck, *Mindset: The New Psychology of Success* (New York: Ballantine, 2006), p. 16.

talented. Many new college students are "fixed" in their beliefs about themselves and their abilities. People with a growth mindset believe that their abilities can be improved—that there is no harm in being wrong or making a mistake. They think that the effort they make is what makes them smart or talented. Some of us have a different mindset for different tasks. For instance, you may find that you have a fixed mindset for your athletic abilities but a growth mindset for music.

Consider Amber, a second-year college student. In high school, Amber was in the top 10 percent of her class, and had never earned a grade lower than an A minus. Her high school was pretty small and lacked some advanced courses, but Amber assumed that she was prepared for college. During her first college year, however, Amber earned Bs, Cs, and even a D in calculus. The extrinsic motivation that had come from good grades was long gone, which turned her fixed-mindset world upside down. For several months, Amber was disinterested in almost everything; she completely lost her motivation to study and learn when earning an A had seemingly become impossible.

Slowly, though, Amber turned things around. She began watching how other students studied and interacted with instructors. Not all of the examples were good ones. Some students would brag about skipping class and staying up all night to study instead of managing their time better. But others had a deliberate plan that included taking really good notes, studying every day, trying to sit close to the front of the classroom, and talking with instructors after class. Amber started adopting these behaviors. Little by little, she practiced new study strategies, began to accept criticism without falling apart, and gained an understanding that sometimes she could learn more from her mistakes than from her successes. It took Amber about a year to regain her positive attitude and a willingness to do her best, no matter what the outcome.

How would you describe how Amber's mindset changed? How would you describe your own? What can you learn about your mindset by walking through the exercise in Table 2.1?

Whether you're in your college classes, your student activity center, or your home, your mindsets—similar to your attitude—can influence how you think about yourself and others, your opportunities, and your

Embrace Change

"The same old thinking yields the same old results." "Stay positive." "Attitude is everything." We've heard sayings like these before. As you read this section, you might agree that these sayings ring true.

Aysezgicmeli/Shutterstock.com

TABLE 2.1 > Mindsets: Which Sounds More like You?

For each pair of statements, select the one that sounds more like you.

A. You believe that your efforts won't change your grades.
B. You believe that you can improve your grades with effort.

A. You believe that a good grade means you have learned everything you need to know.
B. You believe that you can always learn more, even if you have received an A.

A. You tend to blame the world around you when things go wrong.
B. You try to solve the problems when things go wrong.

A. You are often afraid to try new things because you fear you will fail.
B. You believe that failure is an opportunity to learn more.

A. You believe that some jobs are for "women only" or for "men only."
B. You are open to exploring all job opportunities.

A. You believe that leaders are born, not made.
B. You believe that leadership can be developed.

A. You tend to believe negative things that others say about you.
B. You don't allow others to define who you are.

If you selected mostly "A" statements, you likely have a fixed mindset; if you selected mostly "B" statements, you have a growth mindset.

As mentioned above, your mindset can change depending on the task. Which tasks do you approach with more of a growth mindset? Which tasks do you approach with more of a fixed mindset? Remember that a mindset that is fixed today might not be fixed tomorrow—with some motivation you can challenge yourself, take some risks, and develop a positive attitude about your ability to grow and change.

relationships. A fixed mindset will cause you to limit the things you do, the people you meet, the classes you take, and even the activities you choose in college. A growth mindset will help you be more willing to explore classes and activities out of your comfort zone. It will help you stay motivated because you will see disappointments or failures as opportunities to learn.

RESILIENCE

Motivation requires a clear vision, courage, and persistence. And it takes **resilience**—not giving up or quitting when faced with difficulties and challenges. A resilient person maintains a positive attitude even when faced with difficult situations. Students who are resilient—who bounce back quickly from difficult situations—will have a higher probability of success in college and in life. They stay focused on achieving their purpose. Learning to keep going when things are hard is one of the most important lessons you'll learn in this class.

There are many other terms that are used to describe resilience and determination. One of these terms is **grit**, a combination of perseverance, passion, and resilience. Psychologist Angela Duckworth has studied grit and has found that people who are "gritty" are more likely to be both academically and personally successful.[2] Another term that encompasses resilience comes from Finland: **Sisu** is a word that dates back hundreds of years and is described as being central to understanding Finnish culture.

---
[2] See apa.org/monitor/nov07/grit.

It means going beyond one's mental or physical ability, taking action even when things are difficult, and displaying courage and determination in the face of challenge and repeated failures. A similar example is the Mexican word **ganas**, meaning the desire to win or gain.

Resilience is such an important concept in psychological health that the American Psychological Association has developed a list of resilience strategies: "10 Ways to Build Resilience."[3] These strategies are described as follows:

1. **Make connections.** Good relationships with close family members, friends, or others are important. Accepting help and support from those who care about you and will listen to you helps you become more resilient. Some people find that being active in civic groups, religious organizations, or other community groups gives them support and encouragement. Assisting others in their time of need also can benefit the helper.

2. **Avoid seeing crises as problems that can't be overcome.** You can't change the fact that highly stressful events happen, but you can change how you view and respond to those events. Try looking beyond the present and think about how things will be better in the future.

3. **Accept that change is a part of living.** Obstacles might keep you from achieving certain goals. Accepting situations that cannot be changed can help you focus on those that you *can* change.

4. **Move toward your goals.** Develop some realistic goals. Do something regularly—even if it seems like a small accomplishment—that enables you to move toward your goals. Instead of focusing on tasks that seem impossible, ask yourself, "What's one thing I know I can accomplish today that will help me move in the direction I want to go?"

5. **Take decisive actions.** Don't wait for problems to disappear on their own. Take decisive actions rather than staying away completely avoiding problems and wishing they would just go away.

6. **Look for opportunities for self-discovery.** Struggles often make people stronger and teach them what they're made of. Consider what you have learned about yourself from going through tough times.

7. **Nurture a positive view of yourself.** Developing confidence in your ability to solve problems and trusting your instincts helps build resilience.

8. **Keep things in perspective.** Even when facing a very painful event, try to consider the big picture and keep a long-term perspective. Avoid blowing the event out of proportion.

9. **Maintain a hopeful outlook.** An optimistic outlook enables you to expect that good things will happen in your life. Try visualizing what you want, rather than worrying about what you fear.

10. **Take care of yourself.** Pay attention to your own needs and feelings. Engage in activities that you enjoy and find relaxing. Exercise regularly. Taking care of yourself helps keep your mind and body ready to deal with situations that require resilience.

---

[3] American Psychological Association. (2020, February 1). "Building Your Resilience." http://www.apa.org /topics/resilience. No further reproduction or distribution is permitted without written permission from the American Psychological Association.

Don't Let Anything Stop You

Show your grit. Develop sisu. Be resilient. If your goal is to graduate, overcome the obstacles that get in your way, no matter what they are.

Tony Anderson/DigitalVision/Getty Images

There are other ways to deal with challenges and stressful situations. For example, some people write about their deepest thoughts and feelings related to trauma or other stressful events in their life. Meditation and spiritual practices help some people to build connections and restore hope.

Think about your own reactions to frustration and stress. Do you often give up because something is just too hard or because you can't figure it out? Do you take responsibility for what you do, or do you blame others if you fail? For example, how have you reacted to receiving a D or F on a paper, losing a student government election, or getting rejected for a work-study job? Do you have trouble making connections with others in class?

Negative experiences might cause you to question whether you should be in college at all. Resilient students look past negative experiences, learn from them, and try again. For instance, what could you do to improve your grade on your next paper? Perhaps you didn't allow yourself enough time to do the necessary research. Why did someone else get the work-study job that you wanted? It's possible that you need to work on your interview skills. How can you feel more comfortable in your classes? Maybe it would help to join a study group or go to the learning center. You were born with the ability to be resilient.

high-impact practice 3

Many well-known and successful people overcame tough circumstances and failure. For instance, J. K. Rowling, the author of all the Harry Potter books, was divorced and penniless when she wrote the first book in the Harry Potter series. That book was rejected by twelve publishers before it was finally accepted. Walt Disney's first animation company went bankrupt, and he was fired by a news agency because he "lacked imagination." Michael Jordan was cut by his high school basketball team. Jordan has been quoted as reporting that he missed 9,000 shots in his career. These people and many others did not let failure get in the way of their ultimate success.

So far in this chapter we have asked you to consider how thoughts and feelings affect behavior. We've discussed motivation, attitude, and resilience, and have asked you to explore what motivates you, to think about your own attitude and how it helps or hurts you sometimes, and to reflect on whether you are able to bounce back from difficulty. These topics are part of a broader discussion of emotions, which we turn to next.

your turn | **Feeling Connected**

Past Challenges

Think about a challenge you faced in the past. How did you feel and respond to this challenge? Be prepared to share your strategies in dealing with this challenge in class in a small group.

UNDERSTANDING EMOTIONAL INTELLIGENCE

Emotional intelligence (EI) is the ability to recognize, understand, use, and manage emotions—moods, feelings, and attitudes. It should come as no surprise that your emotional intelligence is related to how resilient you are, and it affects your ability to stay motivated and committed to your goals. As we said earlier in the chapter, how you think and feel makes all the difference in whether you succeed or give up. Developing an awareness of emotions allows you to use your feelings to improve your thinking. If you are feeling sad, for instance, you might view the world in a negative way. If you feel happy, you are likely to view the same events differently. Once you start paying attention to emotions, you can learn not only how to cope with life's pressures and demands but also how to use your knowledge of the way you feel for more effective problem solving, decision making, and creativity. This is all part of developing your emotional intelligence; because your ability to deal with life's challenges is based on your emotional intelligence, it's critical to understand this concept.

is this you?

Older Than Average

Are you an older student, maybe in your thirties or forties, who is back in college? As an adult you may have a great deal of life experience in dealing with tough times. You might have real strengths in emotional intelligence that you have developed at work, at home, or with your family, but you may also have some areas that you need to improve. How are you using your strengths and your experience to stand up for yourself and negotiate with others as you face challenges in college? You might want to give some advice to younger students who are struggling with the day-to-day interactions that are part of college life and help them find ways to be more adaptable, resilient, and assertive.

Particularly in the first year of college, many students have difficulty establishing positive relationships with others, dealing with pressure, or making wise decisions. Other students are optimistic and happy and seem to adapt to their new environment without any trouble. Being optimistic doesn't mean that you ignore your problems or pretend that they will go away, but optimistic people believe in their own abilities to address problems successfully as they arise. You'll recall the discussion earlier in this chapter of the impact that attitude has on college success and success in life.

Emotions are a big part of who you are; you should not ignore them. Being aware of your own and others' feelings helps you gather correct information about the world around you and allows you to respond in appropriate ways. If you are a returning student, you probably have a great deal of life experience in dealing with tough times, and you can draw on this experience in college.

As you read this section and the next, think about the behaviors that help people, including yourself, do well and the behaviors that interfere with success. Get to know yourself better, and take the time to examine your feelings and the impact they have on the way you act. You can't always control the challenges of life, but with practice you *can* control how you respond to them. Remember that emotions are real, can be changed for the better, and can significantly affect whether a person is successful.

 high-impact practice 3

your turn | **Feeling Connected**

Considering People Skills

Using an online dictionary, look up the term "people skills." Rate yourself on two or more of these skills and share your ratings with a classmate. How might you and your classmate improve your skills in this area?

Perceiving and Managing Emotions

Perceiving emotions involves the ability to monitor and identify feelings (nervous, happy, angry, relieved, and so forth) correctly and to determine why you feel the way you do. It also involves predicting how others might feel in a given situation. Emotions contain information, and the ability to understand and think about that information plays an important role in behavior.

Managing emotions is based on the belief that feelings can be modified, even improved. At times, you need to stay open to your feelings, learn from them, and use them to take appropriate actions. Other times, it is better to disengage from an emotion and return to it later. Anger, for example, can blind you and lead you to act in negative or antisocial ways; used positively, however, anger can help you take a stand against bias or injustice. It is important that you recognize your mood and your emotions and that you learn when the time is right for you to handle different situations.

The Role of Emotional Intelligence in Everyday Life

Emotional intelligence may be a new term for you, but your emotions guide your behavior throughout your life, even if you do not realize it. For example, whether you just graduated from high school or have worked for several years, you have now decided to pursue higher education. This decision might have been based on your family's encouragement, your career goals, or changes in your current job. You may even have wanted to go to a different college but found out that you and your family could not afford to do that. In that case, how do you think your emotions played a role in making your final decision about college?

Naming and labeling emotions, in addition to focusing on related experiences, improves emotional intelligence. For example, new college students often face the fear of social rejection. Did you think that you would see lots of people from your neighborhood or high school but have found that you don't know anyone? If you are an older student, are your classes filled with younger students who have little in common with you? If you can acknowledge and name what you are feeling, you will be less likely to be controlled by it. You will be in a better place to confront certain fears by walking up to other students, even those of a different age, introducing yourself, and perhaps asking to join their discussions. As you work to develop your emotional intelligence, consider how to use logic rather than your own emotional reactions to evaluate a situation and be helpful to yourself and to others.

Your daily life gives you many opportunities to take a hard look at how you handle emotions. Here are some questions that can help you begin thinking about your own EI.

Don't Roll the Dice

As you learn to identify and manage your emotions, you won't be rolling the dice when it comes to responding to the challenges of everyday life and establishing positive relationships with others.
kostasgr/Shutterstock

Anger Management. Humans experience a wide range of emotions and moods. On the one hand, we can be very generous and positive, and on the other hand, we can lash out in anger. Anger management is an EI skill that is important to develop. Anger can hurt others and can harm your mental and physical health. You may even know someone who uses his or her anger to manipulate and control others.

In spite of the problems it creates, anger does not always lead to negative results. Psychologists see anger as a primary and natural emotion that has value for human survival because it can help us to stand up for what is right.

your turn	**Write and Reflect**

high-impact practice 2

Anger: Friend or Foe?

How do you use anger? Are you in control of how you express this emotion, or does your anger occasionally control you? In a journal entry, explore how anger has affected you, both positively and negatively.

Emotional Intelligence Questionnaire

1. What do you do when you are under stress?
- ☐ a. I tend to deal with it calmly and rationally.
- ☐ b. I get upset, but it usually blows over quickly.
- ☐ c. I get upset but keep it to myself.

2. My friends would say that:
- ☐ a. I play, but only after I get my work done.
- ☐ b. I am ready for fun anytime.
- ☐ c. I hardly ever go out.

3. When something changes at the last minute:
- ☐ a. I adapt easily.
- ☐ b. I get frustrated.
- ☐ c. I don't care because I don't really expect things to happen according to plan.

4. My friends would say that:
- ☐ a. I am sensitive to their concerns.
- ☐ b. I spend too much time worrying about other people's needs.
- ☐ c. I don't like to deal with other people's petty problems.

5. When I have a problem to solve, such as having too many assignments due at the end of the week:
- ☐ a. I write down a list of the tasks I must complete, come up with a plan indicating specifically what I can accomplish and what I cannot, and follow my plan.
- ☐ b. I am very optimistic about getting things done and just dig right in and get to work.
- ☐ c. I get a little overwhelmed. Usually I get a number of things done and then push aside the things I can't do.

Review your responses: "**a**" responses indicate that you probably have a good basis for strong EI; "**b**" responses indicate that you may have some strengths and some challenges in your EI; "**c**" responses indicate that your success in life and in school could be negatively affected by your EI.

Managing Priorities. Using healthy emotional intelligence to prioritize involves deciding what's most important to you and then allocating your time and energy according to these priorities. For example, if exercise, a healthy diet, friends, and studying are most important to you, then you must make time for them all. When you successfully make time in your schedule for what is most important to you, your emotional health benefits. You feel more confident, more in control, and more capable of handling your life with a positive attitude and others with patience. On the other hand, if you cannot keep what is most important to you at the top of your list of priorities, your attitude becomes more negative, you feel stressed out, and you have less patience for other people. Part of developing strong emotional intelligence involves paying attention to your priorities and making adjustments when needed.

Improving Emotional Intelligence

As you reflect more on your own attitudes and behaviors and learn why you have the emotions that you do, you'll improve your emotional intelligence. Studying unfamiliar subjects and interacting with new and diverse people will challenge your EI skills and force you to step outside your comfort zone. Your first year of college is especially critical and gives you a significant opportunity to grow as a person.

Emotional intelligence includes many capabilities and skills that influence a person's ability to cope with life's pressures and demands. Researcher Reuven Bar-On[4] developed the model that is adapted in Table 2.2. This model shows how categories of emotional intelligence directly affect general mood and lead to effective performance.

TABLE 2.2 ❯ Emotional Skills and Competencies

Skills	Competencies	Rank
Intrapersonal	**Emotional self-awareness.** Knowing how and why you feel the way you do.	
	Assertiveness. Standing up for yourself when you need to without being too aggressive.	
	Independence. Making important decisions on your own without having to get everyone's opinion.	
	Self-regard. Liking yourself in spite of your flaws (and we all have them).	
	Self-actualization. Being satisfied and comfortable with what you have achieved in school, work, and your personal life.	
Interpersonal	**Empathy.** Making an effort to understand another person's situation or point of view.	
	Social responsibility. Establishing a personal link with a group or community and cooperating with other members in working toward shared goals.	
	Interpersonal relationships. Seeking out healthy and mutually beneficial relationships—such as friendships, professional networks, family connections, mentoring, and romantic partnerships—and making a persistent effort to maintain them.	
Stress management	**Stress tolerance.** Recognizing the causes of stress, responding in appropriate ways, and staying strong under pressure.	
	Impulse control. Thinking carefully about potential consequences before you act and delaying gratification for the sake of achieving long-term goals.	
Adaptability	**Reality testing.** Ensuring that your feelings are appropriate by checking them against external, objective criteria.	
	Flexibility. Adapting and adjusting your emotions, viewpoints, and actions as situations change.	
	Problem solving. Approaching challenges step-by-step and not giving up in the face of obstacles.	
	Resilience. Being able to bounce back after a setback.	
General mood	**Optimism.** Looking for the bright side of any problem or difficulty and being confident that things will work out for the best.	
	Happiness. Being satisfied with yourself, with others, and with your situation in general.	

---

[4] "What Is Emotional Intelligence?" from Bar-On EQ-i Technical Manual @ 1997,1999, 2000 Multi Health Sytems Inc. Toronto, Canada. Reproduced by permission of Multi-Health Systems.

Identifying Your EI Skills and Competencies

Table 2.2, which is based on Bar-On's work, lists skills that influence a person's ability to cope with life's pressures and demands. Which skills do you think you already have? Which ones do you need to improve? Which ones do you lack? Consider the emotional intelligence skills and competencies listed below and rank them accordingly:

A = Skills I already have, **B** = Skills I need to improve, **C** = Skills I lack

Then go back and rank each one in terms of the priority you assign it right now to your challenges of being a successful college student.

HOW EMOTIONS INFLUENCE SUCCESS AND WELL-BEING

Emotions are strongly tied to physical and psychological well-being. For example, some studies have suggested that cancer patients who have strong EI live longer than those with weak EI. People who are aware of the needs of others tend to be happier than people who are not. An extensive study done at the University of Pennsylvania found that the best athletes succeed in part because they're extremely optimistic. A number of studies link strong EI skills to college success in particular. These studies indicate that emotionally intelligent students get higher grades. Researchers looked at students' GPAs at the end of their first year of college. Students who had tested high for intrapersonal skills, stress tolerance, and adaptability when they entered college did better academically than those who had lower overall EI test scores. Strong EI also affects students' willingness to persist in college. Persistent students keep moving forward through challenging situations, even if progress is slow. And finally students who can delay gratification tend to do better overall. This means that while you are in college you will often have to delay certain fun activities so that you will have more time to succeed in your academic work.

Healthy EI contributes to overall academic success; positive professional and personal relationships, including romantic ones; and career development and satisfaction. EI skills can be enhanced in a college success course. Studies show that, because these skills can be learned, infusing them in a college success course can improve first-year students' emotional intelligence and thus their ultimate success.[5] Here are a few other highlights of these studies:

- Students with intrapersonal skills (emotional self-awareness, assertiveness, independence, self-regard, and self-actualization), stress tolerance, adaptability skills (reality testing, flexibility, and problem solving), and stress management skills (stress tolerance and impulse control) do better academically than those who lack these skills.

---

[5] N. S. Schutte and J. M. Malouff, "Incorporating Emotional Skills in a College Transition Course Enhances Student Retention," *Journal of the First-Year Experience and Students in Transition* 14 (2002): 7–21.

EI Is in Demand
More and more, employers are looking for strong interpersonal skills in job applicants.
Jacob Lund/Shutterstock

- Students who can't manage their emotions struggle academically. Some students experience stress, anxiety, or depression, and too many students turn to risky behaviors (such as drug and alcohol abuse) in an effort to cope.
- Even students who manage to succeed academically in spite of emotional difficulties can be at risk if unhealthy behavior patterns follow them after college.

If you think you need help developing some of these skills, especially if you feel that you are not happy or optimistic, do something about it. You can get by in college without strong EI, but you might miss out on the full range and depth of competencies and skills that can help you succeed in your chosen field and have a fulfilling and meaningful life. Although you can look online for tips about being an optimistic person, there is nothing like getting some in-person help from a professional. Consider visiting your academic adviser or a wellness or counseling center on campus. Look for any related workshops that are offered on campus or nearby.

BUILD A DIGITAL PERSONA

You are active on social media—Facebook, Instagram, Twitter, Snapchat, and others—but you have been told that employers or others might be looking at your profiles, posts, and pictures. You are concerned that people might see parts of your private life that will embarrass you.

If you wonder what people might see, find out. Type your full name into a search engine like Google or Bing and see what comes up. You will see what is connected to you, and you might also see information connected to people who share your name. How can you take charge in order to enjoy a safe digital life?

The Problem

You're open and honest with just about everyone online, but you don't know how to create a professional digital profile that will ensure that employers or others see you at your best.

The Fix

Carefully manage your online image to ensure it sends the appropriate message and reflects the person you want the world to know.

Simon Belcher/Alamy

How to Do It

1. *Exercise caution.* The best way to manage your image online is to be proactive and aware. Make sure that your privacy settings on all social media are updated. For instance, allow only your friends to see your page, and if you list your birthday, don't put the year. If you're choosy about who can have your phone number and address in the real world, be choosy online, too.

2. *Reflect on your values.* You want your online persona to be a version of yourself that you will be proud to be connected to for the rest of your life. Honesty is the best policy, but oversharing is not, especially in the digital age. If you find yourself tagged in a compromising picture, address it right away. Remember that once something goes online, it is public forever, regardless of your privacy settings or if it is taken down.

3. *Delete old accounts.* Delete any accounts that are open to the public but are not updated. Not only do these accounts include out-of-date and possibly embarrassing information, it's likely that you rarely, if ever, check these sites and won't notice if your account has been hacked. The last thing you want is for an employer to find a site full of spam and questionable promotional links.

4. *Stay one step ahead.* Google yourself regularly, especially when applying for jobs. Make sure you know what potential employers can see, and take steps to protect your virtual reputation.

5. *Build your online professional self.* Find a professional social networking site like LinkedIn (linkedin.com) and begin to build a professional persona on that site. Build your professional profile to show where you have gone to college, where you have worked, and awards you have received. The information in this profile should match other professional documents that prospective employers will see, such as your résumé and your job applications.

A professional profile that you control will allow you to connect to other people in your profession, give and receive recommendations and endorsements, join groups of people who share your professional interests, and post comments in those groups. When someone conducts an online search for you, your professional profile will come up first.

EXTRA STYLE POINTS: Have the right mindset when it comes to posting and sharing photos—or even taking them at all—and help adjust the mindset of others. Remind your friends and family to check with you before posting anything about you—especially photos—on a social media site, and think about the purpose and the message of your posts before you share them.

checklist for success

■ **Reflect on your own motivations for being in college and which of them are extrinsic or intrinsic.** If your sources of motivation are entirely extrinsic (for instance money or employment), think of some intrinsic reasons that college will be good for you (for instance, more learning or more satisfaction with life in general).

■ **How do you describe your attitude about the work you're required to do in college?** If your attitude is more often negative than positive, talk to a college counselor about strategies for change.

■ **Think about your mindsets before you came to college.** Were there any fixed mindsets that needed to change in order for you to be successful? Think about your progress so far and how you might still need to alter those stubborn mindsets.

■ **What is emotional intelligence?** Define the most significant abilities of EI and reflect on your connection to those abilities.

■ **Be aware of how your emotions affect the way you react to difficult or frustrating situations.** Use your awareness to try to control your negative reactions before you get into a potentially frustrating situation.

■ **Identify how you develop EI in college.** What can you learn from other students?

■ **Learn and then practice EI improvement strategies such as** identifying your strengths and weaknesses, setting realistic goals, formulating a plan, and checking your progress on a regular basis.

REFLECT ON CHOICES

 **high-impact practice 2** This chapter offers several opportunities for self-reflection and writing in an effort to encourage you to develop an awareness of your noncognitive characteristics—those personal thoughts, feelings, and behaviors that can affect your college success. You can improve your attitudes, mindsets, and overall emotional intelligence. You just have to choose to do so. Remember a time when you faced a difficult problem but overcame it. What choices did you make that helped you through that tough situation? Reflect on these choices and questions in a journal entry or readily accessible file.

APPLY WHAT YOU'VE LEARNED

Now that you have read and discussed this chapter, consider how you can apply what you have learned to your everyday life, both academically and personally. The following prompts will help you reflect on the chapter material and its relevance to you, both now and in the future.

1. Managing stress is an important skill in college, and balancing priorities is a component of emotional intelligence. Look through your course syllabi and list assignments, exams, and important dates. Can you anticipate times when you might be especially likely to get stressed? What can you do in advance to avoid becoming overwhelmed and overstressed?

2. Your emotional reactions, whether positive or negative, affect your interactions with other people. Pretend that you are your own therapist. In what kinds of situations have you reacted with defensiveness, anger, sadness, annoyance, resentment, or humiliation? Take a step back and process these reactions: Think about what you said or did in response to your feelings, and why. What can you do to take control and make good choices the next time you are faced with a potentially volatile situation?

3. No one has the same mindset in all situations. You may be willing to challenge yourself on the playing field but not in the classroom. In what areas are you the most fixed in your self-assessment, and where do you welcome opportunities for challenge and growth?

USE YOUR RESOURCES

> **Your College Library.** Your college library offers books and articles about noncognitive attributes such as motivation, mindsets, and attitude.

> **Your College Counseling Center.** Counselors who work in these centers have special training in stress management, anger management, conflict resolution, and other behavioral issues.

> **Health or Wellness Center.** If personal problems are affecting your overall health—your sleep, diet, or ability to concentrate—visit your campus health center and talk to a health professional about strategies to deal with these issues.

> **Special Workshops That Focus on Personal Emotional Issues.** Be alert for any workshops offered at your institution or in the local community that can help you improve your overall emotional intelligence.

> **Disability Services.** If you are a student with a physical or learning disability that causes additional emotional problems for you, the office of disability services may be your best source of support.

> **Adult Student Services.** Professionals in this office have special training in helping nontraditional students manage the social, personal, and emotional challenges that often arise when adults return to college.

> **Your Peer Leader.** Your peer leader can be a sounding board for you if you are having problems with relationships, stress, anger, or any other personal issues. A peer leader can also refer you to an appropriate office for additional support.

 LaunchPad
macmillan learning

LaunchPad for *Your College Experience* is a great resource. Go online to master concepts using the LearningCurve study tool and much more. **Launchpadworks.com**

nycshooter/Getty Images

3

TIME MANAGEMENT

YOU WILL EXPLORE

Ways to manage your time

Time-management tools

Procrastination and how to overcome it

Setting priorities and achieving balance

The value of time and energy and the importance of allocating these resources wisely

⌖ High-impact practices 2 (writing) and 3 (collaboration)

Hongqi Zhang/Alamy

66 One key to my success with time management is organization. 99

When Abby started college, she had already begun to build a solid foundation in time-management skills. She was born in New York City and moved to Los Angeles, California, when she was three years old. During her senior year of high school, she participated in a college preparation program, which meant taking all her classes at a local college to gain transferable credits. The curriculum included information on learning how to manage time and set priorities. She credits that course with helping her learn how to manage time in her first year of college and beyond. But even with a solid foundation, Abby didn't make it through her first year of college without a few time-management roadblocks. "Sometimes I just got overwhelmed with school and just wanted to work or hang out with my friends and would put my schoolwork on the back burner. This had some bad side effects. Once I saw the drop in my grades, I knew that I had to reprioritize and get back on track."

Now a sophomore, she acknowledges, "one key to my success with time management is organization. I use both paper and electronic organizational tools. If my computer ever goes down, I still have all my information, plans, and due dates in my planner, and vice versa, if I lose my planner, I still have everything on my computer."

This year, Abby is also a resident assistant in a first-year residence hall. She receives free room and board, so this job really helps out with her expenses. But as she says, "it's just one more thing to do, and it's a challenge."

Abby recognizes that prioritizing is the key to maintaining her busy schedule and her sanity. "My priorities are school, work, and family. Then there are all the other things I like to do such as volunteering, exercising, and spending time with my friends," she says. "I find places in my schedule to fit them in, but not necessarily every week. Sometimes, my family comes first, but work helps pay the bills, and I don't want to forget to study. I've actually become pretty good at juggling my most important responsibilities."

LaunchPad
macmillan learning

To access the LearningCurve study tool, video activities, and more, go to LaunchPad for *Your College Experience.*
Launchpadworks.com

Time management is a challenge for almost all first-year college students, many of whom don't use their time wisely at first. As the weeks go by, they begin to realize they will have to change their behavior to ensure that they have sufficient time to give to their coursework. How did Abby deal with the time-management roadblocks that she encountered? How do you deal with those you face? This chapter covers many challenges to time management, such as procrastination and distractions, and it offers techniques you can use to meet your obligations and use your time effectively.

assess your strengths

Time management is challenging for almost all college students. What time-management tools are you already using to manage your time? How do you set and manage your priorities? As you begin to read this chapter, consider the strengths you have in this area.

set goals

Think about challenges you have had in the past with managing your time. Use this chapter to help you understand some strategies and develop goals that relate to time management, such as developing an hour-by-hour record this week of how you spend your time.

MANAGING YOUR TIME

People approach the concept of time differently based on their personalities and backgrounds. Some people are always punctual, while others are almost always running behind schedule. Some students enter all due dates for assignments on a calendar as soon as they receive the syllabus for each class. Other students take a more laid-back approach and prefer to go with the flow rather than follow a daily or weekly schedule. These students might deal well with the unexpected, but they might also leave everything to the last minute and be less successful than if they managed their time more effectively. Even if you prefer to go with the flow, improving your organizational skills can help you do better in college, work, and life. Think of it this way: If *you* were hiring someone for a job, wouldn't you choose an organized person who gets things done on time?

Taking Control of Your Time

The first step to effective time management is recognizing that you can be in control of most areas of your life. While things happen that are out of your control—accidents, sickness, family problems—most decisions relating to your success in college are made by you.

As we discussed in Chapter 1, psychologists use the term *locus of control*—*locus* means "place"—to refer to a person's beliefs about how much control they have over the events that affect them. Being in control means that you make your own decisions and accept responsibility for the outcomes of those decisions.

Some people believe that their locus of control is internal, or within themselves; others believe that it is external, or beyond their power. If you frequently find yourself saying "I don't have time," you may have an external locus of control. The next time you find yourself saying this, stop and ask yourself whether it is actually true. Do you *really* not have time, or have you made a choice not to make time for a particular task or activity? When we say we don't have time, we imply that we don't have a choice. We do have a choice because we have control over how we use our time and how many commitments and small decisions we choose to make every day.

For example, we have control over when we get up in the morning; how much sleep we get; and how much time we spend studying, working, and exercising. All of these small decisions have a big impact on our success in college and in life.

Your Memory Cannot Be Your Only Planner

How you manage your time reflects what you value—what is most important to you and what consequences you are willing to accept when you make certain choices. For instance, if you value time with friends above everything else, your academic work likely takes a backseat to social activities. How you manage your time also corresponds to how successful you will be in college and throughout life. Almost all successful people use some sort of calendar or planner to help them keep up with their appointments, assignments, tasks, and other important activities. Some students are using "bullet journals," which combine the features of a planner, diary, and place for you to write down your thoughts and plans. Bullet journals also allow you to be creative and artistic—to create a planner that reflects your own personality. Also, investigate the features of your college's learning management system (LMS). This system may work well for you and is included in the cost of tuition. But if you try to use your memory as your only planner without writing anything down, you will probably forget some important events or deadlines.

---

your turn | **Making Decisions**

Does Your Planner Work for You?

What kind of planner do you currently use, if any? Do you use a paper planner or the calendar on your phone? Do you think you have chosen the best kind of planner for you? Why or why not? Can you think of a different planner that might work even better?

USING TIME-MANAGEMENT TOOLS

Getting a bird's-eye view—or big picture—of each college term will allow you to plan ahead effectively. An **academic calendar** is a calendar that shows all the important dates that are specific to your campus: financial aid, registration, and add/drop deadlines; midterm and final exam dates; holidays; graduation deadlines; and so forth. You may have received an academic calendar when you registered for classes, or your campus bookstore may have one for sale.

Knowing your big-picture academic deadlines will be helpful as you add deadlines for specific assignments, papers, and exams into your calendar. It is important to refer to your college's academic calendar to add important dates and deadlines, such as when the registration period starts and ends and when you need to pay your tuition or file your application for financial aid or scholarships. Remember, also, that you have to keep track of important dates, not only in your own life, but also in the lives of those close to you—birthdays, doctor's appointments, work schedules, travel, visits from out-of-town guests, and so on. Different aspects of your life have different sorts of time requirements, and the goal is to stay on top of all of them.

You might prefer to use an electronic calendar on your phone, tablet, laptop, or other devices. (See the Tech Tip in this chapter for different options.) Regardless of the format you prefer, it's a good idea to begin the academic term by reviewing the syllabus for each of your courses and then completing a preview (Figure 3.1), recording all of your commitments for each day, and using different colors for each category:

- Classes, tests, quizzes, and major assignment due dates (pink)
- Homework and study time for each class you're taking (green)
- Personal and familial obligations, social activities, and other events (yellow)
- Work, including any commuting time (blue)

Recording your daily commitments allows you to examine your toughest weeks during each month and each term. If research paper deadlines and test dates fall during the same week, find time to finish some assignments early to free up study time. If you use an electronic calendar, set reminders for these important deadlines and dates so that you leave yourself time to get them done. A reminder set for the day the project is due won't help you!

Overall, you should create monthly (Figure 3.1), weekly (Figure 3.2), and daily (Figure 3.3) views of your calendar. All three views are available in an electronic planner, but you can also create monthly, weekly, and daily calendars with paper planners.

Once you complete your monthly templates, you can put them together to preview your entire academic term. Remember to provide details such as the number of hours you anticipate spending on each assignment or task.

As you create your schedule, try to reserve study time for each class and for each assignment. Not all assignments will take an equal amount of time to complete. Estimate how much time you will need for each one, and begin your work well before the assignment is due. A good time manager frequently allows for emergencies by finishing assignments before actual due dates. If you are also working on or off campus, reconsider how many hours per week it will be reasonable for you to work on top of your academic commitments, and whether you need to reduce your credit load to ensure that you have enough time for both work and school.

Remember that managing your time effectively requires practice. You may have to rearrange your schedule a few times, rethink some priorities, and try to use your time differently. The more you apply time-management skills, the more time you can save.

Being a good student does not necessarily mean studying day and night and doing little else. Scheduling time for work and pleasure is important, too. After all, most students have to juggle a *lot* of responsibilities. You might have to work to help pay for college, and you probably want to spend

FIGURE 3.1 › Monthly Calendar

Using the course syllabi provided by your instructors, create your own monthly calendars for your entire term. Provide details such as the number of hours you anticipate spending on each assignment or task. Make sure you can edit your calendar since details on the syllabus might change.

Calendar ˅	◂ September ▸					
● Classes ● Homework ● Work ● Events	Sunday	Monday	Tuesday	Wednesday	Thursday	Friday	Saturday

Sunday	Monday	Tuesday	Wednesday	Thursday	Friday	Saturday
				1	2	3
4	5	6 First Day of Classes 9-12 Psychology 2-5 Work 8-9 Psychology: Read Ch. 1	7 9-12 Work 1-4 Math 8-10 Math HW 1	8 10-1 English 2-5 Work 8-10 English: Read Ch. 1	9 10-12 Work 2-4 Mom's Doctor's Appointment 9-10 Psychology: Review Notes	10 10-4 Work 8-9 Math HW 1 9-10 English: Read Ch. 1
11 2-4 Review Math Notes 6-10 Party at Susan's [555-523-6898]	12 9-12 Work 1-5 Biology 6-8 Nina's Parent-Teacher Conference	13 9-12 Psychology 2-5 Work 8-10 Biology: Read Ch. 1	14 9-12 Work 1-4 Math 8-10 Psychology: Read Ch. 2	15 10-1 English 2-5 Work 7-8 Math HW 2 9-11 Biology: Read Ch. 1	16 10-12 Work 1-3 Lunch with Mary 6-8 Start English Summary Paper	17 10-4 Work 4-6 Shopping 9-11 Finish English Summary Paper
18 10-1 Study for Psychology Test 6-8 Review Math notes for Quiz 1	19 9-12 Work 1-5 Biology 7-10 Study for Psychology Test	20 9-12 Psychology Psychology Test 1 2-5 Work 8-9 Review Math Notes for Quiz 1 (1 hr)	21 9-12 Work 1-4 Math Math Quiz 1 8-9 Revise English Summary Paper	22 10-1 English English Summary Paper due 2-5 Work 8-10 Biology: Read Ch. 2	23 10-12 Work 1-2 Attend Student Club Meeting 6-9 Math HW 3	24 10-4 Work 5-7 Psychology: Read Ch. 3 9-10 English: Read Ch. 2
25 10-12 Biology: Read Ch. 2 1-2 Lunch with James 4-6 Biology: Lab Report 1	26 9-12 Work 1-5 Biology 6-8 Math Tutoring 10-11 Math HW 3	27 9-12 Psychology 2-5 Work 8-10 Biology: Read Ch. 3 10-11 Math HW 3	28 9-12 Work 1-4 Math 8-9 Psychology: Read Ch. 4 9-10 Prepare English Paper Outline	29 10-1 English 2-5 Work 7-9 Math HW 9-10 Review Biology Notes	30 10-12 Work 1-3 Meet with Biology Study Group 8-9 Biology: Lab Report 2 9-11 Stop by Celeste's	1 10-4 Work 4-6 Nina's Birthday Party Preparation 8-9 English: Read Ch. 3

FIGURE 3.2 › Weekly Timetable

Using your term calendar, create your own weekly timetable using a conventional template or one that uses an app such as iCal or LifeTopix. At the beginning of each term, track all of your activities for a full week by entering into your schedule everything you do and how much time each task requires. Use this record to help you estimate the time you will need for similar activities in the future.

time with family or friends to recharge your battery. And most people also need time to relax and unwind; that time can include getting some exercise, reading a book for pleasure, or seeing a movie. Note that the daily planner (see Figure 3.3) includes time for other activities as well as time for classes and studying.

When using an electronic calendar, it's a good idea to print a backup copy in case you lose your phone, cannot access the internet, experience a computer crash, or leave your charger at home or in your residence hall.

FIGURE 3.3 › Daily Planner
Notice how college, work, and personal activities are noted on this daily planner.

Friday, September 30	
8 am	
9 am	
10 am	Work
11 am	
12 pm	
1 pm	Meet with Biology Study Group
2 pm	
3 pm	
4 pm	
5 pm	
6 pm	
7 pm	
8 pm	Biology: Lab Report 2
9 pm	Stop by Celeste's
10 pm	
11 pm	

Carry your calendar with you in a place where you're not likely to lose it. Checking your calendar regularly helps you keep track of commitments and maintain control of your schedule. This practice will become invaluable to you in your career. Check your calendar daily for both the current week and the coming week. It takes just a moment to be certain that you aren't forgetting something important, and it helps relieve stress. Consider setting regular times to check your calendar every day, perhaps right after eating breakfast and then again in the evening, to see what's coming in the days and weeks ahead.

Keep the following points in mind as you organize your day:

- **Set realistic goals for your study time.** Assess how long it takes to read a chapter in your different textbooks and how long it takes you to review your notes from different instructors.
- **Use waiting, commuting, and travel time to review.** Allow time to review your notes as soon as you can after class. You can review your notes if you have a break between classes or while you're waiting for

or riding the bus or train. Consider formally budgeting this commuting time in your planner. If you have a long drive, consider listening to recorded notes or asking those riding with you to quiz you. Make a habit of using waiting time wisely, and it will become bonus study time to help compensate for unexpected events that might pop up in your day and throw off your schedule.

- **If you want or need to work, look for a job that allows you to study during your down time.** This is one of the real advantages to working on campus, but some off-campus employers will also allow you to study during times when you're not busy.
- **Limit distracting and time-consuming communications.** Check your phone, tablet, or computer for messages or updates at a set time, not whenever you're tempted to do so. Constant texting, browsing, or posting on social media can become an addiction that keeps you from achieving your academic goals. Remember that when time has passed, you cannot get it back.
- **Avoid multitasking.** Doing more than one thing at a time, referred to as multitasking, requires that you divide your attention among tasks. You might think that you are good at multitasking. However, the reality is (and research shows) that you can get tasks done faster and more accurately if you concentrate on one at a time.[1] Don't take our word for it: Try setting up your schedule to focus on one important task at a time. You'll probably find you do a better job on your assignment, test, or project.
- **Be flexible.** You cannot anticipate every disruption to your plans. Build extra time into your schedule so that unexpected events do not prevent you from meeting your goals.
- **Schedule breaks.** Relax, catch up with friends and family, or spend time in the cafeteria or student center.

---

your turn | **Making Decisions**

Select Your Best Study Times

What times of day or night do you usually study? Have you selected times when you can concentrate and be productive, or do you just study whenever you can fit it in, even if you're really tired and distracted? For instance, have you already figured out that early morning is your best time to read and remember what you're reading, or that studying after 10:00 p.m. is a waste? Everyone is different, so based on your college experience so far, make a list of the best and worst times for you to study. Most instructors will expect you to study two hours out of class for every hour you spend in class. Using your list as a guide, be intentional about the times you set aside for studying.

---

[1] E. Ophir, C. Nass, and A. Wagner, "Cognitive Control in Media Multitaskers," *Proceedings of the National Academy of Sciences* 106, no. 37 (2009).

PROCRASTINATION

Procrastination is the habit of delaying something that needs your immediate attention. Putting things off can become a serious problem for college students. Dr. Piers Steel, a leading researcher and speaker on the science of motivation and procrastination, writes that procrastination is on the rise, with 80–95 percent of students in college spending time procrastinating.[2] According to Steel, half of college students report that they procrastinate on a regular basis, spending as much as one-third of their time every day in activities solely related to procrastination. All this procrastination takes place even though most people, including researchers who study the negative consequences of procrastination, view procrastination as a significant problem. These numbers, plus the widespread acknowledgment of the negative effects of procrastination, provide evidence that it is a serious issue that trips up many otherwise capable people. Researchers at Carleton University in Canada have found that college students who procrastinate in their studies also avoid confronting other tasks and problems and are more likely to develop unhealthy habits, such as higher levels of alcohol consumption, smoking, insomnia, a poor diet, or lack of exercise.[3]

An article in a 2018 issue of the *Journal of Ergonomics* reports the results of a study of the correlation between overuse of smartphones and procrastination in college students. The study found that there was a correlation between these two behaviors and that male students were somewhat more likely than female students to engage in excessive smartphone usage and to procrastinate.[4]

The good news is that, of those people who procrastinate on a regular basis, 95 percent want to change their behavior.[5] As a first step toward initiating change, it is important to understand why people procrastinate. According to Steel, some people who are highly motivated fear failure, and some people even fear success, although that might seem counterintuitive. Consequently, some students procrastinate because they are perfectionists; not doing a task might be easier than having to live up to your own very high expectations or those of your parents, teachers, or peers. Many procrastinate because they are easily distracted—a topic we'll explore below. Often they have difficulty organizing and regulating their lives, have difficulty following through on goals, view the assigned task as too far into the future, or find an assigned task boring or irrelevant[6] or consider it "busy work," believing they can learn the material just as effectively without doing the homework.

---

[2] Piers Steel, "The Nature of Procrastination: A Meta-Analytic and Theoretical Review of Quintessential Self-Regulatory Failure," *Psychological Bulletin* 133, no. 1 (2007): 65–94.

[3] Timothy A. Pychyl and Fuschia M. Sirois, "Procrastination: Costs to Health and Well-Being," presentation at the American Psychological Association convention, Aug. 22, 2002, Chicago.

[4] Li-Qin Liu, Gao-Min, Shu-Ting Yue, and Le-Sen Cheng , "The Influence of Mobile Phone Addiction on Procrastination: A Moderated Mediating Model" https://www.longdom.org/open-access/the-influence-of-mobile-phone-addiction-on-procrastination-a-moderatedmediating-model-2165-7556-1000232.pdf.

[5] Piers Steel, 65–94.

[6] Ibid.

techtip

ORGANIZE YOUR TIME

Mapping out your schedule — and sticking to it — doesn't have to be a chore. Think of a complete and up-to-date calendar as your compass for college. Besides being a guide for navigating your current term, it will also keep you pointed toward your long-term goals.

The Problem

You keep forgetting or putting off your assignments and can't seem to utilize your work time effectively.

The Fix

Use a free electronic calendar or phone app to arrange your schedule and keep you on track.

iStudiez Pro App for Android Devices

Courtesy of iStudiez Team

How to Do It

Select the device and platform you would be most likely to use.

- Would you check your phone, tablet, or computer?
- Do you have a Gmail account already? (These will also allow you to share files with classmates for group projects using programs like Google Drive and will allow you to create and store files in the "cloud" using the internet like a hard drive.)
- Look at platforms like iStudiez (istudentpro.com) or Studious, which allow you to coordinate and sync your schedule across devices.

Collect schedule information. Look at the syllabi you have gotten from your classes, especially if your instructors provided schedules for assignments, tests, quizzes, and projects. Also, go to your college's website and get a copy of the academic calendar, which will include dates that the college is closed, registration dates, and other important information. Add these important dates to your calendar, and set up alerts for major events (tests, registration deadlines, holiday closings, etc.). Your electronic calendar will send you text or e-mail reminders — set these reminders in advance so that you have time to work on the project or study for the test before the actual due dates.

Avoid distractions online. Set aside time to work or study, and put away or silence any technology that will distract you. Depending on what web browser or smartphone you use, you can download web extensions like **Block Site** (blocksite.co) or apps like **FocusON**, which will block you from accessing time-wasting websites or apps for the amount of time you'll need to work. If you need to take a break, set alarms on your phone or computer so that you don't overextend your break time.

Optional: Add your work schedule or other regular commitments and social events, so that you see them in real time next to your class schedule. Doing so will help you make time for the things you really want to do, without risking the time you need for your course work.

Remember: Setting up your schedule at the beginning of the term does take time, but fortunately, this is usually the time when fewer assignments are due. Having a schedule will pay you big dividends in fewer missed assignments and deadlines or worse, showing up for class on a day when there are no classes.

EXTRA STYLE POINTS: Sync your phone or tablet with your calendar so that if you make changes on your phone, they appear on your online system (Google Calendar, etc.), and if you make changes on your online system, they appear on your phone. Go to YouTube, search "Sync (your phone's name) with (the name of your online system)," and view some videos that show you exactly how to sync them. If you tied your Gmail or Outlook account to your campus e-mail as suggested in the Tech Tip in Chapter 1, you should already be synced.

Overcoming Procrastination

Many of the traits most associated with people who chronically procrastinate can make change more difficult. Fortunately, though, there is hope. With certain changes in behaviors and mindset you can reduce procrastination and become more effective at managing your time. In college, changing how you think about and approach less enjoyable assignments is key to decreasing procrastination and increasing your success.

For instance, simply disliking an assignment is not a good reason to put it off; it's an *excuse*, not a valid *reason*. Throughout life you'll be faced with tasks you don't find interesting, and in many cases you won't have the option not to do them. Whether it is cleaning your house, filing your taxes, completing paperwork, or responding to hundreds of e-mails, tedious tasks will find you, and you will have to figure out strategies to complete them. College is a good time to practice and hone your skills at finishing uninteresting tasks in a timely manner. Perhaps counterintuitively, research indicates that making easier or less-interesting tasks more challenging can decrease boredom and increase your likelihood of completing the tasks on time.[7]

high-impact practice 3

yourturn   Feeling Connected

Staying on Task and on Time

With two or three other students, discuss ways to avoid procrastination. What works for you? Share examples from your experiences.

When you're in college, procrastinating can signal that it's time to reassess your goals and objectives; maybe you're not ready or able to make a commitment to academic priorities at this point in your life. Only you can decide, but an academic adviser can help you sort it out. If you cannot get procrastination under control, it is in your best interest to seek help at your campus counseling service before you begin to feel as though you are also losing control of other aspects of your life. Taking the Procrastination Self-Assessment in this chapter will help give you a sense of whether or not procrastination is a problem for you.

Here are some strategies for beating procrastination and staying motivated:

- Remind yourself of the possible consequences if you do not get down to work, and then get started. Also, remind yourself that simply not enjoying an assignment is not a good reason to put it off; it's an *excuse*, not a valid *reason*.
- Create a to-do list. Check off items as you get them done. Use the list to focus on the things that aren't getting done. Move them to the top of the next day's list, and make up your mind to do them. Working from a list will give you a feeling of accomplishment.

[7] Ibid.

Procrastination Self-Assessment

Place a number from 1 to 5 before each statement. (For example, if you "agree" with a statement, place a 4 before the statement.)

1 = **Strongly Disagree**
2 = **Disagree**
3 = **Mildly Disagree**
4 = **Agree**
5 = **Strongly Agree**

_____ I have a habit of putting off important tasks that I don't enjoy doing.

_____ My standards are so high that I'm not usually satisfied enough with my work to turn it in on time.

_____ I spend more time planning what I'm going to do than actually doing it.

_____ The chaos in my study space makes it hard for me to get started.

_____ The people I live with distract me from doing my class work.

_____ I have more energy for a task if I wait until the last minute to do it.

_____ I enjoy the excitement of living on the edge.

_____ I have trouble prioritizing all my responsibilities.

_____ Having to meet a deadline makes me really nervous.

_____ My biggest problem is that I just don't know how to get started.

If you responded that you "agree" or "strongly agree" with two questions or fewer, then you may procrastinate from time to time, but it may not be a major problem for you. Reading this chapter will help you continue to stay focused and avoid procrastination in the future.

If you responded that you "agree" or "strongly agree" with three to five questions, then you may be having difficulties with procrastination. Revisit the questions to which you answered "agree" or "strongly agree" and look in the chapter for strategies that specifically address these issues to help you overcome obstacles. You _can_ get a handle on your procrastination!

If you responded that you "agree" or "strongly agree" with six or more questions, then you may be having a significant problem with procrastination, and it could interfere with your success in college if you do not make a change. Revisit the questions to which you answered "agree" or "strongly agree" and look in the chapter for strategies that specifically address these issues. Also, if you are concerned about your pattern of procrastination and you aren't having success in dealing with it yourself, consider talking to a professional counselor in your campus counseling center. It's free and confidential, and counselors have extensive experience working with students who have problems with procrastination.

- Break big jobs into smaller steps. Tackle short, easy-to-accomplish tasks first.
- Avoid doing other things that might seem more fun, and promise yourself a reward for finishing the task, such as watching your favorite TV show or going out with friends. For completing larger tasks and assignments, give yourself bigger and better rewards.
- Find a place to study that's comfortable and doesn't allow for distractions and interruptions.

- Say "no" to friends and family members who want your attention; agree to spend time with them later, and schedule that time.
- Shut off and put away all electronic devices during planned study sessions. If you *need* to use an electronic device for studying, turn off all social media and any other applications that are not part of your studying—and *keep* them off.
- Consider asking those living with you to help keep you on track. If they see that you are not studying when you should be, ask them to remind you to get back to the books. If you study in your room, close your door.

Dealing with Distractions

Overcoming procrastination and planning your time effectively are closely associated with achieving your goals. What you do on a daily basis affects your outcomes for that week, that month, that year, and so on. Distractions may push you off course and away from your intended goals. A good first step is becoming aware of what distractions trip you up and considering how much control you have over them.

Table 3.1 lists possible distractions that may or may not be a problem for you. Choose Yes (a problem) or No (not a problem) for each one.

TABLE 3.1 > Solving the Problem of Distractions

Distraction	Yes (Y) No (N)	Controllable (C) Uncontrollable (U)	Solutions
Texting/Messaging			
Social media			
Gaming/Videos/Music			
Sports/Hobbies			
Television/Streaming			
Lack of sleep			
Relationships			
Meals/Snacking			
Daydreaming			
Perfectionism			
Errands/Shopping			
Lost items			
Worries/Stress			
Family			
Socializing/Friends			
Multitasking			
Illness, self or others			
Work schedule			
Pleasure reading			

Then note whether the distraction is controllable or uncontrollable and write down possible solutions.

What did you learn about yourself, the distractions that get in your way, and some ideas for taking control? What choices are you willing to make to maximize your time?

MANAGING YOUR ENERGY

Your best plans will not work if you do not have the energy to make them happen. You may plan to spend a couple of hours on your math homework before you go to bed in the evening after a busy day. However, you may find that you are too tired to concentrate and solve the math problems. While learning to manage your time effectively, you must also learn to manage your energy so that you have more control over your life and can achieve success in college.

Along with time, energy is an essential resource, and we have a choice in how we use it. Although energy is renewable, each one of us has a limited amount of it in the 24-hour day. Each person has a daily pattern of physical, emotional, and mental activity. For instance, some people are early risers and have a lot of energy in the morning to get things done; others feel the least energetic and productive in the morning and can accomplish tasks at the end of the day more effectively, especially those tasks that require mental energy and concentration. You can better manage your energy by recognizing your daily pattern and establishing a routine around it. Use Table 3.2 to record your high, average, and low energy level every day for one week. Use **H** for high, **A** for average, and **L** for low to identify which times of day you feel more or less energetic.

TABLE 3.2 > Monitoring Your Energy Level

Time	Sun	Mon	Tues	Wed	Thurs	Fri	Sat
				Energy Level			
Early morning							
Late morning							
Early afternoon							
Late afternoon							
Evening							
Late evening							
Late night							

What did you learn about yourself by completing Table 3.2? What are the best and worst times for you to study? Considering your daily energy level, obligations, and potential distractions, decide whether you study more effectively in the morning, afternoon, evening, or some combination. Determine whether you are capable of getting up very early in the morning to study or how late you can stay up at night and still get to morning classes on time.

Your energy level also depends on your diet and other habits such as exercise or lack of it. If you are juggling many responsibilities across several locations, you can use some very simple strategies to take care of yourself:

- Take some time just for yourself to relax and restore your energy.
- Take brief naps when possible. Research shows that naps are more effective than caffeine.[8]
- Carry healthy snacks with you, such as fruit, nuts, or yogurt. You'll save time and money by avoiding trips to snack bars and convenience stores, and you'll keep your energy up by eating better.
- Drink plenty of water.

---

your turn | **Feeling Connected**

Saying "No"

Energy management often requires the use of the word *no*. Discuss with another student how saying "no" relates to the way you can manage your energy.

Establishing a Routine

Consider what you have learned about yourself by completing Table 3.2. Now that you have a sense of the best and worst times for you to study, establish a study routine that is based on your daily energy pattern. The more firmly you set a specific time to study, the more effective you will be at keeping up with your schedule. If you have more energy on the weekend, for example, take advantage of that time to review or catch up on major projects, such as term papers, that can't be completed effectively in short blocks of time. Break down large tasks and focus on one thing at a time to make progress toward your academic goals.

Schedule some down-time for yourself to regain your energy. Different activities help different people relax and get energized. For example, you may watch TV for an hour or take a nap before you start doing your

---

[8] S. Medrick, D. Cai, S. Kanady, and S. Drummond, "Comparing the Benefits of Caffeine, Naps and Placebo on Verbal, Motor and Perceptual Memory," *Behavioural Brain Research* 193, no. 1 (2008): 79–86.

Stay Awake
Like this student, you probably have a lot of demands on your time. Make sure to manage your energy effectively by getting enough rest, eating properly, and pacing yourself, or you might find yourself falling asleep while studying.
PeopleImages/Getty Images

homework. Just make sure that you do not go over the amount of time you set aside as your down-time.

SETTING PRIORITIES

As you work to overcome procrastination and limit distractions, think about how to **prioritize**, which means putting your tasks, goals, and values in order of importance. (Below, we'll discuss strategies to avoid becoming overextended, which goes hand in hand with setting priorities.) Ask yourself which goals are most important, but also which ones are most urgent. For example, studying in order to get a good grade on tomorrow's test might have to take priority over attending a job fair today, or completing an assignment that is due tomorrow might have to take priority over driving your friend somewhere.

However, don't ignore long-term goals in order to meet short-term goals. With good time management, you can study during the week prior to the test so that you can attend the job fair, too. Skilled time managers often establish priorities by maintaining a term calendar and to-do lists on which they rank the items in order of importance to determine schedules and deadlines for each task.

From the beginning of the term, plan your work on term papers and major projects that might not be due for several weeks or even months. Consult with a tutor or a more experienced student to help you break large assignments down into smaller steps, such as choosing a topic, doing research, creating an outline, or writing a first draft. Once you have entered your future commitments in a term planner and decided how

Time Flies

Do you find yourself wondering where your time has gone at the end of a long day? Are you aware of how you spend your time when you're not in class, or does this time just seem to vanish? Of all the time-management strategies presented in this chapter, developing an awareness of how you spend your time might be the most important. Using a day planner or your smartphone, develop an "ideal" hour-by-hour schedule that covers the next week. At the end of each day, go back and check to see if you used your time as planned. If not, make sure your projections were realistic, adjust them if necessary, and then try some of the strategies presented in this chapter to improve your ability to control the way you spend your time.

your time will be spent each week, create your to-do list, which is especially handy for last-minute reminders. A to-do list helps you keep track of errands to run, appointments to make, and anything else you might forget. You can keep this list on your cell phone or tablet, in a notebook, or on a bulletin board in your room. Use your to-do list to keep track of all the tasks you need to remember, not just academics (see Figure 3.4). Consider developing a system for prioritizing the items on your list: using different colors of ink for different groups of tasks; highlighting the most important assignments; marking items with one, two, or three stars; or adding letters A, B, C, and so on to indicate which tasks are most important.

Find a Balance

Another aspect of setting priorities while in college is finding a way to balance your academic schedule with the rest of your life. Social and extracurricular activities (for instance, participating in a club, writing for the college newspaper, attending special lectures, concerts, athletic events, or theater performances) are important parts of the college experience. Time spent alone and time spent thinking are also essential to your overall well-being.

Set Priorities Like an Olympian

Olympic athletes set priorities to achieve their goals, whether it's qualifying for the Olympics, winning a gold medal, or winning five world all-arounds in as many tries, like Simone Biles, pictured here. In setting your own priorities, take a lesson from athletes: Prioritize your long-term plans while making sensible decisions every day.

Tom Weller/picture alliance/Getty Images

FIGURE 3.4 › To-Do List

You can keep a to-do list on a mobile device, in a notebook, or on a bulletin board. Use it to keep track of all the tasks you need to remember, not just academics. Consider adding Saturday and Sunday as these are productive days for many busy people. As you complete a task, cross it off your list. Enjoy the satisfaction of each accomplishment.

THIS WEEK	COLLEGE	WORK	PERSONAL
Monday	Schedule a math tutoring session	Meet with the department chair about my schedule	Make a haircut appointment
Tuesday	Make appointment with Prof. Velez to discuss paper topic		Order birthday gift for dad
Wednesday	Meet my history study group at 4:00 p.m.	Work in department, 9:00 a.m.–noon	
Thursday	Finish English essay		Pick up dry cleaning
Friday		Work in department, 9:00 a.m.–noon	Make eye appointment

Don't Overextend Yourself

Being **overextended**, or having too much to do given the resources available to you, is a primary source of stress for college students. Determine what a realistic workload is for you, but note that this can vary significantly from one person to another, and only you can determine what is realistic. Although being involved in social life is very important, don't allow your academic work to take a backseat to other time commitments. Take on only what you can handle. Learn to say "no," as this is an effective time-management strategy! Say "no" to requests that will prevent you from meeting your academic goals. Remember that even if you can find the time for extra tasks, you may not be able to find the energy.

If you are feeling stressed, assess your time commitments and let go of one or more. If you choose to drop a course, make sure you do so before the drop deadline so that you won't have a low grade on your permanent record. If you receive financial aid, keep in mind that you must be registered for a minimum number of credit hours to maintain your current level of financial aid. Read more about financial aid in the chapter on managing money (see Chapter 15).

Stay Focused

Many students of all ages question their decision to attend college and sometimes feel overwhelmed by the additional responsibilities it brings. Some first-year students, especially recent high school graduates, might temporarily forget their main purposes for coming to college and spend their first term of college engaging in a wide array of new experiences.

high-impact practice

your turn | Setting Goals

The Predicament of Too Many Obligations

Are you trying to do too much, and is your packed schedule reducing your motivation for college? Are you overinvolved in campus organizations? Are you working too many hours off campus? Are you feeling really stressed out? In a small group, discuss strategies for reducing your stress level and maintaining your motivation for being successful in your academic work.

Allowing yourself a little time to adjust to college is OK within limits, but you don't want to spend the next four or five years trying to make up for poor decisions made early in your college career, such as skipping class and not taking your assignments seriously. Such decisions can lead to a low grade point average (GPA) and the threat of academic probation or, worse, academic dismissal.

A great way to focus and to keep your priorities on track is to finish what *needs* to be done before you move from work to pleasure. From time to time, you will have competing responsibilities; for example, you might have to work additional hours at your job just when you need additional time to study for an exam. In cases like these, talk to the people involved, including your instructors and your employer, to see how you can manage the conflict.

Work Study

Did you know that the majority of college students have jobs? If you need to work, try to find a job that is flexible and allows you to study during down-time. Use every available minute to stay up to date with your classwork.
Sue McDermott Barlow

> **your turn**   Write and Reflect
>
> **What Are Your Priorities?**
>
> List your current priorities, and assign a value to each on a scale of 1–5 with 1 as most important and 5 as least important. Write a short paper about why you consider some things more important than others. Think about whether your personal priorities support your goals for college success.
>
> _____   _____
> _____   _____
> _____   _____
> _____   _____
> _____   _____

APPRECIATING THE VALUE OF TIME

Time is a valuable resource, perhaps your most valuable resource. You've likely heard the expression "Time is money." Just as you don't want to waste your money, you shouldn't waste your time or the time of others. Did you ever make an appointment with someone who either forgot the appointment entirely or was very late? How did you feel? Were you upset or disappointed because the person wasted your time? Most of us have experienced the frustration of having someone else disrespect our time. In college, if you repeatedly arrive late for class or leave early, you are breaking the basic rules of politeness and showing a lack of respect for your instructors and your classmates.

Punctuality, or being on time, is expected in college, work, and elsewhere in our society. Being strictly on time may be a difficult adjustment for you if you grew up in a home or culture that is more flexible in its approach to time, but it is important to recognize the value of punctuality. Although you should not have to alter your cultural identity to succeed in college, you must be aware of the expectations that instructors typically have for students.

Here are a few basic guidelines for respectful behavior in class and in other interactions with instructors:

- Get to class on time. This means you need to get enough sleep at night so that you can wake up at a time that allows you to arrive in class early enough to take off your coat, shuffle through your backpack, and have your completed assignments and notebooks ready to go by the time the class starts.
- Be on time for scheduled appointments, such as during office hours.
- Avoid behaviors that show a lack of respect for both the instructor and other students, such as leaving class to answer your cell phone.

Getting from Here to There

College students have the responsibility to get themselves to class on time and must plan transportation carefully, whether walking, driving, bicycling, ridesharing, taking public transportation, or using another method of getting from place to place. If you have an emergency situation that causes you to run late, talk to your instructor. He or she will understand a real emergency and help you make up work you missed.

wong yu liang/Shutterstock

Similarly, texting, doing homework for another class, falling asleep, or talking (even whispering) during a lecture are all considered rude.

• Make transportation plans in advance, and have a backup plan.

Not only is time management important for you, but it is also a way in which you show respect for your coworkers, friends, family, college instructors, and yourself. Can you think of the number of times you may have been late (one of the symptoms of procrastination) this week alone? Think back and then take the quiz shown here in Table 3.3:

TABLE 3.3 ❯ Time Management Quiz

Situation	Number of Times This Week
How many times were you late to class?	
How many times were you late for appointments/dates?	
How many times were you late for work, a carpool, or another job and/or responsibility?	
How many times were you so late returning an e-mail, phone call, or text that a problem resulted from this lateness?	
How many times were you late paying a bill or mailing any important document?	
How many times were you late getting to bed or waking up?	
TOTAL	

Did the total number of times you were late surprise you? Two to five incidences of being late in a week is fairly normal. Everyone is late sometimes. Being late more than eight times this week might indicate that you are avoiding situations and tasks that are unpleasant for you. Or maybe you find it difficult to wait for other people, and so you would rather have others wait for you. Try to think of lateness from the other person's perspective. Getting more organized might help if you find that you don't have enough hours in the day to get everything done the way you think it should be. Position yourself for success and develop a reputation for being dependable!

Creating a Workable Class Schedule

Building your class schedule so that it works for you is part of using your valuable time wisely. If you live on campus, you might want to create a schedule that situates you near a dining hall at mealtimes or allows you to spend breaks between classes at the library. Alternatively, you might need breaks in your schedule for relaxation, catching up with friends, or spending time in a student lounge, college union, or campus center. You might want to avoid returning to your residence hall to take a nap between classes if the result is that you could feel lethargic or oversleep and miss later classes. Also, if you attend a large university, be sure to allow adequate time to get from one class to another.

Scheduling Your Classes in Blocks

One option for building a class schedule is using blocks of time when you can schedule several classes in a row, back-to-back, without any breaks. If you're a commuter student or if you must carry a heavy workload to afford going to school, you might prefer block scheduling, which allows you to cut travel time by attending school one or two days a week. Block scheduling might also provide more flexibility if you have to schedule a job or family commitments.

Scheduling classes in blocks, however, can also have significant drawbacks. When all your classes are scheduled in a block of time, you run several risks. If you become ill on a class day, you could fall behind in all your classes. You might also become fatigued from sitting in class after class. When one class immediately follows another, it will be difficult for you to have a last-minute study period immediately before a test because you will be attending another class and are likely to have no more than a 15-minute break in between. Finally, remember that if you take back-to-back classes, you might have several exams scheduled for the same day. Scheduling classes in blocks might work better if you have the option of attending lectures at alternative times in case you are absent, if you alternate classes with free periods, and if you seek out instructors who are flexible with due dates for assignments.

If your classes are offered at more than one time of day or more than one day a week, you will find it easier to design a schedule that works best for you. Often, however, you will be forced to take a class at an inconvenient time because that's the only time the class is offered. Remember that any schedule you develop will have pros and cons, but with advance planning, you can make the most of your in-class and out-of-class time.

 high-impact practice 3

your turn **Feeling Connected**

Scheduling Your Classes

In a small group or with a partner, share your current schedule and explain what you like or dislike about it. If your current schedule is not working well, discuss why that might be and identify changes you can make for the next term.

checklist for success

Time Management

■ **Make sure that you set clear priorities for the way you spend your time.** All your time doesn't have to be spent studying, but remember that your instructors will expect you to study two hours out of class for each hour in class.

■ **Get organized by using a calendar or planner.** Choose either an electronic or a paper calendar. Your campus bookstore will have a campus-specific version. Your calendar can help you allocate time in the present for completing large assignments that are due in the future.

■ **Create and use daily paper or electronic to-do lists.** Crossing off those tasks you have completed will give you a real sense of satisfaction.

■ **Quickly identify and address common time-management problems you are having before they spiral out of control.** Be aware of problems with procrastination, distractions, overscheduling, and motivation. As you notice them happening, take stock and make changes. If any of these issues becomes a serious problem, seek help from your campus counseling center.

■ **Remember the relationship between time and respect.** Be aware of how others might perceive your behavior. If you disregard formal or informal appointments or if you are consistently late for class, you are showing a lack of respect for others even if that's not your intent.

■ **Develop energy-level awareness.** Understand how your energy level changes throughout the day, and allocate your highest-energy time periods to activities that are most challenging.

■ **Think about your course schedule.** As you plan for next term, try to schedule your classes in a way that works best for you, given your other obligations.

REFLECT ON CHOICES

high-impact practice 2 | College presents you with choices. One of them is whether you are going to pay close attention to how you spend your time. If you choose to neglect the issue of time management, you will risk losing a resource that you can never recover and sabotaging your chances for success in college. Did any of the time-management tips in this chapter appeal to you? If so, which ones? Do you still have questions about time management? If so, what are they? Write about these choices and questions in a journal entry or readily accessible file. Revisit these questions throughout your first-year experience.

APPLY WHAT YOU'VE LEARNED

Now that you have read and discussed this chapter, consider how you can apply what you have learned to your academic and personal life. The following prompts will help you reflect on chapter material and its relevance to you both now and in the future.

1. Review the procrastination section of this chapter. Think of one upcoming assignment in any of your current classes and describe how you can avoid waiting until the last minute to get it done. Break down the assignment and list each step it will take to complete the assignment. Give yourself a due date for each step and a due date for completing the assignment.

2. After reading about effective time-management strategies, consider how you manage your own time. If you were grading your current set of time-management skills, what grade (A, B, C, or lower) would you give yourself? Why? What is your biggest impediment to becoming a more effective time manager?

USE YOUR RESOURCES

> **Academic Skills Center.** Your campus academic skills center offers more than just assistance in studying for exams. Head here for time-management advice specific to you. For instance, if you are struggling with managing the process of writing a paper, talk with a writing tutor about how to break the process into manageable steps, and create a timetable for those steps so you can meet course deadlines. If you are an online student, communicate with your instructors and other online students about how to manage time in an online environment.

> **Counseling Center.** Make an appointment at your campus counseling office if your time-management problems involve emotional issues.

> **Your Academic Adviser or Counselor.** If you have a good relationship with your academic adviser, ask him or her for time-management advice or for a referral to another person on campus.

> **Office for Commuter Students.** If you commute back and forth to campus, visit the office for commuter students to see what kinds of suggestions they offer about transportation to and from campus. You may be able to reduce the amount of time you spend in transit.

> **Your Peer Leader.** Peer leaders in college success classes are selected for their wisdom and experience. Talk to your peer leader about how he or she has developed time-management strategies.

> **A Fellow Student.** Don't overlook your closest resources! If you feel your time slipping away, ask a friend who is a good student for advice.

LaunchPad
macmillan learning

LaunchPad for *Your College Experience* is a great resource. Go online to master concepts using the LearningCurve study tool and much more. **Launchpadworks.com**

Huntstock/Brand X Pictures/Getty Images

4

HOW YOU LEARN

YOU WILL EXPLORE

Theories that explain how people learn and what learning preferences are

Tools for determining your learning preference

Strategies for handling a mismatch between how you learn best and how you are being taught

How to understand and recognize a learning disability

⌖ High-impact practices 2 (writing), 3 (collaboration), and 6 (learning communities)

> ❝ **Use multiple learning strategies in your classes. Eventually you will learn in a different, smarter, and more efficient way.** ❞

eurobanks/Shutterstock

Before starting college, Daniel didn't know much about how he learned. When he was in high school, he struggled with some of his courses—so much so that he decided not to attend college right after graduation. But a few years later, Daniel was ready to give college a try.

In his first term at Northeastern Illinois University in Chicago, he enrolled in a college success course and discovered that people prefer to learn in different ways. He took a learning preferences inventory and discovered that he enjoys learning by *doing* more than by listening or reading and writing. Daniel wasn't surprised: "I work part-time outdoors for a landscaping business," he says. "I like being able to use my hands, and I like figuring things out just by playing with them for a bit." He uses this hands-on approach in college by doing things like taking practice exams until he feels ready for the real exam.

Daniel has also come to realize that even though reading and writing aren't his favorite things to do, he can still use those skills to learn more effectively. For example, he rewrites terms and concepts in his own words so that he understands more clearly what they mean. Daniel says, "I've improved my performance not only by understanding how I prefer to learn but also by adding other learning strategies."

After completing his bachelor's degree, Daniel plans to transfer to the University of Illinois at Chicago to pursue a master's degree in computer information systems. He advises fellow students: "Use multiple learning strategies in your classes. Eventually, you will learn in a different, smarter, and more efficient way."

LaunchPad
macmillan learning

To access the LearningCurve study tool, video activities, and more, go to LaunchPad for *Your College Experience*.
Launchpadworks.com

To do well in college, understanding how you learn is important, as is considering which learning environments you like best. Maybe you have trouble paying attention in a long lecture, or maybe listening is the way you prefer to take in information. You might love classroom discussion, or you might consider hearing what other students have to say in class a big waste of time.

Understanding your own learning preferences is helpful, but so is making sure that you don't limit yourself by those preferences. After all, college instructors have their own ways of teaching and communicating, and you will likely find yourself in a course or courses that require you to go outside your comfort zone. This flexibility is part of being a successful college student. College courses are organized and taught in a variety of ways:

- Many instructors lecture; others use lots of visual aids.
- In science courses, instructors will help you conduct experiments or lead field trips where you can observe or touch what you are studying.
- In dance, theater, or physical education courses, learning takes place in both your body and your mind.

assess your strengths

Understanding your own learning preferences will help you study and earn good grades. Do you know the ways you learn best? Were your learning preferences evaluated in high school? As you begin to read this chapter, consider the insights you already have about your own learning preferences.

set goals

Think about challenges you have had with relating to the way some instructors teach and expect you to learn. Use this chapter to help develop strategies and goals that link your preferred style of learning to what you are experiencing in the classroom such as thinking about your favorite and least favorite classes and how your preferences might relate to how you prefer to learn.

You've read about the importance of building relationships with your instructors; to do this, you'll have to navigate how your instructors communicate. These differences may be frustrating, but they will help you to become more aware of your preferred learning environments, and they will challenge you to find ways to succeed in a wide variety of situations.

HOW PEOPLE LEARN

People learn differently, and understanding how the brain functions helps explain why. An entire field of study called cognitive neuroscience focuses on the brain. Neuroscientists and psychologists have developed many theories about how and why people learn differently. Some of the many theories about learning are relevant for college students, especially first-year students.

Learning Theories

One of the most well-known learning theories comes from Abraham Maslow, a psychologist.[1] Using Maslow's "hierarchy of needs" (see Figure 4.1), one might logically argue that in order for students to learn, their needs must be met—basic needs such as food, water, and shelter; safety and security needs such as employment and property; needs for love and belonging; the need for self-esteem that comes from achievement; and self-actualization that can be reached through having a purpose and meeting your potential. You probably have found that when you're hungry, fearful, or lonely, it is very hard—nearly impossible—to learn effectively. If your basic needs are met, you develop friendships and you experience success. Then, it becomes easier to focus on your courses and continue to learn.

Albert Bandura, a psychological researcher, developed a theory of social learning, which suggests that people learn from each other by observing others' actions and the results of those actions.[2] These observations help them repeat or avoid certain attitudes and behaviors.

---

[1] A. H. Maslow, *Motivation and Personality* (New York: Harper & Row, 1970).
[2] A. Bandura, *Social Learning Theory* (Englewood Cliffs, NJ: Prentice Hall, 1977).

FIGURE 4.1 ▶ The Hierarchy of Needs Pyramid
This figure illustrates Maslow's theory.
iQoncept/Shutterstock

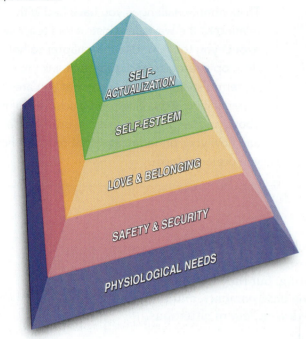

SELF-ACTUALIZATION

SELF-ESTEEM

LOVE & BELONGING

SAFETY & SECURITY

PHYSIOLOGICAL NEEDS

If you had older brothers and sisters, you probably observed their interactions in the family and learned how to stay out of trouble with your parents. In college you will observe other students—those who are successful and those who are not. If you pay attention, you can figure out what behaviors actually lead to success. It's not just about "being smart." Successful students come to class, spend time studying, interact with instructors, and take advantage of the academic support available on campus.

In her work on how adult students learn, Nancy Schlossberg, a counseling psychologist, developed a theory of transition.[3] She found that adults learn new roles when they go through change or transition in their lives. As adults, we constantly change our roles; for example, we change from being a high school student to a college student, from a college student to an employee, or from an employee to a college student. Often we juggle multiple roles at the same time. We also experience changes in our personal roles when we get married or divorced or have children. The transition theory states that change actually helps adults grow and learn new ways of thinking and behaving. During the transition process, the more help and support we receive from people around us, the more easily we will adapt to change. For example, college students who ask for help from their instructors, classmates, tutors, advisers, and even their families and friends can make a more successful transition to college life and deal with the challenges of a new environment more effectively than students who do not seek such assistance.

While the concept of learning may seem simple, educational researchers have discovered that not everyone learns in the same way. Not only do we have different learning styles, we also have unique preferences for the speed at which we learn, the mode of learning (online or face-to-face), and whether we learn better alone or in a group. Your college or university may offer courses that run four to six weeks or "flipped" classes in which you learn material on your own before class and spend class time in discussion groups or working problems.

high-impact practice 6

If your college success course is linked with one or more other courses so that you share other classes with the same group of students, you are in a learning community. About 50 percent of U.S. colleges and universities offer learning communities in the first year. Being in a learning community will help you learn in a different way by emphasizing the connections between different courses. This experience will also help you develop stronger relationships with students in the linked classes.

---

[3] M. Anderson, J. Goodman, and N. Schlossberg, *Counseling Adults in Transition: Linking Theory with Practice in a Diverse World* (New York: Springer, 2011).

LEARNING PREFERENCES

In addition to looking at theories about learning, we can think about how people learn by focusing on personal learning preferences. Simply put, learning preferences are ways that people prefer to learn. Through work and other prior experience, you may have some sense of how you like or don't like to learn. At the start of the chapter, we asked you to consider which learning environments appeal to you. Whether it's listening in lectures, reading your textbooks, doing experiments in science labs, or working in groups, these suggest your learning preferences. Researchers have developed formal methods and tools—some simple, some complex—to identify, describe, and understand different learning preferences. These tools help students learn to adapt their learning preferences to different classroom situations. Remember, it is your responsibility to take charge of your learning in order to be successful in college—even when you find yourself in a course that doesn't match your preferences.

In this chapter, we introduce three of the most commonly used tools and theories for understanding learning preferences: the VARK Inventory, the Myers-Briggs Type Indicator, and multiple intelligences. These tools can help you begin to discover your preferences for learning as well as strategies for improving your learning. As you are making these discoveries, keep in mind that learning preferences cannot be boiled down to one or two defining characteristics; preferences are complex and can vary based on content, context, and situation. But the knowledge you will gain about yourself from working through this chapter is a significant step in taking responsibility for your learning and adapting to any learning environment.

isthisyou?

Disappointed in My Classes

Have you found that some of your classes aren't as interesting and engaging as you expected? Is one of the problems a mismatch between the way you like to learn and the instructor's teaching method? Perhaps you're a visual learner but are forced to sit through mostly lecture classes, or perhaps you really don't enjoy working with others even though your chemistry course requires you to complete lab assignments with a partner. This chapter will help you understand your own learning preferences and adapt them to any classroom situation.

The VARK Learning-Styles Inventory

The VARK is a sixteen-item questionnaire that focuses on how learners prefer to use their senses (hearing, seeing, writing, reading, experiencing) to learn. The acronym VARK stands for "Visual," "Aural," "Read/Write," and "Kinesthetic." As you read through the following descriptions, see which ones ring true to how you learn.

- **Visual** learners prefer to learn information through charts, graphs, symbols, and other visual means. If you can most easily remember data that is presented in graphic form or in a picture, map, or video, you may be a visual learner.
- **Aural** learners prefer to hear information and discuss it with friends, classmates, or instructors. If talking about information from lectures or textbooks helps you remember it, you may be an aural learner.

Bodies in Motion

As you'll learn in the next section, the theater arts have strong appeal for kinesthetic learners who prefer to learn through experience and practice.

Hill Street Studios/Getty Images

- **Read/Write** learners prefer to learn information through words on a printed page. During a test, if you can sometimes visualize where information appears in the textbook, you may be a read/write learner.
- **Kinesthetic** learners prefer to learn through experience and practice, whether simulated or real. They often learn through their sense of touch. Recopying or typing notes helps them remember the material. They also learn better when their bodies are in motion, whether participating in sports, dancing, or working out. If you are a kinesthetic learner, you may find that even your sense of taste or smell contributes to your learning process.

Two or three of these modes probably describe your preferred ways of learning better than the others. At the college level, faculty members tend to share information primarily via lecture and the textbook, but many students like to learn through visual and interactive means. This difference creates a mismatch between learning and teaching preferences. Is this a problem? Not necessarily, if you know how to handle such a mismatch. Later in this chapter you'll learn strategies to adapt lecture material and the text to your preferred modes of learning. First, though, to determine your learning style(s) according to the VARK, respond to the questionnaire.

The VARK Questionnaire, Version 8.01

This questionnaire is designed to tell you about your preferences for how you work with information. Choose answers that explain your preference(s). Check the box next to those items. For each question, select *as many boxes as apply to you.* If none of the response options applies to you, leave the item blank. (You can also take the VARK questionnaire online at **vark-learn.com/the-vark-questionnaire/**.)

1. When learning from the internet I like:
   - ☐ V. interesting written descriptions, lists, and explanations.
   - ☐ A. videos showing how to do or make things.
   - ☐ R. interesting design and visual features.
   - ☐ K. audio channels where I can listen to podcasts or interviews.

2. I have finished a competition or test and I would like some feedback. I would like to have feedback:
   - ☐ V. using graphs showing what I achieved.
   - ☐ A. using examples from what I have done.
   - ☐ R. from somebody who talks it through with me.
   - ☐ K. using a written description of my results.

3. I need to find the way to a shop that a friend has recommended. I would:
   - ☐ V. ask my friend to tell me the directions.
   - ☐ A. find out where the shop is in relation to somewhere I know.
   - ☐ R. use a map.
   - ☐ K. write down the street directions I need to remember.

4. A website has a video showing how to make a special graph or chart. There is a person speaking, some lists and words describing what to do, and some diagrams. I would learn most from:
   - ☐ V. seeing the diagrams.
   - ☐ A. watching the actions.
   - ☐ R. reading the words.
   - ☐ K. listening.

5. I prefer a presenter or a teacher who uses:
   - ☐ V. diagrams, charts, maps, or graphs.
   - ☐ A. question and answer, talk, group discussion, or guest speakers.
   - ☐ R. handouts, books, or readings.
   - ☐ K. demonstrations, models, or practical sessions.

6. I want to learn to do something new on a computer. I would:
   - ☐ V. follow the diagrams in a book.
   - ☐ A. read the written instructions that came with the program.
   - ☐ R. talk with people who know about the program.
   - ☐ K. start using it and learn by trial and error.

7. I want to assemble a wooden table that came in parts (kitset). I would learn best from:
   - ☐ V. advice from someone who has done it before.
   - ☐ A. diagrams showing each stage of the assembly.
   - ☐ R. watching a video of a person assembling a similar table.
   - ☐ K. written instructions that came with the parts for the table.

8. When I am learning I:
   - ☐ V. use examples and applications.
   - ☐ A. like to talk things through.
   - ☐ R. see patterns in things.
   - ☐ K. read books, articles, and handouts.

9. When choosing a career or area of study, these are important for me:
   - ☐ V. Communicating with others through discussion.
   - ☐ A. Using words well in written communications.
   - ☐ R. Applying my knowledge in real situations.
   - ☐ K. Working with designs, maps, or charts.

(continued)

10. I want to learn how to take better photos. I would:

- ☐ V. use the written instructions about what to do.
- ☐ A. use examples of good and poor photos showing how to improve them.
- ☐ R. ask questions and talk about the camera and its features.
- ☐ K. use diagrams showing the camera and what each part does.

11. I want to find out more about a tour that I am going on. I would:

- ☐ V. look at details about the highlights and activities on the tour.
- ☐ A. use a map and see where the places are.
- ☐ R. talk with the person who planned the tour or others who are going on the tour.
- ☐ K. read about the tour on the itinerary.

12. I want to save more money and to decide between a range of options. I would:

- ☐ V. read a print brochure that describes the options in detail.
- ☐ A. consider examples of each option using my financial information.
- ☐ R. talk with an expert about the options.
- ☐ K. use graphs showing different options for different time periods.

13. I have a problem with my heart. I would prefer that the doctor:

- ☐ V. gave me something to read to explain what was wrong.
- ☐ A. showed me a diagram of what was wrong.
- ☐ R. used a plastic model to show me what was wrong.
- ☐ K. described what was wrong.

14. I want to find out about a house or an apartment. Before visiting it I would want:

- ☐ V. a printed description of the rooms and features.
- ☐ A. to view a video of the property.
- ☐ R. a plan showing the rooms and a map of the area.
- ☐ K. a discussion with the owner.

15. I want to learn how to play a new board game or card game. I would:

- ☐ V. listen to somebody explaining it and ask questions.
- ☐ A. watch others play the game before joining in.
- ☐ R. use the diagrams that explain the various stages, moves, and strategies in the game.
- ☐ K. read the instructions.

16. I want to learn about a new project. I would ask for:

- ☐ V. an opportunity to discuss the project.
- ☐ A. diagrams to show the project stages with charts of benefits and costs.
- ☐ R. examples where the project has been used successfully.
- ☐ K. a written report describing the main features of the project.

Totals: Please add up the number of answers with V, then A, then R, and finally K. Enter your results in the boxes below.

	V	A	R	K
Totals				

Source: The VARK Questionnaire™, Version 8.1. © Copyright 2019 held by VARK Learn Limited, Christchurch, New Zealand.

Interpreting Your VARK Results

Now that you've taken the VARK, it's time to interpret your results. Your strongest preference is the area where you received your highest score. For example, if your score is V = 3, A = 2, R = 2, and K = 9, you likely have a strong kinesthetic preference. However, you can also have scores that are more evenly distributed, or have more than one strong preference. If your VARK score is V = 8, A = 7, R = 1, and K = 2, for example, that would mean that you likely have both a visual and an aural preference. If you find yourself with more than one preference (if two, three, or all four scores are close to one another), that means you are considered *multimodal*.

---

your turn **Feeling Connected**

Sharing Different Approaches to Learning

Did you know what your preferred learning style was before you took the VARK? Find one or two other students in your class with different learning preferences. Share thoughts on strategies you are using to study in all your classes, referring to the examples in Table 4.1. What strategies are working for everyone in the group?

high-impact practice 3

Use VARK Results to Study More Effectively

How can knowing your VARK score help you do better in your college classes? The following table offers suggestions for using learning preferences to develop your own study strategies. Consider also how online course management systems (see this chapter's Tech Tip) provide opportunities for different types of learners to connect with the material they are studying.

TABLE 4.1 > Study Strategies by Learning Style

Visual	Aural	Read/Write	Kinesthetic
Underline or highlight your notes.	Talk with others to verify the accuracy of your lecture notes.	Write and rewrite your notes.	Use all your senses in learning: sight, touch, taste, smell, and hearing.
Use symbols, charts, or graphs to display your notes.	Put your notes on audio-tape, or audiotape class lectures.	Read your notes silently.	Supplement your notes with real-world examples.
Use color to highlight important concepts.	Read your notes out loud; ask yourself questions and speak your answers.	Organize diagrams or flowcharts into statements.	Move and gesture while you are reading or speaking your notes.
Create a graphic representation of your notes (e.g., a mind map) and redraw it from memory.		Write imaginary exam questions and respond in writing.	

The Kolb Inventory of Learning Styles

The Kolb Inventory of Learning Styles is a widely used and referenced learning model that is more complex than the VARK Inventory. While the VARK Inventory investigates how learners prefer to use their senses in learning, the Kolb Inventory focuses on the abilities we need to develop so we can learn. This inventory, developed in the 1980s by David Kolb, is based on a four-stage cycle of learning (see Figure 4.2 below).

According to Kolb, effective learners need four kinds of abilities:

1. **Concrete experience** abilities, which allow them to be receptive to others and open to other people's feelings and specific experiences. An example of this type of ability is learning from and empathizing with others.
2. **Reflective observation** abilities, which help learners reflect on their experiences from many perspectives. An example of this type of ability is remaining impartial while considering a situation from a number of different points of view.
3. **Abstract conceptualization** abilities, which help learners integrate observations into logically sound theories. An example of this type of ability is analyzing ideas intellectually and systematically.
4. **Active experimentation** abilities, which enable learners to make decisions, solve problems, and test what they have learned in new situations. An example of this type of ability is being ready to move quickly from thinking to action.

Kolb's Inventory of Learning Styles measures differences along two basic dimensions that represent opposite styles of learning. The first dimension is *abstract-concrete,* and the second is *active-reflective.* See Figure 4.2 below to visualize how these opposing characteristics combine to create four discrete groups of learners: *divergers, assimilators, convergers,* and *accommodators.*

Doing well in college will require you to adopt some behaviors that are characteristic of each of these four learning preferences. Some of them might be uncomfortable for you, but that discomfort will indicate that you're growing, stretching, and not relying on the learning style that might be easiest or most natural for you.

If you are a diverger, you are adept at reflecting on situations from many viewpoints. You excel at brainstorming, and you're imaginative,

FIGURE 4.2 > Kolb's Four-Stage Cycle of Learning

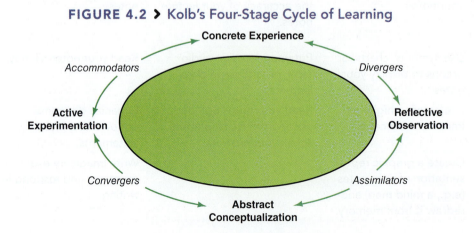

people-oriented, and sometimes emotional. On the downside, you sometimes have difficulty making decisions. Divergers tend to major in the humanities or social sciences.

If you are an assimilator, you like to think about abstract concepts. You are comfortable in classes where the instructor lectures about theoretical ideas without relating the lectures to real-world situations. Assimilators often major in math, physics, or chemistry.

If you are a converger, you like the world of ideas and theories, but you are also good at thinking about how to apply those theories to real-world, practical situations. You differ from divergers in your preference for tasks and problems rather than social and interpersonal issues. Convergers tend to choose health-related and engineering majors.

If you are an accommodator, you prefer hands-on learning. You are skilled at making things happen, and you rely on your intuition. You like people, but you can be pushy and impatient at times, and you might use trial and error, rather than logic, to solve problems. Accommodators often major in business, especially in marketing or sales.[4]

---

yourturn | **Setting Goals**

Where Are You on the Cycle of Learning?

On the basis of the descriptions we have provided here, where do you see yourself in the Kolb Inventory? Are you more like a diverger, assimilator, converger, or accommodator? Do you sometimes feel forced to engage in behaviors that are uncomfortable for you? Is it hard to be motivated when you want hands-on experience but find that some courses require you to consider abstract theories, or when you want to use your imagination but find you must come up with concrete answers? Choose to adopt behaviors that are characteristic of each of Kolb's learning styles. Don't let some initial discomfort hamper your motivation.

The Myers-Briggs Type Indicator

One of the best-known and most widely used personality inventories that can also be used to describe learning preferences is the Myers-Briggs Type Indicator, or MBTI.[5] Whereas the VARK measures your preferences for using your senses to learn and the Kolb Inventory focuses on learning abilities, the MBTI investigates basic personality characteristics and how they relate to human interaction and learning. The MBTI was created by Isabel Briggs Myers and her mother, Katharine Cook Briggs. The inventory identifies and measures psychological types as developed in the personality theory of Carl Gustav Jung, the great twentieth-century psychoanalyst. The MBTI is given to several million people around the world each year. Employers often use this test to give employees insight

---

[4] Adapted from Arthur W. Chickering, *The Modern American College: Responding to the New Realities of Diverse Students and a Changing Society.* Copyright © 1981. Reprinted with permission of John Wiley & Sons, Inc.
[5] Isabel Briggs Myers, *Introduction to Type,* 6th ed. (Mountain View, CA: CPP, 1998).

Take a Time-Out

Do you find that you need some occasional time by yourself? Although introverts are more likely to enjoy time alone, even extraverts can benefit from private time to relax or escape from the hustle and bustle of daily life.

Marc Romanelli/Getty Images

into how they perceive the world, make decisions, and get along with other people. Many first-year seminar or college success courses also include a focus on the MBTI because it provides a good way to begin a dialogue about human interaction and how personality types affect learning.

All the psychological types described by the MBTI are normal and healthy. There is no good or bad or right or wrong; people are simply different. When you complete the MBTI, your score represents your "psychological type," or the combination of your preferences on four different scales. These scales measure how you take in information and how you then make decisions or come to conclusions about that information. Each preference has a one-letter abbreviation. The four letters together make up your type. Although this book doesn't include the actual survey, you will find a description of the basic MBTI types below. Based on these scales, you can be any combination of these eight types.

 high-impact practice 2

yourturn Write and Reflect

Discerning the Extraverts from the Introverts in Your Life

Read the following descriptions of extraverts and introverts. Make a list of your friends and family members, and indicate with an "E" or an "I" which are extraverts and which are introverts. How about you? Which type describes you best? Would you like to be different from the way you are? Reflect on these questions in a journal entry.

Extraversion (E) versus Introversion (I): The Inner or Outer World. The E-I preference indicates whether you direct your energy and attention primarily toward the outer world of people, events, and things or the inner world of thoughts, feelings, and reflections. Personality characteristics of extraverts and introverts are summarized here:

Extraverts	Introverts
Outgoing, gregarious, talkative (may talk too much)	Shy, reflective; careful listeners
People of action (may act before they think)	Consider actions deeply (may think too long before acting or neglect to act at all)
Energized by people and activity	Refreshed by quiet and privacy
Good communicators and leaders	Less likely to voice their opinions; often viewed as unaware of people and situations around them

Sensing (S) versus Intuition (N): Facts or Ideas. The S-N preference indicates how you perceive the world and take in information: directly, through your five senses, or indirectly, by using your intuition. Personality characteristics of sensing and intuitive types are summarized here:

Sensing Types	Intuitive Types
Interested above all in the facts, what they can be sure of; dislike unnecessary complication; prefer practicing skills they already know	Fascinated by concepts and big ideas; prefer learning new skills over those already mastered
Relatively traditional and conventional	Original, creative, and nontraditional
Practical, factual, realistic, and down-to-earth	Innovative but sometimes impractical; need inspiration and meaning; prefer to look to the future rather than at the present
Accurate, precise, and effective with routine and details; sometimes miss the "forest" for the "trees"	May exaggerate facts unknowingly; dislike routine and details; work in bursts of energy

Thinking (T) versus Feeling (F): Logic or Values. The T-F preference indicates how you prefer to make your decisions: through logical, rational analysis or through your subjective values, likes, and dislikes. Personality characteristics of thinking types and feeling types are summarized here:

Thinking Types	Feeling Types
Logical, rational, analytical, and critical	Warm, empathetic, and sympathetic
Relatively impersonal and objective in making decisions, less swayed by feelings and emotions; sometimes surprised and puzzled by others' feelings	Need and value harmony; often distressed or distracted by argument and conflict; reluctant to tackle unpleasant interpersonal tasks
Need and value fairness; can deal with interpersonal disharmony	Need and value kindness and harmony
Fair, logical, and just; firm and assertive	Facilitate cooperation and goodwill in others; sometimes unable to be assertive when appropriate
May seem cold, insensitive, and overly blunt and hurtful in their criticisms	Occasionally illogical, emotionally demanding, and unaffected by objective reason and evidence

Judging (J) versus Perceiving (P): Organization or Adaptability.

The J-P preference indicates how you characteristically approach the outside world: by making decisions and judgments or by observing and perceiving instead. Personality characteristics of judging and perceiving types are summarized here:

Judging Types	Perceiving Types
Orderly, organized, punctual, and tidy	Spontaneous and flexible
In control of their own world and sphere of influence	Adapt to their world rather than try to control it; comfortable dealing with changes and unexpected developments
Quick decision makers; like to make and follow plans	Slow to make decisions; prefer a wait-and-see approach
Sometimes judgmental and prone to jump to conclusions or make decisions without enough information; have trouble changing plans	Tendency toward serious procrastination and juggling too many things at once without finishing anything; sometimes messy and disorganized

To learn more about these personality types and to access a questionnaire to find out more about your type, visit the Myers & Briggs Foundation at **myersbriggs.org/my-mbti-personality-type/take-the-mbti -instrument**. Remember that while some Myers-Briggs personality types may be particularly advantageous in certain situations, no one type is inherently superior to another. Be alert to both the positive and negative effects your type might have on your success in college.

Multiple Intelligences

Another way of measuring how we learn is the theory of **multiple intelligences,** which suggests that all human beings have at least eight different types of intelligence. This theory was developed in 1983 by Dr. Howard Gardner, a professor of education at Harvard University. Gardner's theory is based on the idea that the traditional definition of human intelligence is very limited. Gardner argues that students should be encouraged to develop the abilities they have, and that evaluation should measure all forms of intelligence.

Gardner's work is controversial because it questions our traditional definitions of intelligence. According to Gardner's theory, all human beings have at least eight different types of intelligence, as follows:

1. A **verbal/linguistic** learner likes to read, write, and tell stories, and is good at memorizing information.
2. A **logical/mathematical** learner likes to work with numbers and is good at problem solving and logical processes.
3. A **visual/spatial** learner likes to draw and play with machines and is good at puzzles and reading maps and charts.
4. A **bodily/kinesthetic** learner likes to move around and is good at sports, dance, and acting.

A Knack for Music

Consider the checkmarks you made under musical/rhythmic intelligence in the Multiple Intelligences Inventory in this chapter. Do you play an instrument? Do you find yourself tapping out rhythms? Can you listen to a song and then play it "by ear"? If music comes naturally to you, you probably have a strong musical/rhythmic intelligence.

Peter Muller/AGE Fotostock

5. A **musical/rhythmic** learner likes to sing and play an instrument and is good at remembering melodies and noticing pitches and rhythms.

6. An **interpersonal** learner likes to have many friends and is good at understanding people, leading others, and mediating conflicts.

7. **Intrapersonal** learners like to work alone, understand themselves well, and are original thinkers.

8. A **naturalistic** learner likes to be outside and is good at preservation, conservation, and organizing a living area.

Where do you think you see yourself? In your opinion, which of these eight intelligences best describes you? As you think of your friends and family, what kinds of intelligences do you think they have? Verify your assumptions about the intelligences of friends and family members together by taking the Multiple Intelligences Inventory on the next two pages. Were there any surprises or were your assumptions confirmed?

| **your turn** | Write and Reflect |

 high-impact practice 2

Is There Really More than One Type of Intelligence?

Do a Google search for the phrase *multiple intelligences debate*. Write a one-page paper that describes different opinions about Howard Gardner's theory. Do you agree with the theory? Why or why not?

Multiple Intelligences Inventory

Put a check mark next to all the items within each intelligence that apply to you.

Verbal/Linguistic Intelligence

_____ I enjoy telling stories and jokes.

_____ I enjoy word games (e.g., Scrabble and puzzles).

_____ I am a good speller (most of the time).

_____ I like talking and writing about my ideas.

_____ If something breaks and won't work, I read the instruction book before I try to fix it.

_____ When I work with others in a group presentation, I prefer to do the writing and library research.

Logical/Mathematical Intelligence

_____ I really enjoy my math class.

_____ I like to find out how things work.

_____ I enjoy computer and math games.

_____ I love playing chess, checkers, or Monopoly.

_____ If something breaks and won't work, I look at the pieces and try to figure out how it works.

Visual/Spatial Intelligence

_____ I prefer a map to written directions.

_____ I enjoy hobbies such as photography.

_____ I like to doodle on paper whenever I can.

_____ In a magazine, I prefer looking at the pictures rather than reading the text.

_____ If something breaks and won't work, I tend to study the diagram of how it works.

Bodily/Kinesthetic Intelligence

_____ My favorite class is gym because I like sports.

_____ When looking at things, I like touching them.

_____ I use a lot of body movements when talking.

_____ I tend to tap my fingers or play with my pencil during class.

_____ If something breaks and won't work, I tend to play with the pieces to try to fit them together.

Musical/Rhythmic Intelligence

_____ I enjoy listening to CDs and the radio.

_____ I like to sing.

_____ I like to have music playing when doing homework or studying.

_____ I can remember the melodies of many songs.

_____ If something breaks and won't work, I tend to tap my fingers to a beat while I figure it out.

Interpersonal Intelligence

_____ I get along well with others.

_____ I have several very close friends.

_____ I like working with others in groups.

_____ Friends ask my advice because I seem to be a natural leader.

_____ If something breaks and won't work, I try to find someone who can help me.

Intrapersonal Intelligence

_____ I like to work alone without anyone bothering me.

_____ I don't like crowds.

_____ I know my own strengths and weaknesses.

_____ I find that I am strong-willed, independent, and don't follow the crowd.

_____ If something breaks and won't work, I wonder whether it's worth fixing.

Naturalist Intelligence

_____ I am keenly aware of my surroundings and of what goes on around me.

_____ I like to collect things like rocks, sports cards, and stamps.

_____ I like to get away from the city and enjoy nature.

____ I enjoy learning the names of living things in the environment, such as flowers and trees.

____ If something breaks and won't work, I look around me to see what I can find to fix the problem.

Review your responses. Now, count up the check marks for each intelligence, and write the total for each intelligence here. Your score for each intelligence will be a number between 1 and 5:

TOTAL SCORE

____ Verbal/Linguistic

____ Logical/Mathematical

____ Visual/Spatial

____ Bodily/Kinesthetic

____ Musical/Rhythmic

____ Interpersonal

____ Intrapersonal

____ Naturalist

Your scores of 3 or more will help you to get a sense of your own multiple intelligences.

Depending on your background and age, some intelligences are likely to be more developed than others. Now that you know where your intelligences are, you can work to strengthen the other intelligences that you do not use as often. How do college courses measure ways in which you are intelligent? Where do they fall short? Looking to the future, you can use your intelligences to help you choose a major, choose activities, and investigate career options. This information will help you appreciate your own unique abilities, and also those of others.

Source: Greg Gay and Gary Hams, "The Multiple Intelligences Inventory." Copyright © Learning Disabilities Resource Community, www.ldrc.ca. Reprinted by permission of the authors.

WHEN LEARNING STYLES AND TEACHING STYLES CONFLICT

Do you enjoy listening to lectures, or do you find yourself gazing out the window or dozing? When your instructor assigns a group discussion, what is your immediate reaction? Do you dislike talking with other students, or is that the way you learn best? How do you react to lab sessions when you have to conduct an actual experiment? Is it an activity you look forward to, or one you dread? Each of these learning situations appeals to some students more than others, but each is inevitably going to be part of your college experience. Your college or university has intentionally designed courses for you to have the opportunity to listen to professors who are experts in their field, to interact with other students in structured groups, and to learn through doing. Because they are all important components of your college education, it's important for you to make the most of each situation.

Instructors tend to teach in ways that fit their *own* particular styles of learning. So an instructor who learns best in a read/write mode or aural mode will probably just lecture and give the class little opportunity for either interaction or visual and kinesthetic learning. But an instructor who prefers a more interactive, hands-on environment will likely involve students in discussion and learning through experience.

NAVIGATE ONLINE LEARNING WITH YOUR COLLEGE LMS

Do you like the idea of taking an online class? Maybe that would be a good fit for your work or family schedule. Maybe it would be easier than looking for a parking space on campus. But would you still learn, even if you don't go to a class meeting?

Many colleges and universities use an online learning management system (LMS) for online learning. An LMS is a website that helps you connect with the material you're studying—as well as with your instructors and classmates. There is something for every learning style in the LMS environment.

Warchi/iStock/Getty Images

The Problem

You're considering taking an online course, but you don't really understand what an LMS is or how to use one.

The Fix

Understand your strengths, your preferences, and basic LMS functionality.

How to Do It

Explore your school's LMS. Be open-minded and patient with yourself. Find out if there is an orientation seminar or video you can watch; you can ask your instructors or visit the student learning center. In addition, consider what you've learned about yourself and your learning preferences in this chapter.

Develop learning strategies that work for you. An LMS offers lots of ways to connect with your instructors, classmates, and material. It lets you keep track of your grades and assignments and offers a digital drop box where you can submit your work. It can also offer a lot of fun things, such as online discussion forums and interactive group project spaces where you can sketch ideas on whiteboards that other students can view, or even collaborate on written assignments in real time. Some platforms have videos, recorded lectures, or even your instructor's lecture notes. Consider the following suggestions:

1. If you're an **auditory learner**, you'll love audio recordings. Read your notes and textbook aloud as you study (you can even record yourself doing this so you can play back it back later). Consider listening to audiobooks and joining a study

loaded into your course LMS, there may even be a setting that directs the computer to read chapters aloud to you. Another tip: view videos once, then play them back with your eyes closed.

2. If you're a **visual learner**, you'll love videos, pictures, maps, and graphs. Whenever you take notes, illustrate them, playing up key points with colored highlighters, pictures, or symbols. You can also create your own graphs or charts.

3. If you're a **hands-on learner**, you'll love labs, group projects, and fieldwork. Be sure to take notes and read things aloud as you study. Build models or spreadsheets. Take a field trip with others or even by yourself.

IS IT FOR YOU?

Now that you know more about your learning preferences and something about your college's LMS, ask yourself these questions:

- Are you disciplined enough to work independently?
- Would you miss interacting with your instructor or classmates if you didn't attend classes in person?

You need to know yourself because learning is really

When you recognize a mismatch between how you best learn and how you are being taught, it is important that you take control of your learning process. Use Table 4.2 as a guide to identify these mismatches and discover strategies for how to handle them. Don't depend on the instructor or the classroom environment to give you everything you need to maximize your learning. Employ your own preferences, talents, and abilities to develop many different ways to study and retain information. For instance, if you don't like listening to a lecture, you will want to sit close to the front of the classroom to reduce distractions. You might also want to record the lecture (with the instructor's permission) so that you can listen to it again. Look back through this chapter to remind yourself of the ways that you can use your own learning preferences to be more successful in any class you take.

TABLE 4.2 › Using the VARK to Adapt

Try to use the VARK to figure out how your instructors teach their classes. List your classes, your instructors' teaching styles, and then your learning style. Do they match? If not, list a strategy you can use to adapt.

My Classes	Teaching Style	My Learning Style	Match: Yes or No?
Example: *Psychology*	*Uses PowerPoint with her lecture so:* *Visual and Auditory*	*I am kinesthetic and visual.*	*No, but I can ride a stationary bike while looking over my notes.*

"As we start a new school year, Mr. Smith, I just want you to know that I'm an Abstract-Sequential learner and trust that you'll conduct yourself accordingly!"

Browning

Learn to Adapt

In college you will find that some instructors may have teaching styles that are challenging for you. Seek out the kinds of classes that conform to the way you like to learn, but also develop your adaptive strategies to make the most of any classroom setting.

William G. Browning, Minneapolis, MN

Look back through this chapter to remind yourself of the ways that you can use your own learning preference to be more successful in any class you take. If you are interested in reading more about learning preferences, the library and your college learning center will have many resources.

LEARNING WITH A LEARNING DISABILITY

While everyone has a learning preference, some people have a **learning disability**, a general term that covers a wide variety of specific learning problems resulting from neurological disorders that can make it difficult to acquire certain academic and social skills. A learning disability is a very common challenge to learning for students of any age. Learning disabilities are usually recognized and diagnosed in grade school, but some students can enter college without having been properly diagnosed or assisted.

Learning disabilities can show up as specific difficulties with spoken and written language, coordination, self-control, or attention. Such difficulties can impede learning to read, write, or do math. The term *learning disability* covers a broad range of symptoms and outcomes. Because of this, it is sometimes difficult to diagnose a learning disability or pinpoint the causes. The types of learning disabilities that most commonly affect college students are **attention disorders**, which affect the ability to focus and concentrate, and **cognitive disorders**, which affect the development of academic skills, including reading, writing, and mathematics.

You might know someone who has been diagnosed with a learning disability, such as dyslexia, a reading disability that occurs when the brain does not properly recognize and process certain symbols, or an attention deficit disorder that affects concentration and focus. It is also possible that you have a special learning need and are not aware of it. This section seeks to increase your self-awareness and your knowledge about such challenges to learning. The earlier in life—and college—you address any learning challenges you might have, the better you will perform.

Attention Disorders

Attention disorders are common in children, adolescents, and even adults. Some students who have attention disorders appear to daydream a lot; even if you do get their attention, they can be easily distracted. Individuals with attention deficit disorder (ADD) or attention deficit/hyperactivity disorder (ADHD) often have trouble organizing tasks or completing their work. They don't seem to listen to or follow directions, and their work might be messy or appear careless. Although in legal and medical terms they are not strictly classified as learning disabilities, ADD and ADHD can seriously interfere with academic performance, leading some educators to classify them along with other learning disabilities.[6]

---

[6] Adapted and reprinted from the public domain source by Sharyn Neuwirth, *Learning Disabilities* (Darby, PA: National Institute of Mental Health, 1993), pp. 9–10.

If you have trouble paying attention or getting organized, you won't really know whether you have ADD or ADHD until you are evaluated. It may be that you simply have too much to do or that you're trying unsuccessfully to multitask. Do not assume that you have a learning disability until you consult with an expert in your learning center or in the community. After you have been evaluated, follow the professional advice you get, which may or may not mean taking medication. If you do receive a prescription for medication, be sure to take it according to the doctor's directions. In the meantime, if you're having trouble getting and staying organized, whether or not you have an attention disorder, you can improve your focus through your own behavioral choices. The world-famous Mayo Clinic website offers the following suggestions for adults with ADD or ADHD.[7]

- Make a list of tasks to be accomplished each day. Make sure you're not trying to do too much.
- Break down tasks into smaller, more manageable steps.
- Use sticky pads to write notes to yourself. Put them on the fridge, on the bathroom mirror, in the car, or in other places where you'll benefit from having a reminder.
- Keep an electronic calendar to track appointments and deadlines.
- Carry a notebook or electronic device with you so that you can note ideas or things you'll need to remember.
- Take time to set up systems to file and organize information, both on your electronic devices and for paper documents. Get in the habit of using these systems consistently.
- Follow a routine that's consistent from day to day and keep items, like keys and your wallet, in the same place.
- Ask for help from family members or friends.

Cognitive Learning Disabilities

Cognitive learning disabilities are related to mental tasks and processing. Dyslexia, for example, is a developmental reading disorder classified as a cognitive learning disability. A person can have problems with any of the tasks involved in reading. However, scientists have found that a significant number of people with dyslexia are not able to distinguish or separate the sounds in spoken words. For instance, dyslexic individuals sometimes have difficulty assigning the right sounds to letters, either individually or when letters combine to form words.

There is, of course, more to reading than recognizing words. If the brain is unable to form images or relate new ideas to those stored in memory, the reader can't understand or remember the new concepts. So other types of reading disabilities can appear when the focus of reading shifts from identifying words to comprehending a written passage.[8]

Writing, too, involves several brain areas and functions. The networks of the brain that control vocabulary, grammar, hand movement, and

---

[7] See mayoclinic.org/diseases-conditions/adult-adhd/basics/lifestyle-home-remedies/con-20034552.
[8] See ldaamerica.org/types-of-learning-disabilities/dyslexia/.

memory must all be in good working order. So a developmental writing disorder might result from problems in any of these areas. Someone who can't distinguish the sequence of sounds in a word will often have problems with spelling. People with writing disabilities, particularly expressive language disorders (the inability to express oneself using accurate language or sentence structure), are often unable to write complete, grammatical sentences.[9]

A student with a developmental arithmetic disorder will have difficulty recognizing numbers and symbols, memorizing facts such as the multiplication table, and understanding abstract concepts such as place value and fractions.[10]

The following questions may help you determine whether you or someone you know should be screened for a possible learning disability:

Do you perform poorly on tests, even when you feel that you have studied and are capable of performing better?
Do you have trouble spelling words?
Do you work harder than your classmates at basic reading and writing?
Do your instructors point out inconsistencies in your classroom performance, such as answering questions correctly in class but incorrectly on a written test?
Do you have a really short attention span, or do your family members or instructors say that you do things without thinking?

Although responding "yes" to any of these questions does not mean that you have a disability, your campus learning center or the office for student disability services can help you address any potential problems and devise ways for you to learn more effectively.

If you have a documented learning disability, make sure to notify the office of student disability services at your college or university to receive reasonable accommodations, as required by law. Reasonable accommodations might include use of a computer during some exams, readers for tests, in-class note-takers, extra time for assignments and tests, or the use of audio textbooks, depending on your needs and the type of disability you have.

Anyone who is diagnosed with a learning disability is in good company. According to national data, between 15 and 20 percent of Americans have a learning disability. Pop star Jewel, National Football League host and former player Terry Bradshaw, actor Patrick Dempsey, and CNN news anchor Anderson Cooper are just a few of the famous and successful people who have diagnosed learning disabilities. Here is a final important message: A learning disability is a learning *difference*, but is in no way related to intelligence. Having a learning disability is not a sign that you are stupid. In fact, some of the most intelligent individuals in human history have had a learning disability.

---

[9] Ibid.

[10] See **ldaamerica.org/types-of-learning-disabilities/dyscalculia/**.

Accept the Challenge to Do Your Best, No Matter What!

Although you generally won't be able to select courses and instructors based on your learning preference you can choose how to handle yourself in each class. Think about your courses this term and look at how you filled in Table 4.2. Which classes are challenging you because of the way the instructors teach? If you are using an instructor's teaching style as an excuse for your poor performance, you are making a choice that may affect your overall college success. Your college or university has plenty of resources available to help you. Seek them out and choose to get the assistance you need to do your best.

checklist for success

How You Learn

- **Take an inventory of your learning preferences or styles, either in this chapter or at your campus learning or counseling center(s).** See if the results might explain, at least in part, your level of performance in each class you are taking this term.

- **Learn about and accept your unique learning preferences.** Make a special note of your strengths, in terms of those things you learn well and easily. See if those skills could be applied to other learning situations.

- **Adapt your learning preference to the teaching styles of your professors.** Consider talking to your professors about how you might best be able to adapt to their teaching strategies.

- **Use your learning preference to develop study strategies that work best for you.** You can walk, talk, read, listen, or even dance while you are learning.

- **If you need help with making the best use of your learning preference, visit your learning center.** Consider taking some courses in the social and behavioral sciences, which could help you better understand how people learn.

- **If you think you might have a learning disability, go to your campus learning center and ask for a diagnostic assessment so that you can develop successful coping strategies.** Make sure to ask for a personal interpretation and follow-up counseling or tutoring.

4 | buildyourexperience

REFLECT ON CHOICES

high-impact practice 2 | This chapter has introduced you to the ways people prefer to learn from their environment. The choice of what to do with that information is up to you. Successful college students learn to adapt to teaching styles that they may not prefer. They know what they have to do to be successful learners, they set goals, and they monitor their progress toward their goals. In a journal entry or readily accessible file, reflect on and write about what you have learned about learning preferences and learning disabilities in this chapter and how you can apply the chapter information and strategies in college and in your career. Revisit and build upon your observations throughout your first-year experience.

APPLY WHAT YOU'VE LEARNED

Now that you have read and discussed this chapter, consider how you can apply what you have learned to your academic life and your personal life. The following prompts will help you reflect on chapter material and its relevance to you both now and in the future.

1. It is almost certain that you will find yourself in a class where your learning preference conflicts with your instructor's preferred way of teaching. After reading this chapter, describe what you can do to take control and make the most of your strongest learning preferences.

2. It is important to understand various learning preferences in the context of education, but it is also important to understand how learning preferences affect career choices. Considering your own learning preferences, what might be the best careers for you? Why?

USE YOUR RESOURCES

> **Campus Learning Center or Center for Students with Disabilities.** Whether you are an online or on-campus student, a recent high school graduate, or someone who is older, your college or university will have resources to help students learn more about learning preferences or to diagnose a learning disability.

> **Your Instructors or Your Peer Leader.** To gather information about the support services your campus has to offer, talk to your first-year seminar instructor or instructors in education or psychology, who have a strong interest in the processes of learning. You'll find that your peer leader can also steer you in the right direction. If you *are* a peer leader, make sure you have a working knowledge of the learning preferences covered in this chapter.

> **Campus Library.** A great deal of published information is available that describes how we learn. A campus librarian can help you locate books and online resources on learning preferences and learning disabilities.

> **Social Media.** You will find groups on Facebook that were created by students who have learning disabilities or ADHD. Connect with other students with learning disabilities at your college or university or at other institutions. If you have been diagnosed with a learning disability, the members of these groups can offer support and help you seek out appropriate resources to be successful in college.

LaunchPad
macmillan learning

LaunchPad for *Your College Experience* is a great resource. Go online to master concepts using the LearningCurve study tool and much more. **Launchpadworks.com**

Jacob Lund/Shutterstock

8 STUDYING

Student Goals

- Learn how to make good choices for better concentration and efficient studying
- Understand how memory works and become familiar with myths about memory
- Gain skills to improve your memory
- Explore high-impact practices 2 (writing) and 3 (collaboration)

Chris Ryan/Getty Images

9 TEST TAKING

Student Goals

- Prepare yourself for tests and exams physically, emotionally, and academically
- Learn strategies for taking different types of tests and handling various question types
- Recognize the symptoms of test anxiety and gain strategies to overcome it
- Understand what cheating is and how to avoid it, and learn guidelines for maintaining academic honesty
- Explore high-impact practices 2 (writing) and 3 (collaboration)

Blend Images-Hill Street
Studios/Getty Images
Phase4Studios/Shutterstock

10 INFORMATION LITERACY AND COMMUNICATION

Student Goals

- Understand what it means to be information literate
- Learn how to choose a research topic, narrow it down, and research it
- Know how to use your college library with assistance from librarians
- Apply the guidelines for evaluating sources
- Gain an understanding of how to move from research to writing and use each step of the writing process
- Learn the guidelines for successful public speaking
- Explore high-impact practices 2 (writing) and 3 (collaboration)

Phase4Studios/Shutterstock

5

THINKING IN COLLEGE

YOU WILL EXPLORE

What college-level thinking involves

How to become a critical thinker

Bloom's taxonomy and how it relates to critical thinking

⌖ High-impact practices 2 (writing), 3 (collaboration), and 4 (diversity)

David Aaron Troy/Getty Images

> **Thinking for ourselves and coming up with new conclusions will be really helpful when we enter the workforce.**

As a sophomore psychology student, Alyssa understands the importance of thinking skills both inside and outside the classroom. When Alyssa arrived on campus last fall, she learned that she would be living in the international residence hall with students from all over the world. She quickly learned that interacting with people who don't know anyone else in the area and who have different customs, study habits, and food presented some unique challenges and tested her thinking skills. "Some of the questions the international students ask about America make me think in a different way because I never question the U.S. way of doing things." One way she has been able to reach out to these students is by joining an international student organization, which helps bring new international students to campus and get them settled into campus life.

Alyssa grew up in Philadelphia and decided to attend a university that would give her an opportunity to conduct research in psychology as an undergraduate. So far, her favorite class has been social psychology. She has found good thinking skills to be essential to succeeding in all her classes. "Professors will give you a lot of facts and general information, but they expect you to be able to synthesize all the information and come up with your own conclusions. Thinking for ourselves and not relying on opinions of others will be really helpful when we enter the workforce," she says.

After Alyssa graduates, she's open to new experiences and opportunities, but she hopes to continue on to medical school. As an aspiring psychiatrist, she says that "thinking skills will help a lot when dealing with cases and needing to diagnose disorders and develop treatment plans. They will also be helpful in clinical settings." Her advice to other first-year students? Look for ways to recognize problems and come up with unique solutions.

LaunchPad
macmillan learning

To access the LearningCurve study tool, video activities, and more, go to LaunchPad for *Your College Experience*. **Launchpadworks.com**

Learning to think—using the mind to produce ideas, opinions, decisions, and memories—is part of normal human development. Just as our bodies grow, so does our ability to think logically and rationally about abstract concepts. The Nobel-prize–winning economist, Daniel Kahneman, describes two types of thinking: "fast thinking" and "slow thinking." He characterizes fast thinking as automatic, emotional, stereotypic, and subconscious; this type of thinking is certainly appropriate in some circumstances. Slow thinking takes more effort, more conscious attention, and is more logical, rational, and deep.[1] By improving your slower and more logical thinking abilities and strategies, you will become a better learner and problem solver.

---

[1] Daniel Kahneman, *Thinking, Fast and Slow* (New York: Farrar, Straus and Giroux, 2013).

assess your strengths

Thinking is one of the most valuable skills you can practice for success in college and in the workplace. What strengths do you currently have in solving problems and making decisions? How do you approach such issues? Do you make quick decisions, or are you more deliberate and thoughtful? Think of a couple of issues you have dealt with in the recent past. How has your approach helped or hurt each situation?

set goals

What are your most important objectives in learning the material in this chapter? Do you think deeply before making decisions? Consider an issue that you are currently dealing with. Are you investigating all sides of it rather than making a snap decision? Use this chapter to help you develop strategies and goals that relate to thinking.

The concept of "critical thinking" might not be new to you; you have probably heard the term before. Here we define **critical thinking** as the thoughtful consideration of the information, ideas, observations, and arguments that you encounter. In essence, critical thinking is a search for truth. It is similar to slow thinking as described by Kahneman, but it also emphasizes the importance of analyzing and evaluating information to guide belief and action—this is the kind of thinking you will do in college, and it's what this chapter is all about. We will explain how developing and applying your critical-thinking skills can make the search for answers a worthwhile and stimulating adventure.

COLLEGE-LEVEL THINKING: HIGHER AND DEEPER

In college, the level of thinking that your instructors expect from you exceeds that which you did in high school, both in terms of the questions that are asked and the answers that are expected. For instance, if a high school teacher asked, "What are the three branches of the U.S. government?" you would be expected to give the one right answer: "legislative, executive, and judicial." A college instructor, on the other hand, might ask, "Under what circumstances might conflicts arise among the three branches of government, and what do the circumstances and the conflicts reveal about the democratic process?" There is no simple, quick, or single acceptable answer to the second question—that's the point of higher education. Questions that suggest complex answers engage you in the process of deep thinking. The shift to this higher or deeper level of thinking can be an adjustment—it might even catch you off guard and cause you some stress.

One step toward deep and critical thinking is becoming comfortable with uncertainty. In college, it's important to challenge assumptions and conclusions, even those presented by so-called experts. Rather than just taking in information, studying it, and then recalling it for a test, in college you'll go far beyond these skills and gain the ability and the confidence to arrive at your own conclusions—to think for yourself. Educational researchers describe this process as "constructing" knowledge for yourself rather than merely "receiving" knowledge from others. Courses in every discipline will encourage you to ask questions, sort through competing information and ideas, form well-reasoned opinions, and defend them.

It is natural to feel frustrated by answers that are neither entirely wrong nor right, yet the complicated questions are usually the ones that are the most interesting and worthy of study. Working out the answers can be both intellectually exciting and personally rewarding.

Problem Solving in and out of Class

College will give you experience in decision making and problem solving—processes that are linked to your abilities to use logical thinking processes, to weigh evidence, and to formulate conclusions. Your success both in college and in your future life will depend on how well you make decisions and solve problems. Here are some examples of situations commonly encountered in college that will call upon these skills:

- Deciding how to allocate your research and writing time when you have two papers due on the same day
- Finding a way to ask your roommate to compromise on a suitable lights-out time because you're not getting the sleep you need
- Mapping out how to incorporate time for exercising into your busy schedule in order to maintain a healthy fitness level and avoid weight gain
- Deciding whether to go home on the weekends or stay on campus to study and participate in campus events
- Understanding the advantages and disadvantages of the variety of readily available information sources, including Facebook, Twitter feeds, CNN, *USA Today*, *The New York Times*, the *Onion*, and your campus newspaper

In addition to these situations, which provide opportunities for you to flex your problem-solving muscles on a more personal level, the college years also represent a time in your life when you get to know yourself. You will begin to develop your own positions on societal and political issues, learn more about what is important to you, and develop into a contributing citizen of your country and the world.

In college, you'll be exposed to ideas and conflicting opinions about contemporary issues such as same-sex marriage, U.S. military operations, global human rights, animal rights, comprehensive sex education, food safety, the state of public education in the United States, student loan debt and loan forgiveness, and economic inequality. The list goes on and on. Before accepting any opinion on any issue as "the truth," look for evidence that supports different positions on these debates. In fact, look for opportunities to participate in such debates. In most colleges, it's easy to find these opportunities.

Making a Choice between Slow and Fast Thinking

At the start of the chapter, we introduced the concepts of slow and fast thinking. While fast, or spur-of-the-moment thinking has its place, improving your more logical and slower thinking abilities will allow you to become a better learner. But you might notice that some people seem to do no real thinking at all, or at least no thinking of their own.

People who do not develop their thinking skills often make quick decisions based on what seems easiest, results in the least conflict, or conforms to preconceived notions. You probably know a lot of people like that—who do not think critically, depend on others to think for them, and assume that what they believe is true simply because they wish, hope, or feel that it is true. You might also know people who like things just because they are popular, and still others who base their beliefs on what they heard growing up, without ever examining the underlying assumptions that support those beliefs. As you might have noticed, the followers, the wishful believers, and the rigid thinkers tend not to have much control over their lives or any real power in business or society.

Those who think deliberately and use critical-thinking skills are different. They examine problems, ask questions, suggest new answers that challenge the existing situation, discover new information, question authorities and traditional beliefs, make independent judgments, and develop creative solutions. Being a good critical thinker does not mean that you are "critical" or negative in your dealings with others. Rather, the term refers to thoughtful consideration of the information, ideas, and arguments that you encounter. When employers say they want workers who can find reliable information, analyze it, organize it, draw conclusions from it, and present it convincingly to others, that means they want employees who are good critical thinkers.

How can you sharpen your critical-thinking skills while you're in college? It won't happen overnight. But this is a skill that all of us in the digital age can improve. With practice you will be less likely to be fooled by false information, especially information that is being spread online. Thinking carefully and critically will help you make better decisions, come up with fresh solutions to difficult problems, and communicate your ideas effectively.

your turn   Making Decisions

If You Had a "Do-Over"

Think about a past problem or difficult situation you were unsuccessful in solving. If you could go back in time, how would you choose to solve the problem to get the outcome you desire? What would you do differently? What different choices would you make? Could you more deliberately use slow thinking in approaching the situation?

Rate Your Critical-Thinking Skills

It will be interesting to see how your critical-thinking skills change over the next few weeks and months. Given where you are currently, rate yourself as a "critical" thinker. At the end of the term, return to this table, and see how much you've changed.

Circle the number that best fits you in each of the critical situations described below.

Critical Situations	Never				Sometimes				Always	
In class, I ask lots of questions when I don't understand.	1	2	3	4	5	6	7	8	9	10
If I don't agree with what the group decides is the correct answer, I challenge the group opinion.	1	2	3	4	5	6	7	8	9	10
I believe there are many solutions to a problem.	1	2	3	4	5	6	7	8	9	10
I admire those people in history who challenged what was believed at the time, such as "the earth is flat."	1	2	3	4	5	6	7	8	9	10
I make an effort to listen to both sides of an argument before deciding which side I will take.	1	2	3	4	5	6	7	8	9	10
I read lots of different views on a political candidate before making up my mind.	1	2	3	4	5	6	7	8	9	10
I am not afraid to change my belief system if I learn something new.	1	2	3	4	5	6	7	8	9	10
Authority figures do not intimidate me.	1	2	3	4	5	6	7	8	9	10

The more 7–10 scores you have circled, the more likely it is that you use your critical-thinking skills often. The lower scores indicate that you may not use critical-thinking skills very often, or that you use them only during certain activities.

 high-impact practice 3

Collaboration

One way to become a better critical thinker is to practice with other people. By getting feedback from others, you can see the possible flaws in your own position or approach. Whether debating an issue in a political science class or creating an original painting, appreciate how people bring their own life experiences, personal taste, knowledge, and expertise to the table. Most questions do not have clear-cut answers, and there are often several ways of approaching any task. Getting input from others can help make your finished product a masterpiece.

Researchers who study thinking in populations of elementary school students, high school students, and college students find that critical thinking and collaboration go hand in hand. Students at all levels are more likely to exercise their critical-thinking abilities when they are confronted by the experiences and opinions of others. Having more than one student involved in the learning process generates a greater number of ideas than one person can generate alone. People think more clearly when they talk as well as listen, which is a very good reason to participate actively in your classes. Creative brainstorming and group discussion encourage original thought. These habits also teach participants to consider alternative points of view carefully and to express and defend their own ideas clearly. As a group negotiates ideas and learns to agree on the most reliable concepts, it moves closer to a conclusive solution.

As you leave college and enter the working world, you will find that collaboration—not only with people in your work setting but also with others around the globe—is essential to almost any career you may pursue. Whether in person or through electronic communication, teamwork improves your ability to think critically.

Creativity

Our society is full of creative individuals who think outside the box, challenge the status quo, or simply ask questions that others are not asking. Many have achieved fame by using their thinking skills and actions to change the world. Even a single thought can have a ripple effect that leads to major progress. Lin-Manuel Miranda, pictured here, won the Pulitzer Prize for his hit musical *Hamilton*. In this play, non-white actors play the roles of Hamilton himself as well as Thomas Jefferson, George Washington, Aaron Burr, James Madison, and others. This diverse cast makes the play relevant to today's audiences and can spark a discussion of how history is made and retold.
Tinseltown/Shutterstock

your turn Setting Goals

Rethink Your Goals

How can good critical thinking help you set goals? Think about the goals you have for college—what you want to do when you graduate. When did you decide on these goals—recently or a long time ago? Have any of your experiences in college, either in or out of class, caused you to question your thinking? Now is a good time to rethink your goals. Get some feedback from others who know you, and use that feedback plus your own critical-thinking skills to make sure that your goals are realistic, achievable, and make the most sense for you.

BECOMING A CRITICAL THINKER

As you've read, a high-priority goal in college is to develop strong thinking and decision-making skills. Not only will you develop your own competence and confidence, you will contribute to the larger society by helping solve community and national problems.

Asking Questions

The first step of thinking at a deeper level, of true critical thinking, is to be curious. This involves asking questions. Instead of accepting statements and claims at face value, question them. Here are a few suggestions:

- When you come across an idea or a statement that you consider interesting, confusing, or suspicious, first ask yourself what it means.
- Do you fully understand what is being said, or do you need to pause and think to make sense of the idea?
- Do you agree with the statement? Why or why not?
- Can the statement or idea be interpreted in more than one way?

Don't stop there.

- Ask whether you can trust the person or group making a particular claim, and ask whether there is enough evidence to back up that claim (more on this later).
- Ask who might agree or disagree and why.
- Ask how a new concept relates to what you already know.
- Think about where you might find more information about the subject, and what you could do with what you learn.
- Ask yourself about the effects of accepting a new idea as truth.
  - Will you have to change or give up what you have believed in for a long time?
  - Will it require you to do something differently?
  - Will it be necessary to examine the issue further?
  - Should you try to bring other people around to a new way of thinking?

© Randy Glasbergen.
www.glasbergen.com

WATER 99¢

LO-CARB WATER $2.99

GLASBERGEN

Comparison Shopping

Use your critical-thinking abilities to practice healthy skepticism in your life. Shopping is a great opportunity to practice. What questions do you need to ask to find out if what seems like a good deal really is a good deal? Can you think of a time when you had to think hard about a purchase to make sure it was a wise choice?

Randy Glasbergen

Considering Multiple Points of View and Drawing Conclusions

Before you draw any conclusions about the validity of information or opinions, it's important to consider more than one point of view. College reading assignments might deliberately expose you to conflicting arguments and theories about a subject, or you might encounter differences of opinion as you do research for a project. Your own belief system will influence how you interpret information, just as others' belief systems and points of view might influence how they present information. For example, consider your own ideas about the issue of K–12 education in the United States. American citizens, politicians, and others often voice opinions on options such as charter, private, and public schools. What kind of pre-college education do *you* think is best, and *why* do you hold this viewpoint?

The more ideas you consider, the more sophisticated your thinking will become. Ultimately, you will discover not only that it is okay to change your mind but also that a willingness to do so is the mark of a reasonable, educated person. Considering multiple points of view means synthesizing material, evaluating information and resources that might contradict each other or offer multiple points of view on a topic, and then honoring those differences. After considering multiple viewpoints and drawing conclusions, the next step is to develop your own viewpoint based on credible evidence and facts, while staying true to your values and beliefs. Critical thinking is the process you go through in deciding how to align your experience and value system with your viewpoint.

This process isn't necessarily a matter of figuring out the right idea. Depending on the goals of the activity, the "right" idea might simply be the one that you think is the most fun or the most practical, or it might be a new idea of your own creation.

Drawing conclusions based on your consideration of many opinions and other types of evidence involves looking at the outcome of your inquiry in a more demanding, critical way. If you are looking for solutions to a problem, which ones seem most promising after you have conducted an exhaustive search for materials? If you have found new evidence, what does that new evidence show? Do your original beliefs hold up in the face of new evidence? Do they need to be modified? Which notions should be abandoned? Most important, consider what you would need to do or say to persuade someone else that your ideas are valid. Thoughtful conclusions are the most useful when you can share them with others.

 high-impact practice 3

---

your turn **Feeling Connected**

Moving from Opinion to Logical Conclusion

Imagine that your state has just approved a license plate design incorporating a cross and the slogan, "I Believe." Almost immediately, a number of organizations begin protesting that this license plate is a violation of the First Amendment of the U.S. Constitution. Work with a small group of other students in your class and decide whether you agree or disagree with the state's action. Ask all members of the group to set aside their personal opinions and try to reach the best conclusion using solid evidence.

Making Arguments

What does the word *argument* mean to you? If you're like most people, the first image it conjures up might be an ugly fight you had with a friend, a yelling match you witnessed on the street, or a heated disagreement between family members. True, such unpleasant confrontations are arguments, but the word also refers to a calm, reasoned effort to persuade someone of the value of an idea.

When you think of it this way, you'll quickly recognize that arguments are central to academic study, work, and life in general. Scholarly articles, business memos, and requests for spending money all have something in common: The effective ones make a general claim, provide reasons to support it, and back up those reasons with evidence. That's what argument is.

It's important to consider multiple points of view, or arguments, in tackling new ideas and complex questions, but arguments are not all equally valid. Good critical thinking involves analyzing assumptions that might have been omitted and scrutinizing the quality of the evidence used to support a claim. Whether examining an argument or making one, a good critical thinker is careful to ensure that ideas are presented in an understandable, logical way.

Challenging Assumptions and Beliefs

To some extent, it's unavoidable to have beliefs based on gut feelings or blind acceptance of something you've heard or read. However, some assumptions should be examined more thoughtfully, especially if they will influence an important decision or serve as the foundation for an argument.

We develop an understanding of information based on our value systems and how we view the world. Our family backgrounds influence these views, opinions, and assumptions. College is a time to challenge those assumptions and beliefs and to think critically about ideas we have always had.

Well-meaning people will often disagree. It's important to listen to all sides of an argument before making up your mind. If you follow the guidelines in this chapter, we can't promise that your classes will be easier or that you'll solve major problems, but you will be better equipped to handle them. You will have the skills to use critical thinking to figure things out instead of depending purely on how you feel or what you've heard. As you listen to a lecture, debate, or political argument about what is in the public's best interest, try to predict where it is heading and why. Ask yourself whether you have enough information to justify your own position.

isthisyou?

When New Knowledge and Old Beliefs Collide

Are you having conversations in class or with your friends about topics or ideas that go against what you have been taught? Do you feel anxious that these new ideas don't align with what you have heard all your life? Ideas presented by college instructors are almost always supported by evidence and research, much of which is derived from data and cutting-edge technology. It is important to keep an open mind, even if it makes you uncomfortable. Being exposed to new ways of thinking will help you grow intellectually and personally. Develop a relationship with a mentor or colleague who can help you process new information you hear that challenges or concerns you.

Examining Evidence

Another important part of thinking critically is checking that the evidence supporting an argument—whether someone else's or your own—is of the highest possible quality. To do that, simply ask a few questions about the argument as you consider it:

- What is the general idea behind the argument?
- Are good and sufficient reasons given to support the overall claim?
- Are those reasons backed up with evidence in the form of facts, statistics, and quotations?
- Does the evidence support the conclusions?
- Is the argument based on logical reasoning, or does it appeal mainly to emotions?
- Do I recognize any questionable assumptions?
- Can I think of any counterarguments, and if so, what facts can I muster as proof of one position or the other?
- If other people or organizations are making the argument, what do I know about them?
- What credible sources can I find to support the information?

If you have evaluated the evidence used in support of a claim and are still not certain of its quality, it's best to keep looking for more evidence. Drawing on questionable evidence for an argument has a tendency to backfire. In most cases, a little persistence will help you find better sources.

Recognizing and Avoiding Faulty Reasoning

Although logical reasoning is essential to solving any problem, whether simple or complex, you need to go one step further to make sure that an argument hasn't been compromised by faulty reasoning. Here are some of the most common missteps—referred to as logical fallacies or flaws in reasoning—that people make in their use of logic:

- **Attacking the person.** Arguing against other people's positions or attacking their arguments is perfectly acceptable. Going after their personalities, however, is not. Any argument that resorts to personal attack ("Why should we believe a cheater?") is unworthy of consideration.
- **Begging.** "Please, officer, don't give me a ticket! If you do, I'll lose my license, and I have five little children to feed, and I won't be able to feed them if I can't drive my truck." None of the driver's statements offer any evidence, in any legal sense, as to why she shouldn't be given a ticket. Pleading *might* work if the officer is feeling generous, but an

Logic That Just Doesn't Fly

This cartoon presents an obvious example of faulty reasoning. Some conversations or arguments tend to include reasoning like this. Can you think of a similarly illogical leap that someone used in an argument with you? Did you use critical thinking to counter it, or did your emotions get the best of you?

Randy Glasbergen

appeal to facts and reason would be more effective: "I fed the meter, but it didn't register the coins. Since the machine is broken, I don't believe I should get a ticket."

- **Appealing to false authority.** Citing authorities, such as experts in a field or the opinions of qualified researchers, can offer valuable support for an argument. However, a claim based on the authority of someone whose expertise is questionable relies on the appearance of authority rather than on real evidence. We see examples of false authority all the time in advertising: Sports stars who are not doctors, dieticians, or nutritionists urge us to eat a certain brand of food; famous actors and singers who are not dermatologists extol the medical benefits of a costly remedy for acne.

- **Jumping on a bandwagon.** Sometimes we are more likely to believe something that many others also believe. Even the most widely accepted truths can turn out to be wrong, however. At one time, nearly everyone believed that the world was flat, until someone came up with irrefutable evidence to the contrary.

- **Assuming that something is true because it hasn't been proven false.** If you go to a bookstore or look online, you'll find dozens of books detailing close encounters with flying saucers and extraterrestrial beings. These books describe the people who had such encounters as beyond reproach in their integrity and sanity. Because critics could not disprove the claims of the witnesses, the events are said to have actually occurred. Even in science, few things are ever proved completely false, but evidence can be discredited.

- **Falling victim to false cause.** Frequently, we make the assumption that just because one event followed another, the first event must have caused the second. This reasoning is the basis for many superstitions. The ancient Chinese once believed that they could make the sun reappear after an eclipse by striking a large gong, because they knew that on a previous occasion the sun had reappeared after a large gong had been struck. Most effects, however, are usually the result of a complex web of causes. Don't be satisfied with easy before-and-after claims; they are rarely correct.

- **Making hasty generalizations.** If someone selected a green marble from a barrel containing a hundred marbles, you wouldn't assume that the next marble drawn from the barrel would also be green. After all, you know nothing about the colors of the ninety-nine marbles still in the barrel. However, if you were given fifty draws from the barrel, and each draw produced a green marble after the barrel had been shaken thoroughly, you would be more willing to conclude that the next marble drawn would be green, too. Reaching a conclusion based on the opinion of one source is like assuming that all the marbles in the barrel are green after pulling out only one marble.

- **Slippery slope.** "If we allow tuition to increase, the next thing we know, it will be $30,000 per term." Such an argument is an example of "slippery slope" thinking. Fallacies like these can slip into even the most careful reasoning. One false claim can derail an entire argument, so be on the lookout for weak logic in what you read and write. Never forget that accurate reasoning is a key factor in succeeding in college and in life.

your turn Write and Reflect

Tempted to Use a Logical Fallacy?

Have you ever used a logical fallacy to justify decisions you have made? In looking back, did your flawed argument convince anyone that you were right? Why or why not? Describe your experiences in a journal entry.

APPLYING BLOOM'S TAXONOMY

Benjamin Bloom, a professor of education at the University of Chicago during the second half of the twentieth century, worked with a group of other researchers to design a system of classifying goals for the learning process. This system is known as Bloom's taxonomy, and it is now used at all levels of education to define and describe the process that students use to understand and think critically about what they are learning.

Bloom's Six Levels of Learning

Bloom identified six levels of learning, as represented in Figure 5.1. The higher the level, the more critical thinking it requires. Bloom's taxonomy is used in developing curricula, textbooks, learning management systems, and other academic work. You have been using the levels of Bloom's taxonomy throughout your education, perhaps without being aware of it.

Bloom's Taxonomy and the First Year of College

As you progress through your first year of college, you will notice that your level of comprehension and reflection begin to deepen as you engage with material and apply it to your experience in order to retain and synthesize it. If you pay close attention, you will discover that Bloom's taxonomy is often the framework that college instructors use to design classroom activities and out-of-class assignments. No matter what the topic is, this framework will help move you to deeper understanding and an ability to apply what you learn to other situations and concepts. Now we'll take a closer look at Bloom's taxonomy and then we'll take a concept you're likely to encounter in your first year of college—diversity—and match your cognitive development of the concept to Bloom's taxonomy.

FIGURE 5.1 > The Six Levels of Learning of Bloom's Taxonomy

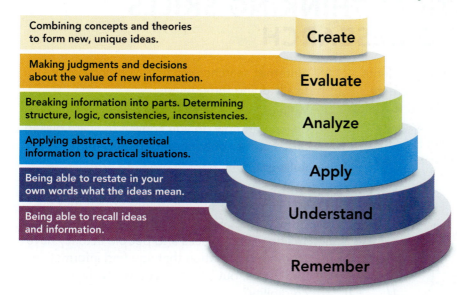

Combining concepts and theories to form new, unique ideas. — **Create**

Making judgments and decisions about the value of new information. — **Evaluate**

Breaking information into parts. Determining structure, logic, consistencies, inconsistencies. — **Analyze**

Applying abstract, theoretical information to practical situations. — **Apply**

Being able to restate in your own words what the ideas mean. — **Understand**

Being able to recall ideas and information. — **Remember**

Concept: Diversity

high-impact practices 2, 4

Level 1 (Remember) Read a dictionary definition of the word *diversity*.

Level 2 (Understand) Explain the concept of diversity to another student without reading the dictionary definition.

Level 3 (Apply) Write about all the types of human diversity that exist within the student body at your college or university and possible categories of human diversity that are not represented there.

Level 4 (Analyze) Conduct two separate analyses to break down the issue into components or questions. The first analysis will consider why your institution has large numbers of certain types of students. The second analysis will investigate why your institution has small numbers of other types of students.

Level 5 (Evaluate) Write a paper that combines your findings in Level 4 and hypothesizes what components of your college or university culture either attract or repel certain students.

Level 6 (Create) In your paper, evaluate the institution's "diversity profile" and suggest new ways for your campus to support diversity.

USE YOUR CRITICAL-THINKING SKILLS IN CONDUCTING RESEARCH

Colleges and universities expect their students to conduct research for their papers or create projects. In high school or a casual setting, doing research usually means going to a search engine like Google, Yahoo, or Ask.com. But is a Google search all professors are looking for when they ask you to conduct research?

"How do we know that's true?"

Royston-Robertson/Cartoon Stock

Internet searches will help you find people basically doing three things:

Yelling: Someone has an opinion and shares it online, but how do you know if they are biased or a member of a fringe or hate group?

Selling: Often, people promote products or services in a way that makes them sound like credible sources of information when they are simply trying to get you to buy something.

Telling: These places and people actually have credible information that you find informative and useful, but how can you verify their credibility?

The Problem

You need to conduct research for a paper, but you're not sure how to evaluate the types of information found on the internet.

The Fix

Use a critical-thinking system to conduct your research.

How to Do It

Start with good questions. If you are researching a topic, such as "marijuana legalization," generate some questions you have about that subject rather than just going to Google and typing "marijuana" into the search box:

- What is the history of marijuana use in the U.S.?
- Why was it made illegal in the first place?
- Where has it been legalized and why?
- What have been some of the positive and negative outcomes of making it legal?

Generating questions will save you time by clarifying what you need to know, so you will recognize useful results and ignore the ones that won't help you.

Go to the library. Show the reference librarians your list of questions. They can help you fine-tune them and will recommend good places to find answers.

Use databases. Your school pays for research databases, which collect a variety of credible, scholarly research. When you use research databases, you can be sure that the information is reliable, and you can refine your search terms to produce twenty

or thirty hits, as opposed to twenty or thirty million. Most databases are available online with login information that your college can provide, so you can use them anytime from home or on your laptop.

Use a variety of locations to confirm information. When you see the same information in a variety of credible sources, you can start to trust its accuracy. *Remember that there are still good sources of information in print form that are not available online.*

Consider the quality of the information. Where did it come from? Who said it and why? How current is it? Has anything major happened in this area since this information was published?

EXTRA STYLE POINTS: Get in the habit of reading (not just watching) a variety of information sources. If you get news only from TV or links on Facebook, you will miss important stories and current events. Professionals need to be up to date in their areas of expertise, but they also must have a broad knowledge in order to place their professional knowledge in context.

checklist for success

Thinking in College

■ **Make sure that you understand what kind of thinking you will develop in college.** If you are not clear, discuss it with the instructor of this course, another instructor, or a staff member in the learning center.

■ **Find ways to express your imagination and curiosity, and practice asking questions.** If you have the impulse to raise a question, don't stifle yourself. College is the perfect venue for self-expression and exploration.

■ **Challenge your own and others' assumptions that are not supported by evidence.** To help you better understand someone's position on a given issue, practice asking for additional information in a calm, polite manner that does not reject his or her ideas.

■ **During class lectures, presentations, and discussions, practice thinking about the subjects being discussed from multiple points of view.** Start with the view that you would most naturally take toward the matter at hand. Then, force yourself to imagine what questions might be raised by someone who doesn't see the issue the same way you do.

■ **Draw your own conclusions and explain to others what evidence you considered that led you to these positions.** Don't assume that anyone automatically understands why you reached your conclusions.

■ **Seek out opportunities for collaboration.** Join study groups or class project teams so you can collaborate with other students. When you are a member of a team, volunteer for roles that challenge you. That is how you will really experience significant gains in learning and development.

■ **Learn to identify false claims in commercials and political arguments.** Then look for the same faulty reasoning in people's comments you hear each day.

■ **Practice critical thinking, not only in your academic work, but also in your everyday interactions with friends and family.** Your environment both in and out of college will give you lots of opportunities to become a better critical thinker.

REFLECT ON CHOICES

high-impact practice 2 This chapter has introduced you to critical thinking—the kind of thinking you will be expected to do in college. Reflect on what you have learned and how you would explain college-level thinking to someone else. Create a written summary of your ideas.

APPLY WHAT YOU'VE LEARNED

Consider how you can apply what you have learned to your academic and personal life. The following prompts will help you reflect on chapter material and its relevance to you both now and in the future.

1. After reading this chapter, think of professions (for example, health care, engineering, marketing) for which problem solving and thinking outside the box are necessary. Choose one career and describe why you think critical thinking is a necessary and valuable skill for that job.

2. In your opinion, is it harder to think critically than to base your arguments on how you feel about a topic? Why or why not? What are the advantages of finding answers based on your feelings versus based on problem solving and evidence? How might you use both approaches in seeking answers to questions?

USE YOUR RESOURCES

> **Logic Courses.** If you are interested in learning more about critical thinking and how to apply critical-thinking skills, check out the introductory course in logic offered by your college's philosophy department. It might be the single best course designed to teach you critical-thinking skills, and nearly all colleges and universities offer such a course. Also, talk with a philosophy or logic instructor about in-class and out-of-class opportunities on your campus. A major in either area might be right for you.

> **Argument Courses and Critical-Thinking Courses.** Does your institution offer either an argument or a critical-thinking course? Check your campus catalog to see what you can find. Such courses will help you develop the ability to formulate logical arguments and avoid such pitfalls as logical fallacies.

> **Debating Skills.** Some of the very best thinkers developed debating skills during college. Go to either your student activities office or your department of speech and drama to find out whether your campus has a debate club or team. Debating can be fun, and chances are you will meet some interesting student thinkers that way.

> *12 Angry Men* **by Reginald Rose (New York: Penguin Classics, 2006).** This reprint of the original teleplay, which was written in 1954, was made into a film in 1958. Read the teleplay or watch the movie version of this stirring courtroom drama that pits twelve jurors against one another as they argue the outcome of a murder trial in which the defendant is a teenage boy. Although critical thinking is needed to arrive at the truth, all the jurors except one use noncritical arguments to arrive at a guilty verdict. The analysis of that one holdout, however, produces a remarkable change in their attitudes.

> **Bloom's Taxonomy.** The University of Arkansas provides a helpful resource about understanding and using Bloom's taxonomy at **https://tips.uark.edu/using-blooms-taxonomy/**.

> **Evaluating Resources.** The University of California, Berkeley provides a guide to evaluating resources you'll encounter when doing research in college at **http://guides.lib .berkeley.edu/evaluating-resources**.

 **LaunchPad** macmillan learning

LaunchPad for *Your College Experience* is a great resource. Go online to master concepts using the LearningCurve study tool and much more. **Launchpadworks.com**

track5/Getty Images

6

READING TO LEARN

YOU WILL EXPLORE

The four steps in active reading: previewing, marking, reading with concentration, and reviewing

Ways to improve and monitor your reading

How to apply strategies for reading textbooks across different subject areas

⚙ High-impact practices 2 (writing) and 3 (collaboration)

Intellistudies/Shutterstock

> **While my habits have worked well for me, students should get to know their own learning habits and find a reading method that works best for them.**

Keira was born in Texas and then spent most of her childhood in Baton Rouge, Louisiana, where she learned study habits that have helped throughout her education. Just before high school, her family moved back to Texas. She decided to go to Sam Houston State University after visiting the campus and speaking with faculty and current students in the communications program. In addition, she thought that the campus was beautiful, and she liked the community. Last, it put her only an hour away from her family.

As someone who loves to learn, Keira came to college with some strategies in place. "There is definitely a lot more reading involved in college than in high school," she says. "However, the good thing is that professors give out syllabi that detail when readings will be due, so you can plan accordingly." Like many first-year students, she also had to learn to balance the amount of reading required. "I had to get used to measuring how long it took to read and then manage my time accordingly."

Many of the other strategies Keira employs revolve around good time management and organization. "Learning how to juggle other coursework, meals, a social life, and sleep can be difficult, but it is possible. I mostly organize my time in order of priorities, usually based on due dates and how much time it takes to do [the assignment]," she says. Keira explains that once she starts reading, "I usually write down headings within the chapter as I go to keep me guided in the right direction. I then read through and write down any important dates, names, words, or anything that better explains the concept or explains it in a different way. This way I have multiple views on the subject that further enhance my understanding. It also doesn't hurt to reread sections and go over notes." She adds, "While my habits have worked well for me, students should get to know their own learning habits and find a reading method that works best for them."

Keira also has some simple advice for other first-year students: "As overwhelming as college can feel sometimes, *don't stress too much*. College is one of the best times of life. Enjoy it!"

LaunchPad
macmillan learning

To access the LearningCurve study tool, video activities, and more, go to LaunchPad for *Your College Experience*.
Launchpadworks.com

As Keira mentions, reading college textbooks is more challenging than reading high school texts or reading for pleasure. College texts are loaded with concepts, terms, and complex information that you are expected to learn on your own in a short period of time. To accomplish it all, you will find it helpful to learn and use the active-reading strategies in this chapter. They are intended to help you get the most out of your college reading. This chapter will also explore different techniques you can use when reading textbooks across the

assess your strengths

Are you a good reader? Do you make it a practice to do all the assigned reading for each of your classes, and do you have strategies for highlighting, annotating, or taking notes on what you read? Do you understand what you read so that you can explain it to others? As you read this chapter, consider your strengths in reading college textbooks and other academic materials.

set goals

What are your most important objectives in learning the material in this chapter? Do you want to improve your reading abilities and strategies? Use this chapter to help you develop techniques and goals for improving your reading of college texts. Check your course syllabi regularly to make sure you're up to date with all your assigned reading. Set a goal to catch up when you get a little behind.

academic disciplines. These include building your overall vocabulary and increasing your familiarity with terms that are unique to your particular field of study. Choose to make your textbook reading something you do every day. Reading in small chunks will help you concentrate and will increase your comprehension.

Depending on how much reading you did before coming to college—reading for pleasure, for your classes, or for work—you might find that reading is your favorite or least favorite way to learn. When you completed the VARK learning styles inventory in the chapter "How You Learn," you determined your preferences about reading and writing as a learning strategy. Even if reading *isn't* your favorite thing to do, it is absolutely essential if you want to do well in college and at work—no matter your major or profession.

A PLAN FOR ACTIVE READING

Active reading involves using strategies, such as highlighting and taking notes, that help you stay focused. Active reading is different from reading for pleasure, which doesn't require you to do anything while you are reading. By choosing active rather than passive reading, you will increase your focus and concentration, understand more of what you read, and prepare more effectively for tests and exams.

These are the four active-reading steps designed to help you read college textbooks:

1. Previewing
2. Marking
3. Reading with concentration
4. Reviewing

high-impact practice 3

your turn | **Feeling Connected**

Comparing Textbook Reading Strategies

With a group of your classmates, share which of these four steps you always, sometimes, or never do. Have one member of the group keep a tally and report results to the class. Are there steps that almost everyone avoids? If so, discuss the reasons why.

Previewing

Previewing involves taking a first look at your assigned reading before you really tackle the content. Think of previewing as browsing in a newly remodeled store. You locate the pharmacy and grocery areas. You get a feel for the locations of the men's, women's, and children's clothing departments; housewares; and electronics. You pinpoint the restrooms and checkout areas. You get a sense for where things are in relation to each other and compared to where they used to be. You identify where to find the items that you buy most often. You get oriented.

Previewing a chapter in your textbook or other assigned reading is similar. The purpose is to get the big picture, to understand the main ideas covered in what you are about to read and how those ideas connect both with what you already know and with the material the instructor covers in class. Here's how you do it:

- Begin by reading the title of the chapter. Ask yourself: What do I already know about this subject?
- Next, quickly read through the learning objectives, if the chapter has them, or the introductory paragraphs. **Learning objectives** are the main ideas or skills that students are expected to learn from reading the chapter.
- Then turn to the end of the chapter and read the summary, if there is one. A **summary** highlights the most important ideas in the chapter.
- Finally, take a few minutes to skim the chapter, looking at the headings, subheadings, key terms, tables, and figures. You should also look at the end-of-chapter exercises.

As you preview, note how many pages the chapter contains. It's a good idea to decide in advance how many pages you can reasonably expect to cover in your first study session. This can help build your concentration as you work toward your goal of reading a specific number of pages. Before long, you'll know how many pages are practical for you to read in one sitting.

Previewing might require some time up front, but it will save you time later. As you preview the text material, look for connections between the text and the related lecture material. Remember the related terms and concepts in your notes from the lecture. Use these strategies to warm up. Ask yourself: Why am I reading this? What do I want to know?

Keep in mind that different types of textbooks can require more or less time to read. For example, depending on your interests and previous knowledge, you might be able to read a psychology text more quickly than a biology text that includes many unfamiliar scientific words. Ask for help from your instructor, another student, or a tutor at your institution's learning center.

Mapping. **Mapping** is a preview strategy in which you draw a wheel or branching structure to show relationships between main ideas and secondary ideas and how different concepts and terms fit together; it also helps you make connections to what you already know about the subject (see Figure 6.1). Mapping the chapter during the previewing process provides a visual guide for how different chapter ideas work together. Because many students identify themselves as visual learners, visual mapping is an excellent learning tool, not only for reading, but also for test preparation.

In the wheel structure, place the central idea of the chapter in the circle. The central idea should be in the chapter introduction; it might even be in the chapter title. Place secondary ideas on the lines connected to the circle, and place offshoots of those ideas on the lines attached to the main lines. In the branching map, the main idea goes at the top, followed by supporting ideas on the second tier, and so forth. Fill in the title first. Then, as you skim the chapter, use the headings and subheadings to fill in the key ideas.

FIGURE 6.1 > Wheel and Branching Maps

Wheel Map

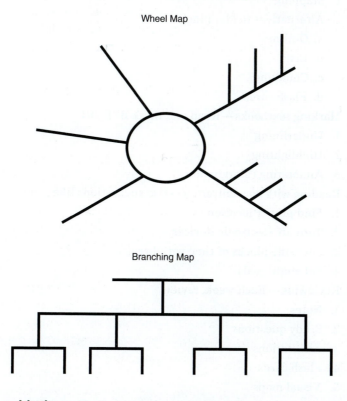

Branching Map

Outlining or Listing. Perhaps you see yourself as more of a read/write learner than a visual learner and prefer a more step-by-step visual image. If so, consider making an outline of the headings and subheadings in the chapter. You can usually identify the text's main topics, subtopics, and specific terms within each subtopic by the size of the print. Notice, also, that the different levels of headings in a textbook look different. In a textbook, headings are designed to show relationships among topics and subtopics covered within a section. Flip through this textbook to see how the headings are designed. See a sample outline of this chapter in Figure 6.2 below. (Review the chapter "Getting the Most from Class" for more on outlining.)

To save time when you are outlining, don't write full sentences. Rather, include clear explanations of new technical terms and symbols. Pay special attention to topics that the instructor covered in class. If you aren't sure whether your outlines contain too much or too little detail, compare them with the outlines your classmates or members of your study group have made. You can also ask your instructor to check your outlines during office hours. In preparing for a test, review your chapter outlines so you can see how everything fits together.

FIGURE 6.2 > Sample Outline
Here is how an outline of the first section of this chapter might look.

I. Active Reading
   A. Previewing—Get lay of the land, skim
      1. Mapping
      2. Alternatives to Mapping
         a. Outlines
         b. Lists
         c. Chunking
         d. Flash cards
   B. Marking textbooks—Read and think BEFORE
      1. Underlining
      2. Highlighting
      3. Annotating (Margin notes)
   C. Reading with concentration—Use suggestions like
      1. Find proper location
      2. Turn off electronic devices
      3. Set aside blocks of time with breaks
      4. Set study goals
   D. Reviewing—Each week, review
      1. Notes
      2. Study questions
      3. Annotations
      4. Flash cards
      5. Visual maps
      6. Outlines

Another previewing technique is listing. A list can be effective when you are dealing with a text that introduces many new terms and their definitions. Set up the list with the terms in the left column, and fill in definitions, descriptions, and examples on the right as you read or reread. Divide the terms on your list into groups of five, seven, or nine, and leave white space between the clusters so that you can visualize each group in your mind. This practice is known as **chunking**. Research has shown that we learn material best when it is presented in chunks of five, seven, or nine.

Creating Flash Cards. **Flash cards** are like portable test questions—you write a question or term on the front of a small card and the answer or definition on the back. In a course that requires you to memorize dates, like American history, you might write a key date on one side of the card and the event that correlates to that date on the other. To study chemistry, you would write a chemical formula on one side and the ionic compound on the other. You might use flash cards to learn vocabulary words or practice simple sentences for a language course (see Figure 6.3). Creating the cards from your readings and using them to prepare for exams are great ways to retain information, and they are especially helpful for visual and kinesthetic learners. Some apps, such as Chegg Flashcards, enable you to create flash cards on your electronic devices.

FIGURE 6.3 › Examples of Flash Cards

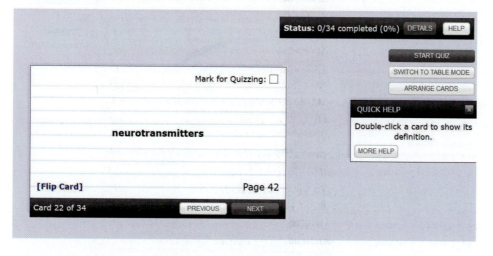

Strategies for Marking Your Textbook

After completing your preview, you are ready to read the text actively. With your map, outline, list, or flash cards to guide you, mark the sections that are most important. To avoid marking too much or marking the wrong information, first read without using your pencil or highlighter. This means you should read the text *at least* twice.

Marking is an active reading strategy that helps you focus and concentrate as you read. When you mark your textbook, you underline, highlight, or make margin notes or annotations. **Annotations** are notes or remarks about a piece of writing. Figure 6.4 provides an example

FIGURE 6.4 ❯ Examples of Marking

Using a combination of highlighting, underlining, and margin notes, the reader has made the content of this page easy to review. Without reading the text, review the highlighted words and phrases and the margin notes to see how much information you can gather from them. Then read the text itself. Does the markup serve as a study aid? Does it cover the essential points? Would you have marked this page any differently? Why or why not?

Source: Adapted from *Discovering Psychology*, 6th ed., p. 534, by D. H. Hockenbury and S. E. Hockenbury. Copyright © 2013 by Worth Publishers. Used with permission.

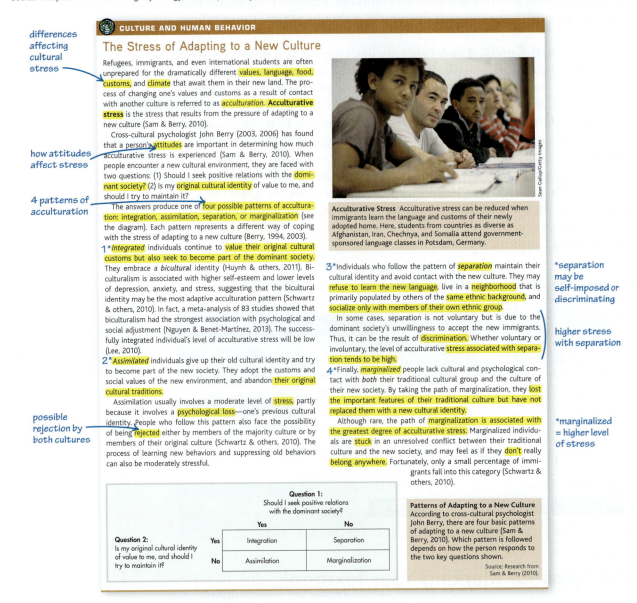

of each method. No matter what method you prefer, remember these important guidelines:

1. **Read before you mark.** Finish reading a section before you decide which ideas and concepts are most important.

2. **Think before you mark.** When you read a text for the first time, everything can seem important. After you complete a section, reflect on it to identify the key ideas. Ask yourself: What are the most important ideas? What terms has the instructor emphasized in class? What will I see on the test? Knowing the likely answers to

these questions can help you avoid marking too much material. On a practical note, if you find that you have made mistakes in how you have highlighted or that your textbooks were already highlighted by another student, use a different color highlighter.

3. **Take notes along with marking.** If you only make notes or underline in your textbook, you will have to read all the pages again. Rather than relying on marking alone, consider taking notes as you read. You can add your notes to the map, outline, list, or flash cards that you created while previewing the text. These methods are also more practical if you intend to review with a friend or study group. One more step in the note-taking process—putting your notes in your own words—will help you learn the material. When you rewrite your notes in your own words, you are not only predicting exam questions but also evaluating whether you can answer them.

A few words of caution about marking: For some students, highlighting or underlining is actually a form of procrastination and can lead to a false sense of security—just noting what's most important doesn't mean you've learned the material. Some students highlight or underline nearly everything they read, which does more harm than good. Remember, highlights and underlines are intended to pull your eye to key words and important facts. You won't be able to identify important concepts quickly if they're lost in a sea of color or lines. Ask yourself whether highlighting or underlining helps you take a more active role in your learning process. If not, you might want to try a different technique, such as making margin notes or adding annotations.

Reading with Concentration

Students often have trouble concentrating or understanding the content when they read textbooks. This is normal, and many factors contribute to this problem: the time of day, your energy level, your interest in the material, and your study location.

high-impact practice 2

your turn   Write and Reflect

Improving Your Powers of Concentration

The next time you are reading a textbook, monitor your ability to concentrate. Check your watch when you begin and check it again when your mind begins to wander. How many minutes did you concentrate on your reading? Write a journal entry listing some strategies to keep your mind from wandering.

Consider these suggestions and decide which would help you improve your reading ability:

- **Find a quiet place to study.** Choose a room or location away from traffic and distracting noises, such as the campus library. Avoid studying in your bed because your body is conditioned to go to sleep there.
- **Negotiate for quiet time.** If you live off campus with family members or friends, negotiate with them to guarantee a quiet time—perhaps a time

when others are studying. If children are a distraction, wait until they go to bed or create an "off-limits" location in your house for study.

- **Mute or turn off your electronic devices.** Store your cell phone in your book bag or some other place where you aren't tempted to check it. If you are reading on a device like a laptop or tablet, download what you need and disconnect from wi-fi so that you aren't tempted to e-mail, chat, or check social media sites.
- **Read in blocks of time, with short breaks in between.** Some students can read for 50 minutes, while others may find that a 50-minute reading period is too long. By reading in small blocks of time throughout the day instead of cramming in all your reading at the end of the day, you should be able to process material more easily.
- **Set goals for your study period.** A realistic goal might be "I will read twenty pages of my psychology text in the next 50 minutes." Reward yourself with a 10-minute break after each 50-minute study period.
- **Engage in physical activity during breaks.** If you have trouble concentrating or staying awake, take a quick walk around the library or down the hall. Stretch or take some deep breaths, and think positively about your study goals. Then go back to studying.
- **Actively engage with the material.** Write study questions in the margins, take notes, or recite key ideas. Reread confusing parts of the text, and make a note to ask your instructor for clarification on any material that remains unclear.
- **Focus on the important portions of the text.** Pay attention to the first and last sentences of paragraphs and to words in italics or bold type.
- **Understand the words.** Use the text's glossary or a dictionary to define unfamiliar terms.
- **Use organizers as you read.** Have the maps, outlines, lists, or flash cards you created during your preview available as you read, and add to them as you go. Table 6.1 on the next page shows an example of an organizer to use when you are reading; you can use it to organize a chapter you are currently reading in this or any other class.

Take a Break

While studying, you will be able to stay alert and concentrate more effectively if you take short breaks to stretch or walk.

Paul Bock/Alamy

TABLE 6.1 › Example of an Organizer

Date:	Course:
Textbook:	Chapter # and Title:

What is the overall idea of the reading?

What is the **main idea** of each major section of the reading?

Section 1:

Section 2:

Section 3:

What **supporting ideas** are presented in each section of the reading?
Examples? Statistics? References to research?

1.

2.

3.

4.

5.

What are the **key terms**, and what do they mean?

What are the **conclusions** from the reading?

What are two or three things I remember after reading?

1.

2.

3.

Reviewing

The final step in active textbook reading is reviewing. **Reviewing** involves looking through your assigned reading again. Many students expect to be able to read through their text material once and remember the ideas four, six, or even twelve weeks later when it's time for their exam. More realistically, you will need to include regular reviews in your study process. Your notes, study questions, margin notes and annotations, flash cards, visual maps, or outlines will prove very useful during the reviewing process. Your study goal should be to review the material from each chapter every week. Here are some strategies:

- Consider ways to use your senses to review.
- Recite aloud.
- Tick off each item on a list on your fingers.
- Post diagrams, maps, or outlines around your living space so that you will see them often and will likely be able to visualize them while taking the test.

IMPROVING YOUR READING

With effort, you *can* improve your reading. Remember to be flexible and to adjust *how* you read depending on *what* you are reading. Here are a few suggestions:

- Evaluate the importance and difficulty of the assigned readings, and adjust your reading style and the time you set aside to do the reading. How you read your math textbook is different than how you read your psychology textbook. When reading your math textbook, you should have a notebook to record your solutions to the problems. When you read your psychology textbook, you should highlight the important ideas or make margin notes.
- Connect one important idea to another by asking yourself: Why am I reading this? Where does this fit in? Writing summaries and preparing notes and outlines can help you connect ideas across chapters.
- When the textbook material is exactly the same as the lecture material, you can save time by concentrating mainly on one or the other.

It takes a planned approach to read and understand textbook materials and other assigned readings and to remember what you have read.

Monitoring Your Reading

You can monitor your comprehension while reading textbooks by asking yourself: Do I understand this? If not, stop and reread the material. Look up words that are not clear. Try to clarify the main points and how they relate to one another.

Another way to check that you understand what you are reading is to try to recite the material aloud, either to yourself or to your study partner. Using a study group to monitor your comprehension gives you immediate feedback and is highly motivating. After you have read with concentration from the first section of the chapter, proceed to each subsequent section until you have finished the chapter.

After you have completed each section and before you move on to the next section, ask again: What are the key ideas? What will I see on the test? At the end of each section, try to guess what information the author will present in the next section.

Developing Your Vocabulary

Textbooks are full of new words and terms. A **vocabulary** is a set of words in a particular language or field of knowledge. As you become familiar with the vocabulary of an academic field, reading the texts related to that field becomes easier.

If words are such a basic and essential component of our knowledge, what is the best way to learn them? The following are some basic vocabulary-building strategies:

- **Notice and write down unfamiliar terms while you preview a text.** Consider making a flash card for each term or making a list of terms.
- **Think about the context when you come across challenging words.** See whether you can guess the meaning of an unfamiliar term by using the words around it.
- **Consider a word's parts.** If context by itself is not enough to help you guess the meaning of an unfamiliar word, try analyzing the term to discover its root (or base part) and any prefixes (parts that come before the root) or suffixes (parts that follow the root). For example, *transport* has the root *port*, which means "carry," and the prefix *trans*, which means "across." Together the word means "carry across" or "carry from one place to another." Knowing the meaning of prefixes and suffixes can be very helpful. For example, *anti* means "against," and *pro* means "for."
- **Use the glossary of the text or a dictionary.** Textbook publishers carefully compile glossaries to help students learn the vocabulary of a given discipline. If the text has no glossary, have a dictionary on hand. If a given word has more than one definition, search for the meaning that fits your text. The online Merriam-Webster's Dictionary (**merriam-webster.com**) is especially helpful for college students.
- **Use new words in your writing and speaking.** If you use a new word a few times, you'll soon know it. In addition, any flash cards you have created will come in handy for reviewing the definitions of new words at exam time.

isthisyou?

The Challenge of Being "First"

Are you the first person in your family to go to college? If so, you are in good company. Many "first-generation" students attend colleges and universities today. Make sure that you understand the rules and regulations and the unique higher-education terminology at your institution. If you or your family members feel lost or confused, talk to your college success instructor and ask about services that are available for first-generation students. Also, remember that some of our nation's most successful individuals were the first in their families to attend and graduate from college.

your turn | Write and Reflect

Building Your Vocabulary

Choose a chapter in this or another textbook. As you read it, list the words that are new to you or that you don't understand. Using a dictionary, write out the definition of each word, and then write a short paragraph using the word in an appropriate context. Set a goal to add at least one new word a week to your personal vocabulary.

What to Do When You Fall Behind on Your Reading

From time to time, life might get in the way of doing your assigned readings on time. You may get sick or have to take care of a sick family member, you may have to work extra hours, or you may have a personal problem that temporarily prevents you from concentrating on your courses. Unfortunately, some students procrastinate and think they can catch up. That is a myth. The less you read and do your assignments, the harder you will have to work to make up for lost time.

A Marathon, Not a Sprint

If you fall behind in your reading, you're not alone—many students do. Remember that your studies are more like a marathon than a sprint; you should take time to catch up, but do so at a steady pace. Do your assigned readings, study with others, get help, and do not give up!

Jerome Prevost/Getty Images

If you try to stay on schedule with your assigned readings but fall behind, do not panic. Here are some suggestions for getting back on track:

- **Add one or two hours a day to your study time to go back and read the material that you missed.** In particular, take advantage of every spare moment to read; for example, read during your lunch hour at work, while you are waiting for public transportation, or in the waiting room at the doctor's office.
- **Join a study group.** If everyone in the group reads a section of the assigned chapter and shares and discusses their notes, summaries, or outlines with the group, you can cover the content more quickly.
- **Ask for help.** Visit your college learning center to work with a tutor who can help you with difficult concepts in the textbook.
- **Talk to your instructor.** Ask for extra time to make up your assignments if you have fallen behind for a valid reason such as sickness or dealing with a personal problem. Most instructors are willing to make a one-time exception to help students catch up.
- **Do not give up.** You may have to work harder for a short period of time, but you will soon get caught up.

STRATEGIES FOR READING TEXTBOOKS

As you begin to read, be sure to learn more about the textbook and its author by reading the sections at the beginning of the book, such as the preface, foreword, introduction, and the author's biographical sketch. The **preface**, which is a brief overview near the beginning of a book, is usually written by the author(s) and will tell you why they wrote the book and what material the book covers. It will also explain the book's organizational structure and give insight into the author's viewpoint—all of which can help you see the relationships among the facts presented and comprehend the ideas discussed throughout the book. Reading the preface can come in handy if you are feeling a little lost at different points in the term. The preface often lays out the tools available in each chapter to guide you through the content, so if you find yourself struggling with the reading, be sure you go back and read this section.

The **foreword** is often an endorsement of the book written by someone other than the author. Some books have an additional **introduction** that describes the book's overall organization and its contents, often chapter by chapter. Some textbooks include study questions at the end of each chapter. Take time to read and respond to these questions, whether or not your instructor requires you to do so.

All Textbooks Are Not Created Equal

Textbooks in different **disciplines**—areas of academic study—can differ in their organization and style of writing. Some may be easier to understand than others, but don't give up if the reading level is challenging.

your turn | **Setting Goals**

Do ALL the Required Reading

Some first-year students, especially those who have trouble managing their time, believe that they can skip some of the required reading and still get good grades on tests and exams. The best students, however, will tell you that this isn't a smart strategy. Instructors assign readings because they believe they're important to your understanding, and concepts and details in the readings will be on the tests. Set a goal to read all the materials assigned by your instructors as well as material they suggest that will introduce you to new ideas.

Math and science texts are filled with graphs and figures that you will need to understand in order to grasp the content and the classroom lectures. They are also likely to have less text and more practice exercises than other textbooks. If you have trouble reading and understanding any of your textbooks, get help from your instructor or your college's learning center.

Textbooks cover a lot of material in a limited space, and they won't necessarily provide all the information you want to know about a topic. If you find yourself interested in a particular topic, go to the **primary sources**—the original research or documents on that subject. You'll find those sources referenced in almost all textbooks, either at the end of each chapter or at the back of the book.

You can also refer to other related sources that make the text more interesting and easier to understand. Your instructors might use the textbook only to supplement their lectures. Some instructors expect you to read the textbook carefully, while others are much more concerned that you understand broad concepts that come primarily from their lectures. Ask your instructors what the tests will cover and what types of questions will be used.

Finally, not all textbooks are written in the same way. Some are better designed and written than others. If a textbook seems disorganized or hard for you to understand, let your instructor know your opinion. Other students likely feel the same way. Your instructor might spend some class time explaining the text or meet with you during office hours to help you with the material.

Math Texts

While the previous suggestions about textbook reading apply across the board, mathematics textbooks present some special challenges because they usually have lots of symbols and few words. Each statement and every line in the solution of a problem needs to be considered and processed slowly. Typically, the author presents the material through definitions, theorems, and sample problems. As you read, pay special attention to definitions. Learning all the terms that relate to a new topic is the first step toward understanding.

Math texts usually include derivations of formulas and proofs of theorems. You must understand and be able to apply the formulas and theorems, but unless your course has a particularly theoretical emphasis, you are less likely to be responsible for all the proofs. If you get lost in the proof of a theorem, go to the next item in the section. When you come to a sample problem, pick up a pencil and paper, and work through it in the book. Think through the problem on your own before you check the solution.

Of course, the exercises in each section are the most important part of any math textbook. A large portion of the time you devote to a math course will be spent completing these assigned exercises. It is absolutely necessary to work out these exercises before the next class, whether or not your instructor collects the work. Success in mathematics requires regular practice, and students who keep up with their math homework, either by working alone or in groups, perform better than students who don't, particularly when they include in their study groups other students who have more advanced math skills.

After you complete the assignment, skim through the other exercises in the problem set. Reading the unassigned problems will increase your comprehension. Finally, talk through the material to yourself, and be sure your focus is on understanding the problem and its solution, not on memorization. Memorizing something might help you remember how to work through one problem, but it does not help you learn the steps involved so that you can use them to solve other, similar problems.

---

your turn   **Feeling Connected**

 high-impact practice 3

Tackle Math as a Team

In a small group, discuss with classmates two or three of your challenges in learning from your math textbooks. Find students who are taking the same math course, share some strategies that you use to study the material for this course, and consider forming a study group.

Science Texts

Your approach to your science textbook will depend somewhat on whether you are studying a math-based science, such as physics, or a text-based science, such as biology. In either case, you need to become familiar with the overall format of the book. Review the table of contents and the **glossary** (a list of key words and their definitions), and check the material in the **appendixes** (supplemental materials at the end of the book). There you will find lists of physical constants, unit conversions, and various charts and tables. Many physics and chemistry books also include a mini-review of the math you will need in those science courses (see Figure 6.5).

Notice the organization of each chapter, and pay special attention to graphs, charts, and boxes. The amount of technical detail might seem overwhelming. Remember that textbook authors take great care to present material in a logical format, and they include tools to guide you through the material. Chapter-opening learning objectives and

FIGURE 6.5 › Reading Science Textbooks

This page from an allied-health–themed chemistry textbook includes abbreviations you'd need to know for dosages, practice exercises, and a formula for calculating medicine dosages. If you need help with any of your textbooks, ask your instructor or classmates.

Source: Excerpt from page 23 of *Essentials of General, Organic, and Biochemistry*, 2nd ed., by Denise Guinn. Copyright © 2012 by W. H. Freeman. Used by permission.

Dosage Calculations

For some medicines prescribed for patients, the dosage must be adjusted according to the patient's weight. This is especially true when administering medicine to children. For example, a dosage of "8.0 mg of tetracycline per kilogram body weight daily" is a dosage based on the weight of the patient. A patient's weight is often given in pounds, yet many drug handbooks give the dosage per kilogram body weight of the patient. Therefore, to calculate the correct amount of medicine to give the patient, you must first convert the patient's weight from pounds into kilograms with an English-metric conversion, using Table 1-3.

It is important to recognize that the dosage is itself a conversion factor between the mass or volume of the medicine and the weight of the patient. Whenever you see the word *per*, it means *in every* and can be expressed as a ratio or fraction where *per* represents a division operation (divided by). For example, 60 miles *per* hour can be written as the ratio 60 mi/1 hr. Similarly, a dosage of 8.0 mg *per* kg body weight can be expressed as the fraction 8.0 mg/1 kg. Hence, dosage *is* a conversion factor:

$$\frac{8 \text{ mg}}{1 \text{ kg}} \quad \text{or} \quad \frac{1 \text{ kg}}{8 \text{ mg}}$$

Dimensional analysis is used to solve dosage calculations by multiplying the patient's weight by the appropriate English-metric conversion factor and then multiplying by the dosage conversion factor, as shown in the following worked exercise.

> Some common abbreviations indicating the frequency with which a medication should be administered include *q.d.* and *b.i.d.*, derived from the Latin meaning administered "daily" and "twice daily," respectively. If the medicine is prescribed for two times daily or four times daily, divide your final answer by two or four to determine how much to give the patient at each administration.

WORKED EXERCISE | Dosage Calculations

1-19 Tetracycline elixir, an antibiotic, is ordered at a dosage of 8.0 mg per kilogram of body weight q.d. for a child weighing 52 lb. How many milligrams of tetracycline elixir should be given to this child daily?

Solution
Step 1: Identify the conversions. Since the dosage is given based on a patient's weight in kilograms, an English-to-metric conversion must be performed. From Table 1-3 this is 1.000 kg = 2.205 lb. The dosage itself is already a conversion factor.

Step 2: Express each conversion as two possible conversion factors. The English-to-metric conversion factors for the patient's weight are

$$\frac{1 \text{ kg}}{2.205 \text{ lb}} \quad \text{or} \quad \frac{2.205 \text{ lb}}{1 \text{ kg}}$$

end-of-chapter summaries can be useful to study both before and after reading the chapter. You will usually find answers to selected problems in the back of the book. Use the answer key or the student solutions manual to make sure that you're solving problems and answering questions accurately.

As you begin an assigned section in a science text, skim the material quickly to gain a general idea of the topic and to familiarize yourself with any new vocabulary and technical symbols. Then look over the end-of-chapter problems so that you'll know what to look for in your detailed reading of the chapter. State a specific goal: "I'm going to learn about recent developments in plate tectonics," or "I'm going to distinguish between mitosis and meiosis," or "Tonight I'm going to focus on the topics in this chapter that were stressed in class."

Should you underline and highlight, or should you outline the material in your science textbooks? You might decide to underline or highlight for a subject such as anatomy, which involves a lot of memorization. In most sciences, however, it is best to outline the text chapters.

Social Sciences and Humanities Texts

Many of the suggestions that apply to science textbooks also apply to reading in the **social sciences** (academic disciplines that examine human aspects of the world, such as sociology, psychology, anthropology, economics, political science, and history). Social science textbooks are filled with special terms that are specific to a particular field of study (see Figure 6.6). These texts also describe research and theory building and contain references to many primary sources. Your social science texts might also describe differences in opinions or perspectives. Social scientists do not all agree on any number of issues, and you might be introduced to several ongoing debates about particular topics. In fact, your reading can become more interesting if you seek out differing opinions. You might have to go beyond your course textbook, but your library is a good source of various viewpoints about ongoing controversies.

Textbooks in the **humanities** (branches of knowledge that investigate human beings, their culture, and their self-expression, such as philosophy, religion, literature, music, and art) provide facts, examples, opinions, and original material such as stories or essays. You will often be asked to react to your reading by identifying central themes or characters.

your turn | **Making Decisions**

Buy Your Course Materials

Textbooks are expensive, and it may be tempting to think that you can borrow one from another student, find the text in the library, or even do well in the course without having access to the textbook. No one will force you to purchase your textbooks—it's really up to you. To succeed in college, however, it's critically important that you choose to buy them and do all the assigned reading. Read the Tech Tip in this chapter for information on the benefits of e-books and for help in evaluating whether these are a good option for you.

FIGURE 6.6 > Social Science Textbook Page

Strategies for reading and note taking should change depending on what kind of textbook you are reading. When reading a social science textbook, such as the economics book shown here, you can see how a section is broken into subsections. Headings help guide you through the content. A table is included with examples that illustrate what is being discussed and help you understand the material.

Source: From *Core Economics*, 3rd ed., by Eric Chiang. Copyright © 2014 by Eric Chiang. Used by permission of Worth Publishers.

The Price System

When buyers and sellers exchange money for goods and services, accepting some offers and rejecting others, they are also doing something else: They are communicating their individual desires. Much of this communication is accomplished through the prices of items. If buyers value a particular item sufficiently, they will quickly pay its asking price. If they do not buy it, they are indicating they do not believe the item to be worth its asking price.

Prices also give buyers an easy means of comparing goods that can substitute for each other. If the price of margarine falls to half the price of butter, this will suggest to many consumers that margarine is a better deal. Similarly, sellers can determine what goods to sell by comparing their prices. When prices rise for tennis rackets, this tells sporting goods store operators that the public wants more tennis rackets, leading the store operators to order more. Prices, therefore, contain a considerable amount of useful information for both consumers and sellers. For this reason, economists often call our market economy the **price system.**

price system A name given to the market economy because prices provide considerable information to both buyers and sellers.

✔ CHECKPOINT

MARKETS

- Markets are institutions that enable buyers and sellers to interact and transact business.
- Markets differ in geographical location, products offered, and size.
- Prices contain a wealth of information for both buyers and sellers.
- Through their purchases, consumers signal their willingness to exchange money for particular products at particular prices. These signals help businesses decide what to produce, and how much of it to produce.
- The market economy is also called the price system.

QUESTION: What are the important differences between the markets for financial securities such as the New York Stock Exchange and your local farmer's market?

Answers to the Checkpoint questions can be found at the end of this chapter.

Supplementary Material

Whether or not your instructor requires you to read material in addition to the textbook, you will learn more about a topic if you go to some of the primary and supplementary sources that are referenced in each chapter of your text. These sources can be journal articles, research papers, or original essays, and they can be found online or in your library. Reading the original source material will give you more detail than most textbooks do.

Many of these sources were originally written for other instructors or researchers, so they often refer to concepts that are familiar to other scholars, but not necessarily to first-year college students. If you are reading a journal article that describes a theory or research study, one

techtip

EMBRACE THE E-BOOK

In college we have textbooks, workbooks, and notebooks. While textbook publishers continue to make traditional books available, the same content is increasingly available in digital formats. In most courses today, students are required to access some course material digitally. For students who are used to buying or renting printed books from the college bookstore, this can be an adjustment.

martin-dm/Getty Images

The Problem

You'd like to read using e-books, but you aren't sure if you should buy an e-reader or a tablet or just use a laptop. You also want to know the advantages and disadvantages that an e-book has when compared to a traditional book.

The Fix

Explore different platforms that deliver e-book content, and discover how reading with a digital reader differs from reading traditional books.

How to Do It

Go to the library. Many libraries have tablets of different kinds. Ask a librarian to download a book in a variety of formats for you, so you can try different tablets out before choosing one to buy.

PROS OF E-BOOKS AND E-READERS

- Digital reading devices are eminently portable and can hold thousands of books.
- E-books save trees, can be bought without shipping costs, and have a low carbon footprint.
- E-readers let you buy books online from anywhere with web access, and you can start reading within minutes.
- You can type notes in an e-book, as well as highlight passages and copy and paste sections.
- You can print out pages simply by hooking the device up to your printer or connecting to a printer on a wireless network.
- You can access many e-books for free from the public library—even rare books.
- Some e-books come with bonus audio, video, or animation features.
- Many digital reading devices accept audio books and can read to you aloud.
- The backlit screen means that you can read in bed with the light off, without disturbing anyone.

- Some e-readers have a built-in dictionary. Others link to reference websites like Google or Wikipedia.
- E-books are searchable and even sharable.

CONS OF E-BOOKS

- Digital reading devices are expensive, breakable, and desirable to thieves.
- Looking at a screen can cause some eye fatigue.
- It's harder to flip through pages of an e-book than a printed book.
- If you have only limited or temporary access to e-books for your courses, your access will expire after the academic term.

GOOD TO KNOW

Some electronic readers are no-frills, basic models designed to replicate the experience of reading a paper book. Others offer web browsers, video, music, and thousands of free and for-purchase apps. Most are web-enabled, so you can use them for other things like listening to music or audio books, checking e-mail, creating presentations, and writing papers. This increased functionality might be distracting, but it can also make you more productive.

EXTRA STYLE POINTS: Price your textbooks in both the print and digital formats. Factoring in the cost of the e-reader or tablet (if you decide to buy

technique for easier understanding is to read the article backward—from the end to the beginning. Read the article's conclusion and discussion sections first, and then go back to see how the author performed the experiment or formed the ideas. In almost all scholarly journals, articles are introduced by an **abstract**, which is a paragraph-length summary of the article's methods and major findings. Reading the abstract is a quick way to get the main points of a research article before you start reading it. As you're reading research articles, always ask yourself: So what? Was the research important to what we know about the topic, or, in your opinion, was it unnecessary?

If English Is Not Your First Language

The English language is one of the most difficult languages to learn. Words are often spelled differently from the way they sound, and the language is full of **idioms**—phrases that cannot be understood from the individual meanings of the words. For example, if your instructor tells you to "hit the books," she does not mean for you to physically pound your texts with your fist, but rather to study hard.

If you are learning English and are having trouble reading your texts, don't give up. Reading the material slowly and more than once can help you improve your comprehension. Make sure that you have two good dictionaries—one in English and one that links English with your primary language—and look up every key word you don't know. Be sure to practice thinking, writing, and speaking in English, and take advantage of your college's services. Your campus might have ESL tutoring and workshops. Ask your adviser or your first-year seminar instructor to help you find out where those services are offered on your campus.

checklist for success

Reading to Learn

- **Be sure to practice the four steps of active reading: previewing, marking, reading with concentration, and reviewing.** If you practice these steps, you will understand and retain more of what you read.

- **Take your course textbooks seriously.** They contain essential information you'll be expected to learn and understand. Never try to "get by" without the text.

- **As you read, be sure to take notes on the material.** Indicate in your notes what specific ideas you need help in understanding.

- **Get help with difficult material before too much time goes by.** College courses use sequential material that builds on previous material. You will need to master the material as you go along.

- **Discuss difficult readings in study groups.** Explain to one another what you do and don't understand.

- **Find out what kind of assistance your campus offers to increase reading comprehension and speed.** Check out your learning and counseling centers for free workshops. Even faculty and staff sometimes take advantage of these services. Most everyone wants to improve reading speed and comprehension.

- **Use reading to build your vocabulary.** Learning new words is a critical learning skill and outcome of college. The more words you know, the more you'll understand, and your grades will show it.

- **Remember that not all textbooks are the same.** They vary by subject area and style of writing. Some may be easier to comprehend than others, but don't give up if the reading level is challenging.

- **Learn and practice the different techniques suggested in this chapter for reading and understanding texts on different subjects.** Which texts are easiest for you to understand? Which are the hardest? Why?

- **In addition to the textbook, be sure to read all supplemental assigned reading material.** Also, try to find additional materials to take your reading beyond what is required. The more you read, the more you will understand, and the better your performance will be.

6 buildyourexperience

REFLECT ON CHOICES

In this chapter you have learned that reading textbooks is an essential part of being a successful student. The choice of how to approach your reading is up to you. Reflect on the strategies that have been suggested, list those that you already use, and make a separate list of those you want to try in the future.

APPLY WHAT YOU HAVE LEARNED

Now that you have read and discussed this chapter, consider how you can apply what you have learned to your academic life and your personal life. The following prompts will help you reflect on the chapter material and its relevance to you both now and in the future.

1. Choose a reading assignment for one of your upcoming classes. After previewing the material, begin reading until you reach a major heading or until you have read at least a page or two. Now stop and write down what you remember from the material. Go back and review what you read. Were you able to remember all the main ideas?

2. It is easy to say that there is not enough time in the day to get everything done, especially when you're faced with a long reading assignment. Your future depends on how well you do in college, however. Challenge yourself not to use that excuse. How can you modify your daily activities to make time for reading?

USE YOUR RESOURCES

> **Learning Center**   Find out about your campus's learning center and any reading assistance that is available there. Most centers are staffed by full-time professionals and student tutors. Both the best students and struggling students use learning centers.

> **ESL Resources**   If English is not your first language and you need assistance with reading and writing, ask your academic adviser or someone in the learning center to help you find the help you need. Your college may offer courses or special tutoring services for ESL students.

> **Peer Leaders**   Peer leaders are a great source of information on campus resources and the availability of tutoring. Ask them for suggestions about where you can go for help with your reading and comprehension.

> **Fellow Students**   Your best help can come from a fellow student. Look for the best students, those who appear to be the most serious and conscientious. Hire a tutor if you can, or join a study group. You are much more likely to be successful.

> **College or University Online Resources** Dartmouth College offers "Reading Techniques: Strategies for Improving Reading Rate and Comprehension." at dartmouth .edu/~acskills /success/reading.html. **Niagara University's Office for Academic Support offers "21 Tips" for better textbook reading** at niagara.edu/oas-21-tips.

LaunchPad
macmillan learning

LaunchPad for *Your College Experience* is a great resource. Go online to master concepts using the LearningCurve study tool and much more. **Launchpadworks.com**

Hero Images/Media Bakery

7

GETTING THE MOST FROM CLASS

YOU WILL EXPLORE

Benefits to your learning that result from being engaged in class

Ways to prepare before class

Why you should participate in class by listening critically and speaking up

Methods for assessing and improving your note-taking skills and how to use your notes to be engaged in learning

⚙ High-impact practices 2 (writing) and 3 (collaboration)

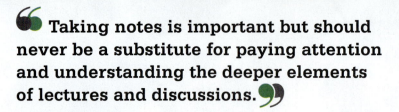

Bobby Coutu/E+/Getty Images

> ❝ **Taking notes is important but should never be a substitute for paying attention and understanding the deeper elements of lectures and discussions.** ❞

In reflecting on his experience in college classes so far, Dillon says, "Most of the time the questions you have are questions that will help the whole class. Everyone in the class benefits from an instructor's answer." He points out, however, that no one appreciates a student asking questions just for the participation points or to show off. "I always try to be direct and simple when asking questions so that the class can get direct and simple answers," Dillon says.

This same no-nonsense attitude is also present in the way he prepares for class. He explains, "I just make sure to be there on time, every time, and to stay until the class is over. I make an effort to pay attention, and I'm careful to write down key points of the lecture. I also do all the assigned reading, and I find it pretty easy to maintain good grades.

"In a class with lots of information, I take detailed notes. Sometimes it makes it harder to actually pay attention to concepts, but it certainly pays off for tests and such. In less formal classes such as speech or ethics, which are very idea-heavy, I tend to take notes only on the major concepts. Taking notes is important but should never be a substitute for paying attention and understanding the deeper elements of lectures and discussions," he says.

Dillon plans to get a master's degree at a California university. In ten years he hopes to be a journalist or a philosophy instructor. He also hopes to put his class-participation skills to good use. "It is my dream to take part in debates and public presentations," he says. His advice to other first-year students: "Do your best and try to get as much as you can out of your classes. It always pays off in the end."

LaunchPad
macmillan learning

To access the LearningCurve study tool, video activities, and more, go to LaunchPad for *Your College Experience.*
Launchpadworks.com

Dillon's advice is sound when you consider that in order to earn high grades in any college class, you'll need to master certain skills such as listening, taking notes, and being engaged in learning. Engagement in learning means that you take an active role in your classes by attending, listening critically, asking questions, contributing to discussions, and providing answers. These active-learning behaviors will enhance your ability to understand abstract ideas, find new possibilities, organize those ideas, and recall the material once the class is over, resulting in strong performance on exams, as many exam questions are based on material covered in class lectures and discussions.

This chapter shows you several note-taking methods. Choose the one that works best for you. Because writing down everything the instructor

assess your strengths

Students who are engaged in college life, both in and out of class, practice many of the behaviors that are reviewed in this chapter. What about you? Were you engaged in classes and activities in high school? Which were your favorites and why? Most students find that engagement makes them more enthusiastic and actually increases their learning. As you begin to read this chapter, consider your strengths in the area of engagement.

set goals

What are your most important objectives in learning the material in this chapter? Do you take good notes? Do you devote time and energy to academic work? Use this chapter to help you develop strategies and goals for engagement in learning. Consider scheduling visits with your instructors during their office hours to clarify any misunderstandings you might have about class lectures and discussions.

says is probably not possible and because you might need some help to determine which are the most important ideas presented, ask questions in class and become comfortable reviewing your notes with your instructor, either after class or during office hours. You might consider making an audio recording of the lecture and discussion, if you have the instructor's permission. Reviewing your notes with a friend from class or in a study group can also help you clarify your understanding of a lecture's most important points.

BECOME ENGAGED IN LEARNING

Engaged students are those who are fully involved with the college experience and spend the time and energy necessary to learn, both in and out of class. Engaged learners who have good listening and note-taking skills get the most out of college.

You can learn by listening to a lecture, and you can better understand that lecture by considering what the information presented means to you. Practice the techniques of **active learning** by talking with others, asking questions in class, studying in groups, and seeking out information beyond the lecture material and required reading. Explore other information sources in the library or on the internet. Think about how the material relates to your own life or experience. For instance, what you learn in a psychology class might help you recognize patterns of behavior in your own family, or the material presented in a sociology class may shed light on the group dynamics in a team or group to which you belong. When you are actively engaged in learning, you will build valuable skills that you can apply to college, work, and your personal life, such as:

- **Working with others.** Learning to work with others is one of the most important skills you can develop for success in college and your career.

Stay Engaged

All students benefit from active learning strategies, whether in arts and sciences courses or professional training situations, requiring students to apply what they learn in their courses.

Hero Images/Getty Images

- **Improving your thinking, listening, writing, and speaking skills.** These are the primary skills that define a college-educated person.
- **Functioning independently and teaching yourself.** Your first year of college will help you become an **independent learner**. Independent learners are self-motivated and do not always wait for an instructor to point them in the right direction.
- **Managing your time.** Time management sounds easy, but it is a challenge for almost all students, regardless of their academic abilities.
- **Gaining sensitivity to cultural differences.** The world we live in requires all of us to develop our own knowledge about, and respect for, cultures that are different from our own.

Engagement in learning requires your full and active participation in the learning process. Your instructors will set the stage, but it's up to you to do the rest. For instance, if you disagree with what your instructor says, politely share your opinion. Most instructors will listen. They might still disagree with you, but they might also appreciate your independent thinking.

Not all instructors teach in a way that includes active learning. Ask your friends to recommend instructors who encourage students to participate in class, work in groups, and explore materials independently.

PREPARE FOR CLASS

Have you ever noticed how easy it is to learn the words of a song? It's easier to remember song lyrics than other kinds of information because they often relate to things in our personal lives. It is easier to remember new information presented in class if you can connect it to what you already know or have experienced.

Preparing for class is a very important first step toward success. Here are some strategies that will help you begin listening, learning, and remembering:

1. **Do the assigned reading.** Doing the assigned reading before class will help you understand new terms, listen better, and pick out the most important information when taking notes. Some instructors assign readings during class; others expect you to follow the **syllabus** (course outline) to keep up with the assigned readings. As you read, take good notes (more on note taking later in this chapter). In books you own, **annotate** (add explanatory notes in the margins), highlight, or underline key points. In books you do not own, such as library books, make a photocopy of the pages and then annotate or highlight the photocopies.

2. **Pay careful attention to your course syllabus.** The syllabus you receive at the start of each course will include the course requirements, your instructor's expectations, and how the course will be graded. Instructors expect students to understand and follow the syllabus with few or no reminders. You might find that this is a key difference between college and high school.

3. **Make use of additional materials provided by the instructors.** Many instructors post lecture outlines or notes in the course management system (CMS) before class. Download and print these materials for easy use during class. CMS materials often provide hints about the topics that the instructor considers most important; they can also create an organizational structure for taking notes.

4. **Warm up for class.** Review chapter introductions and summaries that refer to related sections in your text, and quickly review your notes from the previous class period.

5. **Use organizational tools.** Decide how you want to take notes. If you handwrite your notes, using three-ring binders can help you organize them, as you can punch holes in syllabi and other course handouts and keep them with your class notes. You might want to buy notebook paper with a large left-hand margin, so that you can annotate your lecture notes (more on this later in the chapter). You can also download and print blank notebook paper from several free websites.

   If you take notes on a laptop or tablet, keep your files organized in separate folders for each of your classes, and make sure that the file name of each document includes the date and topic of the class. See the Tech Tip in this chapter for more information on using electronic devices to take effective notes.

PARTICIPATE IN CLASS

Learning is not like watching sports; it's like playing a sport. To play a sport—and not just watch it—you have to participate. To really learn, you must listen carefully, talk about what you are learning, write about it, connect it to past experiences, and make what you learn part of yourself. When you participate in class by asking or answering questions, you are more likely to remember the information discussed than if you listen passively to others.

Listen Critically and with an Open Mind

Listening in class is different from listening to a TV show, listening to a friend, or even listening during a meeting. In such everyday activities, you might not be required to remember or use the information you hear. Knowing how to listen in class can help you get more out of what you hear, understand better what you have heard, and save time. Here are some suggestions:

1. **Be ready for the message.** Prepare yourself to hear, to listen, and to receive the message. If you have done the assigned reading, you will already know details from the text, so you can focus your notes on key concepts from the lecture.
2. **Listen to the main concepts and central ideas, not just to facts and figures.** Although facts are important, they will be easier to remember and will make more sense when you can connect them to concepts, themes, and ideas.
3. **Listen for new ideas.** Even if you are an expert on a topic, you can still learn something new. Do not assume that college instructors will present the same information you learned in a similar course in high school.
4. **Repeat mentally.** Words can go in one ear and out the other unless you make an effort to remember them. Think about what you hear, and say it silently in your own words. If you cannot translate the information into your own words, ask the instructor for more explanation.
5. **Decide whether what you have heard is unimportant, somewhat important, or very important.** While most of what your instructors say and do in class is important, occasionally they may make comments or tell stories that are only somewhat related to the class material or may not be related at all. If an instructor's comment is really unrelated to the focus of the class, you don't need to write it down. If it's very important, highlight or underline it, or use it as a major topic in your outline. If it's somewhat important, try to relate it to a very important topic by writing it down as a part of that topic.
6. **Keep an open mind.** Every class holds the promise of letting you discover new ideas and uncover different opinions. Some instructors might intentionally present information that challenges your ideas and values. College is supposed to teach you to think in new ways and train you to provide support for your own beliefs. Instructors want you to think for yourself; they don't necessarily expect you to agree with everything they or your classmates say. However, if you want people to respect your values and ideas, you must show respect by listening to them with an open mind.

7. **Ask questions.** Most instructors want students to ask questions during lectures. When your instructors answer questions, speak up if you did not hear or understand what was said. Ask for explanations immediately, if possible; other students are likely to have the same questions.

8. **Sort, organize, and categorize.** When you listen, try to match what you are hearing with what you already know. If you find yourself daydreaming during a lecture, quickly refocus your thoughts on the topic and actively take notes. After class or during your instructor's next office hours, ask for help in filling in any gaps in your notes.

isthisyou?

Balancing Sports and Study

Are you a student athlete? If so, you might find that it's tough to balance the demands of team practice and games with being a good student. To keep up with your studies, you'll need to go to every class and take advantage of all the academic help available to you through the athletic department and other campus resources. Whatever your athletic goal might be—whether it is to play on a professional team or just enjoy your sport as a college student—keep your eyes on the prize: a college degree.

Speak Up

Naturally, you will be more likely to participate in a class when the instructor emphasizes class discussion, calls on students by name, shows signs of approval and interest, and avoids criticizing students for an incorrect answer. Often, answers you and other students offer may not be quite correct, but they can lead to new perspectives on a topic.

Whether you are in a large or a small class, you might be nervous about asking a question, fearing you will make a fool of yourself. However, it is likely that other students have the same question but are too nervous to ask. If so, they may thank you silently or even aloud! Many instructors set time aside to answer questions in class, so to take full advantage of these opportunities, try using the techniques listed here:

1. **Take a seat as close to the front as possible and keep your eyes on the instructor.** Sitting close to the front can help you concentrate better and avoid distractions from other students. It will also make it easier to maintain eye contact with your instructors.

2. **Focus on the lecture and class discussions.** Avoid distractions. Sit away from friends who can distract you, do not engage in side conversations, and turn off all electronic devices that you are not using for class.

yourturn | **Feeling Connected**

*high-impact
practice 3*

Do You Ask Questions in Class?

Think about the number of times during the past week you have raised your hand in class to ask a question. How many times has it been? Do you ask questions frequently, or is this something you avoid? Make a list of the reasons you either do or don't ask questions in class. Would asking more questions help you earn better grades? Be prepared to share your reflections with a small group and listen to what others have to say.

Participating in class not only helps you learn but also shows your instructor that you're interested and engaged. You may be anxious the first time you raise your hand, but after that first time, you'll probably find that participating in class raises your interest and enjoyment.

PeopleImages/Getty Images

3. **Raise your hand when you don't understand something.** If you don't understand something, you have a right to ask for an explanation. Never worry that you're asking a stupid question. The instructor might answer you immediately, ask you to wait until later in the class, or throw your question to the rest of the class. In each case, you benefit in several ways. The instructor will get to know you, other students will get to know you, and you will learn from both the instructor and your classmates. But don't overdo it, or you'll risk disrupting class. Office hours provide the perfect opportunity for following up on class lectures.

5. **When the instructor calls on you to answer a question, don't bluff.** If you know the answer, give it. If you're not certain, begin with, "I think . . . , but I'm not sure I have it all correct." If you are sure of an answer that turns out to be incorrect, don't feel bad. Your instructor will appreciate your participation. Of course, if you really don't know, just say so.

6. **If you have recently read a book or article that is relevant to the class topic, bring it in.** Use it either to ask questions about the topic or to provide information that was not covered in class.

TAKE EFFECTIVE NOTES

What are effective notes? They are notes that cover all the important points of the lecture or reading material without being too detailed or too limited. Most important, effective notes prepare you to do well on quizzes and exams. They also help you understand and remember concepts and facts. Becoming an effective note-taker takes time and practice, but this skill will help you improve your learning and your grades in the first year of college and beyond. Research also finds that note taking can help students with organizational and writing skills.[1]

---

[1] https://wac.colostate.edu/journal/vol16/boch.pdf

your turn Making Decisions

Going Back in Time

Think back to high school. Did you choose to save any of your high school notes? Do you remember the note-taking method you used? If you have an old notebook, look at the way you took notes in high school and think about whether this method worked for you then, and whether it works for you now. Is it time to choose a better method of taking notes? Consider this question as you learn about different note-taking formats.

Note-Taking Formats

You can make class time more productive by using your listening skills to take effective notes, but first you have to decide on one of the following four commonly used formats for note taking: the Cornell, outline, paragraph, and list formats. Any format can work as long as you use it consistently.

Cornell Format. Using the **Cornell format**, one of the best-known methods for organizing notes, you create a "recall" column on each page of your notebook or your document by drawing a vertical line about 2 to 3 inches from the left border (see Figure 7.1). As you take notes during class—whether writing down or typing ideas, making lists, or using an outline or paragraph format—write only in the wider column on the right; leave the left-hand recall column blank. You will use the recall column

Serious Business

The importance of developing good note-taking skills cannot be overstated. Carefully read about different note-taking formats presented on the next several pages, study the examples carefully, and try out each one. Find the format that works best for you. Use it in every class, and you're on your way to college success.

benis arapovic/Alamy

FIGURE 7.1 > Note Taking in the Cornell Format

Psychology 101
October 15
Theories of Personality

Personality trait define	Personality trait = "durable disposition to behave in a particular way in a variety of situations"
Big 5: Name + describe them	Big 5–McCrae + Costa–(1)extroversion (or positive emotionality) = outgoing, sociable, friendly, upbeat, assertive; (2)neuroticism = anxious, hostile, self-conscious, insecure, vulnerable; (3)openness to experience = curiosity, flexibility, imaginative; (4)agreeableness = sympathetic, trusting, cooperative, modest; (5) conscientiousness = diligent, disciplined, well organized, punctual, dependable
Psychodynamic Theories: Who?	Psychodynamic Theories–focus on unconscious forces
3 components of personality: name and describe	Freud–psychoanalysis–3 components of personality–(1)id = primitive, instinctive, operates according to pleasure principle (immediate gratification); (2)ego = decision-making component, operates according to reality principle (delay gratification until appropriate); (3)superego = moral component, social standards, right + wrong
3 levels of awareness: name and describe	3 levels of awareness–(1)conscious = what one is aware of at a particular moment; (2)preconscious = material just below surface, easily retrieved; (3)unconscious = thoughts, memories, + desires well below surface, but have great influence on behavior

to write down or type the main ideas and important details for tests and exams as you go through your notes, which you should do as soon as possible after class, preferably within an hour or two. Many students have found the recall column to be an important part of note taking, one that becomes an effective study tool for tests and exams.

Outline Format. Some students find that an outline is the best way for them to organize their notes. In a formal outline, Roman numerals (I, II, III, etc.) mark the main ideas. Other ideas relating to each main idea are

FIGURE 7.2 > Note Taking in the Outline Format

Psychology 101
9/14/20
Theories of Personality

I. Personality trait = "durable disposition to behave in a particular way in a variety of situations"

II. Big 5–McCrae + Costa

    A. Extroversion (or positive emotionality) = outgoing, sociable, friendly, upbeat, assertive

    B. Neuroticism = anxious, hostile, self-conscious, insecure, vulnerable

    C. Openness to experience = curiosity, flexibility, imaginative

    D. Agreeableness = sympathetic, trusting, cooperative, modest

    E. Conscientiousness = diligent, disciplined, well organized, punctual, dependable

III. Psychodynamic Theories – focus on unconscious forces – Freud – psychoanalysis

    A. 3 components of personality

        1. Id = primitive, instinctive, operates according to pleasure principle (immediate gratification)

        2. Ego = decision-making component, operates according to reality principle (delay gratification until appropriate)

        3. Superego = moral component, social standards, right + wrong

    B. 3 levels of awareness

        1. Conscious = what one is aware of at a particular moment

        2. Preconscious = material just below surface, easily retrieved

        3. Unconscious = thoughts, memories, + desires well below surface, but have great influence on behavior

marked by uppercase letters (A, B, C, etc.). Arabic numerals (1, 2, 3, etc.) and lowercase letters (a, b, c, etc.) mark related ideas in descending order of importance or detail. Using the outline format allows you to add details, definitions, examples, applications, and explanations (see Figure 7.2).

Paragraph Format. When you take notes while you read, you might decide to write **summary paragraphs**—two or three sentences that sum up a larger section of material (see Figure 7.3). This method might not work well for class notes because it's difficult to summarize a topic until your

FIGURE 7.3 > Note Taking in the Paragraph Format

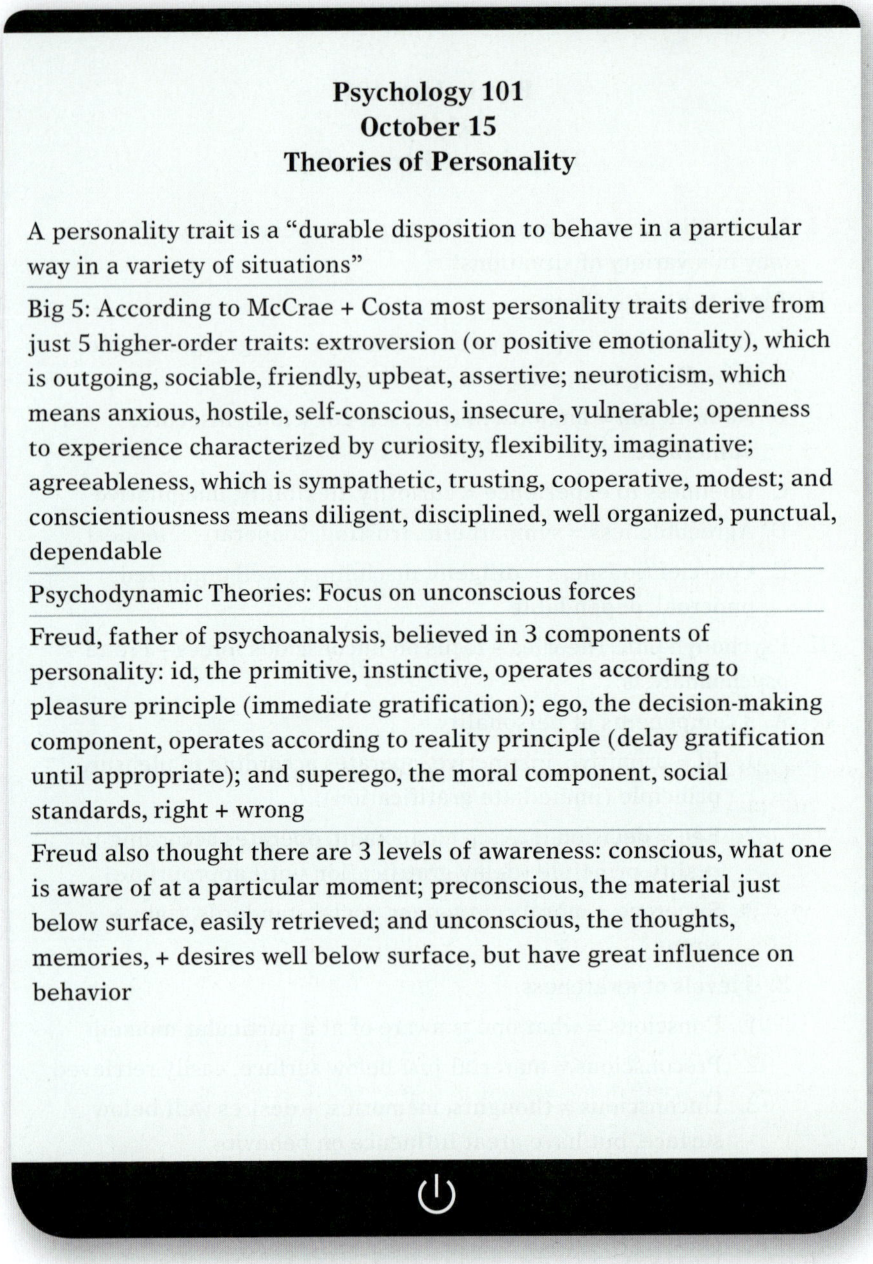

**Psychology 101
October 15
Theories of Personality**

A personality trait is a "durable disposition to behave in a particular way in a variety of situations"

Big 5: According to McCrae + Costa most personality traits derive from just 5 higher-order traits: extroversion (or positive emotionality), which is outgoing, sociable, friendly, upbeat, assertive; neuroticism, which means anxious, hostile, self-conscious, insecure, vulnerable; openness to experience characterized by curiosity, flexibility, imaginative; agreeableness, which is sympathetic, trusting, cooperative, modest; and conscientiousness means diligent, disciplined, well organized, punctual, dependable

Psychodynamic Theories: Focus on unconscious forces

Freud, father of psychoanalysis, believed in 3 components of personality: id, the primitive, instinctive, operates according to pleasure principle (immediate gratification); ego, the decision-making component, operates according to reality principle (delay gratification until appropriate); and superego, the moral component, social standards, right + wrong

Freud also thought there are 3 levels of awareness: conscious, what one is aware of at a particular moment; preconscious, the material just below surface, easily retrieved; and unconscious, the thoughts, memories, + desires well below surface, but have great influence on behavior

instructor has covered it completely. By the end of the lecture, you might have forgotten critical information.

List Format. The list format can be effective in taking notes on terms and definitions, facts, or sequences, such as the body's digestive system (see Figure 7.4). It is easy to use lists in combination with the Cornell format, with key terms on the left and their definitions and explanations on the right.

FIGURE 7.4 > Note Taking in the List Format

Psychology 101
October 15
Theories of Personality

- A personality trait is a "durable disposition to behave in a particular way in a variety of situations"
- Big 5: According to McCrae + Costa most personality traits derive from just 5 higher-order traits
  - extroversion (or positive emotionality), which is outgoing, sociable, friendly, upbeat, assertive
  - neuroticism, which means anxious, hostile, self-conscious, insecure, vulnerable
  - openness to experience characterized by curiosity, flexibility, imaginative
  - agreeableness, which is sympathetic, trusting, cooperative, modest
  - conscientiousness, means diligent, disciplined, well organized, punctual, dependable
- Psychodynamic Theories: Focus on unconscious forces
- Freud, father of psychoanalysis, believed in 3 components of personality
  - id, the primitive, instinctive, operates according to pleasure principle (immediate gratification)
  - ego, the decision-making component, operates according to reality principle (delay gratification until appropriate)
  - superego, the moral component, social standards, right + wrong
- Freud also thought there are 3 levels of awareness
  - conscious, what one is aware of at a particular moment
  - preconscious, the material just below surface, easily retrieved
  - unconscious, the thoughts, memories, + desires well below surface, but have great influence on behavior

Note-Taking Techniques

Whatever note-taking format you choose, follow these important steps:

1. **Identify the main ideas.** The first principle of effective note taking is to identify and write down the most important ideas around which the lecture is built. Although supporting details are important as well, focus your note taking on the main ideas. Some instructors announce the purpose of a lecture or offer an outline of main

ideas, followed by details. Other instructors develop PowerPoint presentations. If your instructor makes such materials available on a website prior to class, you can print them out and take notes on the outline or next to the PowerPoint slides during the lecture. Some instructors change their tone of voice or repeat themselves for each key idea. Some ask questions or provide an opportunity for discussion. If an instructor says something more than once, chances are it is important. Ask yourself, "What does my instructor want me to know at the end of today's class?"

2. **Don't try to write down everything.** Some first-year students try to do just that. They stop being thinkers and become just note-takers. As you take notes, leave spaces so that you can fill in additional details that you might have missed during class but remember or read about later. Take the time to review and complete your notes as soon as you can after class. Once you have decided on a format for taking notes, you might also want to develop your own system of abbreviations. For example, you might write "inst" instead of "institution" or "eval" instead of "evaluation." Just make sure you will be able to understand your abbreviations when it's time to review.

3. **Don't be thrown by a disorganized lecturer.** When a lecture is disorganized, it's your job to try to organize the material presented into general and specific points. When information is missing, you will need to indicate in your notes where the gaps are. After the lecture, review the reading material, ask your classmates to fill in these gaps, or ask your instructor for help. Some instructors have regular office hours for student appointments, while others are willing to spend time after class answering students' questions. However, it is amazing how few students use these opportunities for one-on-one instruction. The questions you ask might help your instructor realize which parts of the lecture need more attention or repetition.

4. **Keep your notes and supplementary materials for each course separate.** Whether you use folders, binders, or some combination, label your materials with the course number and name. Before class, label and date the paper you will use to take notes; after class, organize your notes chronologically. In your folder or binder, create separate tabbed sections for homework, lab assignments, graded and returned tests, and other materials. If you take notes electronically, see the Tech Tip on page 158 for information on using electronic devices to take effective notes.

5. **Download notes, outlines, diagrams, charts, and graphs from the CMS site and bring them to class.** You might be able to save yourself a lot of time during class if you do not have to copy graphs and diagrams while the instructor is talking. Instead, you can focus on the ideas being presented while adding labels and notes to the printouts.

6. **If handouts are distributed in class, label them and place them near your notes.** Buy a portable three-hole punch, and use it to add handouts to your binder or folder as you review your notes each day.

your turn · Write and Reflect

high-impact practice 2

Making the Case for Taking Notes

There are students who complete high school without ever taking notes in class. These students are at a real disadvantage when they come to college, an environment where in-class note taking is an expectation. Develop and write a convincing argument you could present to another student or a younger sibling listing all the reasons that note taking is essential in college classrooms.

Taking Notes in Other Contexts. Always be ready to change your note-taking methods based on the situation. Group discussion is a popular way to teach in college because it engages students in active participation. On your campus, you might also have courses with **Supplemental Instruction (SI)** opportunities, which allow students to discuss the information covered in class lectures and discussions outside of class.

How do you keep a record of what's happening in such classes? Let's assume that you are taking notes on a problem-solving group assignment. You would begin your notes by writing down the problem that the group is being asked to solve. As the group discussion continues, you would list the solutions that are offered. These would be your main ideas. The important details might include the pros and cons of each viewpoint or suggested solution. The important thing to remember when taking notes in nonlecture courses is that you need to record the information presented by your classmates as well as the information presented by your instructor, and you need to consider all reasonable ideas, even those that differ from your own.

When a course has separate lecture and discussion sessions, you will need to understand how the discussion sessions relate to and supplement the lectures. If the material covered in the discussion session differs from what was covered in the lecture, you might need to ask for help in organizing your notes. When similar topics are covered, you can combine your lecture and discussion notes so that you have full coverage of each topic.

How you organize the notes you take in a class discussion session depends on the purpose or form of the discussion. It usually makes sense to begin with a list of the issues or topics under discussion. If the discussion explores reasons for and against a particular argument, divide your notes into columns or sections for each set of reasons. When different views are presented in discussion, record all the ideas. Your instructor might ask you to compare your own opinions to those of other students and explain why and how you formed those opinions.

Taking Notes in Science and Mathematics Courses. Many mathematics and science courses build on one another from term to term and from year to year. When you take notes in these courses, you will

techtip

EXPLORE NOTE-TAKING PROGRAMS AND APPS

Studies have shown that people remember only half of what they hear, which is a major reason to take notes during lectures. Solid note taking will help you better understand key concepts and make them easier to study and remember.

The Problem

You have access to technology but aren't sure how to use it to take notes effectively.

The Fix

Along with making use of the note-taking formats presented in this chapter, use your smartphone, tablet, or laptop to save information and create tools that will help you study.

Erik Isakson/Tetra Images/Corbis

How to Do It

MICROSOFT FEATURES

1. Microsoft **Word** is great for most classes. To highlight main ideas, you can bold or underline text, change the size and color, highlight whole sections, and insert text boxes or charts. You can make bullet points or outlines and insert comments. As you review your notes, you can cut and paste to make things more coherent. You can also create a folder for each class so you can find everything you need easily.
2. Microsoft **Excel** is especially good for any class that involves calculations or financial statements. You can embed messages in the cells of a spreadsheet to explain calculations. (The notes will appear whenever you hover your cursor over that cell.)
3. Microsoft **PowerPoint** can be invaluable for visual learners. Instead of creating one giant, potentially confusing Word file, you can make a slideshow with a new slide for each key point. Some instructors also post the slides that they plan to use in class before class begins. You can write notes on printouts of the slides, or download them and add your notes in PowerPoint.

GOOGLE FEATURES

Google also offers a free suite of products that you can use to take notes and share information.

1. **Docs, Sheets,** and **Slides** allow users to work with text, make calculations, and create slideshows. In addition, Google's collaborative functionality allows users to share files and work simultaneously in one document.
2. Using the comments feature, students can tag other users within a file to ask questions or leave feedback; the system also sends these notes directly to the tagged user's e-mail.
3. Google automatically saves changes with time stamps and tracks which person made edits, which

can be particularly helpful when multiple students work on one set of notes.

APPS FOR NOTE TAKING AND REVIEWING

- **Pocket** (iOS and Android) allows you to store and review written content from your phone.
- **Evernote** (iOS and Android) lets you take a picture of handwritten or printed notes—or anything else you want to recall. Then you can file content and search for it by keyword later.
- **CamScanner** (iOS and Android) allows you to photograph, scan, and store notes.
- **Super Notes** and **Voice Recorder** let you record lectures (with your instructor's permission), and **Speechnotes** transcribes recordings into printable notes.
- **StudyBlue** (iOS, Android, and Web Apps) allows you to make amazing-looking flash cards.

EXTRA STYLE POINTS: No matter what program or app you use, some rules always apply:

- Write down main points using phrases or key terms instead of long sentences.
- Date your notes; keep them in order and in one place; save files using file names with the course number, name, and date of the class; and back up everything.
- Keep a pen and paper handy for sketching graphs and diagrams.
- If you find it hard to keep up, keep practicing your listening and typing skills. Consider a typing class, program, or app to learn how to type properly.
- If you prefer a spiral notebook and a ballpoint pen, that's OK; these formats are tried and true.
- Practice teaching others what you learned in class. You can also learn note-taking strategies from your peers

likely need to go back to them in the future. For example, when taking organic chemistry, you might need to review the notes you took in earlier chemistry courses. This can be particularly important if some time has passed since you completed your last related course, such as after a summer or winter break.

Taking notes in math and science courses can be different from taking notes in other classes. The following tips can help:

- Write down any equations, formulas, diagrams, charts, graphs, and definitions that the instructor puts on the board or screen.
- Write the instructor's words as precisely as possible. Technical terms often have exact meanings that cannot be changed.
- Use standard symbols, abbreviations, and scientific notation.
- Write down all worked problems and examples step by step. The steps are often necessary in answering exam questions. Actively engage in solving the problem yourself as it is being solved during class. Be sure that you can follow the logic and understand the sequence of steps. If you have questions you cannot ask during the lecture, write them down in your notes so that you can ask other students or the instructor.
- Consider taking your notes in pencil or erasable pen. You might need to make changes if you are copying long equations while trying to pay attention to the instructor. You want to keep your notes as neat as possible. Later, you can use colored ink to add other details.
- Listen carefully to other students' questions and the instructor's answers. Take notes on the discussion and during question-and-answer periods.
- Use asterisks, exclamation points, question marks, or symbols of your own to highlight both important points in your notes and questions that you need to come back to when you review.
- Refer to the textbook after class; the text might contain better diagrams and other visual representations than you can draw while taking notes in class. You might even want to scan or photocopy diagrams from the text and include them with your notes in your binder.
- Keep your binders for math and science courses until you graduate (or even longer if you are planning to go to graduate or professional school). They will serve as good review materials for later classes in math and science. In some cases, these notes can also be helpful in the workplace.

Using Technology to Take Notes. While some students use laptops, tablets, or other mobile devices for note taking, others prefer taking notes by hand so that they can easily circle important items or copy equations or diagrams while they are being presented. If you handwrite your notes, entering them on a computer after class for review purposes might be helpful, especially if you are a kinesthetic learner who prefers to learn through experience and practice. After class, you can also cut and paste diagrams and other visuals into your notes and print a copy, since a printout might be neater and easier to read than notes you wrote by hand.

Some students—especially aural learners, who prefer to hear information—find it is advantageous to record lectures. But if you record, don't become passive; listen actively. Students with specific types of learning disabilities might be urged to record lectures or use the services of note-takers, who type on a laptop while the student views the notes on a separate screen.

Review Your Notes

Unless we take steps to remember it, we forget much of the information we receive within the first twenty-four hours; in fact, the decline of memory over time is known as the **forgetting curve**. So if you do not review your notes almost immediately after class, it can be difficult to remember the material later. In two weeks, you will have forgotten up to 70 percent of it! Forgetting can be a serious problem when you are expected to learn and remember many different facts, figures, concepts, and relationships for a number of classes.

Immediate reviewing will help your overall understanding as well as your ability to remember important details during exams. Use the following three strategies:

1. **Write down the main ideas.** For 5 or 10 minutes, quickly review your notes and select key words or phrases. Fill in the details you still remember but missed writing down during class. You might also want to ask your instructor or a classmate to quickly look at your notes to see if you have covered the major ideas.
2. **Repeat your ideas out loud.** Repeat a brief version of what you learned from the class either to yourself or to someone else. For many, the best way to learn something is to teach it to others. You will understand something better and remember it longer if you try to explain it in your own words. This helps you discover your own reactions and find the gaps in your understanding of the material.
3. **Review your notes from the previous class just before the next class session.** As you wait for the class to begin, use the time to quickly review your notes from the previous class session. This will prepare you for the lecture that is about to begin and help you to ask questions about material from the earlier lecture that was not clear to you.

What if you have three classes in a row and no time to study between them? Repeat the information as soon as possible after class. Review the most recent class first. Never delay doing this; if you do, it will take you longer to review, select main ideas, and repeat the ideas. With practice, you can complete the review of your main ideas from your notes quickly, perhaps between classes, during lunch, or while waiting for or riding the bus.

high-impact practice 3

Compare Notes

Comparing notes with other students in a study group, SI session, or learning community has a number of benefits: You will probably take better notes when you know that someone else will see them, you can tell

Many Heads Are Better Than One
Educational researchers have discovered that learning is enhanced by group study. Give it a try.
Kali9/Getty Images

whether your notes are as clear and organized as those of other students, and you can use your comparisons to see whether you agree on what the most important points are.

Take turns testing each other on what you have learned. This will help you predict exam questions and find out if you can answer them. In addition to sharing specific information from the class, you can also share tips on how you take and organize your notes. You might get new ideas that will help your overall learning.

Be aware, however, that merely copying another student's notes, no matter how good those notes are, does not benefit you as much as comparing notes. If you had to be absent from a class, rewriting someone else's notes probably won't help you learn the material. Instead, summarize the other student's notes in your own words to enhance your understanding of the important points.

Class Notes and Homework

Once you have reviewed your notes, you can use them to complete homework assignments. Follow these steps:

1. **Do a warm-up for your homework.** Before doing the assignment, look through your notes again. Use a separate sheet of paper to rework examples, problems, or exercises. If there is related assigned material in the textbook, review it. Go back to the examples. Try to respond to the questions or complete the problems without looking at the answers or solutions. Keep in mind that it can help to go back through your course notes, reorganize them, highlight the important items, and create new notes that let you connect with the material.

2. **Do any assigned problems, and answer any assigned questions.** When you start doing your homework, read each question or problem and ask: What am I supposed to find or find out? What is most important? What is not that important? State the problem in your own words, and then solve it without referring to your notes or the text, as though you were taking a test. In this way, you will test your knowledge and know whether you are prepared for exams.

3. **Don't give up.** Start your homework with the hardest subject first while you are most energetic. When you face a problem or question that you cannot easily solve or answer, move on only after you have tried long enough. After you have completed the whole assignment, come back to any problems or questions that you could not solve or answer. Try again. You might need to think about a particularly difficult problem for several hours or even days. Inspiration might come when you are waiting at a stoplight or just before you fall asleep.

4. **Complete your work.** When you finish an assignment, think about what you learned from it. Think about how the problems and questions were different from one another, which strategies were successful, and what form the answers took. Be sure to review any material you have not mastered. Ask for help from the instructor, a classmate, a study group, the campus learning center, or a tutor to learn how to answer questions that stumped you.

---

your turn Setting Goals

Use What You Have Learned

Now that you've read these suggestions about taking notes and studying for class, which ideas are you motivated to implement in your own note taking? Come to class ready to explain which ideas appeal to you most and why.

checklist for success

Getting the Most from Class

- **Practice the behaviors of engagement.** These behaviors include listening attentively, taking notes, and contributing to class discussion. Engagement also means participating in out-of-class activities without being "required" to do so.

- **Seek out professors who practice "active" teaching.** Ask other students, your seminar instructor, and your adviser to suggest the most engaging professors.

- **Prepare for class before class; it is one of the simplest and most important things you can do.** Read your notes from the previous class and do the assigned readings.

- **Go to class.** A huge part of success is simply showing up. You have no chance of becoming engaged in learning if you're not there.

- **Identify the different types of note taking covered in this chapter and decide which one(s) might work best for you.** Compare your notes with those of another good student to make sure that you are covering the most important points.

- **As you review your notes before each class, make a list of any questions you have and ask both fellow students and your instructor for help.** Don't wait until just before the exam to try to find answers to your questions.

REFLECT ON CHOICES

high-impact practice 2 | This chapter offers several options for effective note taking. Before you make a choice to try a new note-taking format, think back on those we suggested: Cornell, outline, paragraph, and list. Which one is most similar to the method you currently use, and which is most different? Reread the material, and do a brief written comparison of the recommended formats. Which do you think is most complex, which would be the easiest to use, and, given your learning style, which format would help you best understand and remember the material?

APPLY WHAT YOU HAVE LEARNED

Now that you have read and discussed this chapter, consider how you can apply what you have learned to your academic life and your personal life. The following prompts will help you reflect on the chapter material and how you can use it both now and in the future.

1. What is your least engaging class—the one in which the instructor does not encourage you to engage in active learning? Think of some ways you could make this class more engaging, such as asking questions or doing extra reading on the class material. Make a list of your ideas and share it with your college success instructor. The instructor might have other ideas to suggest to you.

2. This chapter makes the point that it is easier to learn and remember new material when you can connect it to something you already know or have experienced. Which of your first-year classes connects most directly to something you learned in the past or something that happened to you? Write a brief paper in which you describe these connections.

USE YOUR RESOURCES

> **Learning Assistance Center** Almost every campus has a learning assistance center, and this chapter's topic is one of their specialties. More and more, the best students—and good students who want to be better students—use learning centers as much as students who are having academic difficulties. Services at learning centers are offered by both full-time professionals and highly skilled student tutors.

> **Fellow College Students** Often, the best help we can get comes from those who are closest to us: fellow students. Keep an eye out in your classes, residence hall, co-curricular groups, and other places for the most serious, purposeful, and directed students. They are the ones to seek out. Find a tutor. Join a study group. Students who do these things are the ones most likely to stay in college and be successful. It does not diminish you in any way to seek assistance from your peers.

> **Computer Center** If you need help using Word, Excel, PowerPoint, or electronic note-taking systems, visit the computer center on your campus.

> **Math Center** Your college may have a special center that provides help for math courses. If you are having difficulty figuring out what kind of notes to take in math classes, visit this center to ask for assistance.

> **Student Disability Services** Your institution's office of disabled student services can help arrange for a note-taker, recorders, or adaptive learning tools for you if you cannot take notes because of a documented disability.

LaunchPad
macmillan learning

LaunchPad for *Your College Experience* is a great resource. Go online to master concepts using the LearningCurve study tool and much more. **Launchpadworks.com**

Monkey Business Images/Shutterstock

8

STUDYING

YOU WILL EXPLORE

Ways to concentrate and study more effectively

How memory works and myths about memory

Skills to improve your memory

⌖ High-impact practices 2 (writing) and 3 (collaboration)

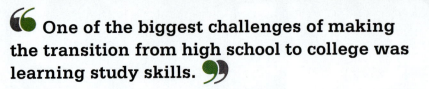

"One of the biggest challenges of making the transition from high school to college was learning study skills. "

Manuela Durson/Shutterstock

Early in high school, Joe did well enough in his classes to be able to play basketball and football. He hoped to be a college athlete, but then a knee injury derailed those plans. In his senior year of high school, one of Joe's teachers recommended that he look into engineering as a profession. Joe had always been interested in math and science, but he hadn't done much planning for college. He researched different careers and types of engineering and found that environmental engineering excited him. He planned to complete his associate's degree in pre-engineering at Spokane Falls Community College (SFCC) and then transfer to Washington State University. While Joe is good at math and science, that doesn't mean his transition to college was easy. "In high school," he says, "my studying habits were slim to none. I was the type of high school student who was able to pass a test just from listening and from what I remembered from class."

But in his first few classes, Joe had to change some of his study habits when he found that he wasn't able to remember everything the instructors required him to learn. "One of the biggest challenges in making the transition from high school to college was learning study skills," Joe says. He notes that, compared with high school, his college classes go twice as fast and instructors expect students to do a lot more work on their own. One of the first steps Joe took to adjust his study habits was to stop setting aside huge blocks of unstructured study time. "I learned that studying for more than four hours straight is not the best for me. I need to study for an hour, take a half hour break, and then study another hour. I realized that after an hour, I had trouble remembering things." By taking breaks to eat, exercise, or watch TV, Joe knows that he's giving his brain time to process information.

His one piece of advice to other first-year students? "The first year is going to be the hardest because it's so different," he says. "Just push through it. You'll find that it all starts making sense."

LaunchPad
macmillan learning

To access the LearningCurve study tool, video activities, and more, go to LaunchPad for *Your College Experience.*
Launchpadworks.com

You might have learned to study effectively while you were in high school, or like Joe, you might find that your high school study habits no longer work now that you're in college. You will need to discover ways of structuring your study time that work best for you. Joe quickly learned that a four-hour study session was too long for him. But however you structure your study sessions, you will need to allocate regular times each week to review course material, do

assess your strengths

What study skills have you learned and practiced, and how do you need to improve? As you read this chapter, consider the strengths you have in studying and remembering course material.

set goals

What are your most important objectives in learning the material in this chapter? Do you need to improve your ability to concentrate, your study skills, and your memory? Consider how you might improve the environment in which you study.

assigned reading, and keep up with your homework. Occasionally, you will also want to do additional (unassigned) reading and investigate particular topics that interest you, as these are strategies that will help you retain knowledge.

Studying, comprehending, and remembering are essential to getting the most from your college experience. Although many students think that the only reason to study is to do well on exams, a far more important reason is to learn and understand course information. If you study to increase your understanding, you are more likely to remember and apply what you learn, not only to tests, but also to future courses and to life beyond college.

This chapter considers two related topics: concentration and memory. It begins with the role of concentration in studying—if you cannot concentrate, you'll find it next to impossible to remember anything. Next, the chapter offers a number of tools to help you make the best use of your study time. It concludes with a thorough discussion of what memory is, how it works, and how you can improve your memory.

is this you?

Making A's without Studying

Were you a straight-A student in high school who spent almost no time studying? In the first few weeks of college, maybe you went to class and listened, and you read through the assigned material on time. But you never took notes, reviewed your reading, or spent extra time preparing for tests and exams. You believed that your brainpower would carry you through college, just like it did in high school. But your first round of college tests gave you a horrible shock: You got Cs and Ds, maybe even an F. You quickly realized that something had to change. If you coasted effortlessly in high school, that probably won't be possible in all your college courses. This chapter will help you develop systematic strategies for studying that will help you maintain good grades throughout the term.

STUDYING IN COLLEGE: MAKING CHOICES AND CONCENTRATING

Learning new material takes a lot of effort on your part. You must concentrate on what you hear and read. This might sound simple, but considering all the responsibilities that college students must balance, the opportunity to concentrate and really focus on what you're learning and studying can be hard to come by. Understanding how to maximize your ability to concentrate through what you do and where you do it is a good place to start.

Making a few changes in your behavior and in your environment will allow you to concentrate better and remember more. With concentration, you'll probably need fewer hours to study because you will use your time more efficiently. What are you willing to do to make this happen? Working through the following exercise in Table 8.1, you'll begin to navigate some tough choices.

Attending a college or university is a major responsibility, one you shouldn't take lightly. It is a lot of work, but it also offers you a lot of opportunities. For most people, a college degree is a pathway to a better, more fulfilling life. As a college learner, you may need to make different choices about how, and how often, you study and the best way to structure your study environment. Depending on your past study habits, some of these choices may not be easy. You may find that you have to invest more time in reading and

TABLE 8.1 > Choose to Upgrade Your Learning

Tough Choices	Your Answer: Yes or No?
Are you willing to work together with others to form study groups or partners?	
Are you willing to do assigned reading before you come to class?	
Are you willing to find a place away from home, either on campus or elsewhere, for quiet study?	
Are you willing to be disconnected from the internet, turn off all notifications on your mobile devices, and turn off your cell phone for reading time with no interruption?	
Are you willing to turn off distracting music or TV while you are studying?	
Are you willing to sit in a spot in class where you can see and hear better?	
Are you willing to go over your notes after class to revise or rewrite them?	
Are you willing to reduce stress through exercise, sleep, or meditation?	
Are you willing to take a few minutes on the weekend to organize the week ahead?	
Are you willing to study for tests four or five days in advance?	

reviewing, and that you have to study in groups with other students. Behaviors such as these can have a direct, positive impact on your ability to remember and learn the information you will need in the months and years ahead.

With these realities in mind, what did you learn about yourself from answering the questions in the exercise on the previous page? Think especially about the questions to which you answered "no." Which of these are you willing or unwilling to change right now? Remember: Making a choice now to change behaviors that disrupt your ability to get the most out of college, both in and out of the classroom, will save you a lot of headaches in the future.

🎯 *high-impact practice 2*

yourturn | **Write and Reflect**

Are You Able to Concentrate?

The next time you sit down to study, monitor your ability to concentrate. Check your watch when you begin, and check it again when your mind begins to wander. How many minutes did you concentrate on your work? List some strategies to keep your mind from wandering. Write a journal entry containing ideas you have heard that you think will work well for you.

HOW MEMORY WORKS

Learning experts describe two different processes involved in memory (see Table 8.2). The first is **short-term memory**, which involves retaining information, such as words or numbers, for about 15 to 30 seconds. After that you will forget the information stored in your short-term memory unless you take action either to keep that information in short-term memory or to move it to long-term memory.

Figure 8.1 is based on the work of Hermann Ebbinghaus, a German psychologist who, in 1885, conducted research on himself to determine his memory over time. Based on this research, he hypothesized that, after nine hours, most people remember less than 40 percent of the information they have learned nine hours before.[1]

TABLE 8.2 ❯ Short- and Long-Term Memory

Short-Term Memory	Long-Term Memory
Stores information for about 15–30 seconds.	Stores information for hours to years
	Can be described in three ways:
Can handle from five to nine chunks of information at one time.	Procedural—remembering how to do something
Information is either forgotten or moved to long-term memory.	Semantic—remembering facts and meanings
	Episodic—remembering events, including their time and place

---

[1] https://www.edubloxtutor.com/hermann-ebbinghaus-first-psychologist-study-learning-memory/

FIGURE 8.1 › Ebbinghaus Forgetting Curve

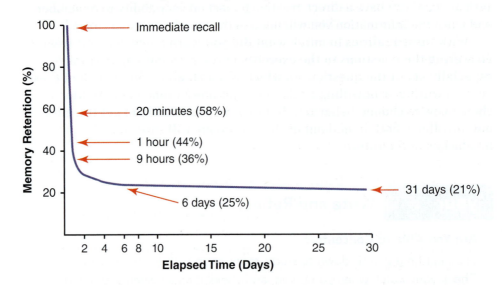

Although short-term memory is significantly limited, it has a number of uses. It serves as an immediate holding tank for information, some of which you might not need for long. It helps you maintain a reasonable attention span so that you can keep track of topics mentioned in conversation, and it also enables you to focus on the goals you have at any given moment. But if you are interrupted in any way, you might find that your attention suffers and that you have to start over to reconstruct the contents of your short-term memory.

The second memory process is also important for college success. **Long-term memory**, the capacity to retain and recall information over the long term, from hours to years, can be divided into three categories:

- **Procedural memory** deals with knowing how to do something, such as solving a mathematical problem or driving a car. You use your procedural memory when you ride a bicycle, even if you haven't ridden one in years; when you cook a meal that you know how to prepare without using a recipe; or when you send a text message.
- **Semantic memory** involves facts and meanings without regard to where and when you learned those things. Your semantic memory is used when you remember word meanings or important dates, such as your mother's birthday.
- **Episodic memory** deals with particular events, their time, and their place. You use episodic memory when you remember events in your life—a vacation, your first day of school, or the moment your child was born. Some people can recall not only the event, but also the very time and place the event happened. For others, although the event stands out, the time and place are harder to remember.

Connecting Memory to Deep Learning

Multitasking has become a fact of life for many of us, but research summarized on the website of the American Psychological Association[2]

---
[2] www.apa.org/research/action/multitask.aspx.

shows that trying to do several tasks at once can make it harder to remember the things that are most important. It is hard to focus on anything for long if your life is full of daily distractions and competing responsibilities—school, work, commuting, and family responsibilities—or if you're not getting the sleep you need. Have you ever had the experience of walking into a room with a specific task in mind and immediately forgetting what that task was? You were probably interrupted, either by your own thoughts or by someone or something else. Or have you ever felt the panic that comes when your mind goes blank during a test, even though you studied hard and knew the material? If you spent all night studying, lack of sleep may have raised your stress level, causing you to forget what you worked hard to learn. Such experiences happen to most people at one time or another.

To do well in college and in life, it's important that you improve your ability to remember what you read, hear, and experience. Concentration is a key element of learning and is so deeply connected to memory that you can't really have one without the other.

The benefits of having a good memory are obvious. In college, your memory will help you retain information and earn excellent grades on tests. After college, the ability to remember important details—names, dates, and appointments—will save you energy and time, and will prevent a lot of embarrassment.

Most memory strategies tend to focus on helping you remember bits and pieces of knowledge: names, dates, numbers, vocabulary words, formulas, and so on. However, if you know the date when the Civil War began and the name of the fort where the first shots were fired but you don't know why the Civil War was fought or how it affected history, you're missing the point of a college education. College is a time to develop **deep learning**, which involves understanding the why and how behind the details. So while remembering specific facts is necessary, to do well in college and in your career you will need to understand major themes and ideas. You will also need to improve your ability to think deeply about what you're learning. For more on the sorts of thinking skills you need to develop in college, see the chapters on "Information Literacy and Communication" and "Thinking in College."

your turn   Setting Goals

The Fun of Improving Your Memory

What might motivate you to improve your memory? Do your friends complain that you keep forgetting the times you had planned to meet? Have you forgotten the due date for a paper, or have you forgotten your mother's birthday? If one of your goals is to develop a better memory, try some fun strategies for memory improvement. For example, many memory games are available that you can play for a few minutes every day; some of them you can find in your daily newspaper, such as crossword puzzles or Sudoku. Others can be accessed online or on your mobile device. Check out apps like Elevate, Lumosity, or Peak.

techtip

USE THE CLOUD

Computer labs, laptops, tablets, and smartphones give you the opportunity to work from almost anywhere. What can you do to keep all your important digital files in one place so that you'll never be without them?

Pixsooz/Shutterstock

The Problem

You store your class files on a drive or laptop that you don't always have with you. How can you access your files anytime you need them?

The Fix

Save your files to the cloud so you can access them from any internet-connected device.

How to Do It

Sign up for a free account from a cloud storage site. These sites allow you to save files to an online location. You'll have your own private, password-protected storage space. Cloud storage is great for collaboration because you can choose to share all or some of your files with your classmates and friends.

The following is a list of sites sites with free storage (though most require payment to increase your storage size):

1. *Dropbox* is one of the best-known cloud storage sites. You can download Dropbox to your own computer or access your Dropbox files from the web. Dropbox is available as a stand-alone app on iPhone, iPad, and Android devices, and it also works with other document-editing mobile apps.
2. *Google Drive* allows users to store and share documents. A great feature of Google Drive is that you can edit documents in real time with your friends and classmates. If you're writing a group paper, all your coauthors can view and edit the same document simultaneously. There is even a chat window so you can talk to each other while editing. Google Drive allows for storage of audio, video, and presentation slides as well. Like Dropbox, Google Drive is available as a stand-alone app and integrates well with iPhone, iPad, and Android apps. If you have a Gmail account, you already have an account for Google Drive.
3. *MediaFire* is newer than Dropbox and Google Drive. MediaFire's key feature is as much as 50 GB of free storage space. Users are able to work together in the cloud and access their files using stand-alone apps on iPhone, iPad, and Android devices.
4. *Microsoft OneDrive* uses the Microsoft Office Suite and allows you to create, store, and share files. It also has a free, stand-alone app for smartphones or tablets.

Myths about Memory

To understand how to improve your memory, let's first look at what we know about how memory works. Although scientists keep learning new things about how our brains function, author Kenneth Higbee[3] suggests some myths about memory, some of which you might have heard, and some you might even believe. Table 8.3 lists four of these memory myths and what experts say about them.

TABLE 8.3 > Dispelling Myths about Memory

Myth	Reality
Some people have bad memories.	Although the memory ability you are born with is different from that of others, nearly everyone can improve their ability to remember and recall. Improving your concentration would certainly benefit your ability to remember!
Some people have photographic memories.	Some individuals have truly exceptional memories, but these abilities result more often from learned strategies, interest, and practice than from the natural ability to remember.
Memory benefits from long hours of practice.	Experts believe that practice often improves memory, but they argue that the way you practice is more important than how long you practice. For all practical purposes, the storage capacity of your memory is unlimited. In fact, the more you learn about a particular topic, the easier it is to learn even more.
People use only 10 percent of their brain power.	No one knows exactly how much of our brain we actually use. However, most researchers believe that we all have far more mental ability than we actively use.

IMPROVING YOUR MEMORY

Just as you can use strategies for improving your ability to concentrate, you can improve your ability to retain information—to store it in your brain for future use. The time you spend in learning memory strategies is a good investment for your academic success.

Strategies for Remembering

Psychologists and learning specialists have developed a number of strategies you can use when studying to remember information. Some of these strategies may be new to you, while others may be familiar. No matter what course you are taking, you need to remember concepts and

[3] Kenneth L. Higbee, *Your Memory: How It Works and How to Improve It*, 2nd rev. ed. (New York: Marlowe, 2001).

ideas in order to complete the course successfully. To store concepts and ideas in your mind, ask yourself these questions as you review your notes and course material:

1. What is the basic idea here?
2. Why does the idea make sense? What is the logic behind it?
3. How does this idea connect to other ideas in the material or experiences in my life?
4. What are some possible arguments against the idea?

To prepare for an exam that will cover large amounts of material, you need to

- Reduce your notes and text pages into manageable study units.
- Review your materials with these questions in mind:
  - Is this one of the key ideas in the chapter or unit?
  - Will I see this on the test?
- Use study tools that are effective to help you remember what you have learned: review sheets, mind maps, flash cards, summaries, and mnemonics.

Review Sheets. Use your notes to develop **review sheets**—lists of key terms and ideas that you need to remember. If you're using the Cornell format to take notes, you can make these lists in the recall column. Also be sure to use your lecture notes to test yourself or others on information presented in class.

Mind Maps. Mapping is an effective way to preview content and also a great strategy to remember content. **Mind maps** are visual review sheets that show the relationships between ideas and whose patterns provide you with clues to jog your memory. Because they are visual, mind maps help many students, particularly English-language learners, to remember the information more easily.

To create a mind map, start with a main idea and place it in the center. Then add major categories that branch out from the center. To these, add pieces of related information to form clusters. You can use different shapes or colors to show the relationships among the various pieces of information. You can find many apps for creating mind maps on your computer or mobile device. Figure 8.2 shows a mind map of this chapter, created by using an app similar to MindMeister and SimpleMind.

Flash Cards. Just as you can create flash cards during the process of active reading, you can also use them as a tool for improving your memory. Flash cards—with a question, term, or piece of information on one side and the answer, definition, or explanation on the other—can serve as memory aids. Flash cards are excellent tools for improving your vocabulary, especially if you are learning English as a second language.

One of the advantages of flash cards is that you can keep them in your backpack or jacket, or you can create flash cards on your mobile device using apps such as Chegg Flashcards and StudyBlue. Flash cards can help you make good use of time that might otherwise be wasted, such as time spent on the bus or waiting for a friend. You can review them anywhere, even when you don't have enough time to take out your notebook to study.

FIGURE 8.2 › Sample Mind Map

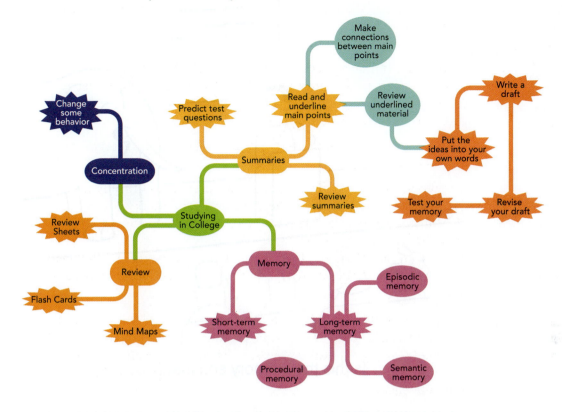

Summaries. An immediate benefit of writing summaries of class topics is that they can help you answer short-answer and essay questions successfully. They also allow you to see connections between ideas and help you identify major and minor details. By summarizing the main ideas and putting them into your own words, you will be able to remember information better. Here's how you can create a good summary in preparation for taking a test:

1. **Read the assigned material, your class notes, or your instructor's presentation slides.** Underline or mark the main ideas as you go, make explanatory notes or comments about the material, or make an outline on a separate sheet of paper. Predict test questions based on your active reading.
2. **Make connections between main points and key supporting details.** Reread to identify each main point and its supporting evidence. Create an outline in the process.
3. **Review underlined material.** Put those ideas into your own words in a logical order.
4. **Write your ideas in a draft.** In the first sentence, state the purpose of your summary. Follow this statement with each main point and its supporting ideas. See how much of the draft you can develop from memory without relying on your notes.
5. **Review your draft.** Read it over, adding missing details or other information.

An Elephant (Almost) Never Forgets

Although elephants apparently do have pretty good memories, they're like the rest of us in that they occasionally forget. Work to develop your memory by using the specific strategies in this chapter. One of the most important strategies you can use is considering the big-picture context behind bits and pieces of information.

Shannon Burns

"Is this the memory seminar?"

6. **Test your memory.** Put your draft away, and try to repeat the contents of the summary out loud to yourself or to a study partner who can let you know whether you have forgotten anything.

7. **Schedule time to review your summary and double-check your memory shortly before the test.** You might want to do this with a partner, but some students prefer to review alone. Some instructors might be willing to help you with this process and give you feedback on your summaries.

 *high-impact practice 3*

your turn   Feeling Connected

What Are You Remembering So Far?

With your other classmates, test your memory of this class so far. Working individually without opening the textbook, list all the topics and subtopics you have already covered in this course. See which member of the class can remember the most topics. Was there a topic that everyone remembered or that no one remembered? Discuss why it might have been harder to remember some topics than others.

Mnemonics. Mnemonics (pronounced "ne-MON-iks") are different methods or tricks to help you remember information. Mnemonics tend to fall into four basic categories:

1. **Acronyms.** Acronyms, which are new words created from the first letters of several words, can be helpful in remembering.

The names of the Great Lakes can be more easily recalled by remembering the word *HOMES* for **H**uron, **O**ntario, **M**ichigan, **E**rie, and **S**uperior.

2. **Acrostics.** An acrostic is a verse in which certain letters of each word or line form a message. Many students are taught the following to remember the planets in their order from the sun: **M**y **V**ery **E**xcellent **M**other **J**ust **S**erved **U**s **N**achos (**M**ercury, **V**enus, **E**arth, **M**ars, **J**upiter, **S**aturn, **U**ranus, **N**eptune).

3. **Rhymes or songs.** Do you remember learning "Thirty days hath September, April, June, and November. All the rest have 31, excepting February alone. It has 28 days' time, but in leap years 29"? If so, you were using a mnemonic rhyming technique to remember the number of days in each month.

4. **Visualization.** You can use visualization to connect a word or concept with a visual image. The more ridiculous the image, the more likely you are to remember the word or concept. For example, if you want to remember the name of George Washington, you may think of a person you know by the name of George. You should then picture that person washing a ton of dishes in the White House. Now every time you think of the first president of the United States, you see George washing a ton of dishes.[4]

---

your turn | **Making Decisions**

Choose Review Methods That Work for You

This chapter has offered several strategies for reviewing material before you take a test or exam, including review sheets, mind maps, flash cards, summaries, and mnemonics. Some of these strategies might work better for certain subject areas. For instance, mnemonics and flash cards will help when you have to remember definitions or other specific bits of information. Review sheets, mind maps, and summaries work more effectively when you need to understand broad concepts. When you begin studying for your next test, let the type of test and the material it will cover help you choose the best study method.

Mnemonics are a sort of mental filing system that provide a way of organizing material. They probably aren't needed if what you are studying is logical and organized, but they can be really useful when material doesn't have a pattern of its own. Although using mnemonics can be helpful in remembering information, it takes time to think up rhymes, associations, or visual images that have limited use when you need to analyze or explain the material.

---

[4] Example from Jim Somchai, "Memory and Visualization," EzineArticles.com, ezinearticles .com/?Memory-and-Visualization&id=569553.

STUDYING TO UNDERSTAND AND REMEMBER

Studying will help you accomplish two goals: understanding and remembering. While memory is a necessary tool for learning, what's most important is that you study to develop a deep understanding of course information. When you really comprehend what you are learning, you will be able to place names, dates, and specific facts in context. You will also be able to exercise your critical-thinking abilities.

Here are some methods that might be useful when you're trying to remember detailed information:

- **Pay attention and avoid distractions.** This suggestion is the most basic, but the most important. If you're sitting in class thinking about everything except what the professor is saying, or if you're reading and you find that your mind is wandering, you're wasting your time. Force yourself to focus. Review your responses to the questions posed in the exercise you completed earlier in this chapter about what you're willing to do to improve your concentration.
- **Be confident that you can improve your memory.** Recall successes from the past when you learned things that you didn't think you could or would remember. Choose memory improvement strategies that best fit your learning preferences: aural, visual, read/write, or kinesthetic. Identify the courses where you can make the best use of each memory strategy.
- **Overlearn the material.** Once you think you understand the material you're studying, go over it again to make sure that you'll remember it for a long time. Test yourself, or ask someone else to test you. Repeat what you're trying to remember out loud and in your own words.
- **Explain the material to another person.** Researchers who study learning know that the best way to learn something is to teach it to someone else.
- **Make studying a part of your daily routine.** Don't allow days to go by when you don't open a book or work on course assignments. Make studying a daily habit!
- **Check the internet.** If you're having trouble remembering what you have learned, Google a key word and try to find interesting details that will engage you in learning more about the subject. Many first-year courses cover such a large amount of material that you might miss some interesting details unless you look for them yourself. As your interest increases, so will your memory about the topic. Make sure to check multiple online sources.
- **Go beyond memorizing words and focus on understanding and then remembering the big concepts and ideas.** Keep asking yourself questions like: What is the main point here? Is there a big idea? Whenever you begin a course, review the syllabus, talk with someone who has already taken the course, and take a brief look at all the reading assignments. Having the big picture will help you understand

and remember the details of what you're learning. For example, the big picture for a first-year college success class is to give students the knowledge and strategies to be successful in college.

- **Look for connections between your life and what's going on in the content of your courses.** College courses might seem unrelated to you and your goals, but if you look more carefully, you'll find many connections between course material and your daily life. Seeing those connections will make your courses more interesting and will help you remember what you're learning. For example, if you're taking a sociology class and studying marriage and the family, think about how your own family experiences relate to those described in your readings or in the lectures.
- **Get organized.** If your desk or your computer is organized, you won't waste time trying to remember where you put a particular document or what name you gave to a file. And as you rewrite your notes, putting them in an order that makes sense to you (for example, by topic or by date) will help you learn and remember them.

---

your turn   **Feeling Connected**

 high-impact practice 3

Is It Worth the Time and Effort to Get Organized?

With a small group of your classmates, share how organized you are in your living space and on your computer. Is your living space more or less organized than your laptop, desktop, or iPad? Do group members think that being organized is important? How does being disorganized affect time management? Work with your peer leader to come up with strategies to be more organized. Keep track of the initial time you spend getting organized, and the time you save over a two- or three-week period by being more organized.

- **Reduce the stress in your life.** Many college students experience stress because they have to juggle college, work, and family life. Stress-reducing habits, such as eating well and getting enough exercise and sleep, are especially important for college students (see the "Wellness" chapter for strategies). Remember, too, that your college probably has a counseling center or health center where you can seek help in dealing with whatever might be causing stress in your daily life.
- **Collaborate.** In your first year of college, join a group of students who study together. Your instructors or the college learning center can help you organize study groups. Study groups can meet throughout the term or can get together only to review for midterm or final exams.

high-impact practice 3

- **Get a tutor.** Tutoring is not just for students who are failing. Often the best students ask for help to make sure that they understand course material. Most tutors are students, and at most community colleges, tutoring services are free.

Work Together

One way to enhance your memory is to study with others. Each of you can check specific facts and details and share the strategies you use to remember them. You can also motivate and support one another.

PeopleImages/Getty Images

As you learned in this chapter, memory and concentration play very important roles in achieving success in college because they help you understand, remember, and deeply learn the material so that you can apply that learning to your career and life.

checklist for success

Studying

■ **Make studying a part of your daily routine.** Don't allow days to go by when you don't crack a book or keep up with course assignments.

■ **Manage your study time wisely.** Create a schedule that will allow you to prepare for exams and complete course assignments on time. Be aware of "crunch times" when you might have several exams or papers due at once. Create some flexibility in your schedule to allow for unexpected distractions.

■ **Collaborate.** One of the most effective ways to study is in a group with other students.

■ **Be confident that you can improve your memory.** Remind yourself occasionally of things you have learned in the past that you didn't think you could or would remember.

■ **Choose the memory improvement strategies that best fit your learning preferences(s): aural, visual, read/write, or kinesthetic.** Identify the courses where you can make the best use of each memory strategy.

■ **Go beyond simply trying to memorize words, and focus on trying to understand and remember the big concepts and ideas.** Keep asking yourself: What is the main point here? Is there a big idea? Am I getting it?

■ **Be alert for external distractions.** Choose a place to study where you can concentrate, and allow yourself uninterrupted time to focus on the material you are studying.

■ **Get a tutor.** Tutoring is not just for students who are failing. Often the best students seek assistance to ensure that they fully understand course material. Most tutors are students, and most campus tutoring services are free.

REFLECT ON CHOICES

🎯 *high-impact practice 2*   Reflect on what you have learned about college success in this chapter and the memory-improvement ideas that are are most interesting to you. Choose one or more of them to learn more about, and describe how you would apply these ideas to your own ways of studying.

APPLY WHAT YOU HAVE LEARNED

Now that you have read and discussed this chapter, consider how you can apply what you have learned to your academic life and your personal life. The following prompts will help you reflect on the chapter material and its relevance to you both now and in the future.

1. Give mnemonics a try. Choose a set of class notes that you need to study for an upcoming quiz or exam. As you study, pick one concept and create your own acronym, acrostic, rhyme, song, or visualization to help you remember.

2. The way that students study in high school is often very different from the way they need to study in college. It can be difficult to adapt to new ways of doing things. Write a one-page paper describing how you studied in high school and how you can improve on those habits to do well in college.

USE YOUR RESOURCES

> **Learning Center**   Here, staff can help you develop effective memory strategies. Pay a visit and ask about specific workshops or one-on-one assistance with memory.

> **Health and Wellness Center**   If you have underlying health issues that are preventing you from concentrating or remembering, seek assistance from your health or wellness center.

> **Peers and Your Peer Leader**   Ask fellow students and your peer leader to share their own tips for improving memory.

> **Your Instructor**   Ask your instructor if there is someone on your campus who is an expert on memory strategies. If so, make an appointment to meet that person.

> **The Library**   Your college or university library will have many books on the topic of memory. Some were written by researchers for the research community, but others were written for people like you. Download or check out a book on memory to see what you can learn. Here are some good options: Tony Buzan, *Memory Book: How to Remember Anything You Want* (Boston: Pearson Education, 2010); Dominic O'Brien, *How to Pass Exams, Accelerate Learning, Memorize Key Facts, Revise Effectively* (London: Duncan Baird Publishers, Ltd., 2007); Harry Lorayne, *The Memory Book: The Classic Guide to Improving Your Memory at Work, at Study and at Play* (New York: Ballantine Books, 2017). Ask your college librarian to help you identify some helpful online resources as well, such as this site from Darmouth University: https://students.dartmouth.edu/academic-skills/learning-resources/learning-strategies/improving-memory-retention.

 **LaunchPad**
macmillan learning

LaunchPad for *Your College Experience* is a great resource. Go online to master concepts using the LearningCurve study tool and much more. **Launchpadworks.com**

Chris Ryan/Getty Images

9

TEST TAKING

YOU WILL EXPLORE

Ways to prepare for exams physically, emotionally, and academically

Tips for test taking

Strategies for taking different types of tests and handling various question types

How to overcome test anxiety

What cheating is, how to avoid it, and how to practice academic honesty

⌖ High-impact practices 2 (writing) and 3 (collaboration)

Wavebreak Media ltd/
Alamy

> ❝ **The first step to improving my test-taking abilities was changing my attitude about my 'academic self.'** ❞

Nicole grew up all over the country, moving with her parents as part of a military family. She finished high school in Spokane, Washington, where she later met her husband. He died in Iraq soon after their son was born, and she had to find work to support herself and her child. College was the furthest thing from her mind, but eventually she realized that she wanted more for her son—and for herself. "Ultimately, being a single mother is what motivates me, not only to provide a better life for both of us but also to set an example that was not always set for me," she explains.

Part of going to college and raising a family involves finding that ever-elusive work–life balance in areas such as preparing for tests. Nicole always thought that she just wasn't good at taking tests or learning, so she usually finished in the middle of the pack on tests and exams. "The first step to improving my test-taking abilities," she says, "was changing my attitude about my 'academic self.'" Once Nicole worked to improve her attitude, she began looking at the test-preparation strategies that worked best for her. One thing she figured out was that note taking was integral to a good performance on tests. "I found that I remember things best by relating them to things that I already know," she says. Now she knows to take careful notes during class, underline key terms, and make additional marginal notes so that when she gets home, she can create associations to help with memory. She also knows that her brain works best when the rest of her body is well cared for and has plenty of rest, good food, exercise, and often meditation and relaxation. "It works better than cram studying, and I get a lot more out of my courses and do better on my exams," she explains.

As with many things in life, Nicole realizes that with test taking, you sometimes have to get it wrong before you get it right. Her advice to other first-year students? "Go back over the questions you got wrong on a test and try to figure out what you got wrong and why."

LaunchPad
macmillan learning

To access the LearningCurve study tool, video activities, and more, go to LaunchPad for *Your College Experience.*
Launchpadworks.com

Tests and exams are the primary ways that instructors will evaluate your learning. In general, tests are shorter than exams and will count less toward your overall course grade. A course might have only a final exam, or it might have a midterm and a final. These exams generally take two or more hours to complete and comprise a major component of your final grade in a course.

You can prepare for tests and exams in many ways. Sometimes you'll have to recall names, dates, and other specific bits of information. Many instructors, especially in courses such as literature and history, will also expect you to have a good overall understanding of the subject matter. Even in math and science courses, your instructors want you not only to

assess your strengths

Tests and exams are an unavoidable component of college life. Good students will practice strategies to improve their exam scores. As you read this chapter, think of specific examples of your strengths in preparing for and taking different kinds of exams.

set goals

What are your most important objectives for learning the material in this chapter? Do you need to improve your abilities as a test taker, or do you need to deal with test anxiety that prevents you from doing your best? Consider what you might do to improve in these areas, such as leaving plenty of time to study in advance of exams.

remember the correct theory, formula, or equation, but also to understand and apply what you have learned. Knowing your preferred learning style, managing your time and energy, and using the study and memory strategies discussed in previous chapters will help you prepare for any kind of test or exam you face. This chapter provides you with several strategies to prepare for and take tests and exams successfully, describes types of tests and test questions you may encounter, and includes tips for managing test anxiety and practicing academic honesty.

GETTING READY . . .

Believe it or not, you actually began preparing for tests on the first day of the term. Your lecture notes, assigned readings, and homework are all part of that preparation. As you get closer to the test day, you should know how much additional time you will need for review, what material the test will cover, and what format the test will take. It is very important to double-check the exam dates on the syllabus for each of your classes, as in Figure 9.1 on the next page, and to incorporate these dates into your overall plans for time management—for example, in your daily and weekly to-do lists.

Prepare for Test Taking

Tests are usually a major portion of your grade in college, so proper preparation for them is essential. Of course you need to understand the material, but there are many ways you can prepare for exams in addition to your regular study routines.

Find Out about the Test. Ask your instructor about the test format, how long the test will last, and how it will be graded. Find out the types of questions and the content that will be covered. Talk with your instructor to clarify any misunderstandings you might have about your reading or lecture notes. If you have part-time instructors who do not have office hours, try to talk to them before or after class. Some instructors might let you view copies of old exams so that you can see the types of questions

FIGURE 9.1 › Exam Schedule from Sample Course Syllabus

**History 111, US History to 1865
Fall Term**

Examinations
Note: In this course, most of your exams will be on Fridays, except for the Wednesday before Thanksgiving and the final. This is to give you a full week to study for the exam and permit me to grade them over the weekend and return the exams to you on Monday. I believe in using a variety of types of measurements. In addition to those scheduled below, I reserve the right to give you unannounced quizzes on daily reading assignments. Also, current events are fair game on any exam! Midterm and final exams will be cumulative (on all material since the beginning of the course). Other exams cover all classroom material and all readings covered since the prior exam. The schedule is as follows:

Friday, 9/9: Objective type

Friday, 9/23: Essay type

Friday, 10/7: Midterm: essay and objective

Friday, 11/4: Objective

Wednesday, 11/23: Essay

Friday, 12/16: Final exam: essay and objective

they use. Never miss the last class before an exam; your instructor might take part or all of that class session to summarize and review valuable information.

Design an Exam Plan. Use information about the test as you design an exam-preparation plan. Create a schedule that will give you time to review for the exam without waiting until the night before. Develop a to-do list of the major steps you need to take to be ready, and schedule review dates. Be sure that your schedule is flexible enough to allow for unexpected distractions or emergencies. If you are able to schedule your study sessions over several days, your mind will continue to process the information between study sessions, which will help you during the test. Be sure you have read and learned all the material one week before the exam. That way, you can use the week before the exam to review. In that final week, set aside several one-hour blocks for review, and make specific notes on what you plan to do during each hour. Also, let your friends and family know when you have important exams coming up and how that will affect your time with them.

Use Online Quizzing. Many textbooks have related websites that offer a number of study tools such as flash cards, videos, or online quizzing. Ask your instructors about these sites, and also check the preface of your textbooks for information on accessing these sites. You might also use Google to find them.

Join a Study Group. As mentioned in previous chapters, joining a study group is one of the best ways to prepare for exams. Group members can share different views of the most important topics to review, quiz one another on facts and concepts, and gain support from other serious students. Some instructors will provide time in class for the formation of study groups, or you might choose to approach classmates on your own. You can always ask your instructor, academic adviser, or the college's tutoring or learning center professionals to help you find other interested students and decide on guidelines for the group. Study groups can meet throughout the term, or they can just review for midterms or final exams. Group members should prepare questions or discussion points before the group meets. If your study group decides to meet just before exams, allow enough time to share notes and ideas.

⊙ *high-impact practice 3*

Talk to Other Students. Other students, especially those who have previously taken a course you are currently taking from the same instructor, may be able to give you a good idea of what to expect on tests and exams. If your college is small, you shouldn't have any trouble finding students who have taken the same courses you are taking now. If you're at a large college, your instructor may be able to suggest a former student who could serve as a tutor. But keep in mind that your instructors might decide to take a different approach in your class than they did in past classes.

Get a Tutor. Most colleges and universities offer free tutoring services. Ask your academic adviser, counselor, or college learning center staff members about arranging for tutoring. Keep in mind that some of the

Strength in Numbers
Study groups can meet anytime, but studying and reviewing with others in your class can be most helpful just before and just after a test or exam.

PeopleImages/E+/Getty Images

best students seek out tutoring, not just students who are struggling. Most students who receive tutoring are successful in their courses. Many learning centers employ student tutors who have done well in the same courses you are taking. These students might have some good advice on how to prepare for tests given by particular instructors. If you earn good grades in a specific course, you could eventually become a tutor and be paid for your services. Serving as a tutor also deepens your own learning and helps you become more successful in your major.

Prepare for Math and Science Exams

Math and science exams often require additional—and sometimes different—preparation techniques. Here are some suggestions for doing well on these exams:

- Do your homework regularly even if it is not graded, and do all the assigned problems. As you do your homework, write out your work as carefully and clearly as you will be expected to on your tests. This practice will allow you to use your homework as a review for the test. Figure 9.2 shows a page from a textbook with practice problems.
- Attend each class, always be on time, and stay for the entire class. Many instructors use the first few minutes of class to review homework, and others may end the class by telling you what will be on the test.
- Build a review guide throughout the term. As you begin your homework each day, write out a problem from each homework section in a notebook that you use solely to review material for that course. Then when you need to review for your exam, you can come back to this notebook to make sure you have a representative problem from each section you've studied.
- Throughout the term, keep a list of definitions or important formulas and put them on flash cards. Review several of them as part of every study session. Another technique is to post the formulas and definitions in your living space—on the bathroom wall, around your computer work area, or on the door of the microwave. Seeing this information frequently will help you keep it in your mind.

If these strategies don't seem to help you, ask a tutor to give you a few practice exams so you can review your responses together.

Prepare Physically

Keeping your body healthy is another key part of preparing yourself for quizzes, tests, and exams. The following strategies will help you prepare physically:

- **Maintain your regular sleep routine.** To do well on exams, you will need to be alert so that you can think clearly, and you are more likely to be alert when you are well rested. Last-minute, late-night cramming does not allow you to get sufficient sleep, so it isn't an effective study strategy. Most students need seven to eight hours of sleep the night before the exam.

- **Follow your regular exercise program.** Exercise is a positive way to relieve stress and to give yourself a much-needed break from long hours of studying.

- **Eat right.** Eat a light breakfast before a morning exam, and avoid greasy or acidic foods that might upset your stomach. Limit the amount of caffeinated beverages you drink on exam day because caffeine can make you jittery. Choose fruits, vegetables, and other foods that are high in energy-rich complex carbohydrates. Avoid eating sweets before an exam; the immediate energy boost they create can be quickly followed by a loss of energy and alertness. Ask the instructor whether you may bring a bottle of water with you to the exam.

FIGURE 9.2 › Solving Practice Problems

Completing plenty of practice problems, like the ones shown here, is a great way to study for math and science classes. So try your hand at all the problems provided in your textbook—even those that your instructor hasn't assigned—and check out websites offering such problems.

Source: Excerpt from page 315, COMAP, *For All Practical Purposes: Mathematical Literacy in Today's World*, 9th ed. Copyright © 2013 by W. H. Freeman. Used by permission.

(c) What is the probability that a randomly chosen household will have a total income less than $50,000?

(d) What is the probability that a randomly chosen household will have a total income less than $100,000?

(e) Suppose two U.S. households were randomly selected. What is the probability that both households will have a total income less than $100,000?

28. Role-playing games like Dungeons & Dragons use many different types of dice. One type of die has a tetrahedral (pyramidal) shape with four triangular faces (see Figure 8.27). Each triangular face has a number (1, 2, 3, or 4) next to each of its edges. Because the top of this die is not a face but a point, the way to read it is by the number at the top of the face that is visible when the die comes to rest. Suppose that the intelligence of a character is determined by rolling this four-sided die twice and adding 1 to the sum of the results.

Figure 8.27 Rolling a pair of tetrahedral dice: red = 1 and green = 3; intelligence of character = 4 + 1 = 5, for Exercise 28.

30. How do rented housing units differ from units occupied by their owners? Here are probability models for the number of rooms for owner-occupied units and renter-occupied units, according to the Census Bureau:

# of Rooms	1	2	3	4	5
Owned	0.000	0.001	0.014	0.099	0.238
Rented	0.011	0.027	0.229	0.348	0.224
# of Rooms	6	7	8	9	10
Owned	0.266	0.178	0.107	0.050	0.047
Rented	0.105	0.035	0.012	0.004	0.005

Make probability histograms of these two models, using the same scale. What are the most important differences between the models for owner-occupied and rented housing units?

31. In each of the following situations, state whether or not the given assignment of probabilities to individual outcomes is legitimate—that is, satisfies the rules of probability. If not, give specific reasons for your answer.

(a) Choose a college student at random and record gender and enrollment status: P(full-time female) = 0.56, P(part-time female) = 0.24, P(full-time male) = 0.44, P(part-time male) = 0.17.

Prepare Emotionally

Just as physical preparation is important, so is preparing your attitude and your emotions. You'll benefit by paying attention to the following ideas:

- **Know the material.** If you have given yourself enough time to review, you will enter the classroom confident that you are in control. Study by testing yourself or quizzing others in a study group so that you will be sure you really know the information.
- **Practice relaxing.** Some students experience test anxiety, which can lead to upset stomachs, sweaty palms, racing hearts, and other unpleasant physical symptoms. The section on test anxiety later in this chapter includes an anxiety quiz; if that quiz reveals that test anxiety is a problem for you, consult your counseling center about relaxation techniques. Some campus learning centers also provide workshops on reducing test anxiety.
- **Use positive self-talk.** Instead of telling yourself, "I never do well on math tests" or "I'll never be able to learn all the information for my history essay exam," make positive statements, such as "I have always attended class, done my homework, and passed the quizzes. Now I'm ready to do well on the test!"

---

your turn   Setting Goals

On Track or Wandering?

When you announced your decision to go to college, family, friends, and teachers may have asked you repeatedly about your goals. Some students can state educational, career, and life goals clearly, but others are just looking to make the most of college now and focus on the future later. What are the advantages or disadvantages of either approach? Do you already have a plan for what you want to do after college? Why or why not?

TIPS FOR TEST TAKING

Throughout your college career, you will take tests in many different formats, in many subject areas, and with many different types of questions. It may surprise you to find that your first-year tests are likely to be more challenging than those in later years because, as a new student, you are still developing your college test-taking skills. The following test-taking tips apply to any test situation.

1. **Write your name on the test.** Usually you will have to write your name on a test booklet or answer sheet. Some instructors, however, may require you to fill in your student ID number.
2. **Look over the whole test and stay calm.** Carefully read all the directions before beginning the test so that you understand what

to do. Ask the instructor or exam monitor for clarification if you don't understand something. Be confident. Don't panic. Answer one question at a time.

3. **Make the best use of your time.** Quickly review the entire test and decide how much time you will spend on each section. Be aware of the point values of different sections of the test. If some questions are worth more points than others, you need to spend more of your time answering them.

4. **Jot down idea starters before the test.** Check with your instructor ahead of time to be sure that it is OK to write some last-minute notes on the test or on scrap paper. If so, then before you even look at the test questions, turn the test paper over and take a moment to write down the formulas, definitions, or major ideas you have been studying. This will help you go into the test with confidence and knowledge, and your notes will provide quick access to the information you may need throughout the test.

5. **Answer the easy questions first.** Expect that you won't completely understand some questions. Make a note to come back to them later. If different sections have different types of questions (such as multiple-choice, short-answer, and essay questions), first finish the types of questions that are easiest for you to answer. Be sure to leave enough time for any essays.

6. **If you feel yourself starting to panic or go blank, stop whatever you are doing.** Take a deep breath, and remind yourself that you will be OK and you do know the material and can do well on this test. If necessary, go to another section of the test and come back later to the item that triggered your anxiety.

7. **Try to answer each question, even if you can only provide a partial answer.** You may not be able to answer all the questions fully; provide as much information as you can remember. Particularly for math and science test questions, you may get some credit for writing down equations and descriptions of how to solve the problems even if you cannot fully work them out or if you run out of time before you finish them.

8. **If you finish early, don't leave immediately.** Stay and check your work for errors. Reread the directions one last time.

TYPES OF TESTS

While you are in college, you will take many different types of tests. Some may be used in specific subjects such as English or math; others can be used in any class you might take. This section discusses the different test types and presents helpful tips for succeeding on each one.

Problem-Solving Tests

In science, mathematics, engineering, and statistics courses, some tests will require you to solve problems and show all the steps that led to the solution. Even if you know a shortcut, it is important to document how you got from step A to step B. For these tests, you must also be careful to avoid errors in your scientific notation. A misplaced sign, parenthesis, or bracket can make all the difference.

If you are allowed to use a calculator during the exam, it is important to check that your input is accurate. The calculator does what you tell it to, and if you miss a zero or a negative sign, the calculator will not give you the correct answer to the problem.

Read all directions carefully. Whenever possible, after you complete the problem, work it in reverse to check your solution. Also check to make sure that your solution makes sense. You can't have negative bushels of apples, for example, or a fraction of a person, or a correlation less than negative 1 or greater than 1.

Machine-Scored Tests

For some tests, you may have to enter your answers on a Scantron form. The instructor will feed those forms into a machine that scans the answers and prints out your score. When taking any test, especially a machine-scored test, carefully follow the directions. In addition to your name, be sure to provide all other necessary information on the answer sheet. Each time you fill in an answer, make sure that the number on the answer sheet corresponds to the number of the item on the test.

Although scoring machines have become more sophisticated over time, they might still misread stray marks or incomplete bubbles on your answer sheet. When a machine-scored test is returned to you, check your answer sheet against the scoring key, if one is provided, to make sure that you received credit for all the questions you answered correctly.

Example of a Scantron Answer Sheet

Each time you fill in a Scantron answer sheet, make sure that the number on the answer sheet corresponds to the number of the item on the test, and make sure that all bubbles are filled in completely.

Vixit/Shutterstock

Computerized Tests

Computerized tests are often taken in a computer lab or testing center and are usually *not* administered online. (Read this chapter's Tech Tip about *online* tests.) Computerized tests and test questions can be significantly different from one another depending on the kind of test, the academic subject, and whether the test was written by the instructor, a textbook company, or another source. Be sure to take advantage of any practice test opportunities to get a better sense of what these tests and test questions will be like. Often they are timed, as is the case with most computerized placement tests. The more experience you have with computerized tests, the more comfortable you will be taking them, which is true with the other test types.

Some multiple-choice computerized tests allow you to scroll through all the questions, while others only allow you to see one question at a time. Some computerized tests might not allow you to return to questions you've already completed to double-check your answers.

For computerized tests in math and other subjects that require you to solve problems, be sure to check each answer before you submit it. Also, know in advance whether you are allowed to use additional materials, such as a calculator or scratch paper, for working the problems.

Laboratory Tests

In many science courses, you will have laboratory tests that require you to move from one lab station to the next to solve problems, identify parts of models or specimens, or explain chemical reactions. To prepare for lab tests, always attend your labs, take good notes, and study your lab notebook carefully before the test.

You might also have lab tests in foreign language courses that can include both oral and written sections. Work with a partner or study group to prepare for oral exams. Have group members ask one another questions that require the use of key vocabulary words.

Open-Book and Open-Notes Tests

Although you may like the idea of being able to refer to your book or notes during an exam, open-book and open-note tests are usually harder than other tests, not easier. You won't really have time to read whole passages during an open-book exam. Study as completely as you would for any other test, and do not be fooled into thinking that you don't need to know the material. The best way to prepare for an open-book test is to study as you would for any other test. But as you prepare, you can develop a list of topics and the page numbers where they are covered in your text or in your lecture notes. Type a three-column grid (or use an Excel spreadsheet) with your list of topics in alphabetical order in the first column and corresponding pages from your textbook and lecture notebook in the second and third columns so that you can refer to them quickly when necessary.

During the test, keep an eye on the time. Don't waste time looking up information in your text or notes if you are sure of your answers. Instead, wait until you have finished the test, and then, if you have extra time, go back and look up answers and make any necessary changes.

techtip

CONQUER ONLINE TESTS

The Problem

You don't know how to take an online test—a test that is administered online.

The Fix

Avoid rookie errors that can trip you up, and apply effective techniques you use when taking other tests.

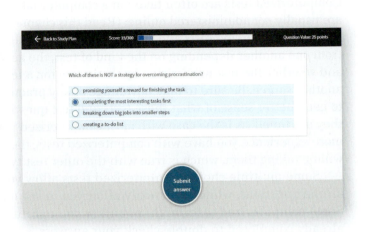

How to Do It

1. **Don't rely strictly on your notes.** Many instructors will allow you to reference your notes when taking an online test, but open-book online tests can take longer than normal tests if you're not sure where to locate the information you need. When you prepare, study like you would for a normal, in-class, timed test; your notes and books should be for occasional reference only.

2. **Resist the temptation to look online for the answers.** The answer you find might not be what your instructor is looking for. It's much better to check your notes to see what you were taught in class.

3. **Collaborate if it is allowed.** If your instructor allows collaboration on tests, open up an instant message window with a fellow student. Take the test together, and take it early.

4. **Stay focused.** When you're taking an online test, it's easy to fall prey to real-life diversions like Twitter, Netflix, or a sudden urge to rearrange your closet. Whatever you do, take the test seriously. Go somewhere quiet where you can concentrate—not Starbucks. A quiet, remote spot in the library is ideal. You might also try wearing noise-canceling headphones.

5. **Practice using the test interface.** Ask your instructor if you can practice with a "zero-point" quiz so you can familiarize yourself with the testing site and the question setup. You don't want to be nervous about how the site works

while you are answering questions on a test that will affect your grade.

6. **Ask about special rules.** Online tests can be set up differently than regular tests. For example, some online tests won't let you change your answer once you hit "submit," and others might have time limits for how long you can spend on each question. Some online tests will let you skip around, provided you finish the test in a certain amount of time. Be sure to ask your instructor what you can expect.

7. **Plan for an intermittent connection.** There's always the risk of losing your internet connection in the middle of the test. To be on the safe side, type your answers and essays into a Word document. Then leave time at the end of the test session to cut and paste them into the test itself.

8. **Use all the time allotted.** If you finish early, take a few minutes to check your answers and spelling carefully. (That's good advice for traditional tests, too.)

EXTRA STYLE POINTS: Use study guides or a study session from each class to create your own online practice test. If you use Google Drive, you can create a file called a "form," which allows you to create a test, quiz, or survey that you can use with your study group. Everyone in the group can use it at times that are convenient for them, rather than only when the group can get together.

Take-Home Tests

Some instructors may allow you to take tests outside class and refer to your textbook, notes, and other resources. Take-home tests are usually more difficult than in-class tests. Read the directions and questions as soon as you receive the test to help you estimate how much time you will need to complete it. Remember that your instructor will expect your essay answers to look more like out-of-class papers—proofread and edited—than like the essays you would write during an in-class test.

It is probably no surprise that issues of academic honesty can arise for take-home tests. If you usually work with a study group or in a learning community for the course, check with the instructor in advance to determine if any type of group work is allowed on the test.

TYPES OF QUESTIONS

Your instructors choose not only what types of exams they give you but also what types of questions to include on the test so you can demonstrate what you are learning in the course. You may take an exam that has one type of question or multiple types of questions. This section includes strategies to help you answer different types of questions successfully.

Essay Questions

Essay questions require students to write a few paragraphs in response to each question. Many college instructors have a strong preference for essay questions for a simple reason: They require deeper thinking than other types of questions. Generally, advanced courses are more likely to include essay exams. To be successful on essay exams, follow these guidelines:

1. **Budget your exam time.** Quickly go over the entire exam, and note the questions that are the easiest for you to answer. Estimate the approximate amount of time you should spend on each essay question based on its point value. Remember, writing long answers to questions that have low point values can be a mistake because it takes up precious time you might need to answer questions that count more toward your total grade. Be sure you know whether you must answer all the questions or if you should choose which questions to answer. Wear a watch so that you can monitor your time, and don't forget to leave a few minutes to review and proofread your essay.

2. **Actively read the whole question.** Many well-prepared students write good answers to questions that were not asked, or write good answers to only part of the question. When that happens, they may lose points or even fail the exam.

3. **Develop a brief outline of your answer before you begin to write.** Make sure that your outline responds to all parts of the question. Use your first paragraph to introduce the main points; use the other paragraphs to describe each point in more depth. If you begin to lose

your concentration, you will be glad to have the outline to help you regain your focus. If you find that you are running out of time and cannot complete an essay question, provide an outline of key ideas at the very least. Instructors usually assign points on the basis of your coverage of the main topics from the material. That means you will usually earn more points by responding briefly to all parts of the question than by addressing just one part of the question in detail. You might receive some credit for your outline even if you cannot finish the essay.

4. **Write concise, organized answers.** Some students answer essay questions by quickly writing down everything they know on the topic. Long answers are not necessarily good answers. Answers that are too general, unfocused, or disorganized may not earn high scores.

5. **Know the key task words in essay questions.** Being familiar with key task words that appear in an essay question will help you frame your answer more specifically. Table 9.1 lists common key task words. If your instructor allows you to do so, consider circling or underlining key words in the question so that you are sure of how to organize your answer.

TABLE 9.1 ❯ Key Task Words in Essay Questions

Analyze	Break the whole topic into parts to explain it better; show how the parts work together to produce the overall pattern.
Compare	Identify similarities in ideas, events, or objects. Don't just describe the elements; state how they are alike.
Contrast	Identify the differences between ideas, events, or objects. Don't just describe the ideas; state how they are different.
Criticize/Critique	Judge something; give your opinion. Criticism can be positive, negative, or mixed. A critique should generally include your own judgments (supported by evidence) and those of experts who agree with you.
Define	Give the meaning of a word or expression.
Describe	Give more information about a topic.
Discuss	Give broad statements backed up by detailed information. Discussion often includes identifying the important questions related to an issue and trying to answer these questions.
Evaluate	Discuss the strengths and weaknesses of an idea or a position. When you evaluate, you stress the idea of how well something meets a certain standard.
Explain	Clarify a statement. Explanations generally focus on why or how something has come about.
Justify	Argue in support of a decision or conclusion by showing evidence or reasons that support the argument. Try to support your argument with both logical and concrete examples.
Narrate	Relate a series of events in the order they occurred, as you do when you tell a story.
Outline	Present a series of main points in order. Some instructors want a formal outline with numbers and letters.
Summarize	Give information in brief form, without examples and details. A summary is short but covers all the important points.

Multiple-Choice Questions

Multiple-choice questions provide a number of possible answers, often between three and five. The answer choices are usually numbered (1, 2, 3, 4, . . .) or lettered (a, b, c, d, . . .), and the test taker is supposed to select the correct or the best one. Preparing for multiple-choice tests requires you to actively review all of the material that has been covered for a specific period, such as a week or a month. Reviewing flash cards, summary sheets, mind maps, or the recall column in your lecture notes is a good way to review large amounts of material efficiently.

Look for particular cues and quirks that multiple-choice questions include. Take extra care when choosing the answer to questions that contain words such as *not, except, all*, and *but*. Also read each answer choice carefully; be suspicious of choices that use words such as *always, never*, and *only*. These choices are often (but not always) incorrect. Often the correct answer is the option that is the most comprehensive.

In some multiple-choice questions, the first part of the question is an incomplete sentence called the stem, and the answer choices complete the sentence. In these questions, any answer choices that do not fit the grammar of the stem correctly are usually wrong. For example, in Figure 9.3, "Margaret Mead was an" is the stem. Which of the four answer options does not grammatically fit the stem, and can therefore be ruled out?

FIGURE 9.3 > Example of a Multiple-Choice Question

Name __Jack Brown_____ Date __9/23/20____

Examination 1

1. Margaret Mead was an
   a. psychologist
   b. anthropologist
   c. environmental scientist
   d. astronomer

To avoid becoming confused by answer choices that sound alike, predict your own answer to the question before reading the options. Then choose the answer that best matches your prediction.

If you are totally confused by a question, place a check mark in the margin and come back to it later. Sometimes a question later in the exam may provide a clue to the answer of the question you are unsure about. If you have absolutely no idea, look for an answer that at least has some pieces of information. If there is no penalty for guessing, fill in an answer for every question, even if it is just a guess. If there is a penalty for guessing, don't just choose an answer at random; leaving the answer blank might be a wiser choice. Finally, always go back, if you have time at the end, and double-check that you chose the right answer for the right question, especially if you are using a Scantron form.

high-impact practice 3

your turn   **Feeling Connected**

Is One Type of Exam Better than Another?

Many college instructors do not give essay exams in first-year courses, and instead use multiple-choice questions. With a small group of other students, discuss the kind of learning that multiple-choice exams measure and the kind of learning they miss. Which type of exam do students in the group prefer? Share your reactions and ideas with the whole class.

Fill-in-the-Blank Questions

Fill-in-the-blank questions consist of a phrase, sentence, or paragraph with a blank space indicating where the student should provide the missing word or words. In many ways, preparing to answer fill-in-the-blank questions is similar to getting ready to answer multiple-choice items, but fill-in-the-blank questions can be harder because you do not have a choice of possible answers right in front of you.

Not all fill-in-the-blank questions are written the same way. Sometimes the answers will consist of a single word; sometimes the instructor is looking for a phrase. There may be a series of blanks to give you a clue about the number of words in the answer, or there may be just one long blank. If you are unsure, ask the instructor whether the answer is supposed to be one word or more.

True/False Questions

True/False questions ask students to determine whether a statement is correct or not. Remember that for a statement to be true, every detail of the sentence must be correct. That is why questions containing words such as *always, never,* and *only* tend to be false, whereas less definite terms such as *often* and *frequently* suggest the statement might be true. Read through the entire exam to see whether information in one question will help you answer another. Do not begin to second-guess what you know or doubt your answers just because a sequence of questions appears to be all true or all false.

Matching Questions

Matching questions are set up with terms in one column and descriptions or definitions in the other, and you must match the proper term with its definition. Before matching any items, review all of the terms and descriptions. Then match the terms you are sure of. As you do so, cross out both the term and its description, and use the process of elimination to help you answer the remaining items. To prepare for matching questions, try using flash cards and lists that you create from the recall column in your notes.

OVERCOMING TEST ANXIETY

Test anxiety takes many different forms. Part of dealing with test anxiety is understanding why it happens and identifying its symptoms. Whatever the reason for test anxiety, you should know that it is common among college students.

Test anxiety has many causes. It can be the result of the pressure that students put on themselves to succeed. Some stress connected with taking exams is natural and can motivate you to perform better. However, when students put too much pressure on themselves or set unrealistic goals, the result can be stress that is no longer motivating. The expectations of parents, a spouse or partner, friends, and other people who are close to you can also create test anxiety.

Finally, some test anxiety is caused by lack of preparation. The awareness that you are not prepared, that you have fallen behind on assigned reading, homework, or other academic commitments, is usually the source of anxiety. Procrastination can also be a big problem because if you do poorly on the first test in a course, you will be under even more pressure to do well on other tests to pull up your course grade. This situation becomes even more difficult if the units of the course are cumulative—that is, if they build on one another, as in math and foreign languages—or if the final exam includes all the material that has been covered throughout the course.

Some test anxiety comes from a negative prior experience. Forgetting past failures can be a challenge; however, the past is not the present. If you carefully follow the strategies in this chapter, you are likely to do well on future tests. Remember that a little anxiety is OK, but if you find that anxiety is getting in the way of your performance on tests and exams, be sure to ask for help from your college counseling center.

Ace the Test—Any Type of Test

No matter what type of test you are taking, read each question carefully so that you have the best chance of selecting the right answer. And remember, when you take a machine-scored test, one of the simplest and most important steps you can take is to make sure you match the questions with your answer sheet numbers.

fStop Images GmbH/Alamy

Symptoms of Test Anxiety

Test anxiety can manifest itself in many ways. Some students feel it on the very first day of class. Other students begin showing symptoms of test anxiety when it's time to start studying for a test. Others do not get nervous until the night before the test or the morning of an exam day. And some students experience symptoms only while they are actually taking a test.

Symptoms of test anxiety can include:

- butterflies in the stomach
- queasiness
- nausea
- headaches
- an increased heart rate
- hyperventilation, which is unusually deep or rapid breathing as a result of anxiety
- shaking, sweating, or muscle cramps
- "going blank" during the exam and being unable to remember information

Test anxiety can undermine the success of any college student, no matter how intelligent, motivated, and prepared. That is why it is important to seek help from your college's counseling service or another professional if you think that you have severe test anxiety. If you are not sure where to go for help, ask your adviser or counselor, but seek help promptly! If your symptoms are so severe that you become physically ill (with headaches, hyperventilation, or vomiting), you should also consult your physician or campus health center.

Types of Test Anxiety

Students who experience test anxiety don't necessarily feel it in all testing situations. For example, you might do fine on classroom tests but feel anxious during standardized examinations such as a college placement test. One reason such standardized tests can create anxiety is that they can change your future. One way of dealing with this type of test anxiety is to ask yourself: What is the worst that can happen? Remember that no matter what the result, it is not the end of the world. How you do on standardized tests might limit some of your options, but going into these tests with a negative attitude will certainly not improve your chances for success.

Test anxiety can often be subject-specific. For example, some students have anxiety about taking math tests. It is important to understand the differences between anxiety that arises from the subject itself and general test anxiety. Perhaps subject-specific test anxiety relates to old beliefs about yourself, such as "I'm no good at math" or "I can't write well." Now is the time to try some positive self-talk and realize that by preparing well, you can be successful even in your hardest courses. If the problem continues, talk to a counselor to learn about strategies that can help you deal with such fears. Take the following test anxiety quiz to find out more about how you feel before taking tests.

Test Anxiety Quiz

Do you experience feelings of test anxiety? Read each of the following questions and consider your responses. If your answer to a question is "yes," place a check mark in the box. If your answer is "no," leave the box blank.

Mental

☐ Do you have trouble focusing and find that your mind easily wanders while studying the material or during the test itself?

☐ During the test, does every noise bother you—sounds from outside the classroom or sounds from other people?

☐ Do you often "blank out" when you see the test?

☐ Do you remember answers to questions only after the test is over?

Physical

☐ Do you get the feeling of butterflies, nausea, or pain in your stomach?

☐ Do you develop headaches before or during the test?

☐ Do you feel like your heart is racing, that you have trouble breathing, or that your pulse is irregular?

☐ Do you have difficulty sitting still, are you tense, or are you unable to get comfortable?

Emotional

☐ Are you more sensitive and more likely to lose patience with a roommate or friend before the test?

☐ Do you feel pressure to succeed, either from yourself or from your family or friends?

☐ Do you toss and turn the night before the test?

☐ Do you fear the worst—that you will fail the class or flunk out of college because of the test?

Personal Habits

☐ Do you often stay up late studying the night before a test?

☐ Do you have a personal history of failure in taking certain types of tests (essay, math, etc.)?

☐ Do you drink more than your usual amount of caffeine or forget to eat breakfast before a test?

☐ Do you avoid studying until right before a test, choosing to do other activities that are less important because you don't want to think about the test?

TEST ANXIETY REFLECTION SCORE

How many items did you check? Count your total, and then see what level of test anxiety you experience.

13–16 Severe: You may want to see if your college counseling center offers individual sessions to provide strategies for dealing with test anxiety. You have already paid for this service through your student fees, so if you have this level of anxiety, take advantage of help that is available for you.

9–12 Moderate: You may want to see if your counseling center offers a seminar on anxiety-prevention strategies. Such seminars are usually offered around midterms or just before final exams. Take the opportunity to do something valuable for yourself!

5–8 Mild: Be aware of what situations—whether it is certain types of classes or particular test formats—might cause anxiety and disrupt your academic success. If you discover a weakness, address it now before it is too late.

1–4 Slight: Almost everyone has some form of anxiety before tests, and it actually can be beneficial! In small doses, stress can improve your performance, so consider yourself lucky.

Strategies for Dealing with Test Anxiety

In addition to studying, eating right, and getting plenty of sleep, you can try a number of simple strategies to overcome the physical and emotional impact of test anxiety:

- **Breathe.** If at any point during a test you begin to feel nervous or you cannot think clearly, take a long, deep breath and slowly exhale to restore your breathing to a normal level.
- **Stretch.** Before you go into the test room, especially before a long final exam, stretch your muscles—legs, arms, shoulders, and neck—just as you would when preparing to exercise.
- **Sit in a relaxed position.** Pay attention to the way you are sitting. As you take the test, sit with your shoulders back and relaxed rather than hunched forward. Try not to clutch your pencil or pen tightly in your hand; take a break and stretch your fingers now and then.
- **Create positive mental messages.** Pay attention to the mental messages that you send yourself. If you are overly negative, turn those messages around. Give yourself encouraging, optimistic messages.
- **Keep your confidence high.** Do not allow others, including classmates, partners, children, parents, roommates, or friends, to reduce your confidence. If you belong to a study group, discuss strategies for relaxing and staying positive before and during tests.

Clear Your Head

Before a test or exam, it is a good idea to take a few minutes for some positive self-talk and a few deep breaths. Find a peaceful place to relax or visualize being in a peaceful setting.

Digital Vision/Getty Images

Getting the Test Back

Students react differently when they receive their test grades and papers. Some students dread seeing their test grades, but other students look forward to it. Either way, unless you look at your answers—the correct and incorrect ones—and the instructor's comments, you will have no way to evaluate your own knowledge and test-taking strengths. While checking over your graded test, you might also find that the instructor made a grading error that might have cost you a point or two. If that happens, you should let the instructor know.

Review your graded tests, because doing so will help you do better next time. You might find that your mistakes were the result of not following directions, being careless with words or numbers, or even thinking too hard about a multiple-choice question. Mistakes can help you learn, so refer to your textbook and notes to better understand the source and reason for each mistake. If you are a member of a study group, plan a test review with other group members; this allows you to learn from your mistakes and those of the others in the group.

If you have any questions about your grade, that is an excellent reason to visit your instructor during office hours or before or after class; your concern will show the instructor that you want to succeed. When discussing the exam with your instructor, you might be able to negotiate a few points in your favor. Avoid making demands, though, and always be respectful.

Above all, don't let a bad test grade get you down. One characteristic that differentiates successful students from unsuccessful ones is resilience—that is, whether they can bounce back from a disappointing grade or performance. Almost every college student has experienced disappointment—perhaps on a test or paper, the athletic field, or in music or dance. Don't run from a bad grade; learn from it. Review the mistakes you made, and talk with your instructor about what you misunderstood and how you can improve your performance on the next graded activity.

---

yourturn | **Write and Reflect**

🎯 *high-impact practice 2*

What Advice Would You Give?

What do you do when an instructor returns an exam to you? Do you just look at the grade, or do you review the items you answered correctly and incorrectly? Write a one- or two-page paper in which you describe to new first-year students what steps they should take after receiving an exam back from an instructor—an exam on which they earned either a very good or very poor grade. Write persuasively, and then share your position verbally with a few other students in your class.

Bouncing Back from a Bad Grade

You bombed a test, and now you are feeling hopeless and unsure about how to do better. First, know that a bad grade is not the end of the world. Almost every student performs poorly at some point in college. Don't let one D or F get you down. Use the opportunity to build your resilience—to become stronger and show your tough spirit. One way to bounce back from disappointment is to take control of the situation. Talk to the course instructor, work to understand what went wrong, and develop a strategy for improvement. That strategy might be finding a tutor, meeting on a regular basis with your instructor, or working with a learning center professional who can help you improve your skills in reading, studying, remembering, and preparing for tests. Your college success instructor can help you decide what first steps you need to take to improve your academic performance.

CHEATING

Imagine what our world would be like if researchers reported fake results that were then used to develop new machines or medical treatments, or to build bridges, airplanes, or subway systems. Fortunately, few researchers falsify their findings; most follow the rules of academic honesty. That honesty is a foundation of higher education, and activities that jeopardize it can damage everyone: your country, your community, your college or university, your classmates, and yourself.

What Is Cheating?

Different colleges define *cheating* in different ways. Some include the following activities in their definition of cheating: looking over a classmate's shoulder for an answer, using a calculator when it is not permitted, obtaining or discussing an exam or individual questions from an exam without permission, copying someone else's lab notes, purchasing term papers over the internet, watching the video instead of reading the book, and copying computer files. Whatever your college's rules about cheating, it's essential that you follow them.

Many schools do not allow certain activities, in addition to lying or cheating. Here are some examples of prohibited behaviors:

- intentionally inventing information or results
- submitting the same piece of academic work, such as a research paper, for credit in more than one course
- giving your exam answers to another student to copy during an exam or before that exam is given to another class

- bribing anyone in exchange for any kind of academic advantage
- helping or trying to help another student commit a dishonest act

Why Students Cheat and the Consequences of Cheating

Students mainly cheat when they believe they cannot do well on their own. Some college students developed a habit of cheating in high school or even earlier, and do not trust their own ability to succeed in classes. Other students simply don't know the rules. For example, some students incorrectly think that buying a term paper isn't cheating. Some think that using a test file (a collection of actual tests from previous terms) is fair behavior.

Cultural and college differences may cause some students to cheat. In other countries and at some U.S. colleges, students are encouraged to review past exams as practice exercises. Some student government associations or student social organizations maintain test files for use by students. Some colleges permit sharing answers and information for homework and other assignments with friends. Make sure you know the policy at your college.

Pressure from others—family, peers, and instructors—might cause some students to consider cheating. And there is no doubt that we live in a competitive society, where winning can trump all other values. But in truth, grades are nothing if you cheat to earn them. Even if your grades help you get a job, it is what you have actually learned that will help you keep that job and be promoted. If you haven't learned what you need to know, you won't be ready to work in your chosen field.

Sometimes lack of preparation will cause students to cheat. Perhaps they tell themselves that they aren't really dishonest and that cheating "just one time" won't matter. But if you cheat one time, you're more likely to do it again.

Stop! Thief!

When students sit close to each other while taking a test, they may be tempted to let their eyes wander to someone else's answers. Don't let this happen to you. Cheating is the same as stealing. Also, don't offer to share your work or make it easy for other students to copy your work. Reduce temptation by covering your answer sheet.

Lucky Business/Shutterstock

Cheating in college is not uncommon, and researchers have found that first-year students are more likely to cheat than other students are. Although you might see some students who seem to be getting away with cheating, such behaviors can have severe and life-changing results. In some cases, students who have cheated on exams have been suspended or expelled, and graduates have had their college degrees revoked.

Here are some steps you can take to reduce the likelihood of problems with academic honesty.

1. **Know the rules.** Learn the academic code for your college by going to its website or checking the student handbook.
2. **Set clear boundaries.** Refuse when others ask you to help them cheat. This might be hard to do, but you must say no. Leave your cell phone in your book bag; instructors are often suspicious when they see students looking at their cell phones during an exam.
3. **Improve time management.** Be well prepared for all quizzes, exams, projects, and papers.
4. **Seek help.** Find out where you can get help with study skills, time management, and test taking. If your skills are in good shape but the content of the course is too hard, consult your instructor, join a study group, or visit your campus learning center or tutorial service.
5. **Withdraw from the course.** You might decide to drop a course that's giving you trouble. Your college has a policy about dropping courses and a deadline to drop without penalty. Some students choose to withdraw from all classes and take time off before returning to college if they find themselves in over their heads or if a long illness, a family crisis, or something else has caused them to fall behind. But before withdrawing, you should ask about college policies in terms of financial aid and other scholarship programs. See your adviser or counselor before you decide to withdraw.
6. **Reexamine goals.** Stick to your own realistic goals instead of giving in to pressure from family members or friends to achieve impossibly high standards. You might also feel pressure to enter a particular career or profession that doesn't interest you. If that happens, sit down with counseling or career services professionals or your academic adviser and explore your options.

---

your turn   Making Decisions

Understand Academic Integrity

Sometimes students are confused about what constitutes dishonest behavior in their college classrooms. There are some actions that are on the line between cheating and being honest. Do you think it is acceptable to get answers from another student who took an exam you're about to take earlier in the term or in a prior term? What do you believe your instructors think? If you're not sure, ask your instructors how they view such behavior.

checklist for success

Test Taking

- [ ] **Learn as much as you can about the type of test you will be taking.** You will study differently for an essay exam than you will for a multiple-choice test.

- [ ] **Realize that you started preparing for test taking the very first day of the course.** Make the most of the first class sessions of the term—they are the most important ones *not* to miss. If you skip class, you are behind on your test preparation from day one.

- [ ] **Prepare yourself physically through proper sleep, diet, and exercise.** These behaviors are as important as studying the actual material. You may not control what is on the exams, but you can control your physical readiness to do your best.

- [ ] **Prepare yourself emotionally by being relaxed and confident.** Confidence comes from the knowledge that you have prepared well and know the material.

- [ ] **If you experience moderate to severe test anxiety, seek help from your counseling center.** Professionals can help you deal with this problem.

- [ ] **Develop a systematic plan of preparation for every test.** Be specific about when you are going to study, for how long, and what material you will cover.

- [ ] **Join a study group and participate conscientiously and regularly.** Students who join study groups perform better on tests. It's a habit you should practice.

- [ ] **Never cheat or plagiarize.** Experience the satisfaction that comes from learning and doing your own work and from knowing that you don't have to worry about getting caught or using material that may be incorrect.

- [ ] **Make sure that you understand what constitutes cheating and plagiarism on your campus so that you don't inadvertently do either.** If you are not clear about policies, ask your instructors or the professionals in your campus learning center or writing center.

REFLECT ON CHOICES

high-impact practice 2 Test taking is an inevitable part of college life. But you can choose how you are going to prepare for tests, deal with any test anxiety you might feel, and pay attention to your grades and instructor feedback. Reflect on your biggest problem in taking tests. Is it with certain types of tests or all of them? Is it related to certain subjects or any subject? Write a brief summary of strategies you have learned in this chapter to deal with this problem.

APPLY WHAT YOU HAVE LEARNED

Now that you have read and discussed this chapter, consider how you can apply what you have learned to your academic and personal life. The following prompts will help you reflect on the chapter material and its relevance to you both now and in the future.

1. Identify your next upcoming test or exam. What time of day is it scheduled, and what type of test will it be? What strategies have you read about in this chapter that will help you prepare for and take this test?

2. Is there one course you are taking this term that you find especially difficult? If you are anxious about taking tests in that class, adopt a positive self-message to help you stay focused. It could be a favorite quote or even something as simple as "I know I can do it!"

USE YOUR RESOURCES

› **Learning Center** Before you take your first tests, locate your campus's learning center. Almost every campus has one, and helping students study for tests is one of its specialties. The best students, good students who want to be the best students, and students with academic difficulties use learning centers and tutoring services. These services are offered by both full-time professionals and highly skilled student tutors, and they are usually free. Students with learning disabilities can also qualify for certain accommodations to help them do better on tests. Check with disability services on your campus for more information about accommodations. If you are an online student, there may be a special learning center that focuses on helping you do your best in online courses.

› **Counseling Services** College and university counseling centers offer a wide array of services, including workshops and individual or group counseling for test anxiety. Sometimes these services are also offered by the campus health center. Ask your first-year seminar instructor where you can find counseling services on your campus.

› **Fellow College Students and Peer Leaders** Often the best help we can get is the closest to us. Keep an eye out in your classes, residence hall, and extracurricular activities for the best students, those who appear to be the most serious, purposeful, and directed. Find a tutor. Join a study group. Talk with your peer leader. Students who do these things are much more likely to be successful than those who do not.

› **College and University Exam Preparation Resources** Helpful exam preparation resources are available from many institutions. For instance, Florida Atlantic University's Center for Learning and Student Success (CLASS) offers a list of tips to help you prepare for exams: http://www .fau.edu/class/success/test%20tips.jpg. The State University of New York offers some excellent strategies for exam preparation: **blog.suny.edu/2013/12/scientifically-the-best -ways-to-prepare-for-final-exams**. And here is some exam preparation advice from the University of Leicester in England: **www2 .le.ac.uk/offices/healthy-living-for-students /preparation-for-exams**.

LaunchPad
macmillan learning

LaunchPad for *Your College Experience* is a great resource. Go online to master concepts using the LearningCurve study tool and much more. **Launchpadworks.com**

Hill Street Studios/Getty Images

10

INFORMATION LITERACY AND COMMUNICATION

YOU WILL EXPLORE

What it means to be information literate

How to choose a topic, narrow it down, and research it

How to use your college or university library and get help from librarians

Strategies for evaluating sources

How to move from research to writing and effectively use all steps in the writing process

Guidelines for effective public speaking

⌖ High-impact practices 2 (writing) and 3 (collaboration)

> ## " Start researching the topic you will be writing about as soon as possible. "

When Analee was looking into going to college, she found that a nearby state university had everything she wanted: affordability, online courses, and a variety of student clubs and activities. The college also has a good library that allows her to conduct research and write papers while on campus.

Analee grew up in a small town in Puerto Rico where she attended high school, completed a certificate program in medical office billing and coding, and then worked for a few years. When she decided that she wanted to change careers, she realized a degree in criminal justice was just what she needed. "I intend to join a law enforcement agency," she says. "My goal is to join the FBI as a behavior analyst."

Now that she is in college, Analee has had to develop a number of strategies to help her write well-researched papers that are very different from those she wrote in high school. "In high school, they didn't emphasize how important it was to include your opinions," she says. "In college, they want you to research your work, cite as many sources as you can, think about your topic, and form opinions. It is very different for me." She tells us that her best strategy is to start early and prepare to write, rewrite, and edit the same material a few times before handing it in for a grade. "Start researching the topic you will be writing about as soon as possible," she advises. "Every day, look for more data and take additional notes. That way you can prevent procrastination and reduce your stress when it's time to put the research together on the paper."

Analee does most of her research online, where information is at her fingertips. She is careful about checking the validity of material she finds on the web, especially on sites like Wikipedia. "I use Wikipedia and other online encyclopedias to start learning about a topic," she explains, "but I rely on other sources for writing my paper and carefully check any information I pull from the web to ensure accuracy." She can access the databases she needs from her laptop or at the library.

LaunchPad
macmillan learning

To access the LearningCurve study tool, video activities, and more, go to LaunchPad for *Your College Experience.*
Launchpadworks.com

As Analee's story illustrates, developing the skills to locate and use information will increase your ability to keep up with what is going on in the world, participate in activities that interest you, and succeed in college, career, and community. The research skills you learn and use as a student will serve you well as a successful professional in whatever career you choose. Whether you're a student of nursing, political science, or business, one of your main tasks in college is to manage information. In a few years, as a nurse, lawyer, or accountant, one of your main tasks will be the same: to manage and present information for your employers and clients. All colleges and many companies provide libraries for this purpose.

Finding information and using it involves more than operating a computer or browsing the bookshelves. To make sense of the enormous

assess your strengths

Information literacy, writing, and speaking are among the most important skills you will learn in college. Success in your career will also depend on your ability to communicate clearly and think critically about information. As you read this chapter, think about your experiences in communicating and working with information successfully.

set goals

What are your most important objectives in learning the material in this chapter? How can you improve your information-literacy and communication skills? Develop some strategies in this area such as taking advantage of working with staff at the writing center to get feedback on the papers you'll write this term, or becoming familiar with library resources that relate to your classes.

amount of information at your fingertips in a reasonable amount of time, you'll need to develop a few key research and information-literacy skills.

INFORMATION LITERACY

Information literacy is the ability to find, interpret, and use information to meet your needs. It includes computer literacy, media literacy, and cultural literacy:

- **Computer literacy** is the ability to use electronic tools to conduct searches and to communicate and present to others the information you have found and analyzed. This ability involves using different computer programs, digital video and audio tools, and social media.
- **Media literacy** is the ability to think deeply about what you see and read through both the content and context of television, film, advertising, radio, magazines, books, and the internet.
- **Cultural literacy** is understanding and being able to participate in the world around you. You have to understand the difference between the American Civil War and the Revolutionary War, U2 and YouTube, and Eminem and M&Ms so that you can keep up with everyday conversation and with your college reading material.

Information matters. It helps people make good choices. The choices people make often determine their success in careers, their happiness as friends and family members, and their well-being as citizens of our planet.

your turn	Feeling Connected

high-impact practice 3

Information Literacy—A Survival Skill?

Brainstorm with a group of classmates and make a list of the components of "information literacy." How many separate components did your group identify? This chapter asserts that information literacy is the premier survival skill for the modern world. Does your group agree? Why or why not? Share your group's ideas with others in the class.

Stay Connected

In today's world, information literacy is one of the most important skills a person can have. This means developing computer, media, and cultural literacy, along with learning how to find, interpret, and use the information you need.

Hero Images/Getty Images

Learning to Be Information Literate

People are amazed at the amount of information available to them everywhere, especially online. Many think that because they checked out some links they found on a search engine, they are informed or can easily become informed. Most of us, though, are unprepared for the number of available sources and the amount of information we can find at the press of a button. What can we do about information overload? To become an informed and successful user of information, keep three basic goals in mind.

1. **Know how to find the information you need.** Once you have figured out where to look for information, you'll need to ask good questions and learn how to search information systems, such as the internet, libraries, and databases. You'll also want to get to know your college librarians, who can help you ask questions, decide what sources you need to investigate, and find the information you need.

2. **Learn how to interpret the information you find.** It is important to find information, but it is even more important to make sense of that information. What does the information mean? Have you selected a source you can understand? Is the information correct? Can the source be trusted?

3. **Have a purpose for collecting information, and then do something with it once you have it.** Even the best information won't do much good if you don't know what to do with it. True, sometimes you'll hunt down a fact simply to satisfy your own curiosity, but more often, you'll communicate what you've learned to someone else. First you should decide how to put your findings into an appropriate format, such as a research paper for a class or a presentation at a meeting. Then you need to decide what you want to accomplish. Will you use the information to make a decision, solve a problem, share an idea, prove a point, or something else?

In this chapter, we'll explore ways to work toward each of these goals.

What's Research—and What's Not?

In the past, you might have completed assignments that required you to find a book, journal article, or web page related to a particular topic. While finding information is an essential part of research, it's just one step, not the end of the road. Research is not just copying a paragraph from a book or putting together bits and pieces of information without adding any of your own comments. In fact, such behavior could easily be considered plagiarism, a form of cheating that could result in a failing grade or worse. At the very least, repeating information or ideas without thinking about or interpreting them puts you at risk of carelessly using old, incorrect, or biased resources.

Research is a process of steps used to collect and analyze information to increase understanding of a topic or issue. Those steps include asking questions, collecting and analyzing data related to those questions, and presenting one or more answers. Good research is information literacy in action. If your instructor asks you to select and report on a topic, you might search for information about it, find a dozen sources, evaluate and interpret them, discard a few, organize the ones you wish to keep, select related portions, write a paper or presentation that cites your sources, write an introduction that explains what you have done, draw some conclusions of your own, and submit the results. That's research. The conclusion that you make based on your research is new information!

isthisyou?

Dreading Writing Assignments

Does the thought of writing papers cause you to panic? Do you have no idea where to even start on a research project? Has it been years since you were in a library? Do you still think that librarians spend their days checking out dusty books while wearing cardigans and sensible shoes? It's time for a little reality check and a lot of strategies to help you improve your research and writing. Whether you're a novice or a pro, calm and collected, or prone to panic, this chapter will help you tackle any research project and writing assignment.

CHOOSING, NARROWING, AND RESEARCHING A TOPIC

Assignments that require the use of library materials can take many forms and will be a part of most of your classes. We'll consider several ways to search for information later in the chapter. Before you start searching, however, you need to have an idea of what you're looking for.

Choosing a topic is often the most difficult part of a research project. Even if an instructor assigns a general topic, you'll need to narrow it down to a particular aspect that interests you enough to research it. Imagine, for example, that you have been assigned to write a research paper on the topic of climate change. What steps should you take? Your first job is to get a general overview of your topic. You can begin by conducting a Google search to look at a range of references. Once you've found some basic information to guide you toward an understanding of your topic, you have a decision to make: What aspects of the subject will you research? Soon after you start researching your topic, you may realize that it is really large (for example, simply typing "climate change" into Google will return millions of hits) and that it includes many related subtopics.

You can use this new information to create keywords. A **keyword** is a word or phrase that tells an online search tool what you're looking for. You can create a list of keywords by brainstorming different terms and subtopics within your general topic. For example, for the topic "climate change," keywords may include "global warming," "greenhouse effect," "ozone layer," "smog," or "carbon emissions." Even those terms will generate a large number of hits, and you will probably need to narrow your search several times.

What you want are twelve or so focused and highly relevant hits that you can use to write a well-organized essay. Begin by figuring out what you already know and what you would like to learn more about. Perhaps you know a little about climate change's causes and effects, and you're curious about its impacts on animals and plants. In that case, you might decide on a two-part topic: impacts on animals, impacts on plants. By consulting a few general sources, you'll find that you can narrow a broad topic to something that interests you and is a manageable size. You may end up focusing on the impact of climate change on one particular animal or plant in one specific geographical area.

If you are having trouble coming up with keywords, you can begin your research in an encyclopedia. Encyclopedias provide general overviews of topics. They can help you understand the basics of a concept or event, but you will need to use other resources for most college-level research projects. An encyclopedia is a great place to start your research, but not a good place to end it.

You have probably used an encyclopedia recently—you may use one all the time without thinking about it: Wikipedia. A *wiki* is a type of website that allows many different people to edit its content. This means that information on wikis can be constantly changing. Wikipedia is controversial in college work. Many instructors feel that the information on Wikipedia cannot be guaranteed to be reliable because anyone can change it; they instead want students to use sources that have gone through a formal editing and reviewing process. Your instructors might even forbid Wikipedia; if so, avoid it altogether. Even if an instructor permits the use of Wikipedia, it's best to use it only as a *starting point* for your research. Do not plan on citing Wikipedia in your final paper. Rather, check the references at the bottom of Wikipedia pages, or otherwise verify claims made at Wikipedia in another trustworthy source.

Even with an understanding of various types of sources, it can be difficult to determine exactly what you need for your assignment. Table 10.1 provides an overview of when to use different common research sources and gives examples of what you'll find in each source.

USING THE LIBRARY

Whenever you have research to do for a class, your job, or your personal life, visit a library. We can't stress this enough. Although the internet is loaded with billions of pages of information, don't be fooled into thinking it will serve all of your needs. For one thing, you'll have to sort through

TABLE 10.1 › Using Common Research Sources

This information time line helps identify when and how to use each type of source, whether for classwork or for your personal life.

INFORMATION TIME LINE		
Source	**When to access information**	**What it offers**
Newspapers (print and online)	Daily/hourly after an event	Primary-source, firsthand discussions of a current event, and of what happened at the time of the event; short articles
Magazines	Weekly/monthly after an event	Analysis by a journalist or reporter of an event days or weeks after it occurred; longer articles than in newspapers; informally credit sources, might include more interviews or research as well as historical context
Scholarly articles	Months after an event	In-depth analysis of issues; research-based scientific studies with formally credited sources, written and reviewed by experts; contains graphs, tables, and charts
Books	Months/years after an event	A comprehensive overview of a topic with broad and in-depth analyses

a lot of junk to find your way to good-quality online sources. More important, if you limit yourself to the web, you'll miss out on some of the best materials. Although we often think that everything is electronic and can be found through a computer, a great deal of valuable information is still stored in traditional print formats and in your college library databases.

Every library has books, journals, and a great number of items in electronic databases that aren't available on public websites. Librarians at your college work with your instructors to determine the kinds of materials that support their teaching. Librarians carefully select well-respected and credible resources with you and your research in mind. Most libraries also have several other types of collections, such as government documents, microfilm, rare books, manuscripts, dissertations, fine art, photographs, historical documents, maps, music, and films, including archival and documentary productions. A key component of being information literate is determining the kinds of sources you need to satisfy your research questions.

A college library is far more than a document warehouse, however. For starters, most campus libraries have websites and apps that offer lots of help to students. Some provide guidelines on writing research papers, conducting online searches, or navigating the **stacks**—the area of a library where most of the books are shelved.

Of course, no one library can possibly own everything you might need or have enough copies of each item to satisfy demand, so groups of libraries share their materials with each other. If your college library does not have a journal or book that looks promising for your project, or if the item you need is checked out, you can use **interlibrary loan**, a service that allows you to request an item at no charge from another library at a different college or university. The request process is simple, and the librarians can help you get started.

Get to the Library

How often do you go to your campus library? Besides being an important academic resource, the library is a great spot for study groups to meet and be productive, and it is a setting where lasting friendships can grow.

Rawpixel.com/Shutterstock

If it is difficult for you to go to your college library because of commuting, family, work challenges, time constraints, or because you are an online student who lives far from campus, you will still have off-campus, online access to library materials through a school-provided ID and password. You can also have online chats with librarians who can help you in real time. To learn more, check your library's website, or e-mail or phone the reference desk. Be sure to use the handouts and guides that are available at the reference desk or online. You will also find tutorials and virtual tours that will help you become familiar with the collections, services, and spaces available at your library.

The 20-Minute Rule

If you have been working hard by yourself trying to locate information for a research project for 20 minutes and haven't found what you need, stop and ask a librarian for help in figuring out new strategies to get to the books, articles, and other sources you need. In addition, the librarian can help you develop strategies to improve your research and writing skills. Doing research without a librarian is like driving cross-country without a map or GPS—technically, you can do it, but you will get lost along the way and you may not get to your destination on time. Get to know at least one librarian as your go-to expert. College librarians are dedicated to helping students like you.

Scholarly Articles and Journals

Many college-level research projects will require you to use articles from **scholarly journals,** collections of original, peer-reviewed research articles written by experts or researchers in a particular academic discipline. Examples are the *Journal of Educational Research* and the *Social Psychology*

Library of the Future? No, the Present!
College libraries are changing to learning commons as information goes digital and space for group work becomes a priority. This type of facility merges the library, information technology, and classrooms and contains multiple zones for individual, small-group, and team-based learning. What does your college library offer?
Norma Jean Gargasz/Alamy

Quarterly. The term **peer-reviewed** means that other experts in the field read and evaluate the articles in the journal before they are published. You might find that some of your instructors use the terms *peer-reviewed* or *academic* to refer to scholarly articles or journals. Be sure to clarify what kinds of sources your instructor expects you to use before you begin your research.

Scholarly articles focus on a specific idea or question and do not usually provide a general overview of a topic. For example, for the topic of climate change, you might find scholarly articles that compare temperature data over a certain period, analyze the effects of pollution, or explore public and political conversations on the topic. Scholarly articles always include a reference list that contains other sources related to the topic; you may find those sources useful in finding other relevant articles.

The most popular way to find scholarly articles is to use an online **database**, an organized and searchable set of information often categorized by subject areas. Some databases are specific to one subject, like chemistry, while others include articles from many different disciplines. Many libraries have dozens, if not hundreds, of databases. It can be difficult to figure out which ones you should use, but your librarian can help you determine which databases are best for your research.

When you use a database, you can easily add filters to ensure that your results include scholarly articles only, and you can clearly see who the authors are. Your database search should result in article and journal titles, descriptions, and sometimes full articles.

While some databases are available to anyone, whether that person is a student or instructor at a college, most of the databases you'll use for research in college are offered through subscription and are available only to students at a college that pays for the service. Remember, even though databases might look just like websites, they're actually carefully chosen subscriptions paid for by the library. For this reason, you will most likely need to log in with your college ID and password.

techtip

CONDUCT EFFECTIVE SEARCHES

Most of us frequently do casual research. But while Google, Wikipedia, and IMDb.com can provide some helpful answers, you will have to ramp it up a notch for a college-level research project.

When academic research is done properly, the question being researched is clear and the answers that are found become part of the body of research that other professionals in that field would recognize and respect. To do that, researchers use "peer-reviewed" publications, which means that other professionals in that field read their research to verify information before it is published.

The Problem

You understand the basics of online research but don't know how to apply it to an academic setting.

The Fix

Learn what research passes scholarly muster: peer-reviewed academic journals (e.g., Harvard Business Review), government websites (U.S. government websites usually end in .gov), or newspaper websites (e.g., New York Times, Washington Post).

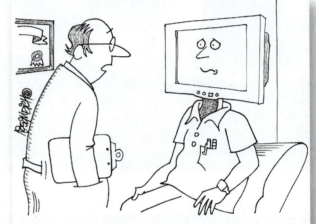

"It's a new syndrome we're seeing more of... "Google-itis"."

Dan Rosandich/Cartoonstock.com

How to Do It

Unlike the examples above, much of the information that you find online isn't objective or factual; the internet is a digital free-for-all. When doing academic research, you need to be picky and filter out what is not helpful by using your critical-thinking skills.

Your college library offers free online access to a wealth of academic databases, LexisNexis, e-journals, and so on. If you have questions about how to use them, or about what kinds of materials qualify as academic research in general, make an appointment with a reference librarian. It's also worth visiting the website of the library at Bowling Green State University at libguides.bgsu.edu/library_basics for helpful "getting started" guides. Here are some quick tips:

- *Hone your online research skills.* Make sure that you understand common Boolean operators such as the words AND, OR, and NOT. How you use them affects your search results.

- *If you are looking for an exact phrase, use quotation marks or asterisks.* For instance, if you search for "rock and roll 1957" or *rock and roll 1957* your results will include that exact phrase. If you get too few hits, omit a search term.

- *In selecting websites for your research, avoid .com sites unless you are looking for the ways that companies advertise a product or service.* The .com ending means "commercial," and you can expect to read material designed to sell you something. Instead, focus on .gov (government), .edu (a college or university), or .org sites (used by not-for-profit organizations); these sites provide the most reliable information.

GOOD TO KNOW: Get familiar with the databases that your college subscribes to; many colleges subscribe to over one hundred. In advance of assignments, make yourself aware of the kinds of information you are likely to find in the various databases. Come up with your own list of questions, and see which database yields the best results in answering them. Databases often offer tools to help you save, store, and cite that information for your research.

EXTRA STYLE POINTS: Avoid internet plagiarism and intentional or unintentional cheating. Check with your instructors about their policies if you are unclear, and always seek research help from reference librarians. You cannot cut and paste whole sentences from the internet into your essays. Instructors can easily catch you, and the penalties are stiff. When in doubt, footnote. Paraphrasing anything off the internet or from any other source without attribution is cheating. Most colleges have a zero-tolerance policy on this issue.

Whenever you copy online research into your notes, be sure to add a URL in brackets at the end. While you're at it, place quotation marks around all cited materials, or highlight them in a bright color.

The second most popular way to find scholarly articles is to use your library's catalog, an online resource accessible on or off campus. Sometimes off-campus access requires you to log in with your college ID and password. When searching the library catalog, you are more likely to find only the names of journals and *not* the titles of the articles within the journal. You might find a link to the electronic version of the journal. You may also be able to find some of the scholarly articles by using Google Scholar as your search engine. This is a specific part of Google that searches only within scholarly journal articles.

Periodicals

You may have heard the word *periodical* before. Many sources that we use in both academic research and our personal lives are periodicals. A **periodical** is a resource such as a journal, a magazine, or a newspaper that is published multiple times a year. Periodicals are designated either by date of publication or by annual volume numbers and issue numbers, which are based on the number of issues published in a given year.

Peer-reviewed scholarly journals are of course periodicals, but most periodicals are classified as popular rather than scholarly. The articles in *Rolling Stone*, a periodical with a focus on popular culture that is published twice each month, do not go through the peer-review process like the articles in scholarly journals. Lack of peer review does *not* disqualify magazines as possible legitimate sources for your research, unless your assignment specifically requires all sources to be scholarly articles or books. Look back at Table 10.1 for a breakdown of different types of sources.

Books

Books are especially useful for research projects. Often students in introductory classes must write research papers on broad topics like the Civil War. While many scholarly articles have been written about the Civil War, they will not provide the kind of general overview of the topic that is available in books.

Searching the library catalog for a book is a lot like searching databases. When you find a source that looks promising, check to see whether it is currently available or checked out by another student. If it's available, write down the title, the author, and the call number. The call number is like an address that tells you where the book is located in the library. After you have this information, head into the stacks to locate your book or journal. If it's checked out by another student or if your library doesn't own the item you're looking for, remember to ask about interlibrary loan. One of the biggest benefits of searching for books is the ability to browse. When you find your book on the shelf, look at the other books around it. They will be on the same topic.

Many books are also available electronically; some of these e-books can be easily accessed online. Your college library may have books available in this format as well. You can browse entire e-book chapters and even print a few pages.

EVALUATING SOURCES

Both the power and the pitfalls of doing research on the internet relate to the importance of knowing how to evaluate sources properly. The internet makes research easier in some ways and more difficult in others. Through internet search engines such as Google and Bing, you have immediate access to a great deal of free information. Keep in mind that many of the entries on a given topic are not valid sources for serious research, and the order of the search results is determined not by their importance, but by search formulas that depend both on popularity and on who pays for their web pages to be on the top of the list. Anybody can put up a website, which means you can't always be sure of the website's credibility and reliability. A web source may be written by anyone—a fifth grader, a famous professor, a professional society, an advertiser, a "bot" (web robot), someone deliberately trying to mislead you, or a person with little reliable knowledge about the topic.

Some students might initially be excited about receiving 243,000,000 hits from a Google search on climate change, but they may be shocked when they realize the information they find is not sorted or organized. Think carefully about the usefulness of the information based on three important factors: relevance, authority, and bias.

Relevance

The first thing to consider in looking at a possible source is whether it is relevant: Does it relate to your subject in an appropriate way? How well does it fit your needs? The answers to these questions depend on your research project and the kind of information you seek.

- **Is it introductory?** Introductory information is basic and elementary. It does not require prior knowledge about the topic. Introductory sources can be useful when you're first learning about a subject, but they are less useful when you're drawing conclusions about a particular aspect of that subject.
- **Is it definitional?** Definitional information provides descriptive details about a subject. It might help you introduce a topic to others or clarify the focus of your investigation.
- **Is it analytical?** Analytical information supplies and interprets data about origins, behaviors, differences, and uses. In most cases, this is the kind of information you want.
- **Is it comprehensive?** The more detail, the better. Avoid unconfirmed opinions, and look instead for sources that consider the topic in depth and offer plenty of evidence to support their conclusions.
- **Is it current?** You should usually give preference to recent sources, although older ones can sometimes be useful (for instance, primary sources for a historical topic or if the source is still cited by others in a field).
- **Can you conclude anything from it?** Use the "So what?" test: So what does this information mean? Why does it matter to my project?

Authority

Once you have determined that a source is relevant to your project, check that it was created by somebody who is qualified to write or speak on the subject and whose conclusions are based on solid evidence. This, too, will depend on your subject and the nature of your research. For example, a fifth grader would generally not be considered an authority, but if you are writing about a topic such as bullying in elementary schools, a fifth grader's opinion might be exactly what you're looking for.

Make sure you can identify the author, and be ready to explain why that author is qualified to write on the subject. Good qualifications might include academic degrees, other research and writing on the subject, or related personal experience.

Understand, as well, whether your project calls for scholarly publications, periodicals such as magazines and newspapers, or both. As mentioned in the previous section, you don't necessarily have to dismiss popular periodicals. Many journalists and columnists are extremely well qualified, and their work might be appropriate for your needs. But as a general rule, scholarly sources will have been thoroughly reviewed, giving the work credibility in a college research project. Use Table 10.1 in this chapter for a review of different sources and what each offers.

 high-impact practice 2

> **your turn**   **Write and Reflect**
>
> **Pros and Cons of Internet Searches**
>
> Do an internet search for the phrase "evaluating internet sources." What ideas did your search yield? List the first ten hits and open each of them. In a brief paper, describe each one and evaluate its usefulness to you. Was the first hit the best one? What did this activity teach you about the value of what's on the Internet?

Bias

When you search for sources, you should realize that all materials have one or more authors who have personal beliefs affecting the way they view the world and approach a topic. This is a normal part of the research process; however, serious authors have adopted ways to ensure that their own opinions don't get in the way of accuracy. While many sources will be heavily biased toward a specific viewpoint or ideology, you will want to find objective (unbiased) sources whenever possible.

Research consists of considering multiple perspectives on a topic, analyzing the sources, and creating something new from your analysis. Signs of bias, such as overly positive or overly harsh language, hints of a personal agenda, or a stubborn refusal to consider other points of view, indicate that you should question the credibility and accuracy of a source. Although nothing may be wrong with someone's particular point of view, as a researcher you need to be aware that the bias exists. You may need to exclude strongly biased sources from your research. For example, if you are writing about climate change, you will want to examine sources for evidence of political or personal agendas. The following questions can help you evaluate your sources:

- Who is the author?
- Why is the author interested in this topic? What is the author's goal in writing about this topic?
- Does the author present facts or personal opinions about the topic?
- Does the author provide evidence that is based on research or information from other sources? Does the author cite these sources?
- Are the conclusions the author makes based on sound evidence, or are they just based on the author's personal interests and opinions?
- What do you think is missing from the article?

 high-impact practice 3

yourturn **Feeling Connected**

What Can You Believe?

Working with a group of your classmates, review the previous list of questions about research sources. Then select approximately 10 blogs, newspapers, magazines, or TV networks that are favorites of yours or your friends. Using the previous questions, how do members of the group evaluate the sources you selected in terms of their potential bias? Discuss ways that you could validate the information presented in these sources.

USING YOUR RESEARCH IN WRITING

You have probably heard the saying "Knowledge is power." But knowledge gives you power only if you put it to use in the form of what might be called a product. You have to decide what form that product will take—a piece of writing or a presentation—and what kind of power you want it to hold. Who is your audience and how will you present the information? What do you hope to accomplish by sharing your conclusions? Remember that a major goal of information literacy is to use information effectively to accomplish a specific purpose. Make it a point to do something with the results of your research. Otherwise, why bother? You researched information to find the answer to a question. Now is the time to formulate that answer and share it with others.

Many students satisfy themselves with a straightforward report that summarizes what they found, and sometimes that's enough. More often, though, you'll want to analyze the information and use that analysis to form your own ideas. To do that, first consider how the facts, opinions, and details you found from your different sources relate to one another. What do they have in common, and how do they differ? What conclusions can you draw from those similarities and differences? What new ideas did they spark? How can you use the information you have on hand to support your conclusions? Essentially, what you're doing at this stage of any research project is **synthesis**, a process in which you put together parts of ideas to come up with a whole result. By accepting some ideas, rejecting others, combining related concepts, and pulling it all together, you'll create new information and ideas that other people can use. Working through the steps of the writing process will get you where you need to go with your paper.

Along with your original ideas, your final paper will include analysis and synthesis of the sources you found through your research. You must make sure that you clearly state which thoughts and ideas came from the sources you found, and which are yours.

THE WRITING PROCESS

In college, your writing provides tangible evidence of how well you think and how well you understand the ideas you are learning in your courses. Your writing is your chance to show what you discovered through your research and to demonstrate your ability to analyze and synthesize sources into a new product that is uniquely your own. Like research, writing takes practice, and asking for help is always a good idea. This section will get you started by providing guidelines for effective and efficient writing.

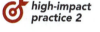 *high-impact practice 2*

Steps to Good Writing

The writing process typically includes three steps as illustrated in Figure 10.1: (1) prewriting, (2) drafting, and (3) revising. Let's look at each of these steps in depth.

Step 1: Using Prewriting to Discover What You Want to Say.
Engaging in prewriting activities is the first step in the writing process. Prewriting simply means writing things down as they come to mind—based

FIGURE 10.1 > The Writing Process

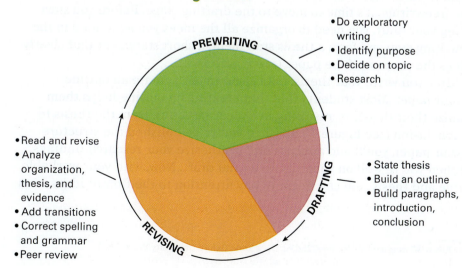

on both the information you found through your research and your own ideas—without consciously trying to organize your thoughts, find exactly the right words, or think about structure. It can involve filling a page, whiteboard, or screen with words, phrases, or sentences.

The most commonly used prewriting activity is called **freewriting**. Freewriting simply means writing without worrying about punctuation, grammar, spelling, and background. Freewriting also helps you avoid the temptation to try to write and edit at the same time. It's impossible to write well while trying to organize, check grammar and spelling, and offer intelligent thoughts to your readers.[1] If you freewrite on your computer or tablet, turn off the grammar and spelling checkers.

When you freewrite, you might notice that you have more ideas than can fit into one paper. This is very common. Fortunately, freewriting helps you choose, narrow, and investigate a topic. It helps you figure out what you really want to say as you make connections between different ideas. When you freewrite, you'll see important issues more clearly, and you can use these issues as keywords to help develop your theme. Remember, keywords are synonyms, related terms, or subtopics that we use to find materials for research papers.

high-impact practice 2

your**turn**   Write and Reflect

Give Freewriting a Try

Have you tried freewriting before? To see what freewriting feels like, write on this general prompt: important issues on our campus. Write for at least 10 minutes, nonstop, about that statement. Don't think about organization, grammar, punctuation, or spelling, and don't stop writing until the time is up.

Step 2: Drafting. When you have completed your research with the help of your librarian, gathered a lot of information sources and ideas, and done some freewriting, it's time to move to the drafting stage. Before you start writing your draft, you need to organize all the ideas you generated in the freewriting step and form a **thesis statement**, a short statement that clearly defines the purpose of the paper (see Figure 10.2).

After you write your thesis, take some time to create an outline for your paper. Most students find that creating an outline helps them organize their thoughts, resulting in a clear structure from the thesis to the conclusion (see Figure 10.3). Once you've established the structure for your paper, you'll add analysis and synthesize your research findings, and then you're well on your way to a final draft. Now, with your workable outline and thesis, you can begin to pay attention to the flow of ideas from

---

[1] Peter Elbow, *Writing without Teachers*, 2nd ed. (New York: Oxford University Press, 1998).

one sentence to the next and from one paragraph to the next, including adding headings and subheadings where needed. If you have chosen your thesis carefully, it will help you evaluate whether each sentence relates to your main idea. When you have completed this stage, you will have the first draft of your paper in hand.

FIGURE 10.2 ❯ Example of a Thesis Statement

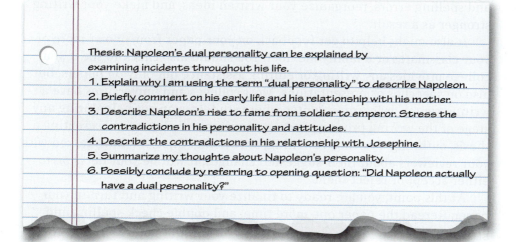

Thesis: Napoleon's dual personality can be explained by examining incidents throughout his life.
1. Explain why I am using the term "dual personality" to describe Napoleon.
2. Briefly comment on his early life and his relationship with his mother.
3. Describe Napoleon's rise to fame from soldier to emperor. Stress the contradictions in his personality and attitudes.
4. Describe the contradictions in his relationship with Josephine.
5. Summarize my thoughts about Napoleon's personality.
6. Possibly conclude by referring to opening question: "Did Napoleon actually have a dual personality?"

FIGURE 10.3 ❯ Example of an Outline

An outline is a working document; you do not need a complete outline to begin writing. Note how this author has a placeholder for another example; she has not yet decided which example from her research to use.

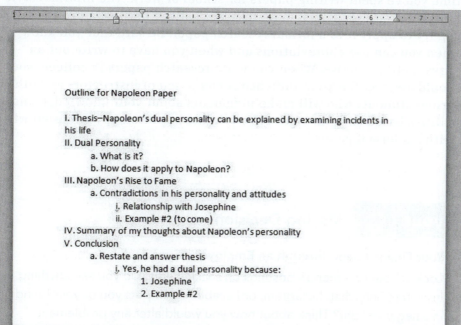

Outline for Napoleon Paper

I. Thesis—Napoleon's dual personality can be explained by examining incidents in his life
II. Dual Personality
    a. What is it?
    b. How does it apply to Napoleon?
III. Napoleon's Rise to Fame
    a. Contradictions in his personality and attitudes
        i. Relationship with Josephine
        ii. Example #2 (to come)
IV. Summary of my thoughts about Napoleon's personality
V. Conclusion
    a. Restate and answer thesis
        i. Yes, he had a dual personality because:
            1. Josephine
            2. Example #2

Step 3: Revising. The key to good writing is rewriting or revising, which is the stage in which you take a good piece of writing and do your best to make it great. After you draft your paper, read it once. You may need to reorganize your ideas, add smoother transitions, cut unnecessary words from sentences and paragraphs, rewrite some sentences or paragraphs, or use stronger vocabulary.

After you revise your paper, put it aside for at least a day and then reread it. Distancing yourself from your writing for a while allows you to see it differently. You will probably find and correct more grammatical and spelling errors, reorganize your written ideas, and make your writing stronger as a result.

It also might help to get feedback on your paper from one or more of your classmates or a family member. You should also check to see if your college provides any writing or editing assistance not only on papers, but also on speeches or presentations. Most colleges and universities have a writing center or learning center where students can get help during any stage of the writing process: finding a topic, narrowing a topic, creating a thesis, outlining, drafting, rewriting, or revising. Once you have talked with your reviewers about their suggested changes, it will be your decision to either accept or reject them.

At this point, you are ready to finalize your writing and turn in your paper. Reread the paper one more time, and double-check spelling and grammar.

Know Your Audience

Before you came to college, you probably spent much more time writing informally than writing formally. Think about all the time you've spent writing e-mails, Facebook posts, texts, and tweets. Now think about the time you've spent writing papers for school or work. The informal style that you use to write an e-mail, text, or post can become a problem if you try to apply it to a formal research paper. Be sure that you know when you can use abbreviations and when you have to write out an entire word or phrase. When you write research papers in college, you should assume that your audience is composed of instructors and other serious students who will make judgments about your knowledge and abilities based on your writing. You should not be sloppy or casual when writing a formal paper.

---

your turn | **Making Decisions**

Your Online Image through an Employer's Eyes

Look at your or a friend's postings on social media. Do you see anything in Twitter, Snapchat, Instagram, or Facebook that puts you or your friend in a negative light? Think about how you would alter any problematic postings.

The Importance of Time in the Writing Process

Many students turn in poorly written papers because they skip the first step (prewriting) and the last step (rewriting/revising), and make do with the middle one (drafting). The best writing is usually done over an extended period of time, not as a last-minute task.

When planning the amount of time you'll need to write your paper, make sure to add enough time for the unexpected. You'll be glad you left enough time for the following:

- asking your instructor for clarification on the assignment
- seeking help from a librarian or from the writing center
- narrowing or expanding your topic, which might require finding some new sources
- balancing other assignments and commitments
- dealing with technology problems

Citing Your Sources

At some point you'll present your findings, whether you are writing an essay, a formal research paper, a script for a presentation, or a page for a website. Remember that you must include complete **citations**, which are references that enable a reader to locate a source based on information such as the author's name, the title of the work, and its publication date.

Citing your sources serves many purposes. For one thing, acknowledging the information and ideas you've borrowed from other writers distinguishes between other writers' ideas and your own and shows respect for their work. Source citations show your audience that you have based your conclusions on good, reliable evidence. They also provide a starting place for anyone who would like more information about the topic or is curious about how you reached your conclusions. Most important, citing your sources is the simplest way to avoid **plagiarism**—taking another person's ideas or work and presenting them as your own—which we will explore in more detail later in this chapter.

Source citation includes many details and can get complicated, but it all comes down to two basic rules. As you write, just remember these two points:

- If you use somebody else's exact words, you must give that person credit.
- If you use somebody else's ideas, *even if you use your own words to express those ideas*, you must give that person credit.

Your instructors will tell you about their preferred method for citation: footnotes, references in parentheses included in the text of your paper, or endnotes. If you're not given specific guidelines or if you simply want to be sure that you do it right, use a handbook or style manual. One standard manual is the MLA Handbook for Writers of Research Papers, published by the Modern Language Association (**mlahandbook.org**). Another is the Publication Manual of the American Psychological Association (**apastyle .org**). You can now download MLA and APA apps on your mobile devices from Google Play or iTunes.

About Plagiarism

Plagiarism is taking another person's ideas or work and presenting them as your own. Plagiarism is unacceptable in a college setting. Just as taking someone else's property is considered physical theft, taking credit for someone else's ideas is considered intellectual theft. In written reports and papers, you must give credit whenever you use another person's actual words, another person's ideas or theories, even if you don't quote them directly, or any other information that is not considered common knowledge.

Occasionally, writers and journalists who have plagiarized have jeopardized their careers. In 2012, columnist Fareed Zakaria was suspended for a week from *Time* and CNN for plagiarizing material from *The New Yorker*, an oversight for which he took full responsibility. In spring 2013, Fox News analyst Juan Williams was criticized for plagiarizing material from a Center for American Progress report in a column he wrote for a political insider publication, but he blamed his research assistant. Also in 2013, Republican senator Rand Paul of Kentucky found himself in trouble over accusations that he plagiarized portions of his book and several of his speeches. Even a few college presidents have been found guilty of borrowing the words of others and using them as their own in speeches and written documents. Such discoveries may result not only in embarrassment and shame but also in lawsuits and criminal actions.

Plagiarism can be a problem on all college campuses, so instructors are now using electronic systems such as Turnitin (**turnitin.com**) to identify plagiarized passages in student papers. Many instructors routinely check their students' papers to make sure that the writing is original. Some

A Speed Trap for Plagiarizers

If knowing that plagiarism is wrong isn't enough of a reason to prevent you from doing it, how about knowing that you will probably get caught? Turnitin's Originality Check checks submitted papers against billions of web papers, millions of student papers, and leading library databases and publications. Just as known speed traps usually get you to slow down when you are driving, knowing about systems like Turnitin can help you resist the urge to plagiarize.

Courtesy Turnitin

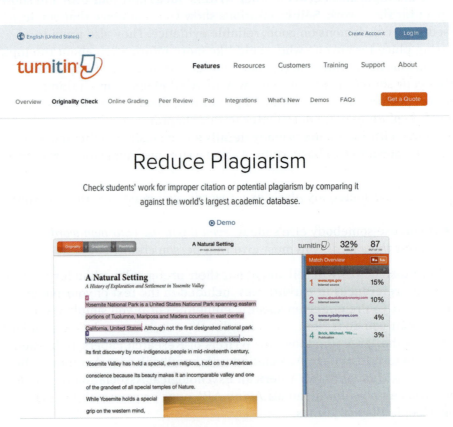

students consider cheating or plagiarizing because they think that doing so will help them get a better grade, but you can avoid the temptation if you keep in mind the high likelihood of getting caught, as well as the serious consequences that will follow if you do get caught.

Because there is no universal rule about plagiarism, ask your instructors about the guidelines they set in their classes. Once you know the rules, plagiarism is easy to avoid. Keep careful notes as you do your research, so that later on you don't mistake someone else's words or ideas for your own. Finally, be sure to check out your college's official definition of what constitutes plagiarism, which you will find in the student handbook, college catalog, college website, course syllabi, or first-year course materials. If you have any questions about what is and isn't acceptable, be sure to ask someone in charge.

It should go without saying (but we'll say it anyway) that intentional plagiarism is a bad idea on many levels. Aside from the possibility of being caught and the potential for punishment—a failing grade, suspension, or even expulsion—submitting a paper purchased from an internet source, copying and pasting passages from someone else's paper, or lifting material from a published source will cause you to miss out on the discovery and skill development that research assignments are meant to teach.

USING YOUR RESEARCH IN PRESENTATIONS

What you have learned in this chapter about writing also applies to public speaking: Both are processes that you can learn and master, and each results in a product. Because the fear of public speaking is a common one—it is more common, in fact, than the fear of death—you might think: What if I plan, organize, prepare, and rehearse my speech, but my mind goes completely blank, I drop my note cards, or I say something totally embarrassing? Remember that people in your audience have been in your position and will understand your anxiety. Your audience wants you to succeed. Be positive, rely on your wit, and keep speaking. Your recovery is what they are most likely to recognize; your success is what they are most likely to remember. The following guidelines can help you improve your speaking skills significantly, including losing your fear of speaking publicly.

Guidelines for Successful Speaking

Just as there is a process for writing a paper, there is a process for developing a good speech. The following guidelines can help you both improve your speaking skills and lose your fear of public speaking.

Step 1: Clarify Your Objective. Begin by identifying the goals of your presentation. Do you want to persuade your listeners that your campus needs additional student parking, or inform your listeners about the student government? What do you want your listeners to know, believe, or do when you are finished?

Speak with Confidence

If you follow the guidelines to successful speaking, you will be able to deliver a meaningful presentation that clearly informs your audience about a topic that matters to them.

Hero Images/Getty Images

Step 2: Understand Your Audience. To understand the people you'll be talking to, ask yourself the following questions:

- What do they already know about my topic?
- What do they want or need to know?
- Who are my listeners?
- What are their attitudes toward me, my ideas, and my topic?

Step 3: Organize Your Presentation. Now comes the most critical part of the process: building your presentation by selecting and arranging blocks of information to guide your listeners through the ideas they already have to the new knowledge, attitudes, and beliefs that you would like them to have. You can use the suggestions from earlier in the chapter for creating a writing outline to create an outline for your speech.

Step 4: Choose Appropriate Visual Aids. You might use presentation software, such as Prezi or PowerPoint, to prepare your presentations. When creating PowerPoint slides or Prezi templates, you can insert images and videos to support your ideas while making your presentations animated, engaging, and interactive. You might also prepare a chart, write on the board, or distribute handouts. As you select and use your visual aids, consider these guidelines:

- Make visuals easy to follow.
- Make sure that words are large enough to be read, and don't overload your audience by including a lot of information on one slide.
- Use font colors to make your slides visually attractive. Use light colors for text on a dark background or dark colors on a light background.
- Explain each visual clearly.
- Allow your listeners enough time to process visuals.
- Proofread carefully. Misspelled words hurt your credibility as a speaker.
- Maintain eye contact with your listeners while you discuss the visuals. Don't turn around and address the screen.

Reach for the Stars

A planetarium probably won't be available when you're giving a speech about astronomy, but you can still use dynamic visual aids that grab your audience's attention and support your major points.

Hill Street Studios/Getty Images

A fancy slideshow can't make up for a lack of careful research or sound ideas, but using clear, attractive visual aids can help you organize your material and help your listeners understand what they're hearing. The quality of your visual aids and your skill in using them can help make your presentation effective.

Step 5: Prepare Your Notes. If you are like most speakers, having an entire written copy of your speech in front of you may tempt you to read much of your presentation, but a speech that is read word for word will often sound artificial. A better strategy is to memorize the introduction and conclusion, and then use a carefully prepared outline to guide you in between. You should practice in advance. Because you are speaking mainly from an outline, your choice of words will be slightly different each time you give your presentation, with the result that you will sound prepared but natural. Since you're not reading, you will be able to maintain eye contact with your listeners. Try using note cards; number them in case you accidentally drop the stack on your way to the front of the room. After you become more experienced, your visuals can serve as notes. A handout or a slide listing key points can provide you with a basic outline.

Step 6: Practice Your Delivery. Practice delivering your speech before an audience: a friend, your dog, even the mirror. As you rehearse, form a mental image of success rather than failure. Practice your presentation aloud several times to control your anxiety. Begin a few days before your speech date, and make sure you rehearse out loud, as thinking through your speech and talking through your speech have very different results. Consider making an audio or video recording of yourself to hear or see your mistakes and reinforce your strengths. If you ask a practice audience to give you feedback, you'll have some idea of what changes you might make.

Step 7: Pay Attention to Word Choice and Pronunciation. As you reread your presentation, make sure that you have used the right words to express your ideas. Get help ahead of time with words that you aren't certain how to pronounce. Try your best to avoid *like, um, uh, you know*, and other fillers. Be careful in using idioms and slang. You want everyone in your audience, including listeners from other countries, to understand the points you're making. Finally, be cautious when using humor. Make sure that a joke you might want to include won't be offensive to someone in your audience.

Step 8: Dress Appropriately and Give Your Presentation. Now you're almost ready to give your presentation, but don't forget one last step: Dress appropriately. Leave the baseball cap, the T-shirt, and the tennis shoes at home. Don't overdress, but do look professional. Experts suggest that your clothes should be a "little nicer" than what your audience is wearing. Some speakers find that when they dress professionally, they deliver a better presentation!

Step 9: Request Feedback from Someone in Your Audience.
After you have completed your speech, ask a friend or your instructor to give you some honest feedback. If you receive written evaluations from your audience, read them and pay attention to suggestions for ways you can improve.

Your first public presentation in college might be a scary experience for you, and you might even try to select courses that allow you to avoid public speaking. You're really not doing yourself any favors, though. Nearly all employers will expect you to make an occasional speech or presentation, and the only way to improve as a speaker is through practice. If you receive negative feedback on a presentation, don't let it get you down. Show your instructors and your fellow students that you are resilient—you can bounce back from a less-than-perfect presentation and can use feedback to improve.

---

your turn | **Setting Goals**

Conquering the Fear of Speaking in Public

If you are afraid to speak in public, now is the time to set a goal to conquer this fear. That will mean taking advantage of speaking opportunities. Start by contributing to class discussions. Then volunteer for a leadership position in a student organization. Take a public speaking course or join a debate team. Ask your college success instructor or your peer leader to help you identify low-stakes (ungraded) ways to practice speaking before a group.

checklist for success

Information Literacy and Communication

■ **Work to learn "information-literacy" skills.** These skills include the abilities to find, evaluate, and use information. They are important not only for college but also for your career because you will be working in the information economy, which uses and produces information.

■ **Become comfortable in your campus library.** Use it as a place to read, relax, study, or just be by yourself.

■ **Accept that research projects and papers are part of college life.** Learn how to do them well. Doing so will teach you how to "research" the information you need in life after college. After all, modern professional life is one big term paper after another!

■ **Get to know your college librarians.** They are eager to help you find the information you need. Ask them for help, even if they look busy. If possible, get to know one as your personal "library consultant."

■ **Early in your college career, take courses that require you to do research and use your library skills.** Yes, these will demand more of you, especially in writing, but you will be thankful for them later. Go ahead, bite the bullet.

■ **Learn about as many new electronic sources as possible.** You must be able to do research and seek the information you need now and after college by doing more than using Google or Wikipedia.

■ **When you use the ideas of others, be sure to give them credit; then create your own unique synthesis and conclusions.** Someday you will create your own "intellectual property," and you will want others to give you credit for your ideas.

■ **Take the time and effort to develop your writing and speaking skills.** Effective writing and speaking are skills for success in college and in life after college. They are skills that employers seek in all their employees.

■ **Learn and practice the three distinct steps of the writing process.** Prewriting, drafting, and revising are separate steps. Going through each step will improve the finished product. Ask for feedback on your writing. Accepting criticism and praise will make you a better writer.

■ **Learn and practice the guidelines for effective speaking.** Clarify your objective, analyze your audience, organize your presentation, choose appropriate visual aids, prepare your notes, and practice delivery. Pay attention to word choice and pronunciation, give your presentation, and request feedback from someone in your audience.

10 build your experience

REFLECT ON CHOICES

Your campus library is a valuable resource for finding information and a great place to study. While your instructors will sometimes require you to use the library, at other times, it will be your choice. Reflect on your use of the library so far in your college experience. Make a list of the pros and cons of going to the library to study or do research, and share that list with other students in your class.

APPLY WHAT YOU'VE LEARNED

Now that you have read and discussed this chapter, consider how you can apply what you have learned to your academic life and your personal life. The following prompts will help you reflect on chapter material and its relevance to you both now and in the future.

1. It is important to get familiar with all the resources in your campus library. Think about a book that you love that was turned into a movie (e.g., *The Lord of the Rings* or the Harry Potter series). Search your library catalog to find the print copy. See if the library has it as an audiobook or in a language other than English. Find the downloadable e-book, DVD, or soundtrack in your library's media collection.

2. The importance of using information-literacy skills in college is a no-brainer, but think beyond your college experience. How will improving your information-literacy skills help you once you are out of college?

USE YOUR RESOURCES

> **Your Instructor** Talk to your instructor after class, drop by during office hours, or make a one-on-one appointment. Check with your instructors to make sure that you understand their expectations for any writing, speaking, or research assignments.

> **Library** Go to the library! Check out your campus library's website or ask for a calendar of upcoming events. Many libraries have drop-in classes or workshops to help you learn specific skills. Head over to the reference desk and talk with a librarian about an assignment that you are working on. If you are an online student, be sure to learn how you can gain access to library sources from your home.

> **Technology Support Centers** Everyone faces some sort of computer crisis in their life. It seems that so many of these emergencies happen just before a deadline for a major paper. Prepare yourself! Check out your school's technology support services *before* you need them. Non-traditional students sometimes feel uncomfortable with technology, especially a campus technology system that is brand new for them. But whatever your age, be sure to get the help you need from the campus's technology experts.

> **Writing Center** Most campuses have one. Frequently it is found within the English department.

> **Online Resources** Purdue University has an excellent resource on documenting both print and electronic sources. Visit **https://owl .purdue.edu/owl/research_and_citation /apa_style/apa_formatting_and_style_guide /reference_list_electronic_sources.html**. Have you ever been confused by government jargon? Here's a guide to using clear communication (also referred to as plain language): **plainlanguage.gov**.

LaunchPad
macmillan learning

LaunchPad for *Your College Experience* is a great resource. Go online to master concepts using the LearningCurve study tool and much more. **Launchpadworks.com**

PhotoAlto/Sandro Di Carlo
Darsa/Getty Images

14 WELLNESS

Student Goals

- Manage the various aspects of wellness, including stress management, nutrition, exercise, weight management, sleep, and emotional health
- Gain strategies for making good decisions about alcohol and other substances
- Explore high-impact practices 2 (writing) and 3 (collaboration)

Getty Images

15 MONEY

Student Goals

- Create a budget and learn how to live within it
- Distinguish between different types of financial aid, and understand how to qualify for and keep it
- Learn how to achieve a balance between working and borrowing
- Get strategies for using and managing credit wisely
- Know why you should plan for your financial future
- Explore high-impact practices 2 (writing) and 3 (collaboration)

Hero Images/Getty Images

11

MAJORS AND CAREERS

YOU WILL EXPLORE

How technology, global competitiveness, and learning shape employment opportunities

Ways to build a professional mindset

Working with academic and career advisers

How to find career resources at your college or university

Strategies and tools for getting to know yourself, including your skills, aptitudes, personality, and interests

How to gain experience through experiential learning and work opportunities

Marketing yourself by developing "You, Inc."

⚲ High-impact practices 2 (writing), 3 (collaboration), 4 (study abroad), 8 (research), and 9 (internships)

Klaus Vedfelt/Getty Images

> **" The more I learn about myself, and the more exploration I do, the more refined my decision making becomes. "**

Tia grew up in Haverhill, Massachusetts, and attended a vocational high school. While she worked two part-time jobs, she was also president of her class and an active member in the National Vocational Technical Honor Society. Her parents instilled in her the values of hard work and dedication and, more important, the expectation that she would be the first in her family to attend college.

Knowing that she would have to commute, Tia applied to four colleges, all within a 30-mile radius of her home. While her parents were emotionally supportive, they were unable to provide financial or informational support during the college application process. Tia would have to find her own way to college. "Being told I needed to pay for my college education all by myself was a real shock," she says. "I knew if I was truly going to be the first in my family to go to college, I was on my own." When Tia is not in class or studying, she splits her time between working as a peer adviser and being an in-home health care aide. "Being a commuter student, juggling academics, family, and two part-time jobs is

definitely difficult," says Tia. "But I know this is what I have to do in order to reach my goals."

Tia entered Salem State University as an undeclared first-year student, unsure of what she wanted to study but knowing that eventually she wanted to work with those suffering from intellectual and developmental disabilities. "I am so grateful to have had professional work experience at an early age. As a health care aide, I have been able to work with adults with various developmental disabilities, which has allowed me to have a clearer understanding of my career goals after college," she explains.

Now in her sophomore year, Tia has decided to major in psychology and minor in interpersonal communications. "I've changed my major twice since coming to Salem State," she says. "The more I learn about myself, the more refined my decision making becomes. I've settled on psychology because I believe it will provide me with a foundation on which to build my education and experiences."

LaunchPad
macmillan learning

To access the LearningCurve study tool, video activities, and more, go to LaunchPad for *Your College Experience.*
Launchpadworks.com

Have you already been thinking about a particular career after college, or are you still exploring a lot of different possibilities? For many students, the road to a career begins with a strong interest in an academic major. For others, selecting a major is harder than deciding on a career path. While the link between major and career is often very direct (for instance, to become a nurse, you have to major in nursing), other careers can link with a variety of majors. For instance, students who want to become lawyers can major in political science, history, English, philosophy, or any number of other academic areas. Tia entered college with a strong sense of purpose and career direction, but at first she still had trouble selecting an academic major that would provide the best foundation for her career plans. And she did what many students do: She entered with one major and changed to another.

assess your strengths

It is important that you honestly appraise your skills and competencies. Many of these will be based on work or life experience before coming to college. By taking advantage of the resources and support available to you, you will be able to make the most of your current strengths and identify those areas where you need to grow. You will be able to match your abilities with the expectations and demands of the classroom and the workplace.

set goals

As you read this chapter, think of what is important as you begin mapping your career path. Has anyone ever asked you where you expect to be in ten years? Not many of us can plan that far ahead because of the rapidly changing world of work. But you do need to plan and set goals, just in shorter chunks. As you read this chapter, consider how your goals will drive your purpose and clarify your desired career outcomes. Commit to exploring and using the resources your college or university makes available to you.

The National Center for Educational Statistics released findings from a recent study reporting that nearly 80 percent of college students who declare their academic majors aren't sure if it was the right choice. The same study revealed that many college students change majors, with the average being about three times before settling into their desired course of study that leads to a career. Whether you do or don't change majors, a wise strategy is to make connections with academic and career advisers who will work with you to ensure that you are on the right path to thrive in today's fast-paced economy.

CAREERS AND THE NEW ECONOMY

During your lifetime, economies in the United States and throughout the world have undergone significant changes as powerful forces, including technology, free markets, health crises, and workforce realignment, collided. Although our economy has experienced extreme ups and downs over the years, today there is hope for a bright economic future for college graduates who have high-level competencies; pre-professional experiences prior to graduation; and pay attention to the importance of resiliency, curiosity, and hard work.

Over the past few years, the labor market for college graduates has steadily improved. In fact, according to the annual recruiting projections made by Michigan State University, in 2019 through 2020, job opportunities will expand by 12 percent across all degree levels. Job opportunities for associate-degree holders will increase by 29 percent and will be especially plentiful in applied engineering, information technology, health, and applied technical fields. Bachelor's degree opportunities will increase by 10 percent.[1]

---

[1] http://www.ceri.msu.edu/recruiting-trends-2019-20/

Although there is good news, economic uncertainty remains a reality. Predictable business cycles mean that we can expect a downturn at some point. To make timely decisions about your major and career path, you need to know about the underlying factors that drive today's economy.

 high-impact practice 2

> ### your turn   Write and Reflect
>
> **The Economy and Your Future Plans**
>
> In a journal entry, describe your understanding of the economy and how these dynamics are shaping the way you approach your career decisions. Do some online research into the economic forecast associated with the major you are considering, and make notes in your journal about what you find and its effect on your plans.

Characteristics of Today's Economy

The characteristics of today's economy are quite different from those of twenty years ago. Our economy today is global, fast, disruptive, innovative, without boundaries, customized, ever-changing, and networked. Think about the potential impact of these characteristics on your program of study and possible career path.

It's GLOBAL. Regardless of their size, many organizations, including education, health, nonprofit, manufacturing, and professional service, are operating in multiple countries. They look for opportunities to expand markets for their goods or services, to identify sources of cheap talent, and to secure access to capital and resources. And they look for employees who have high levels of cultural competence—the understanding of and experience with cultures around the globe. Competition on a global level presents challenges and opportunities for both U.S. and international workers. With open markets, all workers are potentially threatened by cheaper labor somewhere else. Competitive pricing (lowest price point) has become a consumer expectation.

The introduction of so many college-educated individuals worldwide into the economy has and will continue to shape how U.S. college students need to prepare for and make the transition into the labor market. As a U.S. student, you cannot be complacent about the impact of high-quality, highly educated global talent in shaping the competition for employment both here and around the world.

It's FAST. Since the 1990s, the pace of economic activity has quickened significantly. Speed wins. So companies seek ways to produce goods faster, streamline their supply chain, revise services to stay ahead of competitors, or take advantage of new opportunities. Getting a new product to market just a few weeks ahead of a competitor can mean capturing that market niche and returning a profit. This means that new employees have to complete assignments and projects on time; there is no such thing as an extension or a redo.

Thinking Things Through

Your experiences in college will help you make thoughtful decisions about your future.

Blend Images/Peathegee Inc./ Getty Images

It's DISRUPTIVE. A pervasive and threatening disruption to the economy is the rapid infusion of smart technologies based on artificial intelligence (AI), which can be robotic or interactive software. Smart technologies are replacing many human workers and taking over the running of some basic operations. While smart machines and software will not replace workers totally, every occupation will be affected. As technology changes the tasks we do, we also have to change and adapt by learning new skills, identifying opportunities to use the new technology, and understanding the systems we are working in.

It's INNOVATIVE. At no time before has the economy depended more on individual creativity and the ability to innovate. Organizations are seeking talented employees who can employ new work methods; search for and test new technologies, service delivery systems, or processes; and identify new paths to reach team and organizational goals.

It has NO BOUNDARIES. Organizations have learned through this period of economic transformation that the lines separating functional, company, national, and cultural divisions have simply disappeared. No one works or lives in isolation anymore. Organizations are responding by seeking talent that can navigate boundaries. You may be a financial adviser, product designer, or event planner and find that, in order to complete your assignment, you have to interact with different units within your organization, client organizations, several different nation-state governments, and a cross-cultural work team. Being able to cross boundaries means developing strong communication skills, empathy, team-management abilities, cultural awareness, and possibly a foreign language.

It's CUSTOMIZED. In making consumer decisions each day, you face a wide array of choices. Purchasers of goods and services want their purchases tailored to their specific needs. For instance, the popular frozen yogurt franchise, Orange Leaf, allows patrons to "become the master of your dessert" by building their very own yogurt treats. We customize our coffee, ringtones, and playlists. Some colleges and universities even allow students to customize their own majors.

It's CHANGING—all the time. No one likes a lot of change, particularly in the workplace. Yet organizations are constantly changing their missions and their expectations of employees. Workers are changing the landscape as well, with the rise of the "gig" economy and freelance work, along with workers who chose to work remotely instead of from a traditional office. Although change may make you uncomfortable, the simple fact is that you will not be able to avoid it. So turn change into a positive while you're in college by being open to new ideas, continuing to learn, taking advantage of new challenges, and even seeking out change.

It's NETWORKED. Like many of your peers, you are likely to have a Facebook account with hundreds of friends. You may also have LinkedIn, Instagram, Pinterest, YouTube, Twitter, Tumblr, Reddit, VK, Flickr, Vine, and Meetup accounts as well as a number of other social media outlets. We are a highly networked society, and relationships, both personal and professional, are called "social capital." **Social capital**, defined as the value of social networks (who people know) and the tendencies that arise from these networks to do things for each other, has a long and important economic and social role in the development of our country. For a company or organization, the social capital derived from all its employees can be used to advance its ability to produce goods and deliver services. Your personal and professional network or your social capital is a potentially critical resource for you and for your employers.

BUILDING A PROFESSIONAL MINDSET FOR LIFE AFTER COLLEGE

As Professor Andrew Ng of Stanford University reminds us, "What you learn in college isn't enough to keep you going for the next 40 years."[2] You will also need a professional mindset—a point of view about how to be successful in the workplace. While developing this mindset, here are some important things to keep in mind:

- **There are no guarantees.** With a college degree, more employment opportunities, career alternatives, and possible financial security will be available to you compared to those who do not attend college or fail to attain a degree. Research findings are very compelling that a degree pays off. On average, for example, Americans with bachelor's degrees or higher make twice as much in annual income as those with a high school education or less.[3] But a college degree

---

[2] "Re-educating Rita," *The Economist,* June 23, 2016, https://www.economist.com/special-report/2016/06/23/re-educating-rita.

[3] A. P. Carnevale, S. J. Rose, and B. Cheah, "The College Payoff: Education, Occupations, Lifetime Earnings," Georgetown Public Policy Institute, p. 4. Web. 2011.

is not a guarantee. Many hopeful graduates enter the job search confidently, and why not? They have successfully completed their degree, and many have a record of activities that will bolster their employability. These activities might include study abroad, leadership positions, community engagement, and—the crowning jewel—an internship. With this full package, some seniors are surprised at how uncompetitive they still are. The reasons may stem from a failure to integrate their educational experiences; articulate the growth and development of their competencies; and craft their story about how the college experience changed them as learners, professionals, and citizens. Even good students may struggle with the job search if they have limited or no professional experience or if they fail to display work behaviors and attitudes such as cooperation, awareness of others, resiliency, and commitment to the organization.

is**this**you?

No Plan for Life after College

Whenever someone asks you about your plans for employment after college, do you fumble for a response? Do you feel clueless? Are you hoping a flash of insight will put you on the right career path? If so, you're not alone. Many students come to college without firm career plans. This chapter will give you some new ways to think about your major and career choices. It will introduce you to resources that you may not have thought about before. So don't panic. Just make your first year a time to explore your options.

These characteristics of the economy— that it is global, fast, disruptive, innovative, without boundaries, customized, ever-changing, and networked—should provide a roadmap for you as you make decisions throughout your college experience.

- **You will need to take some risks.** In a job interview, a potential employer may ask you whether or not you are a risk taker. Employers generally want to hire people who are comfortable with taking reasonable risks and may ask you to give them an example of something you did in a volunteer, work, or classroom situation that involved a risk. Being a risk taker requires courage, and you will have to take a few chances in order to maintain and even advance your career.
- **Your first job is seldom your dream job.** Everyone wants an ideal job right out of college, but few people get a perfect job right after graduation. Think of your first job as an audition for the next job. Employers want to see how quickly you learn, how well you adapt to and maneuver through the workplace, and how well you perform before providing more demanding and challenging positions. Building a career path is a lifetime endeavor; each job you hold and each professional decision you make contributes to the construction.

Now for the good news: Hundreds of thousands of graduates find jobs every year, even in recessionary times. Some graduates might have to work longer to get where they want to be, but persistence pays off. If you start preparing now and continue to do so over your college years, you'll build a portfolio of academic, co-curricular and pre-professional experiences that add substance to your career profile.

Stiff Competition

The information and strategies in this chapter will help you prepare for job interviews so that when it's your turn to be interviewed, you can walk in with confidence.

Frances Roberts/Alamy

 high-impact practice 2

your turn | Making Decisions

Ponder Your Academic Major Choice

This week, find another student who has the same major as you. Ask that person their reasons for selecting this major. Does that person seem passionate about this major? Why or why not? Why did *you* choose this major? Are you excited or do you have a ho-hum attitude about it? Reflect on your choice of major in a journal entry.

WORKING WITH AN ACADEMIC ADVISER

Academic planning is a vital step to success in college and should be an ongoing process that starts on the first day. Before you register for classes next term, sit down for a strategy session with your academic adviser. On most campuses, you are assigned an adviser who is usually either an instructor or staff person in your field or a professional adviser. A good adviser can help you choose courses, decide on a major, weigh career possibilities, and map your degree requirements. Advisers can also recommend instructors and help you simplify the different aspects of your academic life.

The relationship you form with your academic adviser can become one of the most valuable relationships of your life.
iStock.com/bowdenimages

Prepare for Your First Meeting with Your Academic Adviser

Here are a few ways to make sure that your first meeting with your adviser is a valuable experience. They involve preparation. Take these steps before your first meeting:

- Prepare by looking at the course catalog, thinking about the available majors, and becoming familiar with campus resources. If you haven't decided on a major, ask your adviser about opportunities for taking an aptitude test or a self-assessment to help you narrow down your options.
- Prepare materials to bring to the meeting. Even if you submitted your high school academic transcript with your application, bring a copy of it to the meeting. The transcript is an important tool; it shows your academic adviser what courses you have taken and your academic strengths.
- Make a list of majors that appeal to you. Academic advisers love it when students are passionate and take their futures seriously.
- Map your time frame and goals. Be ready to answer questions such as these: Do you plan to enroll full-time or part-time? When do you plan to graduate, and with what degree? Do you plan to transfer at some point, and are you planning to go to graduate school?

Know the Right Questions to Ask about Your Major

Once you've chosen a major, you'll need to understand how to meet the necessary requirements. You will have *prerequisites*—the basic core courses you need to take before you can enroll in upper-level classes in your major. Your major may also have *corequisites:* courses you have to take in conjunction with other courses during the same term, such as a chemistry lab alongside your chemistry class. With this knowledge, here is what you need to learn:

- How many credits must I take each term to graduate on time?
- What are the prerequisites and corequisites for my major?
- If I have any Advanced Placement (AP) credits or dual enrollment credits, can I use them to fulfill some of my major's requirements?

Leave the meeting with a printout of your current course schedule and plans for classes you might take in the next term and beyond. At many institutions, you and your adviser will set up a five- to seven-term plan online. Finally, find out when you should set up your next meeting with your academic adviser. It's important to stay connected and make sure you're on a positive track, especially if you plan to transfer or apply to graduate school.

Learn How to Select Your Classes

Your academic adviser can help you with rules and regulations and can also help you know how many and which specific classes to take.

- Most full-time students take four to six courses a term. Decide which classes you want to take, find out which days and times they meet, and make sure they don't overlap.
- To get the classes you want, make sure to register as early as possible—in person or online.
- If you can avoid it, resist the temptation to cram all of your classes into one or two days. It's better to aim for a manageable workload by spreading your classes throughout the week.
- Go for a mix of hard and easy classes. Especially at the beginning, you might not realize how challenging college classes can be or how much outside work they entail. If you load up on organic chemistry, Russian 101, and advanced thermodynamics, your grades and general well-being could suffer.

Explore Course Options and Pay Attention to Your Grades

College gives you the opportunity to explore courses, but trying to find easy classes to pad your grades or avoid hard work is not viewed positively by employers or graduate school application committees. Grades are important, especially when you're seeking a position in a field that links directly to an academic discipline, such as accounting, engineering, or finance. Grades also become an easy way to eliminate candidates in a competitive field. Remember that good grades show that you have a solid knowledge base and a strong work ethic—two characteristics that all employers value. Don't risk your chances for a great career or admission to graduate school by letting your grades slide.

Deal with a Mismatch

What if there are problems with your adviser? Your college success instructor will know where you should go if you feel that you need to be assigned to a different adviser. You have a right to make a change. Whatever you do, don't throw in the towel. Academic planning is so critical to your success in college that it's worth making sure you find an adviser with whom you feel comfortable.

---

your turn | Setting Goals

Planning for Your Future

As you plan for your future career, begin by creating a list of career possibilities that you will want to investigate. Talk with a career adviser to make sure that your current or planned academic major will align with the career(s) in which you are most interested. Then with the adviser's help, set some goals for learning about each career during this term. Although your plan may include some common steps for each career, there will undoubtedly be some unique things you need to do to investigate each one.

FINDING CAREER RESOURCES ON YOUR CAMPUS

Your college or university will likely have a number of resources available as you investigate and decide on a career. Career advisers who typically work in your campus career center are partners in your college success who can help you find the resources you need. They know how academic majors link to careers; they can provide one-to-one guidance and direct you to career-related tools, opportunities, and strategies such as these:

- **Explore the career center website.** Your college's career center website is full of great information. You will find resources for planning your career and, later, your job search strategy. Programs and events are highlighted and arranged in a calendar format. You will be able to link to campuswide listings for part- and full-time positions, internships, cooperative (co-op) programs, and seasonal employment. The website will provide details for on-campus interviewing opportunities, employer visits, and special engagements such as career fairs and workshops.
- **Engage in at least one career center–sponsored event per term.** For first-year students, programs and events may be geared toward discovery of possible occupations to consider, introducing you to recent graduates, and allowing you to interact with alumni from different career areas. A common misconception (sadly, on the part

of some of your faculty and staff too) is that the career center's services are just for graduating students who have an immediate need for assistance in finding a job. However, career experts agree that students can benefit from a variety of career services *throughout their entire educational experience.*

- **Build your professional network daily.** Just think about how many new people you have already met during this first year of college. Each new contact—faculty members, guest speakers, alumni, and other students—can potentially become a professional resource in your career. The most important person in your professional network can be a **mentor**. Work to develop a mentor–mentee relationship with an instructor or professional staff member at your campus. Through opportunities off-campus, you can also build a mentor relationship through your internship, employment, or volunteer activities. Most colleges and universities coach students to create and develop a LinkedIn account, which is a professionally structured social media platform. You may have already set up a LinkedIn account; if not, it will be one of the first things you will want to do.

Making Connections

Some career fairs may be specific to disciplines such as health care, information technology, or business. Others may be specific to the audience, such as this career fair for military veterans. Attending events like these is part of planning for your career. Career fairs give job candidates the opportunity to make a strong first impression with potential employers.
Sandy Huffaker/Getty Images

GETTING TO KNOW YOURSELF

Reflecting honestly about yourself while you're in college can help you make decisions about college and life. Don't wait until graduation to think back on what your experiences have taught you about yourself. Here are some questions that you need to think about periodically:

- Do I understand my strengths, aptitudes, and needs for improvement?
- Are my academic experiences preparing me for what I aspire to do?

- Am I gaining confidence to pursue my purpose through developing competencies and strengthening my abilities?
- Do I know what employers or graduate school faculty members expect of me in terms of abilities, attitudes, and behaviors?
- Am I aware of the next steps I need to take to move further toward my goals?

Assess Your Career Competencies

Not everyone is excited about self-assessments. We build up expectations that these assessments should tell us exactly what to do and are disappointed when they don't. Assessments provide insights that should provoke a conversation with yourself, your mentor, and/or your career adviser. These conversations aid you in developing a stronger sense of self, which spurs you into action toward career goals that you establish.

Assessments take many forms. You may take one or more career assessments in your college success course. And you can certainly find self-scored assessments online or through your career center. Never think that you have to make a decision based on the results of only one assessment. Career choices are complex and involve many factors; furthermore, these decisions are reversible. It is important to take time to talk about your assessment results with a career counselor.

Clarify Your Personal and Workplace Values

Your values, formed through your life experiences, are what you feel most strongly about. During your college experience your values will become clearer; sometimes your values will be challenged, and at other times new values will become important to you. You will bring your values into the workplace, making it important that you recognize the values held by the organization where you are seeking employment.

Your **personal values** may reflect your need for family, security, integrity, wealth, compassion, fairness, creativity, ambition, adaptability, and personal fulfillment. People vary widely on the values they hold. What is critical is that you can articulate the values that are important to you and that you are able to do so in a job interview. This is something you may wish to practice and role-play.

Workplace values are the values held by a company or organization. These are usually written in a mission or values statement available on the organization's website. We do not always get the workplace that we want, but knowing that your values are compatible with workplace values before taking a job avoids some early career problems young adults often face. Employers also hold expectations about the values that they want new employees to have when they arrive for the first day of work. Some employers are even shifting to value-based recruiting to ensure that important organizational values are reflected in their candidate pool. Here are some of the values that are important to employers:

- Accountability: taking responsibility for work and behavior
- Strong work ethic: demonstrating a strong willingness to work
- Maturity: displaying sound judgment and controlling feelings/emotions in work situations

- Willingness to cooperate: cooperating with coworkers in respectful, sincere manner
- Passion: conveying passion for work and career
- Adaptability: functioning effectively in an ever-changing environment
- Punctuality: completing assignments and commitments on time
- Integrity: acting and performing with integrity
- Initiative: having the ability to work without immediate supervision

In general, being aware of what you value, as well as what your employers value, is important because a career choice that is closely related to your core values is likely to be the best choice.

Understand Your Skills, Aptitudes, Personality, and Interests

Each job or career is different, and each one you explore will be a good fit or a poor fit for you depending on your personal characteristics. These characteristics include your skills; natural abilities or aptitudes; personality; and, of course, your interests.

Personal, Workplace, and Transferable Skills.
You are continually building your skills and competencies through practice in activities in and out of the classroom. As your skill set grows, new abilities emerge as skills combine in new ways. You can find skills assessments at your campus career center.

Skills typically fall into three categories:

1. **Personal.** Some skills come naturally or are learned through experience. Examples of these skills are teamwork, self-motivation, and conflict management.
2. **Workplace.** Some skills can be learned on the job; others are gained through training designed to increase your knowledge or expertise in a certain area. Examples include designing websites, bookkeeping, and providing customer service.
3. **Transferable.** Some skills gained through previous jobs or hobbies or through everyday life can be transferred to another job. Examples include planning events, motivating others, paying attention to detail, solving problems, and thinking critically.

Employers begin their search for talent by focusing on personal and workplace skills in addition to anticipated educational credentials. Once they have identified potential candidates, their focus shifts to transferable skills. Transferable skills help you because they allow you to adapt quickly to changing situations, extend your career options beyond your academic major, and gain promotions. Table 11.1 provides a list of transferable skills and how they link to specific abilities.

Aptitudes.
Your acquired or natural ability for learning and proficiency in a particular area is referred to as aptitude. Your aptitudes make it easier for you to learn or do certain things. Manual dexterity, musical ability, spatial visualization, and memory for numbers are examples of aptitudes that have a lot to do with the way you learn. Similar to skills, each of us has

TABLE 11.1 ❯ Transferable Skills

Skills	Abilities
Communication	Being a clear and persuasive speaker Listening attentively Writing well Communicating with individuals inside and outside the organization
Presentation	Justifying Persuading Responding to questions and serious critiques of presentation material
Leadership	Taking charge Providing direction Making decisions and solving problems
Teamwork	Working with different people while maintaining control over some assignments
Interpersonal	Relating to others Motivating others to participate Easing conflict between coworkers
Personal traits	Showing motivation Possessing technical knowledge related to the job Recognizing the need to take action Being adaptable to change Having a strong work ethic Being reliable and honest Acting in an ethical manner Knowing how to plan and organize multiple tasks Being able to respond positively to customer concerns
Critical thinking and problem solving	Identifying problems and their solutions by combining information from different sources and considering options Analyzing quantitative data Obtaining and processing information

aptitudes that we can build on. The trick is to shine a light on your aptitudes and discover a path in which your strengths become your best intellectual assets. Remember that navigating the future depends on your aptitude for learning—so uncover the ways you learn best.

Personality. All of us are different. That is what makes college such a fun place as you meet different characters every day among your fellow students, staff, and definitely your professors! But could you work with

Job Candidate Skills and Qualities Ranked as *Very Important* by Employers

Employers seek job candidates who can:

- work in a team structure
- make decisions and solve problems
- plan, organize, and prioritize work
- communicate verbally and/or in writing with persons inside and outside the organization
- obtain and process information
- analyze quantitative data
- demonstrate that they have technical knowledge related to the job

Therefore, the ideal candidate is a team player and a good communicator who can make decisions, solve problems, and prioritize. Does this describe you? If not, don't panic. This chapter is intended as a guide for you to develop into the ideal candidate!

Information from: National Association of Colleges and Employers, *Job Outlook 2014* (Bethlehem, PA: National Association of Colleges and Employers, 2013).

them? Could you do a team project with a randomly selected group of students? How do you feel in new situations? If you are in a rapidly changing workplace and some assignments will be delayed or shifted at the last minute, how will you react? Your personality makes you who you are, and it can't be ignored when you make career decisions.

Matching Passions with a Profession

Are you interested in fashion? Do you enjoy creating things from scratch? Do you value creativity? Do you like to work with others? People who answer "yes" to these questions might find that a career in the fashion industry suits them. How does the career that you plan to pursue align with your values, interests, and personality? If you're coming up empty, you might want to reconsider your plans.

Zero Creatives/Corbis

Interests. From birth, we develop particular interests. These interests help shape our career paths and might even define them. Good career exploration begins with considering what you like to do and relating that to your career choices. For example, if you enjoyed writing for your high school newspaper, you might be interested in writing for the college newspaper with an eye on a career in journalism. Or you might enroll in Psych 101 if you have an interest in human behavior, but then realize halfway through the course that psychology is not what you imagined because it has much more to do with science and research than you anticipated. Don't get trapped trying to live someone else's interests. Too many students grappling with an academic major decision choose one based on what a roommate, best friend, or family member advises. Take time to explore your interests through assessments or job shadowing. Because your interests are unique to you, you are the only person who should determine what you want to do in the future.

Using the Holland Model

John Holland, a psychologist at Johns Hopkins University, developed tools and concepts that can help you categorize the various dimensions of yourself so that you can identify potential career choices (see Table 11.2 on the next page). Holland suggests that people are separated into six general categories based on differences in their interests, skills, values, and personality characteristics: their preferred approaches to life. Holland's system organizes career fields into the same six categories. Career fields are grouped according to the skills and personality characteristics most commonly associated with success in those fields and the interests and values most commonly associated with satisfaction. As you view Table 11.2, highlight or note characteristics that you believe that you have, as well as those that are less closely matched.

Your career choices will involve a complex assessment of the factors that are most important to you. Holland's model is commonly presented in a hexagonal shape (Figure 11.1) to display the relationship between career fields and the potential conflicts people face as they consider them. The closer the types, the closer are the relationships among the career fields; the farther apart the types, the more conflict exists between the career fields.

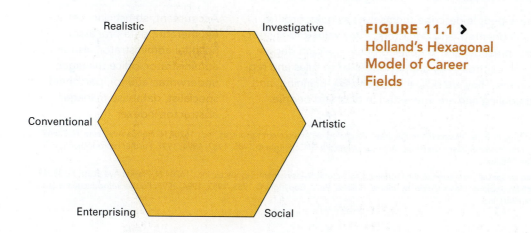

FIGURE 11.1 ›
Holland's Hexagonal Model of Career Fields

TABLE 11.2 > Holland Personality and Career Types

Category	Personality Characteristics	Career Fields
Realistic (R)	These people describe themselves as concrete, down-to-earth, and practical doers. They exhibit competitive/assertive behavior and show interest in activities that require motor coordination, skill, and physical strength. They prefer situations involving action solutions rather than tasks involving verbal or interpersonal skills, and they like taking a concrete approach to problem solving rather than relying on abstract theory. They tend to be interested in scientific or mechanical areas rather than the arts.	Environmental engineer, electrical contractor, industrial arts teacher, navy officer, fitness director, package engineer, electronics technician, web designer
Investigative (I)	These people describe themselves as analytical, rational, and logical problem solvers. They value intellectual stimulation and intellectual achievement, and they prefer to think rather than to act and to organize and understand rather than to persuade. They usually have a strong interest in physical, biological, or social sciences. They are less apt to be people oriented.	Urban planner, chemical engineer, bacteriologist, flight engineer, genealogist, laboratory technician, marine scientist, nuclear medical technologist, obstetrician, quality control technician, computer programmer, environmentalist, physician, college professor
Artistic (A)	These people describe themselves as creative, innovative, and independent. They value self-expression and relating with others through artistic expression and are also emotionally expressive. They dislike structure, preferring tasks involving personal or physical skills. They resemble investigative people but are more interested in the cultural or the aesthetic than the scientific.	Architect, film editor/director, actor, cartoonist, interior decorator, fashion model, graphic communications specialist, journalist, editor, orchestra leader, public relations specialist, sculptor, media specialist, librarian
Social (S)	These people describe themselves as kind, caring, helpful, and understanding of others. They value helping and making a contribution. They satisfy their needs in one-on-one or small-group interaction using strong speaking skills to teach, counsel, or advise. They are drawn to close interpersonal relationships and are less apt to engage in intellectual or extensive physical activity.	Nurse, teacher, social worker, genetic counselor, marriage counselor, rehabilitation counselor, school superintendent, geriatric specialist, insurance claims specialist, minister, travel agent, guidance counselor, convention planner
Enterprising (E)	These people describe themselves as assertive, risk-taking, and persuasive. They value prestige, power, and status and are more inclined than other types to pursue it. They use verbal skills to supervise, lead, direct, and persuade rather than to support or guide. They are interested in people and in achieving organizational goals.	Banker, city manager, FBI agent, health administrator, judge, labor arbitrator, salary and wage administrator, insurance salesperson, sales engineer, lawyer, sales representative, marketing manager
Conventional (C)	These people describe themselves as neat, orderly, detail oriented, and persistent. They value order, structure, prestige, and status and possess a high degree of self-control. They are not opposed to rules and regulations. They are skilled in organizing, planning, and scheduling and are interested in data and people.	Accountant, statistician, census enumerator, data processor, hospital administrator, insurance administrator, office manager, underwriter, auditor, personnel specialist, database manager, abstractor/indexer

Source: Table 11.2 reproduced by special permission of the Publisher, Psychological Assessment Resources, Inc., 16204 N. Florida Ave., Lutz, FL 33549. From *The Self-Directed Search Professional User's Guide*, by John L. Holland, Ph.D. Copyright © 1985, 1987, 1994, 1997. Further reproduction is prohibited without permission from PAR, Inc.

Source: Figure 11.1 reproduced by special permission of the Publisher, Psychological Assessment Resources, Inc., 16204 N. Florida Ave., Lutz, FL 33549. From *The Self-Directed Search Professional User's Guide*, by John L. Holland, Ph.D. Copyright © 1985, 1987, 1994, 1997. Further reproduction is prohibited without permission from PAR, Inc.

Holland's model can help you address the questions surrounding career choice in two ways. First, you can begin to identify career fields that are consistent with what you know about yourself. Once you have identified potential fields, you can use the career center at your college to get more information about those fields, such as the daily activities for specific jobs, the interests and abilities required, the preparation required for entry, the working conditions, salary and benefits, and employment outlook. Second, you can begin to identify the areas of harmony or conflict in your career choices. Doing so will help you analyze the reasons for your career decisions and allow you to be more confident as you make choices.

GAINING PROFESSIONAL EXPERIENCE

Once you have determined your interests and career goals, you can start to gain experience that will move you toward your goals. Gaining professional experience means having experiences in contexts outside the classroom. Students in health professions gain this experience through their clinical rotations, student teachers through their student teaching experience, and social workers and counselors through practice. Most students will gain their experience through an internship or cooperative ("co-op") education.

Internships and Other Professional Work Experiences

high-impact practices 4, 5, 9

Internships come in many different forms and are widely available. You need to plan early to fit an internship into your academic plan. Other options are available should you not want to pursue an internship; for instance, some employers offer paid summer positions but not internships. Start thinking now about the experiential learning opportunities available

Linking Classroom and Career

This student studies computer science and works part-time in the college's computer lab, helping other students with their technology problems. Her work experience links to what she is learning in her courses.

FangXiaNua/Getty Images

techtip

JOIN THE PROFESSIONAL COMMUNITY

If you have ever been to a party where you don't know many people, you know how awkward it can be to stand near a group and not feel comfortable joining it.

Getting started in a new career or profession is similar. Members of different professions have their own ways of doing things: their own terminology, particular leaders, and important events. As a college student, you have to learn about how to join your intended professional community, and you can and should start now.

The Problem

You want to research a professional community that you're interested in joining, but you don't know how.

The Fix

Learn about the industries, companies, and professional groups you would like to work with.

How to Do It

1. *Conduct industry and career research.* A great place to start is O*NET Online (onetonline.org), a site with an interactive application for exploring occupations. Also, get in the habit of visiting the U.S. Bureau of Labor Statistics' Occupational Outlook Handbook (bls.gov/ooh). These sites will give you a very clear picture of thousands of professions. Identify specific companies or organizations that interest you, as well as roles in which you could see yourself. Research individual employers of interest, too. How do your expectations match with reality? Be sure to ask for help from a librarian if you need it.

2. *Do some research on yourself.* Even if you already have an idea about what you want to pursue, online resources, like the O*NET Online Interest profiler (mynextmove.org/explore/ip) or iSeek (iseek.org/careers/clusterSurvey), will give you important feedback about what professions match your interests, personality, values, and skills.

3. *Get familiar with professional organizations.* Every profession has groups whose members exchange ideas, hold events, or conduct training. Explore their websites to find local chapters of the organization or local events you can attend to learn more. For a list of associations, check out https://jobstars.com/professional-associations-organizations/. Also, many professional groups have a presence on LinkedIn, where you can see who is in a group and can join an online conversation about an area of interest.

Courtesy U.S. Department of Labor from https://www.onetonline.org/

4. *Find ways to gain real experience.* Check with your college's career center to find out what kinds of internship opportunities are available. You can look online, too:

- internships.com
- indeed.com
- mediabistro.com
- idealist.com
- experience.com

EXTRA STYLE POINTS: Visit work environments you want to explore. Find a person, either through LinkedIn or your college's alumni or career center, who will grant you an informational interview. You can also seek an opportunity for job shadowing. Here are a few questions to get your interview off to a strong start:

- Describe the moment when you knew this was the job for you.
- What is the most interesting thing that has happened to you in this profession?
- What changes would you make in your career preparation if you were entering this field today?
- Describe the most satisfying professional accomplishment you have had.

After your interview or shadow experience, be sure to send a thank you letter or e-mail to show your appreciation. These letters can be a brief opportunity to share with those you interviewed to you, such as service-learning, volunteer activities, internships, study abroad, co-op programs (alternating studies and work), and student competitions and projects.

Part-Time Work in College

Paid part-time opportunities for getting experience are also beneficial because they can support the attainment of your college goals, provide you with the financial means to complete college, and help you structure your time so that you are a much better time manager. Remember that overextending yourself—working more than 20 hours per week—can potentially interfere with your college success. Be sure to check with a financial aid expert to determine how much money you can earn from a part-time job before it has a negative effect on your financial aid award.

Your first decision will be whether to work on campus or off. If you choose to work on campus, look for opportunities early in the term. One benefit of on-campus employment is that the work schedules are often flexible. Another benefit is that you might be able to connect with instructors and administrators you can later consult as mentors or professional references. Plus, your boss will understand that you occasionally need time off to study or take exams. Finally, students who work on campus are more likely to graduate from college than students who work off campus; keep this fact in mind as you think about mixing college and work.

As a college student, you may decide that you would rather work off campus. An off-campus job might pay better than an on-campus one, or maybe it is closer to your home, or it is in an organization where you want to continue working after you finish college. The best place to start looking for off-campus jobs is your campus career center, which might have listings or websites featuring off-campus employment opportunities.

> **your turn Making Decisions**
>
> **Let Previous Work Experience Guide Future Career Choices**
> What kinds of jobs have you had, either for pay or as a volunteer? Why did you choose those jobs? Which of them was your favorite, and which did you dislike? How could your prior job experience help you make good choices in the future? Be prepared to discuss your ideas in class and offer thoughts about what your work experience has taught you about yourself and which careers you should choose—or avoid—in the future.

MARKETING YOURSELF AND PUTTING IT ALL TOGETHER

You may never have thought that you might be responsible for your own start-up company, but you are. Let's call it "You, Inc." This company is all about understanding your brand (what you bring to the table in

Standing Out from the Crowd

A big part of developing "You, Inc." is figuring out how to set yourself apart from others. Will you do it through commitment to getting good grades, community service, engagement in campus activities, or a unique niche in your industry? At the beginning of college, start thinking about the "end game," continually revisit where you're headed, and make adjustments along the way.
elenabs/iStock/Getty Images

terms of knowledge, skills, attitudes, behaviors, and values) and how to market yourself. You have been building your brand for years, whether you realized it or not, but now you have to take your brand much more seriously.

Branding "You, Inc."

Building your brand begins the day that you arrive on campus. You cannot wait until your junior or senior year to build your brand. How you interact with new people, how you approach your academics, how you engage in campus life—each is an important ingredient in who you are and how you are seen by others. Through your experiences and growing understanding of self, you establish your presence on campus, you create name recognition among professors and peers, and you shape your reputation. This is a personal responsibility that you accept for a lifetime. It is more than getting a job; it is the navigation system—a sort of GPS—that will guide your professional and personal aspirations.

Here are a few points to consider:

- **If you don't do it, no one else will.** You must take control of your own image. No one is better equipped to portray *you* as accurately as *you*. Remember to share your career goals with instructors, academic and career advisers, friends, and family; they can help market you if they get to know you! The more others know about your professional goals, the more they can help you make professional connections.
- **Got ideas? Share them.** People are often hesitant about sharing their ideas or providing direction to others, but guess what? If you don't, you may be left with a good idea that no one else knows about.
- **Realize that it isn't all about you.** Strong candidates whom employers compete to hire not only can bring out the best in themselves but can also bring out the best in others. For team dynamics and success, your ability to assist others to succeed is powerful.

- **Actions speak louder than words.** When you were in high school, you may have realized that your grades and your extracurricular activities were ways to build your college applications. Or you may have learned how poor grades or lack of involvement in school activities made it more difficult to feel confident in your college applications. Professional résumés are similar—you want to be mindful of what makes a strong résumé, and you should act accordingly. It is never too early important to develop your résumé and a well-written cover letter. These two items are critical marketing material for "You, Inc."

Building a Résumé

A good résumé is an excellent and necessary way to market yourself. Before you finish college, you'll need a résumé, whether it's for a part-time job, an internship, a co-op position, or to show to an instructor who agrees to write you a letter of recommendation. Typically, there are two types of résumés. One is written in chronological format, and the other is organized by skills. If you have related job experience, choose the chronological résumé; if you can group skills from a number of jobs or projects under several meaningful categories, choose the skills-based résumé. Your career center can help you choose the format that is right for you given your experience and future goals.

On average, an employer spends 7 to 10 seconds screening each résumé to select their first-round picks when it's time to fill a job. Many employers also use résumé-scanning software to identify key terms and experiences that are most important to the employer. If you are a new professional, a one-page résumé is usually appropriate. Add a second page only if you have truly outstanding skills or work experiences that won't fit on the first page, but consult with your career center for guidance on this point. If you are in college to get retrained and change your career, make sure to update the information on your résumé.

Writing a Cover Letter

A cover letter is *more important* than a résumé—and much harder to write well. When sending a cover letter, think about who will receive it. Different fields have different requirements. Your academic adviser or career counselor can help you address your letter to the right person; so can the internet. Never write, "To whom it may concern." Use the proper formats for date, address, and salutation. Employers pay attention to these details, and a mistake in your letter may cost you an interview. Make sure to ask someone whose writing ability you trust to proofread your cover letter.

A cover letter, written to explain how hiring you will benefit the organization, is an excellent way of marketing yourself to a potential employer. It is important to review the organization's website and find out what skills and experience its employees have. Use the cover letter to highlight your skills for every requirement of the position. Your career center can help you write a cover letter that talks about your education and your experience related to the position. Spending time on writing an excellent cover letter also prepares you for the interview by allowing you to think about how your background matches the needs of the position and the organization.

Putting It All Together

At this point your head may be swimming with tips, strategies, and things you should be doing. It is overwhelming, period. What could happen is that you take one or two suggestions, check them off your list, and leave the rest smoldering on the back burner to be reheated later if ever. Don't let this happen. Take full advantage of the resources in this chapter. Invest the time now in developing "You Inc.," and you'll see that its value will grow in the coming years. Now is a good time to review this chapter and schedule the steps of career preparation throughout your undergraduate years. Plan ahead and work forward—this approach is more effective than trying to play catch-up as you approach the end of your college experience.

high-impact practice 3

your turn Feeling Connected

Marketing Yourself to Employers

Working with a small group of your classmates, help one another develop a "marketing strategy" that each of you could develop to sell yourself to a potential employer. Which characteristics and aptitudes would each group member emphasize? Do other group members agree or disagree? Be honest and respectful in your comments to each other.

Time to Celebrate!

When you are a first-year student, it may be hard for you to imagine graduation day, but we can confidently tell you that successful completion of this course is a good predictor that you will succeed and graduate with a college degree and perhaps a graduate or professional degree some day. Before you know it, you, along with your family and friends, will celebrate your achievements. By making the most of what you have learned in your college success course and your other college experiences, both in and out of class, you will be ready to take the next steps toward a successful career and a bright future.

Ariel Skelley/Blend Images/Getty Images

checklist for success

Majors and Careers

■ **Understand the nature of the new economy that you will be entering.** It is global, fast, disruptive, innovative, without boundaries, customized, ever-changing, and social.

■ **Learn which of your characteristics could and should affect your career choices.** Strive to define your interests, skills, aptitudes, personality, life goals, and work values. Talk them through with a career counselor. It's a normal thing for college students to do.

■ **Keep in touch with your instructors.** Consider keeping in touch with the instructor of this course and with other instructors. Later in college, you may need to ask them to write letters of reference for you as you seek employment or admission to graduate school. When an instructor becomes part of your larger support group, it is a form of networking.

■ **Be responsible for planning your own career.** No one else is going to do it for you, but plenty of people on your campus are willing to help you. Think seriously about your major. You eventually have to get a degree in something, and you want to feel confident and comfortable about the major that you select. Use the insights into yourself that you have gotten from this course as motivation, now and in the future.

■ **Get familiar with online resources for industry research and career exploration.** The more knowledge you have about the industries that interest you, the better your chances of making a sound career decision. Great places to start are **O*NET OnLine (onetonline.org)** and the U.S. Bureau of Labor Statistics' Occupational Outlook Handbook **(bls.gov/ooh).**

■ **Enhance your employability by getting different kinds of work and travel experience during college.** You can get different experiences while taking classes but, better yet, consider maintaining your momentum during the summer. Continuous enrollment is a good thing. See your adviser and career center to learn about experiences that your college offers: volunteer or service-learning, study abroad, internships and co-ops, employment on campus, and student projects and research.

■ **Get professional help from your career center.** Advisers can help you write your résumé and cover letters, learn and practice interview skills, and much more. For example, you can learn how your personality characteristics have been shown to align with particular career fields.

■ **Be aware of what today's employers seek from new employees.** Make sure you can demonstrate both the content and transferable skills necessary for the jobs that interest you most.

11 buildyourexperience

REFLECT ON CHOICES

high-impact practice 2 Most students are in college to prepare for a career. This chapter provides essential information on how you can structure your college experience, both in and out of class, to gain knowledge and skills that will help you, no matter what your employment future holds. Think about careers you are considering, and jot down some steps that you can take in your very first term of college to help you prepare for your first job after graduation.

APPLY WHAT YOU'VE LEARNED

Now that you have read and discussed this chapter, consider how you can apply what you have learned to your academic life and your personal life. The following prompts will help you reflect on chapter material and its relevance to you both now and in the future.

1. Sometimes it's hard to know if you're headed in the right career direction. Describe two steps you can take to make sure your career plans are realistic.

2. Finding a career is about more than just the job itself. It's also about how and where you want to live and with whom. Does the career you envision fit with the way you want to live your life?

USE YOUR RESOURCES

> **Your College Website and Campus Resources** Continue using the institutional services and resources that you learned about in this course, such as the learning center or career center.

> **Academic Advisers** More and more advisers have been trained to help you throughout your college experience. If you are an adult student seeking a new career direction, your academic adviser can help make sure you're taking the right courses and can assist you in finding the help you need.

> **Career Advisers** Seek the kind of specialized help that can come from a career adviser. This professional can be found in either your career center and/or in your campus counseling center.

> **Faculty** On many campuses, faculty members take an active role in helping students connect academic interests to careers. A faculty member can recommend specific courses that relate to a particular career. If you are a racial or ethnic minority student on your campus, seek out faculty or staff members who share your racial or ethnic profile and experiences.

> **Library** All campuses have a main library that contains a wealth of information on careers. Some campuses have a separate library in the career center, staffed by librarians whose job is to help you locate career-related information resources.

> **Upperclass Students and Your Peer Leader** More experienced students can help you navigate courses and find important resources. Many colleges have established peer mentoring programs that connect you to upperclass students for one-on-one guidance. Because they have tested the waters, they can alert you to potential pitfalls or inform you of opportunities.

> **Student Organizations** Professional student organizations that focus on specific career interests meet regularly throughout the year and provide excellent leadership development opportunities. Join them now. If you are a veteran or active duty military student, your campus may have a special organization designed to help you take advantage of special veterans or military benefits.

> **Career Center** Go to your campus career center's home page and check its resources.

> **U.S. Bureau of Labor Statistics' Occupational Outlook Handbook: bls.gov/ooh** This guide to career information about hundreds of occupations is maintained by the U.S. Department of Labor.

> **Mapping Your Future: mappingyourfuture .org** This comprehensive site provides support for those who are just starting to explore potential careers.

LaunchPad for *Your College Experience* is a great resource. Go online to master concepts using the LearningCurve study tool and much more. **Launchpadworks.com**

William Perugini/Shutterstock

12

RELATIONSHIPS

YOU WILL EXPLORE

How to build positive relationships with your college instructors

How to manage family relationships while in college

The role that college friendships and romantic relationships play in your life

Ways to maintain your sexual health and protect yourself and others against sexual assault and violence

Strategies for using digital communication properly

Ways to get involved on campus

⚙ High-impact practices 2 (writing), 3 (collaboration), and 5 (service-learning)

> ❝ **My wife encouraged me to enroll in college when I was just throwing around the idea.** ❞

Even before he enlisted in the U.S. Navy and served for nine years as an electronics technician, Benjamin had a passion for music. He played guitar in high school and on his ship, and he discovered a new interest in professional recording. If it hadn't been for his wife's encouragement, however, he may never have enrolled in Bunker Hill Community College (BHCC) in Boston and begun pursuing music as a career. "My wife encouraged me to enroll in college when I was just throwing the idea around," he said.

At BHCC, Benjamin developed an important relationship with one of his music instructors who taught a course on arranging and composing. Professor Black agreed to mentor Benjamin when he decided to participate in the honors program. "It was a wonderful experience to work so closely with a professor," he says. Benjamin also found plenty of support from friends and family while he was in college. "My father and sisters back in Illinois would listen to me talk about the classes I was taking. My friends were so supportive, to the point of asking about the research papers I was writing and even attending events with me in support of my research."

During his time at BHCC, Benjamin became inspired to become a teacher, and he continued his studies in the music education program at the University of Massachusetts Boston (UMB). "I chose UMass Boston because I could use my military benefits, and I would be set up for job success right out of the gate," Benjamin explained. "I could tack a five-year initial [teaching] license onto my degree plan and teach K–12 music anywhere in the state."

While at UMB, Benjamin tutored second graders in math and reading. "That experience alone made me realize that teaching little kids is what I am meant to do," he said. He also created a ten-week middle school music program that he taught to sixth graders. After three years at UMB, Benjamin landed a job as a K–5 music teacher for the Framingham Public Schools. "I am so incredibly grateful that my college education path brought me here. This is what I was meant to do, and my wife is incredibly proud of my accomplishments. I'm the happiest I've ever been," he said. Benjamin plans to earn a master's degree within the next five years.

📕 **LaunchPad**
macmillan learning

To access the LearningCurve study tool, video activities, and more, go to LaunchPad for *Your College Experience.*
Launchpadworks.com

What does success in college have to do with relationships? As Benjamin's story shows, the quality of both the relationships students have when they begin college and those that they develop in college can have positive effects on their success. As college educators, we have learned from our own experiences and the experiences of others that relationships can also negatively affect success.

Relationships take many forms. You will get to know lots of other students, instructors, and staff members. While many of these relationships will be temporary, some of them will continue throughout your life.

Whether you live on or off campus, you will continue your existing relationships with your parents, partner, children, or other family members.

assess your strengths

One of the best aspects of college life is developing relationships with your peers, your instructors, and upperclass students, including peer leaders in your college success class. As you begin to read this chapter, think about the most important relationships you have developed since coming to college.

set goals

What are your most important objectives in learning the material in this chapter? Think about the relationship challenges you have had in the past, and develop some strategies to improve these relationships in the future. For example, if you want to feel more comfortable with your instructors, make use of their office hours.

Sometimes, the assumptions and expectations that define family interactions will change, and negotiating that change is not always easy. Parents sometimes have trouble letting go of children, and if you are fresh out of high school, you might think that your parents still want to control your life. If you are an adult with a spouse or partner, going to college will give you a new identity that might seem strange or threatening to your partner. If you have children, they might not understand what's going on as you try to balance your need for study time with their need for your undivided attention.

If your friends also go to college, you will have a great deal to share and compare. But if your friends are not college students, they, too, might feel threatened as you take on a new identity. In addition, romantic relationships can support you or can create major conflict and heartbreak, depending on whether your partner shares your feelings and values and whether the relationship is healthy or dysfunctional.

This chapter will help you think about all these different kinds of relationships, including those that you create and continue online.

your turn	Write and Reflect

high-impact practice 2

Your Important Relationships

At this point in your life, what are the three relationships that are most important to you? In a journal entry, reflect on what makes these people special to you.

BUILDING RELATIONSHIPS WITH COLLEGE INSTRUCTORS

Some of the most important relationships you can develop in college are those with your instructors. The basis of such relationships will probably be mutual interests and mutual respect. Instructors who respect students treat them fairly and are willing to help them both in and out of class. Students who respect instructors come to class regularly and take their work seriously.

What Your Instructors Expect from You

Although instructors' expectations might vary depending on a particular course, most instructors expect their students to exhibit attitudes and behaviors that are central to student success. First, and quite simply, be in class on time. Being on time might be a difficult adjustment for some students, but you need to know that this is a basic faculty expectation, no matter where you are in college.

Avoid behaviors that show a lack of respect for both the instructor and other students, such as leaving class to feed a parking meter or answer your cell phone and then returning 5 or 10 minutes later, thus disrupting class twice. Similarly, texting, doing homework for another class, falling asleep, or talking (even whispering) disrupts the class.

Your instructors expect you to come to class, do the assigned work to the best of your ability, listen and participate, think critically about course material, and persist even when a concept is difficult to master. Instructors also expect honesty and candor. Many instructors will invite you to express your feelings about the course anonymously in writing through 1-minute papers or other forms of class assessment.

Generally speaking, college instructors expect you to want to do your best. Your grade school and high school teachers might have spent a great deal of time thinking about how to motivate you, but college instructors usually consider motivation to be your personal responsibility.

 **high-impact practice 3**

your turn | **Feeling Connected**

Evaluating the Rumor Mill: Were Those Stories True?

Make a list of any stories you heard or ideas you developed about college instructors before coming to college. Share these ideas in a small group. See how many stories or rumors were common among all students in the group. Talk about whether these stories are proving to be accurate or inaccurate in your college experience.

What You Can Expect from Your Instructors

The expectations you have for college instructors may be based on the positive and negative things you have heard from friends, fellow students, and family members, but you will find that instructors vary in personality and experience. You might have instructors who are graduate students or new professors in their first year of teaching. Other instructors might be seasoned professors who have taught generations of new students. Some will be introverted and difficult to approach; others will be open, friendly, and willing to talk to you and your classmates.

However, no matter what their level of experience, personality, or skill as a lecturer, you should expect your instructors to grade you fairly and provide meaningful feedback on your papers and exams. They should be organized, prepared, and enthusiastic about their academic fields, and they should be accessible. You should always be able to approach your instructors if you need assistance or if you have a personal problem that affects your academic work.

Exchanging Ideas

Most college instructors have a passion for their field and love to exchange ideas. Many successful college graduates can name a particular instructor who made a positive difference in their lives and influenced their academic and career paths. Embrace opportunities to develop meaningful relationships with your instructors. Doing so could change your life for the better.

Hill Street Studios/Getty Images

What You Can Expect from Your Peer Leader

Many college success courses will include upper-level students who will work as coinstructors or student mentors. If your class has a peer leader, get to know that person and feel free to ask for advice about how to make the most of life on your campus. Peer leaders will usually be juniors or seniors and will remember what it was like to be a first-year student. They are selected because they have good academic records and strong leadership abilities, and because they want to help first-year students like you be successful.

Make the Most of the Learning Relationship

Most college instructors appreciate your willingness to ask for appointments. This may seem a little scary to some students, but most instructors welcome the opportunity to establish appropriate relationships with their students and to get to know them. As discussed in the first chapter of this book, it's up to you to take the initiative to visit your instructors during their office hours. Instructors are almost always required to keep office hours, so don't worry that you are asking for a special favor. Even part-time instructors, who may not be required to have office hours, can be available to help you with your coursework or answer your questions.

You can visit your instructors, either in real time or online, anytime during the term to ask questions, seek help with a difficult topic or assignment, or discuss a problem. If you have problems with one or more instructors, the course, or your grade, set up a meeting with them to work things out. If the problem is a grade, however, keep in mind that your instructors have the right to assign you a grade based on your performance, and no one can force them to change that grade.

People who become college instructors do so because they have a real passion for a particular subject. If you and your professor share an interest in a particular field of study, you will have the opportunity to develop a true friendship based on mutual interests. Instructors who know you well can also write that all-important letter of reference when you are applying to graduate or professional school or seeking your first job after college.

Understanding Academic Freedom

Colleges and universities have promoted the advancement of knowledge by granting instructors **academic freedom**, which is virtually unlimited freedom of speech and inquiry as long as human lives, rights, and privacy are not violated. Such freedom is not usually possible in other professions.

Most college instructors believe in the freedom to speak out, whether in a classroom discussion or at a political rally. You will benefit by listening to what they have to say and respecting their ideas and opinions. Think of where education would be if instructors were required to keep their ideas to themselves. You won't always agree with your instructors, and you might find that different instructors within the same academic field have different viewpoints on a single topic. Don't let this confuse you. This "intellectual diversity" is one of the special features of almost all higher education environments, and it can help you understand that there is seldom one right answer to any complex question.

Academic freedom also extends to students. Within the limits of civility and respect for others, you will be free to express your opinions in a way that might be different from your experiences in high school or work settings.

Handling a Conflict between You and an Instructor

Although there is a potential in any environment for things to go wrong, only rarely are problems between students and instructors impossible to resolve. If you have a conflict with an instructor, you should first ask the instructor for a meeting to discuss your problem. See whether the two of you can work things out. If the instructor refuses, go up the administrative ladder, starting at the bottom: first the department head, then the dean, and so on. Above all, don't let a bad experience sour you on college. Even the most disagreeable instructor will be out of your life by the end of the term. When all else fails, resolve to stick with the class until the final exam is behind you. Then shop carefully for instructors for next term by asking fellow students, your academic adviser, and others whose advice you can trust.

FAMILY CONNECTIONS

Almost all first-year students, no matter their age, are connected to other family members. Your family might be your parents and siblings, a partner, or a spouse and children. The relationships that you have with family members can be a source of support throughout your college years, and it's important that you do your part to maintain those relationships.

If you come from a cultural background that values family relationships and responsibilities above everything else, you will also have to work to balance your home life and your college life. In some cultures, if your grandfather or aunt needs help, that might be considered just as important—or more important—than going to class or taking an exam.

Negotiating the demands of college and family can be difficult. However, most college instructors will be flexible with requirements if you have genuine problems with meeting a deadline because of family obligations. But it's important that you explain your situation to your instructors; don't expect them to guess what you need. As the demands on your time increase, it's also important that you talk with family members to help them understand your role and responsibilities as a student.

Marriage and Parenting during College

Can marriage, parenting, or other family responsibilities coexist with being a college student? The answer, of course, is *yes*, although meeting everyone's needs—your own, a significant other's, your family's—is not easy. If you are married, with or without children, you need to become an expert at time management. If you do have children, make sure you find out what resources your college offers to help you with child care.

Sometimes, going to college can create conflict within a family. Partners and children can be threatened and intimidated if you take on a new identity and a new set of responsibilities. Financial pressures are likely to put an extra strain on your relationship, so both you and your partner will have to work hard at paying attention to each other's needs. Be sure to involve your family members in your decisions. Bring them to campus at every opportunity and let them read your papers and other assignments. Set aside time for your partner and your family just as carefully as you schedule your work and your classes. Most family difficulties can be resolved with good communication. Trust your own ability to be resilient and to maintain your motivation in the face of occasional conflict.

Sweet Success

Whether you are single or have a spouse or partner, being a parent while being a college student is one of the most challenging situations you can face. Find other students who have children so that you have a support system—it can make all the difference. You may not believe it now, but you are functioning as an important role model for your children. They will learn from you that education is worth striving for, even in the face of many obstacles.

Paul Barton/Getty Images

Relationships with Your Parents

Whether you live on campus or at home, your relationship with your parents will never be quite the same as it was before you began college. Your father and mother may have made all or most of your decisions in the past, but now your instructors, academic advisers, and other administrators will expect you to make important choices for yourself, such as what your major will be, where and how much you work, and what you do on weekends. You might find that it's hard to make choices on your own without talking to your parents first. While you should continue to communicate with your parents, don't let them make all your decisions. Your college can help you draw the line between the decisions you should make alone and those that would benefit from seeking advice from your parents. Many college students live in blended families, with more than one set of parents involved in their college experience. If your father or mother has remarried, you might even have to negotiate with both family units.

So how can you have a good relationship with your parents during this period of transition? A first step in establishing a good relationship with them is to be aware of their concerns. Your parents may be worried that you'll harm yourself in some way. They might still see you as young and innocent, and they don't want you to make the same mistakes that they might have made or experience negative aspects of the college experience that they have seen publicized in the media. They might be concerned that your family or cultural values will change or that you'll never really come home again, and, for some students, that is exactly what happens.

Remember, though, that parents generally mean well. Most of them love their children, even if their love isn't always expressed in the best way. Your parents have genuine concerns that you will understand even better if and when you become a parent yourself. To help your parents feel more comfortable with your life in college, try setting aside regular times to update them on how things are going for you. Ask for and consider their advice. You don't have to take it, but it can be useful to think about what your parents suggest, along with the other factors that will help you make decisions.

Even if you're successful in establishing appropriate boundaries between your life and your parents' lives, it's hard not to worry about what's happening at home, especially when your family is in a crisis. If you find yourself in the midst of a difficult family situation, seek help from your campus's counseling center or from a chaplain—people who are available for support even in "normal" times. Just reach out. When you receive help with your emotional needs, you can manage the tough times in more productive ways.

high-impact
practice 3

> **your turn**   Setting Goals
>
> **Determining your Family's Role in your College Success**
>
> In a small group, talk about how your family is adjusting to your college experience. Are they supportive, fearful, meddling, remote? How do their attitudes and reactions affect your motivation with regard to college? Share strategies with other students for handling issues that arise and staying motivated, even when family issues seem to get in the way.

Homesickness

Going to college can be a huge adjustment. You leave everything you have known growing up—your family, friends, your room, your pets, and the familiar routine of your hometown. Even students who stay close to home may choose to live on campus and will have to change their daily patterns to accommodate new demands of independence. The food is different, the professors leave as soon as the class period is over, and there is not a specific meal time when you know you can connect with others. With this big shift in your environment, it is normal to feel lost. You are not alone. According to a 2017 survey conducted at the University of California, Los Angeles, about two-thirds of first-year college students experience homesickness at some point[1]. For some, adjusting to transition happens quickly, and after the first few weeks there will be new friends, lots of classwork, and extracurricular activities occupying your time and your mind. For others transition is more difficult. Here are some tips that will help you as you move from home to college:

- Don't let go of home all at once. Keep in touch with parents, friends from home, and parts of your routine that are important to you like religious activities or exercise routines. These things can help you remember who you are even when you are in a new place.
- Reach out slowly. The choices in college can be overwhelming, so don't take on too much right away. Create your new routine a little at a time by trying new things with other first-year students. You don't have to commit to anything if it doesn't feel right for you.
- Keep in mind that you are not the only new person at your college. Reach out to other first-year students who may also be feeling the same way. You may feel better knowing you are not the only one who is missing home.

If you can't find another student to talk to, go the college counseling center. Counselors are used to helping students make this adjustment every year.

College on Screen

For decades, the college experience has been the basis of numerous television shows like *Felicity, Undeclared, Greek, Community,* and *Grown-ish* (the cast of which is shown here), and movies like *Animal House, Revenge of the Nerds, Old School, Legally Blonde,* and *The Social Network.* What is it about college students that makes for such good storytelling? Have you seen any movies or TV shows that really struck a chord of familiarity with what you are experiencing as a college student?

Freeform/Photofest

---

[1]E. B. Stolzenberg, et al. "The American Freshman: National Norms Fall 2017," Los Angeles: Higher Education Research Institute, UCLA, 2019.

PERSONAL RELATIONSHIPS

One of the best things about going to college is meeting new people. In fact, scholars who study college students have found that you'll learn as much—or more—from other students as you'll learn from instructors. Although not everyone you meet will become a close friend, you will likely find a few relationships that are really special, that expose you to new backgrounds and worldviews, and that might even last a lifetime.

Roommates

Adjusting to a roommate is a significant transition experience. You might make a lifetime friend or end up with an exasperating acquaintance you wish you'd never known. A roommate doesn't have to be a best friend, just someone with whom you can share your living space comfortably.

Perhaps your current roommate is someone you wouldn't have selected if the decision had been up to you. The person may be of a different race or ethnic group or may have different attitudes or experiences than you. Although it's tempting to room with your best friend from high school, that friend might not make the best roommate. In fact, many students lose friends by rooming with them. Many students end up developing a lasting relationship with someone who at first was a total stranger. It's important for roommates to establish, in writing, their mutual rights and responsibilities. Many colleges provide contract forms that you and your roommate might find useful if things go wrong. If you have problems with your roommate, talk them out promptly. Talk directly—politely, but plainly. If the problems persist or if you don't know how to talk them out, ask your residence hall advisers for help; they are trained to help resolve roommate conflicts. Usually you can tolerate, and perhaps even learn from, a less-than-ideal situation, but if things get really bad and do not improve, insist on a change. If you live on campus, talk to your residence hall adviser or to a professional counselor in your campus's counseling center.

> ## your turn | Making Decisions
>
> ### What about Online Relationships?
>
> Have you met someone interesting online? Do you plan to meet that individual in person? While some online relationships can blossom when the parties meet face-to-face, others can be disappointing or even dangerous. If you want to get together in person with someone you've met online, it's a good idea to meet in a public place and to bring a friend along for that first meeting. At that point, based on your interaction, you can choose whether you want to see this person again or whether one "date" was enough. Read "Communicating in a Digital Age" in this chapter for more information on this topic.

Romantic Relationships

You may already be in a long-term, committed relationship as you begin college, or you might have your first serious romance with someone you meet on campus. Since college allows you to meet people from different backgrounds with whom you share common interests, you might find it easier to meet romantic partners in college than it ever was before. Whether you choose to commit to one serious relationship or keep yourself open to meeting different people, you'll grow and learn a great deal about yourself and those with whom you become involved.

If you are seriously thinking about getting married or entering a long-term commitment, consider this: Studies show that the younger you are when you marry, the lower your odds are of enjoying a successful marriage. It is important not to marry before both you and your partner are certain of who you are and what you want. Many eighteen- to twenty-year-olds change their outlook and life goals drastically as they get older, which can negatively affect a romantic relationship.

Breaking Up. Breaking up is hard, but if it's time to end a romantic relationship, do it cleanly and calmly. Explain your feelings and talk them out. If you don't get a mature reaction, take the high road; don't join someone else in the mud.

If your partner breaks up with you, you might find yourself sad, angry, or even depressed. If that breakup happens through a text, an e-mail, or another form of social media, ask to have a face-to-face meeting or at least a telephone conversation with that person. (See the section on Communicating in a Digital Age later in this chapter.) Almost everyone has been rejected or "dumped" at one time or another. Let some time pass, be open to emotional support from your friends and your family, and, if necessary, pay a visit to your college counselor, a chaplain, or another trusted faculty member. These skilled professionals have assisted many students through similar experiences, and they can be there for you as well. You can also find many books in bookstores and in your library that will have good information on the topic of surviving a breakup.

isthisyou?

In a Long-Distance Relationship

Are you a first-year college student who has a romantic partner at another college or university miles away from you? Negotiating long-distance relationships while trying to do well in college can be a significant challenge. You might find yourself feeling guilty if you enjoy activities on campus when your partner isn't around. Try not to let this relationship get in the way of your enjoyment of the whole college experience and your commitment to doing well academically. Depending on you and your partner, the relationship may become stronger, or you may decide that absence doesn't really "make the heart grow fonder," but instead creates problems that seem insurmountable. If you find that it's difficult or impossible to negotiate a long-distance romance, seek some help from your counseling center before making any major decisions. Many students have been in the same situation as you.

---

your turn | **Write and Reflect**

high-impact practice 2

When Romantic Relationships End

On the basis of your experience or the experience of someone close to you, write a journal entry with advice or emotional support that you would give a student who is dealing with a breakup.

Relationship No-Nos. If you find yourself becoming attracted to an instructor or someone else who has the power to affect your grades or your job, remember this: It is never wise to get involved with someone who is in a "power relationship" with you—unbalanced relationships create opportunities for abuses of power and/or sexual harassment. Even dating coworkers is risky; it will be much harder to heal from a breakup if you must continue to work with your ex. You won't be sorry if you choose to maintain strictly professional relationships in the classroom and in the workplace.

MAINTAINING SEXUAL HEALTH

Numerous studies report that about 75 percent of traditional-age college students have engaged in sexual intercourse at least once. Whether or not you are part of this percentage, it can be helpful to explore your sexual values and consider whether sex is right for you at this time in your life. Many students have had different levels of exposure to sex education and have a different view and knowledge base about their sexual experiences. If it is the right time for you to become sexually active, you should know what resources are available and adopt strategies for avoiding the unwanted consequences of unprotected sex. This section provides resources to help you make informed and educated decisions regarding your sexual health.

Communicating about Safe Sex

Communication is the most important aspect of both casual and long-term sexual relationships. You and your partner must share your experiences and communicate needs, backgrounds, and how to be safe. Without communication, partners do not know each other's expectations, intentions can get confused, and emotions can become muddled. Here are some strategies to help with communication:

- Discuss testing for sexually transmitted infections (STIs). Make sure both partners have been tested recently. The rule of thumb for a sexually active person is to get tested at least once a year, and after any unprotected encounter.
- Communicate expectations. Partners should talk about what they expect from the sexual encounter. Partners should be clear about what they are comfortable with and what they want to get out of the experience, and should check in with each other throughout to make sure that they are still comfortable with what is happening. If at any point you or your partner changes their mind or no longer feels comfortable, stop immediately. Discuss how you or your partner would like to continue, if at all.
- Use protection. Protecting yourself and your partner from unwanted consequences—pregnancy or the transmission of STIs—is important, and so is communicating about protection ahead of time. Do you and your partner have what you need, or does one of you need to buy it? One night can change your entire life, so make sure you are prepared.
- Communicate in "I" statements. "I" statements help facilitate open communication. When you use "I" statements, you accept responsibility

for your feelings, you do not accuse or threaten another. A statement like "I feel like we need to explore our options," is more useful than "You don't know what you're talking about." Remember, each individual brings previous personal experiences into an encounter or a relationship; being aware of this helps with communication, whether you are talking or listening.

Avoiding Sexually Transmitted Infections (STIs)

You can avoid STIs and unwanted pregnancies by abstaining from sex entirely. According to national research, 25 percent of college students choose this option. For many people, masturbation is a reasonable alternative to sex with a partner.

If you're in the remaining 75 percent, you'll be safer, in terms of STI transmission, if you have only one partner. As a responsible adult, you have the option to choose your sexual experiences. Whether you're monogamous or not, you should always protect yourself by using a condom or being sure your partner uses one.

In addition to offering contraceptive protection, a condom can help prevent the spread of STIs, including human immunodeficiency virus (HIV) and human papillomavirus (HPV). A condom offers effective protection against the spread of disease during anal, vaginal, and oral intercourse. The most up-to-date research indicates that condoms are 90 to 99 percent effective at both preventing the transmission of STIs and preventing pregnancy when used correctly and consistently for every act of anal, vaginal, and oral intercourse. Note that only latex rubber condoms and polyurethane condoms—not lambskin or other types of natural membrane condoms—provide this protection. The polyurethane condom is a great alternative for individuals who have allergies to latex. Use a water-based lubricant such as K-Y Jelly rather than an oil-based lubricant, which can cause a latex condom to break.

The problem of STIs on college campuses has received growing attention in recent years as epidemic numbers of students have become infected. In general, STIs continue to increase faster than other illnesses on campuses today, and approximately 5 to 10 percent of visits by U.S. college students to college health services are for the diagnosis and treatment of STIs. STIs are usually spread through genital contact. Sometimes, however, these infections can be transmitted mouth-to-mouth. Leaving the light on before intercourse can give you an opportunity to notice symptoms of an STI on your partner, and it can also help with proper condom use.

There are more than twenty known types of STIs; seven are most common on college campuses. One particularly common STI is HPV, a sexually transmitted infection that is closely linked to cervical cancer. In fact, the CDC estimates that twenty million people in the United States are currently infected with HPV. Gardasil, a vaccine that became available in 2006, provides protection for both men and women against the strains of HPV that cause genital warts, anal cancer, and cervical cancer. For more information about this vaccine or to receive the three-injection series, contact your college or university health services or your local health care provider.

Using Birth Control

Sexually active, heterosexual students have to take steps to prevent unwanted pregnancies. Planning is the key. The best method of contraception is any method that you use correctly and consistently each time you have intercourse. Always discuss birth control with your partner so that you both feel comfortable with the option you have selected. For more information about a particular method, consult a pharmacist, your student health center, a local family-planning clinic, or your private physician. Remember, birth control is not the answer to safe sex—it only protects against pregnancy. Use condoms for protection against STIs, in *addition* to your chosen method of pregnancy prevention.

What if the condom breaks or you forget to take your birth control pill? Emergency contraceptive pills can reduce the risk of pregnancy. According to the Planned Parenthood Federation of America, if emergency contraceptive pills are taken within 72 hours of unprotected intercourse, they can significantly reduce the risk of pregnancy. Most campus health centers and local health clinics dispense emergency contraception.

Protecting Yourself and Others against Sexual Assault and Violence

Sexual assault that happens on college campuses is a problem that has existed for many years. Everyone is at risk for becoming a victim of sexual assault, but the majority of victims are women. The results of a recent study conclude that during their first year in college, one in seven women will have experienced incapacitated assault or rape (that is, assault or rape that took place while the women were incapacitated, generally by drugs or alcohol), and nearly one in ten women will have experienced assault or rape committed by force.[2] According to nationwide research, more than 80 percent of these women will be assaulted or raped by someone they know[3]—and most will not report the crime. Alcohol is a factor in nearly 75 percent of the incidents.[4] A disturbing finding reported in a recent issue of the *American Economic Journal* reports a significant increase in reports of sexual assault on college football game day. Experts believe that these incidents are linked to the party culture and alcohol abuse that surrounds college football.[5]

Interventions to reduce sexual violence on campus are urgently needed. In 2013, the federal government instituted an initiative called the Campus Save Act. The act mandates that all universities must provide sexual assault, violence, and harassment education to students. The Campus Save Act provides an amendment to the Clery Act of 1990, which the federal government implemented after a woman was raped and killed. The Clery Act required postsecondary institutions to report

[2]Kate B. Carey et al., "Incapacitated and Forcible Rape of College Women: Prevalence across the First Year," *Journal of Adolescent Health* 56 (2015): 678–80, http://i2.cdn.turner.com/cnn/2015/images/05/20/carey_jah_proof.pdf.

[3]C. P. Krebs et al., *The Campus Sexual Assault (CSA) Study* (Washington, DC: National Institute of Justice, 2007): 2–3, https://www.ncjrs.gov/pdffiles1/nij/grants/221153.pdf.

[4]Meichun Mohler-Kuo et al., "Correlates of Rape While Intoxicated in a National Sample of College Women," *Journal of Studies on Alcohol* 65, no. 1 (2004): 37–45, http://www.jsad.com/doi/10.15288/jsa.2004.65.37.

[5]https://pubs.aeaweb.org/doi/pdfplus/10.1257/app.20160031

sexual and other crimes and related statistics. Colleges can report cases of sexual misconduct, but as always, the student's information must remain confidential. It is always up to the victims to decide how they would like to proceed after a sexual assault has occurred.

Whether sexually assaulted by an acquaintance or by a stranger, a survivor can suffer long-term traumatic effects as well as depression, anxiety, and even suicide. Many survivors essentially blame themselves, but the only person at fault for a sexual assault is the perpetrator. If you are a survivor of sexual assault, regardless of whether you choose to report it to the police, it is useful to seek help by contacting a counselor, a local rape crisis center, campus public safety, student health services, women's student services, or a local hospital emergency room. Here are some steps you can take to help a person who has experienced a sexual assault:

- Remain empathetic and nonjudgmental
- Keep information private, and ensure the survivor's confidentiality
- Listen
- Talk with the survivor about how to proceed; discuss options like contacting campus police or the campus counseling center
- Seek out advice from a professional on how to help the survivor
- Stay in touch, and follow up to see if the survivor is getting help

If you observe a sexual assault or a potential sexual assault, make your presence known. Don't be a bystander; intervene in any way you can. Create a distraction, and if you need help, ask a friend, a resident assistant, or even a bartender or bouncer to help you.

COMMUNICATING IN A DIGITAL AGE

So much of our communication with others occurs through e-mail, text and photo messaging, mobile apps, and posting on social networking sites such as Snapchat, Instagram, or Facebook. Online communication enables us to connect with others, whether we're forming new friendships or romantic relationships or maintaining established ones. Online communication also gives us a broad sense of community, particularly in difficult times.

Whereas people used to gather around the proverbial water cooler to chat, new media continually offer new virtual gathering places. Given how often we use technology to communicate with others, it becomes critically important to use it properly. Here are some helpful suggestions, which are also summarized in Table 12.1.[6]

- **Match the seriousness of your message to your communication medium.** Know when to communicate online versus offline. Texting friends to remind them of a coffee date that you've already set up is likely quicker and less disruptive than calling them. E-mail may be best when dealing with problematic people or trying to resolve certain types of conflicts because it allows you to take the time to

---

[6]Adapted from Steven McCornack, *Reflect & Relate: An Introduction to Interpersonal Communication*, 3rd ed. (Boston: Bedford/St. Martin's, 2013), pp. 24–27.

TABLE 12.1 › Best Practices for Online Communication

Key Points to Remember	Best Practices
1. Match the gravity of your message to your communication medium.	*Online* is best for transmitting quick reminders, linear messages, or messages that require time and thought to craft. *Offline* is better for sharing personal information such as engagement announcements or news of health issues.
2. Online communication is not necessarily more efficient.	If your message needs a quick decision or answer, a phone call or a face-to-face conversation may be better. Use online communication if you want the person to have time to respond.
3. Presume that your posts are public.	If you wouldn't want a message to be seen by the general public, don't post it or send it online.
4. Remember that your posts are permanent.	Even after you delete something, it still exists on servers and may be accessible.
5. Practice the art of creating drafts.	Don't succumb to the pressure to answer an e-mail immediately. Taking time to respond will result in a more competently crafted message.
6. Protect your online identity.	Choose passwords carefully and limit the personal information you put online.
7. Protect yourself when online correspondence turns into face-to-face communication.	Exercise caution and common sense when meeting any online acquaintances in person.

Source: Information from Steven McCornack, *Reflect & Relate: An Introduction to Interpersonal Communication,* 3rd ed. (Boston: Bedford/St. Martin's, 2013), pp. 24–27.

think and carefully draft and revise your responses before sending them, which isn't possible in person.

Use face-to-face interactions for in-depth, lengthy, and detailed explanations of professional or personal problems or important relationship decisions. Although online communication is common, many people still expect important news to be shared in person. Most of us would be surprised if a close friend revealed a long-awaited pregnancy through e-mail or if a family member disclosed a serious illness through a text message.

- **Don't assume that online communication is always more efficient.** Issues that may cause an emotional reaction are more effectively and ethically handled in person or over the phone. So are many simple things—like deciding when to meet or where to go to lunch. Often a 1-minute phone call or a quick face-to-face exchange can save several minutes of texting.
- **Presume that your posts are public.** You may be thinking of the laugh you'll get from friends when you post the funny picture of you drunkenly hugging a houseplant on Snapchat. But would you want family members, future in-laws, or potential employers to see the

picture? Even if you have privacy settings on your personal page, what's to stop friends from downloading your photos and posts and distributing them to others? Keep this rule in mind: Anything you've sent or posted online can potentially be seen by anyone.

- **Remember that your posts are permanent.** What goes online or is shared through a mobile app lives on forever, despite some sites' claims to the contrary. Old e-mails, photos, videos, tweets, blogs, you name it—all of these may still be accessible years later. As just one example, everything you have ever posted on Facebook is stored on the Facebook server, whether or not you delete it from your profile, and Facebook legally reserves the right to sell your content, as long as they first delete personally identifying information such as your name. Think before you post.

- **Practice the art of creating drafts.** Get into the habit of saving text and e-mail messages as drafts, then revisiting them later and editing them for appropriateness, effectiveness, and ethics. Because online communication makes it easy to insult someone without thinking, many of us impetuously fire off messages that we later regret.

- **Protect yourself and your online identity, and protect yourself when online correspondence turns into face-to-face communication.** Choose secure passwords for your social networking sites and for course sites where your grades might be listed. Limit the amount of personal information available on any online profile, ratchet up your security settings, and accept friend requests only from people you know. Exercise caution and common sense when meeting in person someone you've met online. Keep in mind that some people lie in their profiles and posts.

Cyberbullying. In recent years, cyberbullying has been on the rise, not just in grade school and high school, but on college campuses as well. Experts define cyberbullying as "any behavior performed through electronic or digital media by individuals or groups who repeatedly communicate hostile or aggressive messages intended to inflict harm or discomfort on others."[7] According to a recent study, the prevalence of cyberbullying among college populations ranges from 10 to 28.7 percent.[8] These may seem like low numbers, but cyberbullying can go unreported because of embarrassment or privacy concerns. Tragic cyberbullying stories that have resulted in the victim's clinical depression or suicide have been reported in recent years.

Cyberbullying is a serious issue that harms individuals in many ways. It is a crime that should be dealt with immediately. If someone you know has experienced cyberbullying or if you have been a cyberbullying victim, you should report it as soon as possible. Several foundations and resources are available to help students report cyberbullying:

- **Stopbullying.gov**
- The Megan Meier Foundation, **meganmeierfoundation.org**
- National Crime Prevention Council, **ncpc.org**

---

[7]P. K. Smith et al., "Cyberbullying: Its Nature and Impact in Secondary School Pupils," *Journal of Child Psychology and Psychiatry*, no. 49 (2008): 375–76.
[8]Carlos P. Zalaquett and SeriaShia J. Chatters, "Cyberbullying in College: Frequency, Characteristics, and Practical Implications," *SAGE Open* (Jan.–Mar. 2014): 1–8. Web.

Victimized by Cyberbullying?

Have you or a friend ever felt victimized by something someone posted about you on social media? It's tempting to lash out with an equally negative post, but the best strategy is to disengage. Don't let what others say or write about you define who you are.

Owen Franken/Getty Images

GET INVOLVED

A college or university can seem to be a huge and unfriendly place, especially if you went to a small high school or grew up in a small town. To feel comfortable in this new environment, it is important for you to get involved in campus life.

Getting involved is not difficult, but it will take some initiative on your part. Consider your interests and the high school activities you enjoyed most, and choose some related activities to explore. You might be interested in joining an intramural team, performing community service, running for a student government office, or getting involved in your residence hall, or you might prefer to join a more structured campuswide club or organization.

While involvement is the key, it's important to strike a balance between finding a niche where you are immediately comfortable and challenging yourself to have new and different interactions with others. Having an open mind and experiencing diversity will prepare you for the workforce you will enter after you graduate.

Almost every college has numerous organizations you can join; usually, you can check them out through activity fairs, printed guides, open houses, web pages, and so on. If a particular organization interests you, consider attending one of the organization's meetings before you decide to join. Find out what the organization is like, what the expected commitment is in terms of time and money, and whether you feel comfortable with its members.

Be careful not to overextend yourself when it comes to campus activities. Although it is important to get involved, joining too many clubs or organizations will make it difficult to focus on any one activity and will interfere with your studies. Future employers will see a balance in academics and campus involvement as a desirable quality in prospective employees.

> ## your turn | Feeling Connected
>
> **Explore Involvement Opportunities**
>
> After you have been at your institution for a month or so, you will have been presented with opportunities to get involved. Get together with four or five other students in your class and share what you have learned about how to get involved and about participating in clubs or organizations. Share both the positives and the negatives of your involvement experiences, as well as your beliefs about how many extracurricular clubs or organizations a first-year student should join.

To Greek or Not to Greek?

Greek social organizations are not all alike, nor are their members. Fraternities and sororities can be a rich source of friendship and support. Some students love them. Other students find them philosophically distasteful, too demanding of time and money, or too restricting. Greek rush (member recruitment) on your campus might happen before you have decided whether you want to go Greek or before you have determined which fraternity or sorority is right for you. There is nothing wrong with delaying a decision about Greek membership.

If Greek life is not for you, consider the many other ways that you can make close friends. Many campuses have residence halls or special floors for students with common interests or situations, such as first-year students; honors students; students in particular majors; students with strong ethnic or religious affiliations; students who do not use tobacco, alcohol, and drugs; environmentally conscious students; and so on. Check them out. Often, they provide very satisfying experiences.

Working

One of the best ways to develop meaningful relationships on your campus is to get an on-campus job, either through the federal work-study program or directly through the college. You might not make as much money working on campus as you would in an off-campus job, but the relationships that you'll develop with influential people who care about your success in college and who will write those all-important reference letters make on-campus employment well worth it. Consider finding a job related to your intended major. For instance, if you are a film major, you might be able to find on-campus work in a media production lab or

techtip

MAINTAIN A HEALTHY RELATIONSHIP WITH SOCIAL MEDIA

You go online to post a photo or check your e-mail, and before you know it, you've spent three hours scrolling through Facebook, liking memes on Instagram, and watching videos on YouTube.

While you enjoyed some of these, overall you might feel unproductive, lethargic, and a bit gloomy.

The Problem

Your social media use is making you feel more isolated, and you feel like you're spending too much time on your smartphone.

The Fix

Take some breaks from social media and create better boundaries for yourself.

Kornburut Woradee/EyeEm/Getty Images

How to Do It

1. *Track and limit your usage.* Use apps like OFFTIME, Moment, and SPACE to track your phone usage behavior and block yourself from the sites that take up the most of your time. With these apps you can set personal device usage goals and receive gentle reminders when you're falling back into harmful patterns.

2. *Put the phone down.* Try to recognize the moments when your phone should be silent, off, or put away, especially when you're with company. If you're with others, play a game and see who can go the longest without checking their phones. If you take a photo or video, wait until later to post it online so that you can focus on enjoying the moment.

3. *Take breaks.* Take breaks from social media when it distracts you too much or makes you feel negative emotions like loneliness or jealousy. You can delete the apps from your phone and check your accounts only on a computer, or you can deactivate your accounts for a day, week, or month for a real break.

4. *Unfollow negative accounts.* If someone's profile makes you feel bad about yourself—maybe an influencer with perfect-looking photos or an ex-partner—don't be afraid to cut yourself off from them. If you don't want to block their account entirely, sites like Facebook and Instagram allow you to "mute" or "unfollow" accounts without alerting their owners. Also, while online discourse can be fun and enlightening, it can also turn ugly if that discourse isn't respectful. Remember the saying "Don't feed the trolls," and don't engage in online arguments with hostile users.

5. *Don't Compare Yourself to a Profile.* Remember that while someone's life may *seem* perfect on their social media accounts, you're looking at a filtered, curated narrative showing you what they *want* you to see. You're just seeing a highlight of their life, not the full story.

EXTRA STYLE POINTS If you're looking for more connections in real life, use social media to find discussion groups, events, and people with similar interests in your area. Facebook's "Events" page advertises free and open events, and apps like Meetup, Friender, and Bumble BFF may be able to help you find new friends. Be careful, though, to always meet these people in a safe, public place, and not to give away too much identifying information about yourself until you've gotten to renting out film equipment. That work could help you gain knowledge and experience, as well as make connections with faculty experts in your field. If an on-campus job is not available or if you don't find one that appeals to you, an off-campus job can allow you to meet new people in the community as well.

Community Service

As a first-year student, one way to get involved with your college or university or with the community is to consider volunteering for a community-service project. Your campus's division of student affairs might have a volunteer or community-service office that offers many opportunities that match local needs with your particular interests. You can also check the Volunteer Match website (**volunteermatch.org**) for opportunities in your area. Simply enter your ZIP code and, if you wish, keywords to help you find volunteer work in a particular field.

checklist for success

Relationships

■ **Do your part to build a learning relationship with your instructors.** Ask good questions in and out of class, and visit instructors during their posted office hours.

■ **Be open to new relationships.** College may be a great time for you to test out serious relationships, including romantic ones.

■ **Don't hesitate to get help from your campus counseling center.** When counselors are asked, "What is the most common type of problem you help students address?" the answer is "relationship issues."

■ **Work to have a good relationship with your family during the college years.** Family members have your best interests at heart, and college is a time to become closer to them while also setting boundaries.

■ **Get involved.** Join other students in groups sponsored by your college or university. Students who are involved on campus are more likely to graduate from college than those who are not. Getting

involved is fun, easy, free, and rewarding, and employers will be interested in your extracurricular activities. Ways to get involved include social organizations, on- or off-campus jobs, and community service.

■ **Know that social organizations, such as fraternities and sororities, can be very supportive of college success.** They can also be very disruptive, so make careful choices regarding your involvement with these groups.

■ **Practice making good decisions about sexual health.** Make wise choices to protect yourself against unwanted pregnancy and sexually transmitted infections. Learn to communicate about sex, and work to develop and maintain respectful relationships.

■ **Learn about sexual assault.** Know how to define sexual assault, what laws are in place to protect survivors, and what you should do if you witness a sexual assault.

12 buildyourexperience

REFLECT ON CHOICES

high-impact practices 2, 5 College is a great time to build and nurture relationships with instructors, students your age, and students who are younger or older. The choice of whether to find new relationships is up to you. College offers lots of ways to meet new and interesting people. Consider finding an on-campus job, participating in community service, and becoming involved in a campus activity. Write a brief summary of the new relationships you've developed so far and the activities in which you're involved. Then write about whom you'd like to meet and how you would like to be involved during the rest of your college experience.

APPLY WHAT YOU HAVE LEARNED

Now that you have read and discussed this chapter, consider how you can apply what you have learned to your academic life and your personal life. The following prompts will help you reflect on chapter material and its relevance to you both now and in the future.

1. If you are not already involved in on-campus activities and clubs, visit your campus's website or activities office to learn more about the kinds of clubs, organizations, sports teams, and volunteer work that are offered. Find at least one activity that seems interesting to you and learn more about it. When does the group meet, how often, and how many students are involved?

2. Check out some of your fellow students' profiles on a social networking site such as Facebook or Twitter. What kinds of personal information do they share? What kinds of issues are they writing about? Do they use the privacy settings that are available? Do you think that it is important for college students to be careful about the kinds of information they post on social networking sites? Why or why not?

USE YOUR RESOURCES

> **Counseling Center** A helpful campus resource where you can obtain expert, confidential counseling from professionals at no charge. Remember that their support is confidential and that you will not be judged.

> **Chaplains** An often under-recognized way to get help with relationship issues is a session (or more) with a campus chaplain. Your academic adviser might be able to refer you to an appropriate chaplain, or you can seek out the one who represents your faith.

> **Health Center or Infirmary** Pay a visit to your campus health center or infirmary. On most campuses, the professionals who staff the health center are especially interested in educational outreach and practicing prevention. You should be able to receive treatment as well.

> **Student Organizations** The variety of student groups designed to bring together students is virtually unlimited. Explore student organizations on your campus.

> **Your College Success Instructor** Whether you are a student or a peer leader in the classroom, your course instructor can help you locate resources that will help you negotiate relationship issues.

> **Online Resources** The University of Chicago's "Student Counseling Virtual Pamphlet Collection" (**dr-bob.org/vpc**) takes you to dozens of websites devoted to problems in relationships. Browse among the many links to see whether any information applies to you. The University of Texas Counseling Center offers an online brochure that explores the ups and downs of romantic relationships. Visit **cmhc.utexas.edu/vav/vav_healthyrelationships.html**.

The website of the American College Health Association provides a list of resources for various health topics, including sexual health for heterosexual, cisgender, and LGBTQIA students: https://www.acha.org/

The website of the Center for Young Women's Health has helpful advice on sexual health and other issues: **youngwomenshealth .org**

 **LaunchPad**
macmillan learning

LaunchPad for *Your College Experience* is a great resource. Go online to master concepts using the LearningCurve study tool and much more. **Launchpadworks.com**

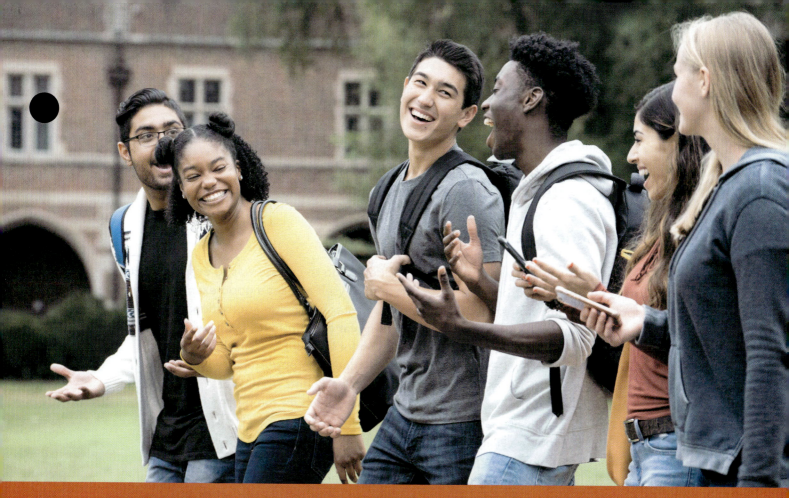

Ariel Skelley/DigitalVision/Getty Images

13

DIVERSITY AND INCLUSION

YOU WILL EXPLORE

What *diversity* and *inclusion* mean and the various kinds of diversity you will experience

How to identify and help overcome discrimination, prejudice, bias, and insensitivity on campus

The value of expanding your worldview in college, in the workplace, and in life

⚙ High-impact practices 2 (writing), 3 (collaboration), and 4 (global learning/diversity)

> **Despite the challenges, the opportunity to meet and interact with students from diverse backgrounds has been enriching for me personally and academically.**

Sam Edwards/Getty Images

Diversity and *inclusion* can mean many things to many people. For the purposes of introducing this chapter, we spoke to a number of students about their personal experiences with diversity.

At Florida Atlantic University in Boca Raton, Florida, we asked five students—Leticia, Wei, Darrell, Simone, and Olivia—to tell us about themselves: where they were from; why they decided to attend college; and how diversity has played a part in their lives, both in college and elsewhere. The students ranged in age from nineteen to twenty-five and grew up in places as varied as New Zealand, the state of Florida, China, New York City, and Mexico City. Most of the students chose Florida Atlantic University because of its numerous academic opportunities and its diverse community. Some of the students are adjusting to life in America for the first time, while others were born and raised here. Some of these students came to Florida Atlantic straight from high school, while others returned to college after a break. These students bring their own unique experiences to Florida Atlantic, and they strive to learn about the differences and similarities among them.

Leticia is the first person in her family to attend college, and she explained, "The reason I decided to go to college was to ensure a better future for myself and set a good example for my younger sister." Being an international student and living far away from his family was a tough transition for Wei, but he said that "despite the challenges, the opportunity to meet and interact with students from diverse backgrounds has been enriching for me personally and academically."

We asked the students to talk a bit about diversity and how it has played a part in their education. Darrell believes that it is important to seek out other people and other opinions. He said, "Your view in life is one of billions. Get to know some different points of view!" Leticia, Olivia, and Simone emphasized getting involved on campus so that you can learn to work with many people toward a common goal. As Simone put it, "Diversity brings language skills, new ways of thinking, and creative solutions to different problems." Darrell reminded us that it's important to reach out to students who may feel they're in the minority on campus. Simone acknowledged that diversity is international, adding, "The internet and improved transportation mean that contact between countries is increasing."

assess your strengths

Your college or university campus offers many opportunities for you to experience diversity. Through classes, clubs, and informal interactions, you will likely have experiences that enable you to explore diverse ideas or meet people from different countries, cultures, or religions. As you begin to read this chapter, think of specific examples of the ways that you've already experienced new ideas and people who are different from you.

set goals

What are your most important objectives in learning the material in this chapter? Think about any experiences that you've had in the past in the area of diversity, and write down three goals for the future, such as taking a course that is part of the diversity curriculum, getting to know someone from another country, or attending a campus event or celebration sponsored by students who are from a unique ethnic group.

 As demonstrated by the diverse group of students profiled here, a college or university can serve as a microcosm of the real world—a world that requires us all to work, live, and socialize with people from various ethnic and cultural groups. In few settings can members of different groups interact in such close proximity as on a college campus. Regardless of the type of institution you are attending, you will be exposed to new experiences and opportunities, all of which can enhance learning and understanding.

Through self-assessment, discovery, and open-mindedness, you can begin to understand your perspectives on diversity. This work, although difficult at times, will intensify your educational experiences, personal growth, and development. Thinking critically about your personal values and belief systems will allow you to have a greater sense of belonging and to make a positive contribution to our multicultural society.

 LaunchPad
macmillan learning

To access the LearningCurve study tool, video activities, and more, go to LaunchPad for *Your College Experience.*
Launchpadworks.com/

 high-impact practice 4

EXPLORING DIVERSITY AND INCLUSION

Colleges and universities attract students from different backgrounds, and therefore the ethnicity, cultural background, economic status, and religion of college students may vary widely. These differences provide opportunities for students to experience diversity.

Diversity is the difference in social and cultural identities among people living together. A diverse community has many advantages that include exposure to various cultures, historical perspectives, and ways of thinking. Diversity, however, can be challenging. An untested bias or assumption about other people or groups can create misunderstanding and suspicion of the beliefs and behaviors of others. A college campus can offer an ideal environment for exploring, understanding, and appreciating human differences.

Inclusion is the achievement of an environment in which everyone feels they belong and are treated fairly and respectfully. In an inclusive college or university all students and staff members have equal access to opportunities and resources, and all are invited to participate in and contribute fully to campus life. What role can you and your friends play in making your campus an inclusive environment?

high-impact practice 3

yourturn   **Feeling Connected**

Exploring Diversity in Your College Success Classroom

Look around your classroom. What kinds of diversity do you see? What other kinds of diversity might exist but can't be seen? With a small group of students, discuss the reasons some college students have an interest in diversity, both seen and unseen, and why other students avoid the topic. Share your ideas with the whole class.

Ethnicity, Culture, Race, and Religion

Often the terms *ethnicity* and *culture* are used interchangeably, but their definitions are different. **Ethnicity** refers to the identity that is assigned to a specific group of people who are historically connected by a common national origin or language. For example, Latinos are one of the largest ethnic groups in the United States, including people from more than thirty countries within North, Central, and South America. **Culture** is defined as the aspects of a group of people that are passed on or learned. Traditions, food, language, clothing styles, artistic expression, and beliefs are all part of culture.

Race commonly refers to visual characteristics that are shared by groups of people, including skin tone, hair texture and color, and facial features. Making generalizations about someone's race or ethnicity, however, is harmful. Even people who share some biological features—such as similar eye shape or skin color—might be ethnically distinct. Many students can trace their genetic make-up to more than one race. In fact, the population of students who are biracial or multiracial is projected to be the fastest growing population over the next several decades, and according to the U.S. Census Bureau, by around 2043 no one race/ethnic category in the United States will be a majority.[1]

All of us come into the world with our own unique characteristics, and the intersection of those identities (race, gender, sexual orientation, physical ability, and more) makes us who we are. Even if we are different

---

[1]https://www.census.gov/newsroom/blogs/random-samplings/2014/06/nation-to-become-a-plurality-but-some -areas-already-are.html

Let Diversity Energize You

Most colleges and universities are diverse environments. Some, however, are not. If you can't find diversity on campus, look for it in your community or region. If you are in a diverse campus environment, make the most of all the opportunities you have to meet, interact, enjoy, and learn from new and different people.

Ariel Skelley/Getty Images

from others in some ways, people around the world have one thing in common: We want to be respected. Whatever the color of your skin or hair, whatever your life experiences or cultural background, you want others to treat you fairly and acknowledge and value your contributions to your community and the world. And, of course, others want the same from you.

Religion is a specific set of beliefs and practices generally agreed on by a number of persons or sects. Freedom to practice one's religion has been central to the American experience from its beginning. In fact, many settlers of the original thirteen colonies came to North America to escape religious discrimination.

Many students come to college with deeply held religious views. Some will create or join faith communities on campus. These faith communities include those with a Judeo-Christian heritage, Islam, Hinduism, Buddhism, and more. Learning about different faith perspectives is another way you can explore human differences. Also, many students and instructors may consider themselves atheists or agnostics: They do not believe in, or are unsure about, the existence of a divine creator.

If you grew up in a home where certain religious beliefs were very important, college may give you a chance to step back and consider your faith from a more neutral standpoint apart from family influence. You may change what you believe, or your beliefs may become even stronger. Whatever *your* religious views may be, it is important that you respect the views of others. Learning more about other religions as practiced in the United States and around the world can help you better understand your own faith perspective.

Other Differences You Will Encounter in College

When you think about diversity, you might first think of differences in race or ethnicity. Although it is true that those are two forms of diversity, you will most likely experience many other types of diversity in college and in the workplace, including age, gender, economic status, physical challenges, learning challenges, and sexuality.

Age. Although many students enter college around age eighteen after they graduate from high school, others choose to enter or return in their twenties, thirties, and beyond. Age diversity in the classroom gives everyone the opportunity to learn from others who have different life experiences. Many factors determine when students enter higher education for the first time or whether they leave college and then reenter. If you are attending a college that has a large population of students who are older or younger than you, this can be an advantage. A campus where students of different ages are in classes together can be an invigorating learning environment. Resist making assumptions about students of different ages (e.g., adult students are "teachers' pets," traditionally aged students are "lazy").

Sex, Gender, and Sexual Orientation. The words *gender* and *sex* are often used interchangeably, but as you become part of an academic community, you might start to think differently about these related terms. While a person's *sex* is often thought of as being either male or female, some students identify as nonbinary, transgender, or intersex (individuals born with both male and female sex characteristics). Beyond sexual anatomy, multiple *gender* definitions and experiences are generally understood as existing on a continuum or spectrum. To offer support to students across the gender spectrum, many colleges and universities are now asking students to identify gender affiliation and gender expression voluntarily on admission applications. *Sexual orientation* is one's pattern of sexual, romantic, and emotional attraction—and a person's sense of identity based on those attractions. Sexual orientation is not the same as gender identity, the internal sense of being male, female, or something else.

You are probably familiar with the terms *gay*, *straight*, and *transgender*, as well as *homosexual*, *heterosexual*, and *bisexual*. You might be less familiar with the categories *queer*, *questioning*, *intersex*, *asexual*, and *ally*. These two sets of terms include people whose sexual orientation or gender identity is represented by the acronym **LGTBQIA** (lesbian, gay, transgender, bisexual, queer, intersex, and asexual). The LGBTQIA community advocates for human rights and fights against laws that do not include protections and just treatment for LGBTQIA individuals. According to the Human Rights Campaign (**www.hrc.org**), critical protections for the LGBTQIA community should be upheld in matters of immigration reform, public restroom use, consumerism, adoption, juror nondiscrimination, marriage, and many more. This movement lobbies for the inclusion of the LGBTQIA community's right to live, love, and pursue happiness in the United States and abroad.

In college, you will meet students, staff members, and instructors whose sexual orientation or gender identity is similar to or different from yours. Some people are lucky enough to have come from accepting environments; for many students, however, college is the first time they have been able to openly express their sexual or gender identity. These topics can be difficult to talk about; avoid making judgments about what you believe is appropriate or inappropriate for one group or another, and give others a chance to become educated without fear of judgment. Your campus might have a center for the LGBTQIA community. Consider attending educational events about sexual or gender identity on your campus to increase awareness, listen to the speakers, and expand your and others' worldviews. Use the resources available to you on campus so that you can learn how to respect all individuals and their unique identities.

You can also ask your college success instructor to suggest resources, which might include written materials in your college library, websites, and faculty members who specialize in human sexuality and gender issues. You might also want to take a gender- or sexuality-studies course if one is available at your college or university. These courses are generally interdisciplinary and explore subject matter from the perspective of gender or sexual orientation. These classes are not necessarily about women or men; rather, they consider how the concepts of gender and sexuality influence the way we see and shape the world around us. Such courses open up new ways of thinking about many aspects of society.

---

your turn **Write and Reflect**

⊕ *high-impact practice 2*

Gender and Opportunities

Has anyone ever tried to convince you to forgo an educational or job opportunity based on your gender expression? Are there special jobs or other life experiences that should be restricted by gender identity? Write a short paper in which you argue that gender expression and identity should or should not narrow life choices or options.

Economic Status. The United States is a country of vast differences in wealth. This considerable economic diversity can be either a positive or a negative aspect of college life. On the positive side, you will be exposed to, and can learn from, students who have had vastly different life experiences as a result of their economic backgrounds. Meeting others who have grown up with either more or fewer opportunities than you is part of learning how to live in a democracy.

Your economic background may influence your access to certain experiences in college or in life, like being able to live in a residence hall or having to live at home, but it does not determine your worth, your abilities, or what you may have in common with other students around you.

Learning and Physical Disabilities. The numbers of students with physical or learning disabilities are rising on most college campuses, as is the availability of services for these students. If you have a physical or learning disability, you're not alone.

Physical disabilities. These disabilities can affect a student's sight, hearing, or movement. If one or more physically disabled students is in any of your classes or your residence hall, don't avoid them even if their disability makes you feel uncomfortable. Treat them just as you would treat anyone else. In your interactions with them, it is okay to offer assistance. Be sure, however, to respect the student's personal space and dignity by asking before assisting.

Learning disabilities. You will interact with many students who have some sort of learning disability or difference (see Chapter 4 for more

Learning with a Disability

Many college students have a learning or physical disability, but that does not stop them from studying and graduating. All colleges must provide support services to students who have documented disabilities.

Huntstock/Getty Images

information on learning disabilities). Sometimes learning disabilities actually become strengths; what might be considered a disability can actually push students to become highly creative as they learn to maximize their unique abilities while adapting to the expectations of academic life. If you have, or think you might have, a learning disability, visit your campus accessibility center, disability services office, or learning center for testing, diagnosis, and advice on getting extra help for learning problems. If you require accommodations, be sure to inform the appropriate office on campus.

Ableism is defined as discrimination against people who have either physical or mental disabilities. Never underestimate what a student with a disability can accomplish. It is important to support and encourage these students and to eliminate negative predictions of what they can achieve.

Bias, Stereotyping, and Microaggressions

Many of our beliefs are the result of our personal experiences. Some of our beliefs may be based on a **bias**, which is an inclination or prejudice for or against one person or group, especially in a way considered to be unfair.

Others are a result of a **stereotype**, which is a generalization, usually exaggerated or oversimplified—and often offensive—that is used to describe or distinguish a group. What we might have heard throughout our lives from family members, friends, or neighbors about their negative views of members of a particular group may result in our stereotyping of people in that group. We may acquire stereotypes about people we have never met before, or we may have bought into a stereotype without even thinking about it. Children who grow up in an environment in which dislike and distrust of certain types of people are openly expressed might adopt those judgments, even if they have had no direct interaction with those being judged.

Sometimes interacting in the diverse environment that college represents can result in **microaggressions**, which are subtle but offensive comments that reinforce bias against or stereotypes of minority populations.[2] For instance, what if a white person interviewed a minority person for a position with an advertising agency or another corporate setting, and said, "Wow, you are very well spoken!" This kind of statement suggests that the interviewer is biased and believes that most of the people in the interviewee's racial or ethnic group are not expected to be well spoken. This is an offensive generalization.

Or what if, in an effort to build rapport or make small talk, a white woman asks an Asian American woman "So, what country are you from?" Assuming a person is not originally from the United States based purely on that person's appearance can be offensive. Consider how you would feel if you were asked this question within your home country—alienated, misunderstood? Consider also what this kind of assumption says about the person who makes it.

In a college classroom, if the discussion topic is race relations, should one minority student be expected to speak on the topic as a spokesperson for an entire race? Of course not, but sometimes this happens. Although most of us would not intentionally insult someone of a different race or ethnic group, we do so when we aren't careful about the language we use or the assumptions we are inclined to make. While you are in college, learn to approach topics with an open mind and appreciation for different cultures, behaviors, and beliefs. Enjoy the diverse perspectives around you and be willing to listen and learn from them.

When meeting people for the first time, keep the following suggestions in mind:

1. **Focus on the Person:** Put aside any of your previous ethnic and racial stereotypes. Get to know the person as a blank slate. You may be fascinated by what you have in common.
2. **Avoid Guesswork:** Do not attempt to guess a person's race, language, diet, expected behavior, age, background, or knowledge based only on appearance. In other words, do not judge a book by its cover.

> ## is**this**you?
>
> **From Another Country**
>
> Are you a student who has recently come to the United States from another country? Perhaps you have immigrated to the United States with family members, or perhaps you immigrated on your own. Whatever your particular situation, learning the unique language, culture, and expectations of an American college or university can be a challenge, especially if English is not your primary language. You might find that instructors' expectations seem different from what you experienced in your home country. In the United States, most instructors want students to speak up in class and work in groups. You will also find that American students sometimes challenge their instructors in ways that might seem disrespectful to you. Even if you don't feel comfortable with your language skills, don't give up. Your college or university probably offers English as a Second Language courses or programs to help you with your English skills. Also, visit the international student office or center to investigate ways to increase your understanding of life in the United States, both on and off campus.

---

[2]McWhorter, J. (2014, March 21). " 'Microaggression' Is the New Racism on Campus." *Time magazine.* Retrieved from http://time.com/32618/microaggression-is-the-new-racism-on-campus/.

FIGURE 13.1 › The Pyramid of Hate

The Pyramid of Hate illustrates the prevalence of bias, hate, and oppression in our society. It is organized in escalating levels of attitudes and behavior that grow in complexity from bottom to top. Like a pyramid, the upper levels are supported by the lower levels. Bias at each level negatively impacts individuals, institutions, and society and it becomes increasingly difficult to challenge and dismantle as behaviors escalate. When bias goes unchecked, it becomes "normalized" and contributes to a pattern of accepting discrimination, hate, and injustice in society. While every biased attitude or act does not lead to genocide, each genocide has been built on the acceptance of attitudes and actions described at the lower levels of the pyramid. When we challenge those biased attitudes and behaviors in ourselves, others, and institutions, we can interrupt the escalation of bias and make it more difficult for discrimination and hate to flourish. *© 2019 Anti-Defamation League, www.adl.org. Reprinted with permission.*

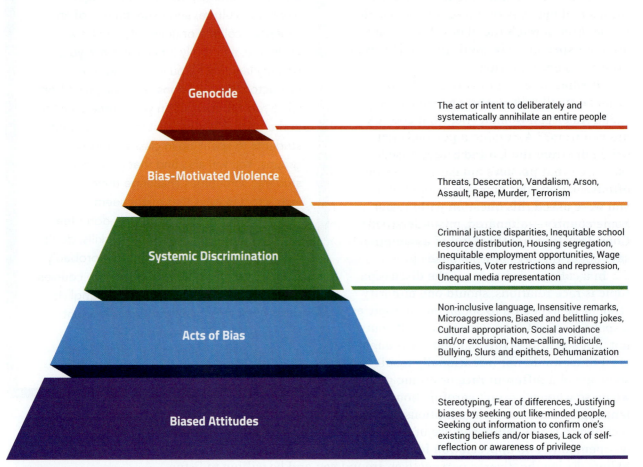

Pyramid of Hate © 2019 Anti-Defamation League

3. **Practice the Golden Rule:** Treat others as you want to be treated. If you are curious about someone's ethnicity or background, use conversation starters like "Tell me about yourself," or "Where did you attend high school?" Avoid questions that reflect assumptions and could cause offense or embarrassment. Questions such as "So, what are you?" are likely to insult the very person you are eager to get to know.

In college, you are likely to encounter personal values and belief systems that run counter to yours. When you find that you and your friends have different values, practice tolerance. Talking about diversity with someone else whose beliefs seem to conflict with your own can be very rewarding. A desired outcome from this kind of discussion is not necessarily to reach agreement but rather to build your understanding of why people have different values and beliefs, and how this understanding can enrich your college experience and your life beyond college. Because we live and work in a global economy, most sought-after job candidates in most industries are those who can respectfully engage with people from all walks of life.

In college, you have the opportunity to learn from many kinds of people, possibly many more than in your home community, which may not have offered the kind of diverse population you see on your college campus. Your lab partner in biology may be a veteran, and your sociology study group may include international students. Your roommate or suitemate in a residence hall may be someone of a different economic background or ethnic group. If you are taking one or more online courses, explore the diversity among other online students. You might find students from other states or countries, adult students, students with disabilities, and others who could be taking classes on campus but prefer to learn in an online format. Your college experience will be enriched if you are open to the possibility of learning from all members of the campus community.

Your openness to diversity, especially in college, will build your understanding of the many ways in which people are different from one another. Learn not to make assumptions, rely on stereotypes, or rush to judgment. Give yourself time to get to know different people before forming opinions about them.

Making New Friends
College is prime time for meeting new people, some of whom will become lifelong friends. Looks can be deceiving. In your first few conversations with new people, invite them to share something about themselves.
FatCamera/iStock/Getty Images

OVERCOMING DISCRIMINATION, PREJUDICE, AND INSENSITIVITY ON COLLEGE CAMPUSES

You might feel uncomfortable when asked about your views on diversity. As we have discussed earlier, we all have certain prejudices or biases, tendencies against or in favor of certain groups or value systems, but it is what we do with our individual beliefs that separates an unbiased and open-minded person from the racist, the bigot, and the extremist. Prejudice refers to preconceived ideas and expectations about a particular group. Racism is an offshoot of prejudice. It is the belief that differences among human racial groups determine achievement and that one's own race is superior or that a particular racial group is inferior to others.

Colleges strive to provide a welcoming and inclusive campus environment for all students that assures an absence of prejudice or racism. Because of acts of violence, intimidation, and stupidity occurring on campuses, college administrations have established policies against any and all forms of discriminatory actions, racism, and insensitivity. Most campuses have adopted zero-tolerance policies that prohibit verbal and nonverbal harassment and **hate crimes** such as physical assault, vandalism, and intimidation. A hate crime is defined as a crime motivated by prejudice. Such a crime occurs when a perpetrator targets victims because of their membership (or perceived membership) in a certain group. A hate crime can include physical assault, vandalism, and intimidation. One of the most common forms of hate crime on campus is graffiti that expresses racial, ethnic, and cultural slurs.

Get Involved

One of the abiding characteristics of the American college campus is that it has long been a haven for free speech and for students to vent their feelings and try out new ideas and forms of expression. See what you can learn from the activism on your campus. Find a cause that means something to you, and take steps to get involved!

Bloomberg/Getty Images

Some students are involved in hate crimes because of deeply held negative views or fears about people who represent a different race, ethnic group, or sexual orientation. Other students might "follow the crowd" or feel pressured by peers to participate in organized harassment of a certain group. Commit to becoming involved in making your campus a safe place for all students. If you have been a victim of a racist, insensitive, or discriminatory act, report it to the proper authorities such as your campus diversity office or, in the case of injury or threatened injury, the campus police. Seek help from your campus mental health resources if you are upset, frightened, or depressed because of the incident.

Raising Awareness

While hate crimes on college and university campuses are, thankfully, infrequent, they do happen. At Howard University in July of 2019, a trans woman of color reported a sexual assault on campus. At Stanford University, police investigated a noose that was placed in July of 2019 near a dorm where high school summer camp students were housed. In May of 2018, a black graduate student at Yale who had fallen asleep in a residence hall common room was awakened by police responding to an "emergency" call from another student who was white. The white student assumed that the black student was an intruder. While this incident didn't rise to the level of a hate crime, it shows an immediate negative reaction based on race.

Whether or not such actions cause tangible harm, they are still damaging. Consider a campus party that was held to celebrate Cinco de Mayo. Party organizers asked everyone to wear sombreros. On arrival, guests encountered a mock-up of a border patrol station on the front lawn and were required to crawl under or climb over a section of chain-link fencing. Student groups voiced their disapproval and hurt over such insensitivity, which resulted in campus probationary measures for the organization that had thrown the party. At a Halloween party at a large university, members of a campus organization decided to dress in Ku Klux Klan outfits while other members dressed as slaves and wore black shoe polish on their faces. The group then simulated slave hangings during the party. When photos of the events surfaced, the university suspended the group from campus, and the community demanded that the group be banned indefinitely.

For a number of years, stereotypes that are used to identify school sports teams and their supporters have disturbed ethnic and cultural groups such as Native Americans. Mascots that incorporate a bow and arrow, a tomahawk, feathers, and war paint have raised awareness about the promotion and acceptance of stereotypes associated with the concept of the "savage Indian." Some schools have responded by altering the images while retaining the mascot. Other schools, such as Southeastern Oklahoma State University and the University of Illinois Urbana-Champaign, have changed their mascots to move away from references to Native Americans. These stereotypes are damaging because they reinforce harmful ideas and are immediately hurtful to the group identified.

your turn | Setting Goals

Plan to be an Active Bystander

Can you recall an occasion in school or college when you were harassed for any reason, or when you witnessed harassment? How could a bystander have safely helped you or the person being harassed in this situation? Maybe they could have intervened by escorting you away, or by calling the authorities and reporting what they saw. What are some ways you can prepare yourself to be an active bystander, should a similar situation ever occur?

What You Can Do to Stand for Inclusion on Campus

Hate crimes, regardless of where they occur, should be taken very seriously. Whatever form these crimes might take on your campus, it is important to examine your thoughts and feelings about their occurrence. The most important question to ask yourself is: Will you do something about it, or do you think that it is someone else's problem? If you or a group to which you belong is the target of the hate crime, you might be compelled to take a stand and speak out against the incident, but will you feel strongly enough to express your discontent if you are not a member of the target group?

Just because you or your particular group has not been targeted in a hate crime doesn't mean that you should do nothing. Commit to becoming involved in making your campus a safe place where students with diverse views, lifestyles, languages, politics, religions, and interests can come together and learn. If nothing happens to make it clear that hate crimes on campus will not be tolerated, it's anyone's guess as to who will be the next target.

Commit to Connect

In a college or university environment, students often learn that there are more commonalities than differences between themselves and others. By learning to coexist respectfully and peacefully and listen to one another and consider other perspectives, students can take the first step toward building a better world.

Rawpixel.com/Shutterstock.com

Many students, whether or not they were directly targeted in a hate crime, find strength in unity, forming action committees and making it clear that hate crimes will not be ignored or tolerated. It is important not to respond to prejudice and hate crimes with violence. It is more effective to unite with fellow students, faculty members, staff members, campus police officers, and administrators to address the issue, educate the greater campus community, and work to promote an environment of respect and tolerance. News reports have also described the use of Twitter to identify and arrest perpetrators of hate crimes, whether the crime is hate speech or more serious instances of physical assault. The use of social media can make identifying harassers and responding to hate crimes quick and effective.

How can you get involved? Work with existing campus services such as the campus police, the multicultural center, faculty members, and administrators to plan and host educational opportunities, including training sessions, workshops, and symposiums centered on diversity, sensitivity, and multiculturalism. Organize an on-campus antidiscrimination event at which campus and community leaders address the issues and provide solutions. Join prevention programs to think of ideas to battle hate crimes on campus or in the community. Finally, look into the antidiscrimination measures your college has in place. Do you think that they need to be updated or revised?

EXPANDING YOUR WORLDVIEW

high-impact practice 4

Making an effort to seek diversity in different aspects of your life will benefit you and others through better relationships; a greater sense of empathy and understanding; increased employment opportunities; and a richer, fuller life. Learn to pay attention to the opportunities for diversity that surround you while you're in college, and consider how these opportunities available to you now can build on each other to enrich the roles you will eventually play in the workplace and in your life.

Embracing Diversity in College

Because research in higher education[3] confirms the importance of diversity to learning, many colleges and universities have committed to ensuring diversity in college admissions and in learning opportunities. Your campus should provide you with opportunities to interact with and learn alongside individuals who represent diversity in religious affiliation, sexual orientation, gender, ethnicity, age, culture, economic status, and ability.

Curriculum. Many institutions offer an **inclusive curriculum**, one that offers courses that introduce students to diverse people, worldviews, and approaches. Today you can find many courses with a diversity focus, and many of them meet graduation requirements. The college setting is ideal for

---

[3]*Does Diversity Make a Difference: Three Research Studies on Diversity in College Classrooms* (Washington, DC: American Council on Education and American Association of University Professors, 2000), and Gloria M. Ameny-Dixon, "Why Multicultural Education Is More Important in Higher Education Now Than Ever: A Global Perspective." *National Forum.* Accessed January 9, 2015.

promoting education about diversity because it allows students and faculty members of varying backgrounds to come together for the common purpose of learning and critical thinking.

College students have led the movement that resulted in a curriculum that reflects disenfranchised groups such as women, people of color, the elderly, the disabled, gays, lesbians, bisexuals, and people who identify as transgender. In public protests, students have demanded the hiring of more instructors from different ethnic groups, the creation of ethnic studies departments, and a variety of initiatives designed to support diverse students academically and socially, including multicultural centers, women's resource centers, enabling services, and numerous academic support programs.

At almost all colleges and universities, you will be required to take some general education courses that will expose you to a wide range of topics and issues. We hope that you will take a course or two with a multicultural focus. Such courses can provide you with new perspectives and an understanding of issues that affect your fellow students and community members. They can also affect you, possibly in ways you had not considered. Just as your college or university campus is diverse, so too is the workforce you will enter. Therefore, a multicultural education can improve the quality of your entire life.

high-impact practice 4

your turn   Making Decisions

Go for Diversity

Whether or not your college or university requires you to include a diversity or multicultural course in your curriculum, you should choose to take at least one. These courses will introduce you to different views on common issues and will help prepare you for the contemporary and multicultural world in which you live and work.

Study-Abroad Programs. If your college or university offers study-abroad opportunities, take advantage of them. Visiting or living in another country for a period of time (a few weeks to an entire year) is a great way to expand your horizons, learn about another culture, and become competent speaking another language. Many colleges and universities offer scholarships or grants for study abroad, and some even have student residential accommodations in the host country.

Student-Run Organizations. Student-run organizations can provide multiple avenues for expressing ideas, pursuing interests, and cultivating relationships. According to our definition of culture, all student-run organizations provide an outlet for the promotion and celebration of a culture. Let's take, for instance, a gospel choir and an animation club and apply the components of culture to both. Both groups promote a belief system that is common among their members: The first is based on a love of

Broadening Your Horizons

These students are spending a semester studying abroad in East Asia, visiting a section of the Great Wall of China in Badaling. Time spent in other countries will not only expose you to new people, a new language, and a new culture, it will also allow you to think of the familiar in new ways.

Rolphus/Getty Images

music in the gospel tradition, and the second is based on the appreciation of animation as an art form. Both have aspects that can be taught: the musical tradition of gospel singing, and the rules and techniques used in drawing. Both groups use a specific language related to the group's belief system.

To promote learning and discovery both inside and outside the classroom, colleges and universities provide programming that highlights ethnic and cultural celebrations, such as Chinese New Year and Kwanzaa; gender-related activities, such as initiatives sponsored by the group Sexual Assault and Relationship Violence Activists; and a broad range of entertainment, including concerts and art exhibits. These events expose you to new and exciting ideas and viewpoints, enhancing your education and challenging your current views.

Career/Major Groups. You can also explore diversity through your major and your career interests. Groups that focus on a specific field of study can be great assets as you explore your interests. Are you interested in helping different groups of people interact more effectively? Consider majoring in sociology or social work. Do you want to learn more about human behavior? Study psychology. If you join a club that is affiliated with the major that interests you, you will find out more about the major and you can also make contacts that could lead to career opportunities.

Political/Activist Organizations. Organizations devoted to specific political affiliations and causes—such as Young Democrats and Campus Republicans, Students for Human Rights, and Native Students in Social Action—add to the diversity mix on campus. These organizations provide debating events and forums and contribute diverse ideas on current issues and events.

Special-Interest Groups. Perhaps the largest subgroup of student organizations is the special-interest category, which encompasses everything from recreational interests to hobbies. On your campus, you might find special-interest clubs such as a Brazilian jujitsu club, a belly dance club, a flamenco club, a sports club, an Ultimate Frisbee group, and a video gamers' society. Students can cultivate an interest in bird-watching or indulge their curiosity about ballroom dance without ever leaving campus. If a club for your special interest is not available, seek out your student activities center and learn what steps you would need to take to create one yourself.

high-impact practice 4

Embracing Diversity in the Workplace

Diversity enriches us all, and understanding the value of working with others and the importance of having an open mind enhances your educational and career goals. Your college campus is diverse, and so is the workforce you will enter.

Expanding your worldview during your time in college prepares you to work successfully with others in any field. For instance, if you plan to major in biology in hopes of becoming a physician, you are highly likely to come into contact with people from other countries; there will always be a need for knowledgeable, open-minded, and nonjudgmental doctors to care for the sick here and around the world. If you are a business major, you may find yourself leading or participating on a team or in a diverse taskforce in college and later in your career. Has your instructor already given you an assignment to join a group of classmates to complete a graded project? The rationale behind group work is not only to help you develop the ability to function in a group setting but also to help you understand all members of the group as individuals in spite of their differences. Learning the characteristics and strengths of each person and using them collectively to complete the goal and ace the project can propel your productivity in a team environment in the workplace.

After you have graduated from college and are pursuing a career, a director or supervisor might come to you to ask if you would lead a team charged with resolving a particular issue that your employer is facing. Your first step will be to get to know and establish rapport with all members

Busy Coworkers

How would you describe this professional setting? What kinds of diversity do you see? Applying the content of this chapter to your college experience will help you develop into the kind of team player who would thrive in this type of diverse workplace.

10'000 Hours/Getty Images

of your team, no matter their age, gender, race, or ethnic group; then you can successfully communicate the goals of the project. In a workplace situation, prejudice against another coworker reduces your ability, and your coworker's ability, to be productive and achieve workplace goals. Prejudiced behavior in the workplace will not be tolerated.

Embracing Diversity in Life

To prepare for your future in this diverse world, challenge yourself to learn about various groups in your community, in your college, and on any part-time job you hold. These settings might differ ethnically and culturally, giving you an opportunity to develop your relationship skills. Attend events and celebrations sponsored by other groups whether they are in the general community or on campus. Taking advantage of special cultural events is a good way to see and hear traditions that are specific to the groups being represented. Not only will you learn about differences, but you will also be able to see similarities between individuals and groups that you may not have thought of before.

One simple way to seek diversity is to incorporate people from different cultures in your inner circle of friends. As you begin your college experience, you will meet people who are not like you but who share common goals and aspirations. Some of these people have the potential to be future business partners, coworkers, managers, and/or employers. If you plan to own your own business, you will more than likely need a good accountant, lawyer, or staff assistant, for instance. Developing friendships with diverse individuals in college and in part-time jobs will increase your understanding of different cultures and abilities, and how others function in the workplace.

You can also become active in your own learning about diversity by making time for travel. Seeing the world and its people can be an uplifting experience. Finally, if you want to learn more about a culture or group, ask a member of that group for information. If you do so in a tactful, genuine way, most people will be happy to share information about their viewpoints, traditions, and history.

techtip

GO BEYOND THE FILTER

When people learn new things, they increase their capacity to learn even more. Technology can help us explore new ideas, products, and opportunities. However, when we are online, our preferences are tracked. The more we use internet technology, the more information we make available about our opinions. Our online experience is continually shaped by our past searches, likes, and preferences. Author Eli Pariser defines this effect as our "filter bubble," which he describes as an unintended consequence of web companies tailoring their services, including news and search results, to our personal tastes.[6] This effect causes us to miss all kinds of information that we might like or learn from—we never see it because it is being filtered away from us.

[6] Eli Pariser, The Filter Bubble: What the Internet Is Hiding from You (New York: Penguin Press, 2011).

The Problem

You want to be exposed to new things, but past preferences are shaping your current online experience.

The Fix

Push back on the filter bubble. Be aware that it exists, and make a concerted effort to obtain information that could challenge or broaden your worldview. Shape your online research and reading so that you automatically receive a variety of sources of online information. And don't restrict yourself to the online world. Get out and experience the diverse world in which you live, in person!

How to Be Exposed to Different People and Ideas

1. *Join clubs or student groups to expand your interests.* Check with your campus center for student services. Most colleges have student activities, clubs, and events. College can be a time for you to meet new people and learn about new things, and not all of this will happen in the classroom. You can develop new interests by talking to new people about new things.

2. *Find ways to be of use.* Volunteering or interning can help you meet new people, explore new interests, understand others, and learn new skills. It can be tempting to avoid these kinds of activities because of the existing demands of your schoolwork or job. But the people you meet, the interests you explore, and the skills you learn can be important to your future career and long-term goals.

3. *When you are online, search in places other than Google or YouTube for new things to see, hear, or experience.* As you saw in the chapter, Information Literacy and Communication, your college maintains access to a number of databases containing all kinds of cool information. These databases are not searchable by external search engines like Google or Bing, and your preferences and interests are not automatically tracked and mirrored back to you. If you take time to explore these databases, many of which contain unusual videos and music as well as text,

you will become a better researcher and find new things to guide your professional interests. If you do search in engines like Google or YouTube, log out, turn off your search history, or open a private browsing window to see new or trending topics you might otherwise miss.

4. *Expand your world.* Travel can be a great way for you to experience new people, music, food, history, and culture. No one will track your interests electronically if you explore the Camden Market in London or the Divisoria, a major market district in Manila. Travel will expose you to diverse ways of thinking that will challenge your ideas about who you are and what you have been taught—things you cannot learn in books or by watching television.

checklist for success

Diversity

■ **Know that successful college students have strong skills in understanding, appreciating, and embracing diversity.** Given the growing diversity of the U.S. workforce, most employers now hold these skills as an expectation, too. It is just good business.

■ **Gain an understanding of the various differences you will encounter in college.** Beyond race, ethnicity, culture, and religion are differences in age, economic status, gender, sexuality, and physical and learning abilities. In college, you have the opportunity to learn from many kinds of people, and these experiences will likely affect any stereotypes you have brought to college with you.

■ **Use college as the ideal environment to learn about and get to know people who are different from you.** Practice acknowledging and respecting other people, even if you don't agree with them.

■ **Take advantage of opportunities to enroll in courses designed to expose you to a wide range of topics and issues.** You can and should study diverse people and

diverse ideas in both the curriculum and the co-curriculum.

■ **Be alert for examples of racism and discrimination.** College is a microcosm of our society. You may therefore see examples of discrimination, prejudice, and insensitivity on your campus. Become aware of what you can do to combat hate on campus.

■ **Learn about and avoid microaggressions.** These are subtle statements, often made unintentionally, that imply prejudice toward or lack of knowledge about an individual or group and can hurt those individuals or groups.

■ **Be prepared for diversity in the workplace and in life.** The nature of our world means that we will continue to encounter diversity in every aspect of our lives and work experiences. Learning how to understand, appreciate, communicate, and interact with others who are different is an essential life skill.

REFLECT ON CHOICES

high-impact practice 2, 4 | Your college experience will probably expose you to more diversity than you have experienced before—diversity of race and ethnicity and diversity of opinions and attitudes. By choosing to get to know others who are different, you will enrich and energize your learning. Write a one-page essay about someone you have already met who helped you understand a different way of thinking.

APPLY WHAT YOU HAVE LEARNED

Now that you have read and discussed this chapter, consider how you can apply what you have learned to your academic life and your personal life. The following prompts will help you reflect on the chapter material and its relevance to you both now and in the future.

1. Use your print or online campus course catalog to identify courses that focus on topics of multiculturalism and diversity. Why do you think that academic departments have included these issues in the curriculum? How would studying diversity and multiculturalism help you succeed in different academic fields?

2. Reflecting on our personal identities and values is a step toward increased self-awareness. Read and answer the following questions to the best of your ability: How do you identify and express yourself ethnically and culturally? Which, if any, aspects of your identity expose you to harm? Which give you certain privileges? What aspects of your identity do you truly enjoy?

USE YOUR RESOURCES

More than ever, colleges and universities are taking an active role in promoting diversity. In an effort to ensure a welcoming and supportive environment for all students, institutions have established offices, centers, and resources to provide students with educational opportunities, academic guidance, and support networks. Look into the availability of the following resources on your campus, and visit one or more.

> **Office of Student Affairs**   Small institutions may group diversity services into a comprehensive office of student affairs.

> **Office of Diversity or Multicultural Center** An office that provides resources for educating students about diversity or multiculturalism is a good place to find the information you need or to report harassment based on race, gender, or sexual orientation.

> **Women's and Men's Centers**   Some institutions provide specialized services to both women and men.

> **Lesbian, Gay, Bisexual, Transgender, Queer, Intersex, and Asexual Student Alliances** These student-run organizations provide valuable programming and sources of support for LGBTQIA students, their friends, and their families.

> **Centers for Students with Disabilities** Students with either learning or physical disabilities can access supportive services through these campus offices.

> **Academic support programs for underrepresented groups**   While academic support programs are generally available for all students, your institution may offer special types of academic support for certain student populations.

> **Diversityedu.com**   This website lists resources related to diversity on campus.

> **Tolerance.org**   This website, a project of the Southern Poverty Law Center, provides numerous resources for dealing with discrimination and prejudice, both on and off campus.

LaunchPad
macmillan learning

LaunchPad for *Your College Experience* is a great resource! Go online to master concepts using the LearningCurve study tool and much more. **Launchpadworks.com**

PhotoAlto/Sandro Di Carlo Darsa/Getty Images

14

WELLNESS

YOU WILL EXPLORE

The many aspects of wellness, including stress management, nutrition, exercise, body image, sleep, and emotional health

Strategies for making good decisions about alcohol and other substances

High-impact practices 2 (writing) and 3 (collaboration)

Gino Santa Maria/ Shutterstock

> ❝ **I realized that eating right, exercising, and sleeping would help me be less anxious and more in control in all my classes.** ❞

When Rahm started attending the University of West Florida, he had no idea what to expect. After the first week of classes, when he received the syllabus for each course, he could tell he was going to have to work hard. "To make more study time, I cut back on going to the gym each week," he explained. "And I started skipping lunch to save time and ate snacks from vending machines between classes instead." He also found himself sleeping less and eating more junk food during exam weeks. It was a perfect storm.

As the weeks went by, stress and anxiety began to get the better of him. It all came to a head just before a scheduled class presentation. Rahm knew he wasn't ready to do his best, so he e-mailed his instructor and asked for an extension, which his instructor, Dr. Cruz, granted. But even with the extension, Rahm's presentation did not go as well as he would have liked. Rahm was frustrated, but he wasn't sure what he could do to get back on track—until the next week.

When he came into class on Monday, Rahm saw that Dr. Cruz had invited a guest speaker: one of the counselors from the campus counseling

center. The counselor talked about strategies students could use to take steps in the right direction if they found themselves struggling. The counselor had a long conversation with the class about how physical and mental wellness connect, and shared some articles about how to eat, exercise regularly, get more sleep, and maintain a positive attitude. As he listened to the discussion, Rahm knew that he had some changes to make. "I realized that eating right, exercising, and sleeping would help me be less anxious and more in control in all my classes," says Rahm. "I also noticed that I really didn't have a relationship with any of my instructors, including Dr. Cruz."

Using some of the resources the counselor had provided, Rahm developed a plan for gaining more control over his life. As part of that plan, he visited Dr. Cruz during office hours to get to know her and to discuss how he could improve his performance in class. In their meeting, Dr. Cruz promised to work with Rahm on his presentation skills and to help him become more organized in his study strategies. Rahm was pleasantly surprised by how much he enjoyed his visit with his instructor.

The first year of college can be one of life's most interesting and challenging transitions. Much of what you experience will be new—new friends, new freedoms, and new responsibilities. You will notice that many students use sensible and healthy coping strategies to handle the transition to college successfully. They watch what they eat and drink, exercise regularly, and get enough sleep. However, some students have more difficulty managing the transition. They stay up late, drink too much, overeat, or engage in other risky behaviors.

assess your strengths

Maintaining your health in college will enable you to feel good about yourself and succeed academically. By making smart choices, getting enough rest, developing an exercise regimen, and eating a healthy diet, you will be ready to make the most of your college experience. As you read this chapter, consider the healthy behaviors that you already practice.

set goals

What are your most important objectives in learning the material in this chapter? Think about the challenges that you have had in the past in the areas of health and wellness. Think of reasonable goals that you would like to achieve, such as eating less junk food or getting the same amount of sleep each night.

The college experience shouldn't only be about studying. To make the most of the college years, it's also important to spend time with friends and enjoy all the activities your college has to offer. The freedoms you experience in this new environment will bring challenges and risks, and your success in college will depend on your ability to make sensible decisions about your personal habits and behaviors. If you stay healthy, you are more likely to achieve your academic and personal goals.

UNDERSTANDING WELLNESS

Wellness is a concept that encompasses the care of your mind, body, and spirit. Wellness involves making healthy choices and achieving balance throughout your life. It includes reducing stress in positive ways, keeping fit, fostering your spirituality, deepening your self-knowledge, maintaining good sexual health, and taking a safe approach to drugs and alcohol—assuming that you are of legal age to drink alcoholic beverages.

Take this short quiz. As you consider each question, rate yourself on a scale of 1–5, with 1 being "never" and 5 being "always."

1. Are you able to manage your stress successfully? _____
2. Do you eat a wide range of healthy foods? _____
3. Do you exercise several times a week? _____
4. Do you get seven or more hours of sleep each night? _____
5. Do you say "no" to others in order to manage your obligations? _____
6. Do you seek help from friends, family, or professionals when you need it? _____
7. Are you in control of your sexual health? _____
8. Do you avoid abusing alcohol, tobacco, or other substances? _____
9. Do you live a balanced life? _____

In what areas did you mark a 4 or 5? _____
In what areas did you mark a 1 or 2? _____

As you read the preview of the nine components of wellness described below, pay special attention to the areas that you scored as ones or twos, so that you can get yourself on track.

1. **Managing stress:** Occasional stress is a normal reaction to the new demands of college life. It is important, though, to recognize when your stress level is getting out of control and to seek help before stress gets in the way of your academic performance.

2. **Paying attention to diet and nutrition:** Eating fast food can have a negative impact on your overall health. Limit the number of sugary drinks or drinks with artificial sweeteners, and opt for fresh, unprocessed foods, and plenty of water.

3. **Getting enough sleep:** Going without sleep will negatively affect your overall health and ability to perform academically. Seven or eight hours of sleep per night can significantly improve your ability to handle stress.

4. **Remembering to exercise:** Exercising stimulates the release of the endorphins needed for stress relief and helps with maintaining your overall health. If you don't have time to work out every day, start with a smaller goal of three or four times a week.

5. **Saying "no" when you need to:** In order to manage your obligations, sometimes you have to say "no" to activities that interest you, and that's okay! Identify your priorities and stick to them. You might want to review Chapter 3, "Time Management," for more help in this area.

6. **Seeking help for emotional problems:** If your emotions are out of control, if you are feeling depressed, or if you are becoming anxious about what's happening in your life, consider professional counseling or talking to a friend or family member. Even writing in a journal can be an effective way for you to combat these symptoms.

7. **Maintaining your sexual health:** Be sure that if you choose to be sexually active you practice safe sex. Understand the resources available to you when you have questions or problems and remember that communication with your partner is key to navigating your sexual experiences in college. (See Chapter 12 for more information on sexual health.)

8. **Avoiding substance abuse:** During the college years, you will encounter substances like alcohol, tobacco, and illegal drugs. First and foremost, you must know the laws that govern the use of these substances in your state. If you are of legal age, remember that moderation is key. Are you a smoker? If so, quit now. There is no such thing as a safe level of smoking.

9. **Achieving balance:** Wellness is about mind, body, and spirit. When you take care of all aspects of your personal wellness, it will be easier for you to identify and handle problems when they develop.

The Lotus Position

When you feel stressed, take a moment to breathe. Focusing on inhaling and exhaling slowly and picturing a serene scene, like a blue sky or a sunny beach, can help slow your heart rate and calm you down. Yoga classes provide opportunities for these relaxation techniques. Check out your campus health and wellness center for a schedule of fitness or relaxation classes.

FatCamera/Getty Images

Managing Stress to Maintain Wellness

Everyone experiences stress at one time or another—it's a normal part of being a human being—but the level of stress affecting college students can undermine their ability to succeed academically.

Consider the level of stress you feel today. Rate your current level of stress on a scale of 1–5: 1 is "little or no stress" and 5 is "extremely stressed."

My current stress level: _____

If your stress level is a 3 or above, describe the symptoms of stress that you are experiencing.

_____

_____

Can you identify *why* you are feeling this level of stress?

_____

_____

If your stress level is a 1 or 2, can you identify why?

_____

_____

When you are stressed, your body undergoes physiological changes. Your breathing becomes rapid and shallow; your heart rate increases; the muscles in your shoulders, forehead, neck, and chest tighten; your hands become cold or sweaty; your hands and knees may shake; your stomach becomes upset; your mouth goes dry; and your voice may sound strained. Over time, stress can develop into chronic health issues such as irritable bowel syndrome, common colds, migraines, and fatigue.

A number of psychological changes also occur when you are under stress. You might experience a sense of confusion, trouble concentrating, memory lapses, and poor problem solving. As a result of stress, you may also make decisions that you regret later. High stress levels can lead to emotions such as anger, anxiety, depression, fear, frustration, and irritability, which might cause you to be unable to go to sleep at night or to wake up frequently. These stress-related changes can turn into more serious psychological ailments such as anxiety disorder, depression, or panic attacks if they are not addressed.

Stress has many sources, but two seem to be prominent: life events and daily hassles. Life events often represent major adversity, such as the death of a parent, spouse, partner, or friend. Researchers believe that an accumulation of stress from life events, especially if many events occur over a short period of time, can cause physical and mental health problems. Daily hassles are the minor irritants that we experience every day, such as losing your keys, having three tests on the same day, quarreling with your roommate, or worrying about money.

The best starting point for handling stress is to be in good physical and mental shape. If you pay attention to your body and mind, you will be able to recognize the signs of stress before they escalate and become uncontrollable.

Being Mindful of Stress

Do you get stressed before an exam or graded performance? Some level of stress might motivate you to do well, but a high stress level can have the opposite effect. The next time that you are stressed before a test or performance, note how you feel, both physically and mentally. Are you more energized, more alert? Or does your stress negatively affect your concentration or self-confidence? Manage your stress so that it helps, not hurts, your preparation and performance. If your stress is out of control, seek help from the campus wellness or counseling center.

Take Control. Modifying your lifestyle is the best overall approach to stress management. You have the power to change your life so that it is less stressful. Lifestyle modification involves identifying the parts of your life that do not serve you well, making plans for change, and then carrying out the plans. For example, if you are stressed because you are always late for classes, get up 10 minutes earlier. If you get nervous when you talk to a certain negative classmate before a test, avoid that person when you have an exam coming up. Learn test-taking skills so that you can manage test anxiety better (see Chapter 8). If doing poorly on a test causes you to give up or become depressed, work to develop your resilience and belief in yourself. Learn from your mistakes, but trust yourself to do better in the future.

Learn to Relax. Check your college website, counseling center, health center, student newspaper, or fitness center for classes that teach relaxation techniques. Learning new techniques for managing stress takes knowledge and practice. You'll find apps, websites, books, and other resources that guide you through many options.

isthisyou?

Making Healthy Choices

Are you struggling to make healthy choices about what to eat? Do you find the choices in the dining halls overwhelming? Are you limiting yourself to familiar foods such as pizza or French fries? This chapter offers nutrition strategies that can help you to establish a healthy routine in your new environment. Which of these strategies are you willing to try? Pick one nutrition strategy and chart your progress for a week. Are you willing to continue for a second week?

The Importance of Good Nutrition

There is a clear connection between what you eat and drink, your overall health and well-being, and stress. Eating a lot of junk food will negatively impact your overall health and reduce your energy level, and when you can't keep up with your work because you're slow or tired, you will experience more stress.

We sometimes choose what to eat or drink based on convenience or what makes us feel good in the moment without thinking about how we'll feel later. Caffeine is probably the best example of a common substance that is linked to high stress levels. College students, like many adults, use caffeine to help with their productivity. Caffeine increases alertness and reduces feelings of fatigue if used moderately. Up to 400 milligrams (mg) of caffeine a day appears to be safe for most healthy adults. That's roughly the amount of caffeine in four cups of brewed coffee, ten cans of cola, or two "energy shot" drinks.[1] However, too much caffeine can cause nervousness, headaches, irritability, upset stomach, and sleeplessness—all symptoms of stress. It is important to limit your intake of caffeine. Many students consume energy drinks, which can contain more than the recommended amount of caffeine. Find other sources of energy, like working out or spending some time outside, to help you feel energized throughout the day.

your turn   Making Decisions

Resist Junk Food Temptations

Let's face it—food is one of life's greatest pleasures, and having a piece of birthday cake or a hamburger and fries is fine every now and then. It is your regular, daily eating habits that will have the most impact on helping you look and feel well. Remember that your choices of what and how much you eat now will not only affect you at your current age but will also make a difference in what you feel like twenty, thirty, or forty years from now.

It might not be easy at first, but if you start making small, positive changes, you can build toward a new way of eating. You will not only feel better, but also be healthier and probably happier. Here are some commonsense suggestions:

- Limit snacks to healthy options such as fruit, vegetables, yogurt, hummus, and small portions of nuts, like pistachios, almonds, cashews, or walnuts.
- Be careful about "fad" diets. Before using diet pills or beginning a diet regimen such as the Paleo, Atkins, or South Beach diet, check with your physician. These diets may show results quicker than maintaining a balanced diet and exercising, but they might cause you to miss essential nutrients, especially if you are an athlete. Simply changing your portion sizes can be a first step toward maintaining a healthy weight.
- Drink plenty of water. Drinking 64 ounces of water a day helps flush your system of toxins, keep your skin healthy, and manage your weight. A rule of thumb: To keep hydrated, drink water before and after a workout and between meals.
- Add variety to your meals. Dining halls can offer several options, and the most important strategy is to eat a balanced and well-portioned meal that includes protein, vegetables, grains, salad, and fruit.

---

[1] www.mayoclinic.org/caffeine/ART-20045678?p=1

FIGURE 14.1 ❯ MyPlate Eating Guidelines

This is the new MyPlate icon, which was introduced by the federal government in 2011 to replace the food guide pyramid. **ChooseMyPlate.gov** provides tips and recommendations for healthy eating and understanding the plate's design.

Courtesy USDA

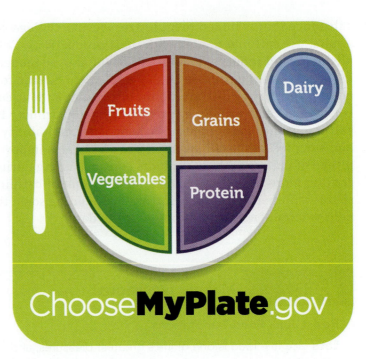

Limit fried and sugary foods. Choose grilled or broiled lean meat and fish instead, or other forms of lean protein. A good reference is **ChooseMyPlate.gov** (see Figure 14.1).

- Watch your portion sizes. Avoid large, jumbo, or king-size fast-food items and all-you-can-eat buffets.
- Always read the nutrition label on packaged foods. Do not let "nonfat/low-fat" options entice you. Often, these products contain chemicals and unhealthy by-products that are worse for you than their full-fat counterparts.

One Healthy Meal at a Time

Balanced meals with the protein and fiber that come from lean meats and vegetables keep you feeling satisfied for longer. Stop at a grocery on the way home to pick up food that's healthy, or consider your options in the dining hall. It's never too late to take better care of yourself, and no step in the right direction is too small.

Barbara Dudzinska/Shutterstock

Risky Eating Habits. Although we advise you to think about what you eat from day to day, we also advise you not to overthink your diet. Remember that the key to good health is achieving balance, and an obsession with food intake may be a sign that things are out of balance. Over the last few decades, an increasing number of both male and female college students have been developing eating disorders such as anorexia nervosa (an extreme fear of gaining weight), bulimia (overeating followed by self-induced vomiting or laxative use), or binge eating disorder (compulsive overeating long past the feeling of being full).

Anyone who is struggling with an eating disorder should seek immediate medical attention. Eating disorders can be life-threatening if they are not treated by a health care professional. Contact your student health center for more information, or contact the National Eating Disorder Association (**nationaleatingdisorders.org** or 1-800-931-2237) to find a professional in your area who specializes in the treatment of eating disorders.

---

your turn | **Feeling Connected**

🎯 *high-impact practice 3*

Knowing When You Are Hungry

In a small group, discuss how you can tell when you are hungry. Do you ever eat because you're tired, stressed, or bored? Focusing on eating only when you are hungry can help you maintain your overall health. In your group, think of ways to determine whether or not you are really hungry, and things you can do to distract yourself when something else is going on, like boredom. You may also brainstorm healthy snacks that will satisfy your hunger without making you crave more.

Body Positivity: Having a Healthy Self-Image

Have you ever heard the term, "the freshman fifteen"? While health care researchers have documented some weight gain among traditional-aged first-year college students, the notion of the freshman fifteen is an urban myth. There are reasons that some weight gain is common in the first year, including stress and the tendency to eat fattening foods, but extreme weight gain is rare. Maintaining your overall health and appearance doesn't mean focusing just on weight. It means learning how your body works, what it needs, and how to keep it feeling good. Many campus health and counseling centers are promoting a Health at Every Size approach. This approach is more inclusive than previous approaches that idealized a particular body type, body mass index (BMI), skin color, or gender expression. We are all designed to look different, but our basic needs for healthy foods, quality sleep, water, activity, medical care, and social belonging are the most important aspects of our health regimen. Focus on developing a lifestyle that ensures you get all the things that help you feel great. When you feel good, you will look good!

Exercising to Maintain Wellness

Exercise is an excellent stress-management technique, the best way to stay fit, and an important element in effective weight management. Whether it's walking to class, going to the campus recreation center, or

Get Moving!

Whether it's running, walking, or playing a sport, every student needs to get moving. What are your exercise habits? Remember that daily exercise can be a great, no-cost way to reduce stress while keeping you in good physical and mental shape.

Michael Doolittle/Alamy

going for a bike ride, it is important to be active every day. Any kind of exercise benefits your body and spirit and is a great choice for reducing stress and maintaining overall health. Choose activities that you enjoy so that you look forward to your exercise time and make it a regular part of your routine. People who exercise report higher energy levels, less stress, better sleep, and an improved self-image compared with people who do not exercise.

Think about ways to combine activities and use your time efficiently. Maybe you can leave your car at home and walk or ride a bike to class. If you must drive, then park at the far end of the parking lot to get in extra steps. Try going to the gym with a friend and asking each other study questions while you're on the treadmills. Take the stairs whenever possible. Wear a pedometer and aim for a certain number of steps each day. If you're a parent, run around with your kids. Play organized sports or use your campus fitness center. Most important, remember that exercise is most effective if you make it part of your day-to-day life.

Getting Enough Sleep to Maintain Wellness

Getting adequate sleep is another way to protect yourself from stress. According to a 2013 Gallup poll, 46 percent of individuals aged eighteen to twenty-nine get less than the recommended seven hours of sleep per night.[2] Lack of sleep can lead to anxiety, depression, and academic problems. Researchers found that students who studied all week but then stayed up late partying on the weekends forgot as much as 30 percent

---

[2]Jeffrey M. Jones, "In U.S., 40% Get Less Than Recommended Amount of Sleep," December 19, 2013, https://news.gallup.com/poll/166553/less-recommended-amount-sleep.aspx.

Catch Some Z's

When you aren't getting enough sleep, you cannot do your best. A brief, 20-minute nap can revive you when you're feeling tired during the day. Establish good sleeping habits and grab opportunities for power naps when you can, like before or after class.

Andersen Ross Photography Inc/ Getty Images

of the material they had learned during the preceding week. Try the following suggestions to establish better sleep habits:

- Avoid daytime naps that last more than 30 minutes.
- Try reading or listening to a relaxation tape before going to bed.
- Exercise during the day.
- Get your clothes, school materials, and food together for the next day before you go to bed.
- Sleep in the same room and bed every night.
- Set a regular schedule for going to bed and getting up.
- Resist checking electronic devices immediately before going to bed.

Spirituality

Many students find that maintaining a connection to their spiritual life helps them maintain strong emotional health. *Spirituality* is a broad term that includes not only religion but also an exploration of questions about life's meaning and ultimate values. For some college students, spirituality is linked to attendance at a church, temple, mosque, or synagogue. Others feel that they have a personal and private relationship with God, or they may explore spirituality through meditation, yoga, or a strong connection to nature or art. Maintaining your sense of spirituality will help you achieve a healthy perspective on whatever difficulties come your way.

Emotional and Mental Health

Your emotional and mental health are important components of your overall health. Particularly in the first year of college, some students have difficulty establishing positive relationships with others, dealing with pressure, or making wise decisions. Other students are optimistic and seem to believe in their own abilities to address problems successfully. Your ability to deal with life's challenges is based on your emotional intelligence (EI); this book devotes a chapter to this topic, with tools for assessing your EI and strategies for improving it (see Chapter 2). Emotional intelligence is part of your personality; if you take a psychology course in college, you will learn more about it.

Taking care of your emotional health is a big part of maintaining wellness. When one's emotional health declines, the consequences can be very serious.

Anxiety. According to the Center for Collegiate Mental Health, anxiety is the most prevalent concern cited by students seeking help at college counseling centers.[3] About 20 percent of students report that they experienced overwhelming anxiety in the last 12 months, according to the 2019 American College Health Association survey. Why is anxiety so prevalent? Anxiety can be related to prolonged stress over time. Today's college students have grown up with persistent war, economic uncertainty, chronic mass violence, and political turmoil, which has had very real effects on how they live. With little reprieve from the consistent anticipation of the next uncontrollable devastating event, the ability to rest, relax, re-center, and rebuild necessary coping stores become diminished. Being on high alert much of the time leads to being less resilient to even routine challenges. Social anxiety, panic disorder, and generalized anxiety can be manifestations of this prolonged stress.

Anxiety may cause:

- Shortness of breath
- Racing heartbeat
- Sweating
- Dizziness
- Fear of losing control
- Difficulty with attention and memory
- Nausea

Fortunately, anxiety can be addressed with professional support. There are many online resources as well as apps that can help someone manage their anxiety. If, however, you experience anxiety that is continuous or results in any of the physical symptoms mentioned above, it is time to seek help from a counselor or a trained therapist.

Loneliness. A 2018 Cigna survey[4] found that Generation Z and Millennials are lonelier than older generations. Why does this matter? For many years social and behavioral health experts have agreed that social connectedness is critical to a person's physical and mental well-being. Loneliness is a predictor of poorer overall health and shorter life expectancy. Paying attention to not just the quantity but the quality of your relationships is an important aspect of managing your health and well-being. While college is a time to engage in activities that enhance your identity as a scholar and a citizen, you should also make time for activities that are just fun with people you enjoy being with. It is also helpful to talk about what you are experiencing with people that are important to you. One measure of your social and emotional well-being is whether you have contact with other people who really know how you feel, your interests, your strengths, and your struggles. If you are with a

---

[3]CCMH, 2018–2018 Annual Report.
[4]https://www.cigna.com/about-us/newsroom/studies-and-reports/loneliness-epidemic-america

lot of people all day long who don't know the real you, that can create a lonely feeling. Minimize loneliness by using these tips:

- Make sure your daily schedule includes activities you do because you like to do them, not just because you must do them. Doing things you enjoy will help you connect with people who have something in common with you.
- Make a list of people you can call or meet when you are feeling disconnected. Your parents would love to hear about your day, and your friends at other colleges or universities would enjoy a video chat while you take breaks from homework. Maybe ask your roommates about what they did today or whom they met.

Depression. According to the American Psychological Association, depression is one of the most common psychiatric disorders in the United States, affecting more than fifteen million adults. College students are at especially high risk for both depression and suicide because of the major life changes and high stress levels some of them experience during the college years.

Depression is not a weakness; it is an illness that needs medical attention. Many college students suffer from some form of depression. The feelings are sometimes temporary and may be situational. A romantic breakup, a disappointing grade, or an ongoing problem with another person can create feelings of despair. Although situational depression may go away on its own, if you or a friend has any of the following symptoms for more than two weeks, it is important to talk to a health care provider:

- feelings of helplessness and hopelessness
- feeling useless, inadequate, bad, or guilty
- self-hatred, constant questioning of one's thoughts and actions
- loss of energy and motivation
- loss of appetite
- weight loss or gain
- difficulty sleeping or excessive need for sleep
- loss of interest in sex
- difficulty concentrating for a significant length of time

Suicide. The CDC reports that students aged fifteen to twenty-four are more likely than any other group to attempt suicide. Most people who commit suicide give a warning of their intentions. The following are common indicators of someone's intent to commit suicide:

- recent loss and inability to let go of grief
- change in personality—sadness, withdrawal, indifference
- expressions of self-hatred
- change in sleep patterns
- change in eating habits
- a direct statement about committing suicide (e.g., "I might as well end it all")
- a preoccupation with death

If you or someone you know threatens suicide or displays any of these signs, it's time to consult a mental health professional. Most campuses have counseling centers that offer both one-on-one sessions

Difficulty Coping
Many events in life can trigger feelings of despair. Know the signs of depression. If you or someone you care about seems to be having trouble, reach out. College campuses have resources to help.
Wavebreak Media Ltd/Veer/Corbis

and support groups for their students, usually for free. If you or someone you know is having suicidal thoughts, contact the National Suicide Prevention Lifeline at 1-800-273-TALK or visit the website: **suicidepreventionlifeline.org**.

Finally, remember that there is no shame attached to having high levels of stress, depression, anxiety, or suicidal tendencies. Unavoidable life events or physiological imbalances can cause such feelings and behaviors. Proper counseling, medical attention, and in some cases prescription medication can help students cope with depression and suicidal thoughts.

ALCOHOL AND OTHER SUBSTANCES

In this section, our purpose is not to make judgments, but to warn you about the ways in which irresponsible use of substances can have a negative impact on your college experience and your life. In today's world, it is easy to obtain substances, both legal and illegal, that can cause serious harm to your health and well-being. For college students, tobacco, alcohol, and marijuana are the substances most commonly used and abused. It is important to observe the laws that pertain to such use to avoid legal consequences. Some of these laws are as follows:

- In the United States, the age at which you can legally consume alcohol is twenty-one.
- The legal age to purchase tobacco in most states is eighteen; however, there are several states and localities that have raised the legal age to twenty-one.
- Recreational marijuana use is legal or decriminalized in only some states (and not at the national level).
- Using controlled substances (like prescription drugs) without a prescription is illegal according to both federal and state laws.

There are always risks involved with using drugs whether over-the-counter medications, prescribed medications, legal drugs like alcohol or tobacco, or illegal substances. In this section we want to focus on the risks involved in using drugs of any type in order to help you make choices that will lead to the best outcomes for your health and safety.

Alcohol Use

Because nearly 60 percent of college students drink alcohol, it is important that all students learn about the effects of alcohol consumption.[5] Alcohol can turn even people who don't drink into victims, such as people who are killed by drunk drivers or family members who suffer as a result of the destructive behavior of an alcoholic relative. Just one occasion of heavy or high-risk drinking can lead to problems.

People experience the pleasurable effects of alcoholic beverages as the alcohol begins to affect the brain. How fast you drink makes a difference, too. Your body gets rid of alcohol at a rate of about one drink—defined as one 12-ounce beer, one 5-ounce glass of wine, or 1.5 ounces of hard liquor—per hour. Drinking more than one drink an hour may cause a rise in Blood Alcohol Content (BAC) because the body is absorbing alcohol faster than it can eliminate it.

At BAC levels of 0.025 to 0.05, a drinker may feel animated and energized. At a BAC level of around 0.05, a drinker may feel rowdy or boisterous. This is where most people report feeling a buzz from alcohol. At a BAC level between 0.05 and 0.08, alcohol starts to act as a depressant, causing the drinker to lose coordination and judgment. Most people become severely uncoordinated with BAC levels higher than 0.08.

Driving is measurably impaired even at BAC levels lower than the legal limit of 0.08. In fact, an accurate safe level for most people may be half the legal limit, or 0.04. As BAC levels climb past 0.08, people become progressively less coordinated and less able to make good decisions. Most people become severely uncoordinated at BAC levels higher than 0.08 and may begin falling asleep, falling down, or slurring their speech.

Most people pass out or fall asleep when their BAC level is above 0.25. Unfortunately, even after you pass out and stop drinking, your BAC level can continue to rise as alcohol in your stomach is released to the intestines and absorbed into the bloodstream. Your body may try to get rid of alcohol by vomiting, but you can choke on your vomit if you are unconscious, semiconscious, or severely uncoordinated. Worse yet, at BAC levels higher than 0.30, most people will show signs of severe alcohol poisoning, such as an inability to wake up, slowed breathing, a fast but weak pulse, cool or damp skin, and pale or bluish skin. Anyone exhibiting these symptoms needs medical assistance immediately. Most campuses have an amnesty policy that allows you to call for help without the fear of getting in trouble for underage drinking. Know your college's policy on helping friends get help when they need it.

Excessive drinking is dangerous, so it's important to keep in mind some simple ways to reduce the harmful effects that alcohol can produce:

- Decide how much you will drink before you begin drinking. Set a safe limit for *your* body and stop when you reach that limit or before if you begin to feel as if you have had enough to drink. Once you start drinking you may lose your ability to determine when you have had enough.

[5]Center for Behavioral Health Statistics and Quality, *Results from the 2014 National Survey on Drug Use and Health: Detailed Tables* (Rockville, MD: Substance Abuse and Mental Health Services Administration, 2015), https://www.samhsa.gov/data/sites/default/files/NSDUH-DetTabs2014/NSDUH-DetTabs2014.htm#tab6-88b.

- Slow down drinking. One way to maintain a "buzz"—the euphoric sensation you experience from drinking—is by drinking one beer per hour or less. Pacing yourself and limiting your drinks can help prevent you from attaining a high BAC level.
- Eat while you drink. Sometimes eating while you consume alcohol helps slow down your drinking and slows down the processing of alcohol. Body weight and gender play a large role in this as well.
- Drink water. Alcohol dehydrates your body, so it is important to drink plenty of water while consuming alcohol.
- Designate a driver before you go out. Walking is always a better option than driving a vehicle, but if you are going to take a vehicle to a destination with alcohol, you should always designate the sober driver before you start out.
- Don't count on home remedies. Popular home remedies for sobering up, like drinking coffee or taking a cold shower, simply don't work. The only remedies are time and reducing your alcohol intake in the first place.

Tobacco

Tobacco is a legal drug that contains nicotine, a highly addictive substance, and is the cause of many serious medical conditions, including heart disease, lung disease, and some forms of cancer. One concern that particularly relates to college students is *social smoking*—smoking when hanging out with friends, drinking, or partying. Most college students feel they will be able to give up their social smoking habit once they graduate, but some find that they have become addicted to cigarettes.

Hookah smoking is possibly even more dangerous than cigarettes, because users can inhale more of the toxic substances. The Centers for Disease Control reports that an hour-long hookah session involves approximately 200 puffs, and the smoke inhalation is equivalent to that of about 165 cigarettes.[6]

Vaping of e-cigarettes, popular among teens, has recently become a major concern of U.S. health officials, and a few states are moving toward banning the sale of vaping products because of the link with breathing illnesses and death. The makers of Juul, a flavored vaping product, are being sued by several states for marketing to younger teens. The American Medical Association has recommended a total ban on e-cigarettes until more is known about why they are causing lung-related illnesses.

Along with the many health reasons for smokers to quit and for others never to start, there is another practical reason: the cost. If you smoke half a pack of cigarettes every day at the national average of $6.16 per pack, you'll spend about $1,121 per year on this habit—and that's in addition to the more expensive health and life insurance costs you'll likely pay (see Table 14.1). If you are a smoker, contact your campus health or counseling centers for more information about quitting.

Marijuana

A growing number of states have legalized recreational marijuana use for individuals 21 years or older, and over half of the states have legalized it for medicinal use. It is still not legal in other states or at the federal

---

[6]https://www.cdc.gov/tobacco/data_statistics/fact_sheets/tobacco_industry/hookahs/index.htm

TABLE 14.1 › Average Cost of Smoking across the United States
(packs of cigarettes continue to increase in cost, but prices differ by geographical location)

Half-Pack-a-Day Smoker
$6.16/pack × 3.5 packs/week = $21.56/week
$21.56/week × 52 weeks/year = $1121.12/year
$1121.12/year × 4 years of college = $4,484.48
In 25 years, you will have spent $28,028.00
Pack-a-Day Smoker
$6.16/pack × 7 packs/week = $43.12/week
$43.12/week × 52 weeks/year = $2,242.24
$2,242.24/year × 4 years of college = $8,968.96
In 25 years, you will have spent $56.056.00

level, however, and as with tobacco, there are health risks associated with smoking it. Some impacts of marijuana use include an increase in anxiety, paranoia, short-term memory loss, and depression. In addition, marijuana smoke increases your risk for lung cancer, much like tobacco does. It is important to understand the risks and be aware of your state and federal laws, as well as your campus policies in states where marijuana is legal.

Prescription Drugs

While some students misuse prescription depressants or stimulants such as Xanax or Adderall, the fastest-growing drug problem today is the overuse or misuse of opioids, a class of drugs that is used to control pain. These medications, which include morphine and codeine, are highly addictive; in fact, the Centers for Disease Control and Prevention (CDC) reports that in 2017, 70,000 Americans died from an opioid overdose.[7]

Patients who become addicted to legal opioids often find that their tolerance for these drugs increases—in other words, they have to take higher doses of the drugs to manage their pain. Some of these patients even turn to cheaper illegal drugs, such as heroin, as a substitute. If you are prescribed an opioid, talk with your physician about how you can be sure to avoid the life-threatening problem of addiction. And never take opioids unless they are legally prescribed.

your turn **Write and Reflect**

high-impact practice 2

The Legalization of Marijuana

A number of states and the District of Columbia have recently legalized the recreational use of marijuana. With a small group of students in your class, discuss possible consequences associated with allowing marijuana to be consumed legally. What are the potential problems? What are the benefits? Based on your group conversations, write a one-page paper arguing either for or against the federal legalization of marijuana.

---

[7] https://www.cdc.gov/drugoverdose/index.html

techtip

TURN OFF YOUR SCREENS FOR BETTER SLEEP

One of the most crucial elements of maintaining your overall wellness of mind, body, and spirit is getting enough sleep. Many of us find this difficult, especially with the constant distractions of television, computer, and smartphone and tablet screens, the blue lights of which can actually keep us awake longer. So instead of letting technology keep you up all night, how can you use it to help you get better sleep?

The Problem

You're not getting enough sleep and it's starting to impact your health, your stress levels, and your ability to study for tests and complete your assignments.

The Fix

Enlist technology to help you get to sleep earlier.

damircudic/Getty Images

How to Do It

1. *Create a sleep schedule for yourself.* Plan to go to sleep and wake up at the same time every day, even on the weekends. To help with this, set an alarm on your phone about an hour before your set sleep time so that you know when to start winding down for bed. Choose a pleasant sound for your alarm so that you don't dismiss it too quickly.
2. *Turn off notifications.* Silence any notifications that might wake you up during the night like text messages, e-mails, or distracting apps. Your phone should have a "Do Not Disturb" mode in its settings to silence all incoming notifications. If you only want to silence one or two apps, you can turn off notifications in the app settings.
3. *Listen to soothing sounds and music.* Apps like Slumber, Sleepo, and Sleep Time feature collections of soothing sounds like nature noises, stories and meditations, and other forms of white noise. Not all of these apps are free, so you may also want to listen to soothing music through apps like YouTube or Spotify. If you don't want to keep your phone on all night, you can also use a white noise machine or fan to help

4. *Track your sleep cycles.* Along with providing soothing noises, some sleep apps like Sleep Cycle, SleepScore, and Sleep Time can track your sleep patterns and cycles, showing you how you might be able to improve your sleep. In some cases, these apps can wake you up with an alarm while you're in your lightest sleep phase to help you feel more refreshed. If you own a fitness or smart watch, see if your model offers sleep tracking. Remember that these trackers are not always 100% accurate, but they can provide a good overview of how you're sleeping and how much more sleep you might need.

EXTRA STYLE POINTS: Turn it off. At the end of the day, the noises, screens, and lights of digital devices are more likely than not to keep you awake and distracted. If trying these tips doesn't help you get to sleep earlier, try turning off all digital devices a half hour before you go to bed. Unwind by reading a book, practicing bedtime yoga, meditating, or writing in a journal. If you currently use your phone as your alarm, buy an alarm clock so that you won't have to keep your phone on at

checklist for success

Wellness

■ **Understand that wellness is about your body, mind, and spirit.** These components can influence each other and can, in turn, affect your success in college.

■ **Remember that managing stress is a key college success strategy.** College, with its very demanding nature, increases stress. Use the strategies from your college success course to learn how to reduce stress in college and beyond.

■ **Learn strategies for managing your diet and your exercise regimen.** There are many sources of advice on ways to maintain your physical and mental health through proper diet and exercise. Check in your library or online for a reputable source that works for you.

■ **Appreciate the role that your emotional health plays in your overall wellness, and recognize the warning signs of anxiety and depression in yourself and others.** Remember that your emotional health can negatively affect your college experience. It's important for any student who is experiencing symptoms of mental health concerns to seek help from the campus counseling center.

■ **Consider the powerful connections between things you control through your decisions.** Make good decisions concerning diet, exercise, sleep, your schedule, and your stress levels.

■ **Practice making good decisions about sexual health.** Make wise choices to protect yourself against unwanted pregnancy and sexually transmitted infections. Learn to communicate about sex, and work to develop and maintain respectful relationships.

■ **Learn about sexual assault.** Know how to define sexual assault, what laws are in place to protect victims, and what you should do if you witness a sexual assault.

■ **Practice moderation in using alcohol and other legal drugs.** Successful college students can still have a good time in college and not let alcohol or marijuana use interfere with their academic success or personal health. Contrary to prevalent stereotypes, it is not the norm for students to abuse these substances.

■ **Learn about the costs of smoking.** There are lots of risks to your health associated with using tobacco products. The small benefits you may achieve can be achieved in ways that don't involve such risks. If you use tobacco, try to stop. If you don't use tobacco, don't start.

REFLECT ON CHOICES

Successful college students reflect deeply on their wellness and experiences. From the strategies you learned in this chapter, what do you remember as being most important? How will you change behaviors and check in with yourself in the future? Reflect on the information found in this chapter.

APPLY WHAT YOU HAVE LEARNED

Now that you have read and discussed this chapter, consider how you can apply what you have learned to your academic life and your personal life. The following prompts will help you reflect on the chapter material and its relevance to you both now and in the future.

1. Identify one area in your life where you need to make changes to become healthier. How do you think that becoming healthier will improve your performance in college? What challenges do you face in becoming healthier? How can friends or campus supports help you to overcome these challenges?

2. If you could make only three recommendations to an incoming first-year college student about managing stress in college, what would they be? Use your personal experience and what you have learned in this chapter to make your recommendations.

USE YOUR RESOURCES

> **Counseling Center**   Locate your college or university's counseling center. Professionals there offer individual and group assistance and lots of information. Remember that their support is confidential and that you will not be judged.

> **Health Center or Infirmary**   Pay a visit to your campus health center or infirmary. On most campuses, the professionals who staff the health center are especially interested in educational outreach and practicing prevention. You should be able to receive treatment as well.

> **Campus Support Groups**   Many campuses provide professionally led support groups for students dealing with problems related to excessive alcohol and drug use, abusive sexual relationships, and other issues. Your campus counseling center can help you identify support groups at your college or in your community. If you are a member of a minority group on campus in terms of your age, sexual orientation, race or ethnic group, or veteran or active-duty status, seek out services that are designed specifically for you.

> **Online Resources**   The Go Ask Alice website, sponsored by Columbia University, has answers to many health questions: **goaskalice .columbia.edu**

The website of the Academy of Nutrition and Dietetics provides advice and information on healthy eating and nutrition: **eatright.org**

Learn more about the health effects of tobacco at the American Cancer Society's website: **cancer.org**

The website of the Center for Young Women's Health has helpful advice on sexual health and other issues: **youngwomenshealth .org**

The National Clearinghouse for Alcohol and Drug Information provides up-to-date information about the effects of alcohol and drug use: **www.addiction.com**

The website of the Centers for Disease Control and Prevention is an excellent resource for information on all the topics covered in this chapter: **cdc.gov**

If you or someone you know is having suicidal thoughts, contact the National Suicide Prevention Lifeline at 1-800-273-TALK or visit their website: **suicidepreventionlifeline.org**

National Eating Disorders Association: **nationaleatingdisorders.org**

U.S. Government's Nutrition Information: **nutrition.gov**

Image Source/Getty Images

15

MONEY

YOU WILL EXPLORE

The importance of living on a budget

Different types of financial aid and how to qualify for and keep them

How to achieve a balance between working and borrowing

Strategies for using and managing credit wisely

Why you should plan for your financial future now

⌖ High-impact practices 2 (writing) and 3 (collaboration)

Mckinsey Jordan / EyeEm/Getty Images

> ❝ **I have had to keep my spending to the bare minimum. That was a tough transition.** ❞

Juliana grew up and attended high school in Massachusetts. During the college application process, she decided that she wanted to attend a big university, one with Greek life and lots to do, and she wanted to find an institution with a highly ranked business program. The University of Arizona fit the bill, and the warm weather far from the harsh New England winters didn't hurt either.

Juliana had worked hard during high school, and she managed to save a lot of money the summer before she left for college, so she opted to try attending the university without holding an outside job. The trade-off was that she had to keep her spending low. "It was a tough transition from having lots of money while working full time," she says, but she quickly learned how important it was to have a balanced budget. "When I first got to the university, I wasn't able to immediately adjust to the thought of not buying things when I wanted them. I have had to keep my spending to the bare minimum. That was a tough

transition." Like many students, Juliana also has a credit card now, which she got to begin building a good credit score. She has to be careful with that, too, and she tries to use it only for necessities. "My parents cosigned for it," she says, "but I am still the one who has to make the monthly payments!"

After a year at the University of Arizona, Juliana has realized that she actually misses New England more than she thought she would and has decided to transfer to a college back East. "The process of applying to colleges as a transfer was exhausting, but worth it in the end," she says. "I am at a point in my life where I need to make decisions that will truly benefit my future and help me set up my career." She sees herself working in hotel management in the future and hopes to get a job at one of Boston's many fine hotels. Her advice for other first-year students? "Save much more than you think you will need. That money can come in handy!"

macmillan learning

To access the LearningCurve study tool, video activities, and more, go to LaunchPad for *Your College Experience.*
Launchpadworks.com

Juliana made a hard choice; she had just enough money to manage expenses without working, but her strict budget didn't allow her to spend her hard-earned dollars on anything but the necessities. Living within a budget during the first year of college can be tough, and that's why some students begin to depend on credit cards. Counting on credit cards to extend your available financial resources can be a slippery slope, however. Problems with managing money can make it more difficult to establish a strong academic record and complete your degree. Money issues can also affect your specific academic goals, causing you to select or reject certain academic majors or degree plans because of their future earning potential.

assess your strengths

Whether they work, receive financial aid, or receive money from their families, successful college students must learn to live on a budget. As you begin to read this chapter, remember times when you have had success managing your money.

set goals

What are your most important objectives in learning the material in this chapter? Think about any challenges you have had in the past with money management, or areas that confuse you or make you nervous. Write down two money-management goals, such as tracking your spending and expenses for one month and using that information to create a monthly budget.

Money is often symbolically and realistically the key ingredient to independence and even, some people have concluded, to a sense of freedom. Money can also stir up problems. You probably know of instances when money divided a family or a relationship, or seemed to drive someone's life in a direction that person would not have taken otherwise.

The purpose of this chapter is to provide some basics of financial literacy—a specialized form of information literacy—and suggestions so that money issues will not be a barrier to your success in college. Sources of financial assistance are available through loans, grants, and work-study programs, and this chapter will help you develop a strategy for investigating your options. Think of this chapter as a summary of needed financial skills; if you want more information, consider taking a personal finance class at your college or in your community.

LIVING ON A BUDGET

Face it: College is expensive, and most students have limited financial resources. Not only is tuition a major cost, but day-to-day expenses can also add up quickly. No matter what your financial situation, a budget for college is a must. A **budget** is a spending plan that tracks all sources of income (student loan disbursements, money from parents, etc.) and expenses (rent, tuition, etc.) during a set period of time (weekly, monthly, etc.). Creating and following a budget will allow you to pay your bills on time, cut costs, put some money away for emergencies, and finish college with as little debt as possible. A budget can help you become realistic about your finances so that you have a basis for future life planning.

Creating a Budget

A budget will condition you to live within your means, put money into savings, and possibly invest down the road. Here are a few tips to help you get started.

Gather Income Information. To create an effective budget, you need to learn more about your income and your spending behaviors. First,

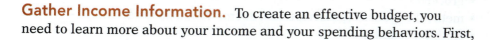

isthisyou?

Too Much Month, Too Little Money

Are you having serious problems managing your money? Were you counting on a source of income that isn't going to be available after all? Do you need a budget, even though you aren't sure how to create one that will work for you? Are you using credit cards to buy things that you don't really need? To stay in college and do your best academically, you have to learn to manage your money. That might mean seeking out loans or scholarships, destroying or hiding your credit cards until they are paid off, or seeking financial counseling at your institution or through a community resource. This chapter will help you figure out what you need to do to be resilient—to stay on top of your financial situation so that money problems don't derail your college plans.

determine how much money is coming in and when. Sources of income might include a job, your savings, gifts from relatives, student loans, scholarship dollars, or grants. List all your income sources, making note of how often you receive each type of income (weekly or monthly paychecks, quarterly loan disbursements, one-time gifts, etc.) and how much money you can expect. Knowing when your money is coming in will help you decide how to structure your budget. For example, if most of your income comes in on a monthly basis, you'll want to create a monthly budget. If you are paid every other week, a biweekly budget might work better.

Gather Expense Information for Your College or University. Your expenses will include tuition, residence hall fees if you live on campus, books and course materials, lab fees, and membership fees for any organizations you join. Some institutions offer a separate January or May term. Although your tuition for these one-month terms is generally covered in your overall tuition payment, you would have extra expenses if you wanted to travel to another location in the United States or abroad.

Gather Information about Living Expenses. First, do a "reality check." How do you *think* that you are spending your money? To find out for sure where your money is going and when, track your spending for a few weeks—ideally for at least a full month—in a notebook, a table, or a spreadsheet. The kinds of expense categories you should consider will vary depending on your situation. If you are a full-time student who lives with your parents or family members, your living expenses won't be the same as students living in a campus residence hall or in an off-campus apartment. If you are a returning student who holds down a job and has a family of your own to support, you will calculate your expenses differently. Whatever your situation, keeping track of your expenses and learning about your spending behaviors are important habits to develop. Consider which of the following expense categories are relevant to you:

- rent/utilities (electricity, gas, water)
- cell phone/cable/internet/wi-fi
- transportation (car payment, car insurance, car repairs, gas, public transportation)
- child care
- groceries
- medical expenses (prescriptions, doctor visits, hospital bills)
- clothing/laundry
- entertainment (dining out, hobbies, movies)

- personal grooming (haircuts, toiletries)
- charitable donations
- personal emergency fund
- miscellaneous (travel, organization dues)

Be sure to recognize which expenses are fixed and which are variable. A *fixed expense* is one that will cost you the same amount every time you pay it. For example, your rent is a fixed expense because you owe your landlord the same amount each month. A *variable expense* is one that may change. Your textbooks are a variable expense because the number and cost of them will be different each term.

Find Out How You Are Doing. Once you have a sense of how your total income compares to your total weekly or monthly expenses, you can get a clearer picture of your current financial situation.

Make Adjustments. Although your budget might never be perfect, you can strive to improve it. In what areas did you spend much more or much less than expected? Do you need to reallocate funds to better meet the needs of your current situation? Be realistic and thoughtful in how you spend your money, and use your budget to help meet your goals, such as planning for a trip or getting a new pair of jeans.

Whatever you do, don't give up if your bottom line doesn't end up the way that you expected it would. Budgeting is a lot like dieting; you might slip up and eat a pizza (or spend too much buying one), but all is not lost. If you stay focused and flexible, your budget can lead you to financial stability and independence.

---

your turn | **Making Decisions**

Miscellaneous Expenses

Trying to get a handle on your "miscellaneous" expenses can be a challenge. Choose to write down everything you purchase over a two-week period, and see how many of those expenses don't fit into any of the categories listed above. Which of your miscellaneous expenses are necessary, and which aren't? The unnecessary expenses are places to reduce your spending. Make some tough choices to cut back, and start immediately. Track your spending for another two weeks. Can you tell the difference?

Cutting Costs

Once you have put together a working budget, tried it out, and adjusted it, you're likely to discover that your expenses still exceed your income. Don't panic. Simply begin to look for ways to reduce those expenses. Here are some tips for saving money in college:

- **Recognize the difference between your *needs* and your *wants*.** A *need* is something that you must have. For example, tuition and textbooks are considered *needs*. On the other hand, your *wants* are goods, services, or experiences that you wish to purchase but could reasonably live without. For example, concert tickets and mochas are *wants*. Your budget should always provide for your *needs* first.

- **Share expenses.** Having a roommate (or several) can be one of the easiest ways to cut costs on a regular basis. In exchange for giving up a little bit of privacy, you'll save hundreds of dollars on rent, utilities, and food. Make sure, however, that you work out a plan for sharing expenses equally and that everyone accepts their responsibilities. For instance, remember that if only your name is on the cable account, you (and only you) are legally responsible for that bill. You'll need to collect money from your roommates so that you can pay the bill in full and on time.

- **Consider the pros and cons of living on campus.** Depending on your school's location, off-campus housing might be less expensive than paying for a room and a meal plan on campus. Be aware, however, that although you might save some cash, you will give up a great deal of convenience by moving out of your campus residence. You almost certainly won't be able to roll out of bed 10 minutes before class, and you will have to prepare your own meals. Living on campus also makes it easier to make friends and develop a sense of connection to your college or university. Before you make the decision about where to live, weigh the advantages and disadvantages of each option.

- **Use low-cost transportation.** If you live close to campus, consider whether you need a car. Take advantage of lower-cost options such as public transportation or biking to class to save money on gasoline and parking. If you live farther away, check to see whether your institution hosts a ride-sharing program for commuter students, or carpool with someone in your area.

- **Seek out discount entertainment options.** Take advantage of discounted or free programming through your college. Most institutions use a portion of their student fees to provide affordable

Go Vintage

Saving money doesn't mean you have to deprive yourself. Shopping at thrift stores for your clothes or apartment furnishings is a fun, affordable way to get one-of-a-kind pieces that won't break the bank.

Andrew Winning/Reuters/Newscom

entertainment options such as discounted or free tickets to concerts, movie theaters, sporting events, or other special events.

- **Embrace secondhand goods.** Use online resources such as Craigslist and thrift stores such as Goodwill to expand your wardrobe, purchase extras such as games and sports equipment, or furnish and decorate your room or apartment. You'll save money, and you won't mind as much when someone spills a drink on your "new" couch.
- **Avoid unnecessary fees.** Making late payments on credit cards and other bills can lead to expensive fees and can lower your credit score, which in turn will raise your interest rates. You might want to set up online, automatic payments to avoid making this costly mistake.

your turn | Setting Goals

Using Money-Saving Strategies

Are you a bargain shopper or a coupon-clipper? Do you get a good feeling when you know you've saved money on a purchase or a service? Do you get an even better feeling when you decide not to purchase something you really don't need? Be on the lookout for ways to trim your budget, and let your successes motivate you to cut your expenses even more. Share your strategies with other students in your college success class.

UNDERSTANDING FINANCIAL AID

Few students can pay the costs of college tuition, fees, books, room and board, bills, and random expenses without some kind of help. Luckily, financial aid—student loans, grants, scholarships, work-study programs, and other sources of money to support your education—is available to help cover your expenses.

Types of Aid

While grants and scholarships are unquestionably the best forms of aid because they do not have to be repaid, the federal government, states, and colleges offer many other forms of assistance, such as loans, work-study opportunities, and cooperative education. A student loan is a form of financial aid that must be paid back with interest. We will discuss student loans in more detail later in this chapter.

Grants are funds that help students pay for college. They are given to students based on their financial needs, and they do not need to be repaid. Some grants are specific to a particular academic major. Grants are awarded by the federal government, state governments, and educational institutions. Students meet academic qualifications for grants by being admitted to a college and maintaining grades that are acceptable to the grant provider.

A **scholarship** is money from your college or another institution that supports your education; it does not have to be repaid. Some scholarships are need-based—that is, they are awarded on the basis of both talent and financial need. "Talent" can refer to your past accomplishments in the arts or athletics, your potential for future accomplishments, or even where you are from. Some colleges and universities place importance on admitting students from other states or countries. "Need" in this context means the cost of college minus a federal determination of what you and your family can afford to contribute toward that cost. Your institution might provide scholarships from its own resources or from individual donors. Donors themselves sometimes stipulate the characteristics of scholarship recipients, such as age or academic major.

Other scholarships are known as **merit scholarships**. These are based on talent as defined above, but they do not require you to demonstrate financial need. It can be challenging to match your talent with merit scholarships. Most of them come through colleges and are part of the admissions and financial aid processes, which are usually described on the college's website. Remember that merit scholarships depend on your grade point average (GPA), both when you enter college and at the end of each term grading period. To retain this kind of scholarship, you have to maintain good grades.

Web-based scholarship search services are another good source for information on merit scholarships. Be certain that the website you use is free, will keep your information confidential unless you release your name, and will send you a notice—usually through e-mail—when a new merit scholarship that matches your qualifications is posted. Also be sure to ask your employer, your family's employers, and social, community, or religious organizations about any available merit scholarships.

Work-study programs provide part-time employment opportunities for students who receive financial aid if their aid amount is not enough to cover all their education costs. Students receive work-study notices as part of the overall financial aid notice and then can sign up to be interviewed for work-study jobs. Although some work-study jobs are relatively menial, the best options provide experience related to your academic studies while allowing you to earn money for college. Your salary is based on the skills required for a particular position and the hours involved. Keep in mind that you will be expected to accomplish specific tasks while on duty, although some supervisors might permit you to study during any down-time.

Cooperative (co-op) education allows you to alternate a term of study (a semester or quarter) with a term of paid work. Co-op opportunities are very common in the field of engineering, and the number of co-op programs in health care fields is growing. Colleges make information about co-ops available through the admissions office and individual academic departments.

Navigating Financial Aid

Financial aid seems complex because it can come from so many different sources. Each source may have a different set of rules about how to receive the money and how not to lose it. Your college's financial aid office and its website can help you find the way to get the largest amount of money that doesn't need to be repaid, the lowest interest rate on loans, and work opportunities that fit your academic program. Do not overlook this valuable campus resource, even if you dread having to fill out lots of forms that ask for personal financial information. In order to get the assistance you need and deserve, you'll have to be resilient and overcome any negative feelings you might have about asking for money.

Other organizations that can help students find the right college and the money to help them attend are located throughout the United States. Many of these organizations are members of the National College Access Network (which helps manage the National College Access Program Directory that can be accessed at casp.nacacnet.org) or participate in a national effort called KnowHow2Go (**knowhow2go.acenet.edu**). You might also be able to obtain funds from your employer, a local organization, or a private group.

The majority of students pay for college through a combination of various types of financial assistance: scholarships, grants, loans, and paid employment. Financial aid professionals refer to this combination as a *package.*

Qualifying for Aid

Most financial assistance requires you to fill out some kind of application form. The application used most often is the Free Application for Federal Student Aid (FAFSA). Every student should complete the FAFSA by the earliest deadline of the colleges you are applying to. Be sure to log on to the FAFSA website at **fafsa.ed.gov**; you will find it very informative. Be alert for scams that offer to file the FAFSA for a fee. If there is a charge for services, it's not the official FAFSA website. If additional forms are also required, such as the College Board's PROFILE form (**cssprofile .collegeboard.org**) or individual scholarship applications, they will

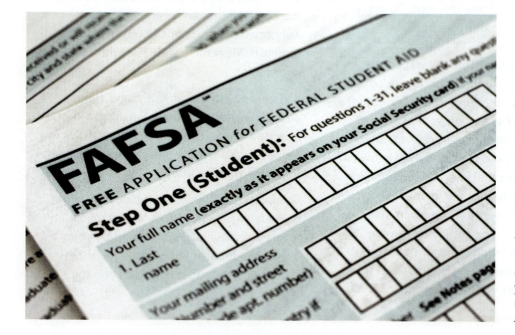

Show Me the Money

Don't let the paperwork scare you away. If you're not already receiving financial aid, be sure to investigate all the available options. Remember that your institution may also offer scholarships or grants that you don't have to repay.

Jon Elswick/AP Images

be listed in colleges' financial aid or admissions materials or by the organizations that offer scholarships. The box on this page outlines the steps you must take to qualify for most scholarships and grants, especially those sponsored by the federal government or state governments.

The amount of financial aid that you receive will depend on the cost of your academic program and what you or your family can pay as determined by the FAFSA. The cost includes average expenses for tuition and fees, books and supplies, room and board, transportation, and personal expenses. The financial aid office will subtract from the cost the amount that you and your family are expected to pay. In some cases, that amount can be as little as zero. Financial aid is designed to make up as much of the balance or "need" as possible.

Steps to Qualifying for Financial Aid

1. Enroll half-time or more in a certificate or degree program at one of the more than 4,500 colleges and universities certified to distribute federal financial aid. A few aid programs are available for less than half-time study; check with your department or college.

2. Complete the FAFSA. The first FAFSA you file is intimidating, especially if you rush to complete it right before the deadline. Completing the FAFSA in subsequent years is easier because you only need to update items that have changed. To make the process easier, get your personal identification number (PIN) a few weeks before the deadline. This PIN will be the same one you'll use throughout your college career. Try to do the form in sections rather than tackling all of it at once. Most of the information is basic: name, address, driver's license number, and things you will know or have in your personal files and records. For many undergraduates, the financial section will require your own and your parents' information from tax materials. However, if you are at least twenty-four, are a veteran, or have dependents, you do not need to submit your parents' tax information. If you

are married, your spouse's tax information will be needed.

3. Complete the College Board PROFILE form if your school or award-granting organization requires it. Review your college's admission information, or ask a financial aid adviser to determine whether this form is required.

4. Identify any additional applications that are required. These are usually scholarship applications with personal statements or short essays. The organizations, including the colleges that are giving the money, will provide instructions about what is required. Most have websites with complete information.

5. Follow instructions carefully, and submit each application on time. Financial aid is awarded from a fixed pool of funds. Once money is awarded, there is usually none left for those who file late.

6. Complete the classes for which you were given financial aid with at least a minimum grade point average as defined by your academic department or college, or by the organization that provided you the scholarship.

How to Keep Your Funding

If you earn average or better grades, complete your courses each term, and finish your program or degree on time, you should have no trouble maintaining your financial aid. It's a good idea to check with the financial aid office before you drop classes to make sure that you will not lose any aid.

Some types of aid, especially scholarships, require that you maintain full-time enrollment and make satisfactory academic progress. Dropping or failing a class might jeopardize all or part of your financial aid unless you are enrolled in more credits than the minimum required for financial aid. Full-time enrollment for financial aid purposes is often defined as twelve credit hours per term. If you initially enrolled in fifteen credit hours and dropped one three-hour course, your aid should not change. Even so, talk with a financial aid counselor before making the decision to drop a course, just to be sure.

Remember that although the financial aid office is there to serve you, you must be your own advocate. These tips should help:

- **File for financial aid every year.** Even if you don't think that you will receive aid for a certain year, you must file annually in case you become eligible in the future.
- **Meet all filing deadlines.** Students who do not meet filing deadlines risk losing aid from one year to the next.
- **Talk with a financial aid officer immediately if you or your family experiences a significant loss** (e.g., loss of a job, death of a parent or spouse). Don't wait for the next filing period; you might be eligible for funds for the current year.
- **Inquire every year about criteria-based aid.** Many colleges and universities have grants and scholarships for students who meet specific criteria. These might include grants for minority students, grants for students in specific academic majors, and grants for students of single-parent families.
- **Inquire about campus jobs throughout the year,** as these jobs might be available at any time, not just at the beginning of the term. If you do not have a job and want or need to work, keep asking.
- **Consider asking for a reassessment of your eligibility for aid.** If you have reviewed your financial aid package and think that your circumstances deserve additional consideration, you can ask the financial aid office to reassess your eligibility. The office is not always required to do so, but the request might be worth your effort.

ACHIEVING A BALANCE BETWEEN WORKING AND BORROWING

After you have determined your budget, decided what (if anything) you can pay from savings, and taken your scholarships and grants into consideration, you might find that you still need additional income. Each term or year, you should decide how much you can work while maintaining good grades, and how much you should borrow from student loans.

Advantages and Disadvantages of Working

The majority of students today find that a combination of working and borrowing is the best way to gain experience, finance college, and complete their educational goals on time. Paid employment while you are in college has benefits beyond the money you can earn. Having a job in a field related to your major can help you develop a credential for graduate school and make you more employable later because it shows that you have the capability to manage several priorities at the same time. Working while you are in college can help you determine whether a particular career is what you will really want after you complete your education. And students who work a moderate amount (fifteen to twenty hours per week) typically get better grades than students who do not work at all.

On the other hand, it's almost impossible to get great grades if you work full time while also trying to be a full-time student. Some students prefer not to take a job during their first year in college while they're making adjustments to a new academic environment. You might find that you're able to work some terms but not others, as family obligations or challenging classes can sometimes make the added burden of work impractical or impossible.

Part-time off-campus jobs that relate to your major or career plan are hard to come by. You'll likely find that most part-time employment has little or no connection to your career objectives. A better option may be to seek a job on campus. Students who work on campus develop relationships with instructors and staff members who can help them make plans for the future and negotiate the academic and social sides of campus life. While off-campus employers are often unwilling to allow their student employees time off for study and exam preparation, college employers will want you to put your studies and exam preparation first. The downside to on-campus employment is that you'll likely earn less than you would in an off-campus job, but if success in college is your top priority, the upside of working on campus outweighs the downside.

Student Loans

Although you should be careful not to borrow yourself into a lifetime of debt, avoiding loans altogether could delay your graduation and your progress up the career ladder. For most students, some level of borrowing is both necessary and prudent.

The following list provides information about the most common types of student loans. The list reflects the order in which you should apply for and accept loans to get the lowest interest rates and the best repayment terms.

- **Subsidized federal student loans** are backed by the government, which pays the loan interest on your behalf while you are enrolled in undergraduate, graduate, or professional school. These loans require at least half-time enrollment and a submitted FAFSA application.
- **Unsubsidized federal student loans** may require that you make interest payments while you are enrolled. If not, the interest is added to the amount you owe; this is called *capitalization*.
- **Parent Loan for Undergraduate Students (called PLUS loans)** are applied for and owed by parents but disbursed directly to students.

The interest on PLUS loans is usually higher than the interest on federal student loans but lower than that on private loans. Parents who apply must provide information on the FAFSA.

- **Private student loans** are offered through banks and credit unions. Private loans often have stricter credit requirements and higher interest rates than federal loans do, and interest payments on private loans begin immediately.

Student loans are a very important source of money for college, but like paid employment, loans should be considered carefully. Loans for costs such as books and tuition are good investments. Loans for a more lavish lifestyle are likely to weigh you down in the future. As one wise person put it, if by borrowing you live like a wealthy graduate while you're a student, you'll live like a student after you graduate. At some point after graduating or even leaving college before graduation, you will have to begin repaying your student loans. When you obtain a loan, be sure to check to see when you will have to begin paying it back. Student loans can be a good way to begin using credit wisely—a skill you are likely to need throughout your life.

MANAGING CREDIT WISELY

When you graduate, you will leave your institution with two significant numbers. The first is your grade point average (GPA), which represents the level of academic success you attained while in college. The second, your credit score, is a numerical representation of your fiscal responsibility. Although this second number might be less familiar to you than the first, it could be a factor that determines whether you get your dream job, regardless of your GPA. In addition, years from now you're likely to have forgotten your GPA, while your credit score will be more important than ever.

Your credit score is derived from a credit report that contains information about accounts in your name. These accounts include credit cards, student loans, utility bills, cell phones, and car loans, to name a few. This credit score can determine whether or not you will qualify for a loan (car, home, student, etc.), what interest rates you will pay, how much your car insurance will cost, and your chances of being hired by certain organizations. Even if none of these things are in your immediate future, now is the time to start thinking about your credit score.

Although using credit cards responsibly is a good way to build credit, federal law prohibits college students under the age of twenty-one from obtaining a credit card unless they can prove that they are able to make the payments, or unless the credit card application is cosigned by a parent or guardian.

Understanding Credit

Even if you can prove that you have the means to repay credit card debt, it is important for you to thoroughly understand how credit cards work and how they can both help and hurt you. Several frequently asked questions about credit cards are answered in the box later in this chapter. Simply put, a credit card allows you to buy something now and pay for it later.

techtip

TRACK YOUR BUDGET WITH DIGITAL TOOLS

Technology can really help you when it comes to keeping track of your money—knowing how much you have, how much you need, and whether there are any problems with transactions moving through your accounts.

The Problem

You want to keep track of your finances, but you don't know where to begin.

The Fix

Start with the financial institutions you already work with and see what technology tools they offer.

How to Do It

1. *Create a budget.* As you learned earlier in this chapter, a budget is a spending plan that tracks all of your sources of income and expenses during a set period of time. Working within a budget helps you meet your goals and obligations. Try creating a spreadsheet that you can easily access from your computer or phone.

2. *Check with your banking institution.* See what apps and online services they offer. Many banks offer free online access to your accounts so that you can deposit funds, make purchases, transfer funds, and receive deposit or withdrawal notifications via your cell phone or e-mail. Many banks will also send you electronic notifications of these transactions so you are always aware of how much money is currently in your account and when activity occurs that will affect your account. These services allow you to review your account information and help you make better decisions about when you use your money.

3. *Use apps and online tools to help you with your budget.* Check out some of these cool apps:

 Mint mint.com
This website and phone app allows you to combine information from all of your financial accounts in one place, so you can see how much money you have in investments, income, loans, and payments. While it is not a bank, it does allow you to see your whole financial picture at once.

 PayPal Mobile paypal.com
This app allows you to spend money online and allows other people to give you money, including money you earn from part-time jobs, gigs, or monetary gifts from friends or family members.

 PocketGuard pocketguard.com
This is a simple way to keep track of your spending compared to your budget.

Splitwise splitwise.com
This website allows you to easily split expenses with your roommates like rent, utilities, or common household items (toilet paper, furniture, etc.), and allows you to pay your share directly through apps like Venmo or PayPal.

4. *Beware of scams.* As you improve how you track your finances, remember to exercise caution in dealing with banks, credit card companies, and all financial institutions:

- Do not transmit personal information (social security number, bank details, credit or debit card numbers, passwords, etc.) through e-mail. Doing so could put you at risk of identity theft. (Read more about identity theft in the box later in this chapter.) If you need to contact a financial institution by phone, place the call yourself, and deal only with banks or other financial institutions you trust.

- Do not answer questions about vital personal information over the phone if you didn't originate the call.

- Do not reply to e-mail, pop-ups, or text messages that ask you to reveal personal information.

- Never click on links in unsolicited e-mails or paste URLs or lines of code into your browser bar.

- Do your research and use good judgment. If an offer sounds too good to be true—like a huge line of credit with 0% annual percentage rate—it probably is.

EXTRA STYLE POINTS: Keep tabs on your credit report. Regularly reviewing your credit history pays off in major ways. It alerts you to any new accounts that might have been opened in your name. It also lets you catch unauthorized activity on accounts that you've closed or haven't used lately.

Each month, you will receive a statement listing all the purchases you made using your credit card during the previous thirty days. The statement will request a payment toward your balance and will set a payment due date. Your payment options will vary: You can pay your entire balance, pay a specified amount of the balance, or pay only a minimum payment, which may be as low as $10.

But be careful: If you make only a minimum payment, the remaining balance on your card will be charged a finance fee, or interest charge, causing your balance to increase before your next bill arrives, even if you don't make any more purchases. Paying the minimum payment is almost never a good strategy and can add years to your repayment time. In fact, assuming an 18 percent interest rate, if you continually pay only $10 per month toward a $500 credit card balance, it will take you more than seven years to pay it off, and you'll pay an extra $431 in interest, almost doubling the amount you originally charged.

Avoid making late payments. Paying your bill even one day late can result in a finance charge of $30 or more; it can also raise the interest rate not only on that card, but also on any other credit accounts you have. If you decide to use a credit card to build credit, you might want to set up online, automatic payments to avoid incurring expensive late fees. Remember that the payment due date is the date that the credit card lender should receive your payment, not the date that you should send it.

If you decide to apply for a credit card while you're in college, remember that it should be used to build credit and for emergencies. Credit cards should not be used to fund a lifestyle that you cannot otherwise afford, or to buy things that you want but don't need (see the "Living on a Budget" section in this chapter). On the other hand, if you use your credit card just once a month and pay the balance as soon as the bill arrives, you will be on your way to a strong credit score in just a few years.

In Case of Emergency

Having a credit card for emergencies is a good practice. Circumstances that might warrant the use of credit include paying critical expenses to care for yourself or your family, dealing with an auto accident or an unforeseen medical expense, or traveling on short notice to handle a crisis. Remember, spring break is *not* an emergency.

Panther Media GmbH/Alamy

Frequently Asked Questions about Credit Cards and Identity Theft

- **I have a credit card with my name on it, but it is actually my parents' account number. Is this card building credit for me?** No. You are considered an authorized user on the account, but your parents are the primary account holders. To build credit, you must be the primary account holder, or at least a joint account holder.

- **I have a credit card and am the primary account holder. How can I resist abusing it?** Use your credit card to help you build credit by making small charges and paying them off in full each month. Stick to two expense categories only, such as gas and groceries, and don't make any exceptions unless you have a serious emergency.

- **I choose the "credit" option every time I use my debit card. Is this building credit for me?** No. Using the credit function of your debit card is more like writing an electronic check because you are still taking money directly out of your checking account. Even if your debit card has a major credit card (Visa, MasterCard, etc.) logo on it, it is not building credit for you.

- **I have a few store credit cards (Target, Best Buy, etc.). Are these accounts included on my credit report?** Yes. However, though they will affect your credit score, store credit cards do not carry as much weight as major credit cards such as Visa or MasterCard. It is OK to have a few store credit cards, but a major credit card will do more to help you build credit.

- **Where can I apply for a major credit card?** A good place to begin is your bank or credit union. Remember that you might have to prove your ability to make payments in order to obtain a card.

- **If one credit card will help me build credit, will several build my credit even more?** Research shows that there is no benefit to having more than two major credit cards. And even if you're able to pay the required monthly amounts, having too many accounts open can make you appear risky to the credit bureaus determining your credit score.

- **What if I forget and make a late payment? Is my credit score ruined?** Your credit report reflects at least the past seven years of activity, but it puts the most emphasis on the most recent two years. In other words, the farther you get from your mistakes, the less impact they will have on your credit score. There is no quick fix for improving a credit score, so beware of advertisements that say otherwise.

- **If building credit is a wise decision, what's so bad about using credit cards to buy some things that I really want but can't afford right now?** It is not wise to use credit cards to

Debit Cards

Although you might want to use a credit card for emergencies and to establish a good credit rating, you might also look into the possibility of applying for a debit card (also called a checkcard). The big advantage of a debit card is that you don't always have to carry cash, and thus you don't run the risk of losing your money. Because the amount of your purchases purchase things that you cannot afford. Living within your means is always the way to go.

- **What is identity theft?** In this insidious and increasingly common crime, someone assumes your identity, secretly opens up accounts in your name, and has the bills sent to another address.

- **How can I protect myself from identity theft?** *Be password savvy.* The more sensitive the information, the stronger your password should be. Aim for passwords with eight to fourteen characters, including numbers, both uppercase and lowercase letters, and, if allowed, a few special characters like @ and #. Never use an obvious number like your birthday or wedding anniversary. Don't use the same username and password for every site. Change the password to your online credit card or bank account at least once a year. If you must keep a written record of your usernames and passwords, keep the list in a secure place at home, not in your wallet. *Beware of scams.* Don't make yourself vulnerable. A few tips: Research a company or organization before submitting your résumé. Don't e-mail any personal information (social security number, bank details, credit or debit card numbers, passwords, etc.) that could put you at risk of identity theft. Don't answer questions about vital personal information over the phone if you didn't originate the call. Don't reply to e-mails, pop-ups, or text messages that ask you to reveal sensitive information. Don't send sensitive data by e-mail. Call instead, and deal only with businesses you trust. Never click on links in unsolicited e-mails or paste URLs or lines of code into your browser bar. If an offer sounds too good to be true, it probably is.

- **Where can I get my credit report?** You can keep an eye on your credit report by visiting the free (and safe) website annualcreditreport.com at least once a year. Regularly reviewing your credit history pays off in major ways. It alerts you to any new accounts that might have been opened in your name. It also lets you catch unauthorized activity on accounts that you've closed or haven't used lately. Everyone is entitled to one free credit report a year from each of the three major national credit bureaus, Transunion, Experian, and Equifax. The federal government has legislation—the Fair Credit Reporting Act (FCRA)—that regulates how these and other credit bureaus can and must operate. They're monitored by the Federal Trade Commission and the Office of the Comptroller of the Currency because they handle sensitive information on so many millions of citizens.

will be limited to the funds in your bank account, a debit card is also a good way to constrain your spending.

The only real disadvantage is that a debit card provides direct access to your checking account, so it's very important to keep your card in a safe place and away from your personal identification number (PIN). The safest way to protect your account is to commit your PIN to memory. If you lose your debit card—or your credit card—notify your bank immediately.

Protect Your Identity

Whether you have a credit or debit card, you'll need to protect yourself from identity theft. Keep your cards safe, use strong passwords, and—if you have a debit card—commit your PIN to memory. If you lose either your debit or credit card, notify your bank immediately.

PeopleImages/Getty Images

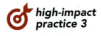 **high-impact practice 3**

your turn | **Feeling Connected**

Credit Danger

Have you or anyone you know ever been in serious credit card debt? Was the debt eventually reduced or eliminated, and if so, how? In a small group, share ways to avoid trouble with credit cards.

 high-impact practice 2

your turn | **Write and Reflect**

It's Easy to Waste Money in College

Write a "warning letter" to a younger sibling (real or imaginary) about ways that students are tempted to waste money in college and what can happen as a result. In your letter, include strategies from this chapter for carefully managing money.

PLANNING FOR THE FUTURE

It's never too early to begin thinking about how you will finance your life after graduation and whether you will begin working immediately or pursue a graduate or professional degree. Your work, whether on or off campus, will help you make that decision. Here are some tips that will help you plan now for your future:

- **Figure out your next step—more education or work?** If you are working on campus, get to know faculty or staff members and seek their advice about your future plans. If you are working off campus, think carefully about whether your current job is one that you would want to continue after you graduate. If not, keep your options open and look for part-time work in a field that more closely aligns with your career plans or long-term educational objectives.

- **Keep your address current with the registrar.** Even when you have finished your degree or program, and especially if you stop classes for a term, alert the registrar of any changes in address. This is doubly important if you have a student loan; you don't want to get a negative report on your credit rating because you missed information about your loan.

- **Establish a savings account.** Add to it regularly, even if you can manage to deposit only a few dollars a month. The sooner you start, the greater your returns will be.

Your education is the most productive investment that you can make for your future and the future of your family. Research shows that completion of programs or degrees after high school increases earnings, opens up career options, leads to greater satisfaction in work, results in more engaged citizenship such as voting and community service, and greatly increases the probability that your children will go to college. Although college is a big investment of time and money, it's an investment you'll be glad you made.

checklist for success

Money

■ **Make learning financial-literacy skills a priority.** Understanding how to manage money has life-long benefits.

■ **Create a budget and then live on it.** Remember that it's your budget, tailor-made by and for you.

■ **Act on some of the suggestions offered in this chapter for cutting your costs.** For most college students, cutting costs is even more important than increasing their income.

■ **Learn as much as you can about the different types of financial aid.** Find out what is offered to U.S. college students by the government and by your particular college, even though the term has already started. It's never too late to take advantage of these opportunities.

■ **Consider the pros and cons of working while in college.** If you do work, consider how much and where you will work. Realize that students who borrow money and attend college full time are more likely to attain their degrees than those who use a different strategy.

■ **Remember that you will finish college with two key numbers: your GPA and your credit score.** Potential employers will check both your transcript and your credit report.

■ **Learn the strategies in this chapter for wise credit card management.** College is a time to learn how to use credit wisely.

■ **Take advantage of help offered on your campus to learn financial-management skills.** You can't help it if you didn't learn these skills before; you may not have had any money to manage!

15 build your experience

REFLECT ON CHOICES

high-impact practice 2 Successful college students learn to manage their money. They are careful to manage their income and their expenditures. Write about the choices you have already made about how to spend your money? This chapter offers lots of good strategies for handling your finances. Which of them will you practice this term?

APPLY WHAT YOU'VE LEARNED

Now that you have read and discussed this chapter, consider how you can apply what you have learned to your academic life and your personal life. The following prompts will help you reflect on chapter material and its relevance to you both now and in the future.

1. Sometimes it's hard to plan for the future. Describe two ways that you can save money each week, such as using public transportation to reduce the expense of owning a car.

2. Money is a difficult subject to talk about, and sometimes it seems easier not to worry about it. Ask yourself hard questions. Do you spend money without much thought? Do you have a lot of debt? Describe your ideal financial picture.

USE YOUR RESOURCES

> **Your Institution's Financial Aid Office** Be sure to visit your institution's financial aid office to take advantage of financial aid opportunities and to learn how to apply for scholarships.

> **Special Scholarships** If you are a veteran, a student from an underrepresented group, or an adult student, your institution may have special scholarship opportunities designed for you. Check with the financial aid office for leads on special scholarship opportunities.

> **Local United Way Office** If your college or university doesn't offer credit counseling, look online or in the telephone book for credit counseling agencies within the local United Way office.

> **Campus Programs** Be on the lookout for special campus programs on money

management. These programs are often offered in residence halls or through the division of student affairs.

> **Business School or College** Faculty or staff members within a school or college of business or a division of continuing education sometimes offer a course in personal finance. Check your college catalog or website, or call the school, college, or division office to see if there are options that you can take advantage of either this term or next.

> **Counseling Center** If money problems are related to compulsive shopping or gambling, be sure to seek counseling at your institution's counseling center.

> **Budget Wizard:** cashcourse.org. The National Endowment for Financial Education (NEFE) offers this free, secure, budgeting tool.

> **Free Application for Federal Student Aid:** fafsa.ed.gov. The online form allows you to set up an account, complete the application electronically, save your work, and monitor the progress of your application.

> **FastWeb:** FastWeb.com. Register for this free scholarship-search service and discover sources of educational funding you never knew existed.

> **Bankrate:** bankrate.com. This free site provides unbiased information about the interest rates, fees, and penalties associated with major credit cards and private loans. It also provides calculators that let you determine the long-term costs of different kinds of borrowing.

> **Susan Knox,** *Financial Basics: A Money-Management Guide for Students* (Columbus: Ohio State University Press, 2004). The author blends money-management experience with her desire to inform and help students master their finances, sharing experiences about money lessons learned in college and offering sound solutions and advice for students and their families.

LaunchPad
macmillan learning

LaunchPad for *Your College Experience* is a great resource. Go online to master concepts using the LearningCurve study tool and much more. **Launchpadworks.com**

glossary

ableism   Discrimination against people who have either physical or mental disabilities.

abstract   A paragraph-length summary of the methods and major findings of an article in a scholarly journal.

academic adviser   A faculty or staff member who provides official advice to students on course selection and academic planning.

academic calendar   A calendar that shows all the important dates specific to your campus: financial aid, registration, and add/drop deadlines; midterm and final exam dates; holidays; graduation deadlines; and so forth.

academic freedom   The virtually unlimited freedom of speech and inquiry granted to professors to further the advancement of knowledge as long as human lives, rights, and privacy are not violated.

academic integrity   Intellectual honesty; the avoidance of cheating and plagiarism.

academic plan/map   A list of the courses you need to take and complete in a program of study to graduate with a degree.

academic planning   Creating a plan of coursework that leads to a college degree.

acronym   A memory device created by forming new words from the first letters of several words.

active learning   Learning by participation, such as listening critically, discussing what you are learning, and writing about it.

active reading   Participating in reading by using strategies that help you stay focused, such as highlighting and note taking. The steps in the active reading process are previewing, marking, reading with concentration, and reviewing.

adaptability   The ability to adjust your thinking and behavior when faced with new or unexpected situations.

analyze   The fourth level of Bloom's taxonomy; involves breaking information into parts and determining structure, logic, consistencies, and inconsistencies.

annotate   To add critical or explanatory margin notes (or annotations) on a page as you read.

anorexia nervosa   An eating disorder characterized by an extreme fear of gaining weight.

apply   The third level of Bloom's taxonomy; involves applying abstract, theoretical information to practical situations.

aptitude   Natural talent or an ability an individual has acquired through life experience, study, or training.

argument   Reason and evidence brought together in logical support of a claim.

assertiveness   Standing up for yourself when you need to, without being too aggressive.

attention disorder   Officially termed attention-deficit hyperactivity disorder or ADHD; characterized by an inability to be attentive or to control impulses.

attitude   The way you think and feel in relation to the events around you.

autonomy   Self-direction or independence. College students usually have more autonomy than high school students.

balance   A state in which different things occur in proper amounts.

behavioral interview   An interview in which the interviewer questions the candidate about past experiences and how they helped the candidate learn and grow. This type of interview helps assess skills and behaviors.

bias   A tendency against or in favor of certain groups or value systems.

binge eating disorder   Compulsive overeating long past the feeling of being full.

Bloom's Taxonomy   A system of classifying goals for the learning process, now used at all levels of education to define and describe the process that students use to understand and think critically about what they are learning.

budget   A spending plan that tracks all sources of income (financial aid, wages, money from parents, etc.) and expenses (rent, tuition, books, etc.) during a set period (weekly, monthly, etc.).

bulimia   An eating disorder characterized by overeating followed by self-induced vomiting or laxative use.

Campus SAVE Act   A federal law passed in 2013 mandating that all colleges and universities provide sexual assault, violence, and harassment education to students.

capstone course or project   A course or experience taken during the senior year that requires students to reflect on what they learned in all their courses and create a project of some sort that integrates and applies that knowledge (a high-impact practice).

cheating   Acting dishonestly or unfairly to gain an advantage. Different colleges define cheating in different ways. The following activities are often included in definitions of cheating: looking at the work or test of a classmate for an answer, using a calculator when it is not

347

permitted, purchasing term papers, or copying someone else's lab notes.

chunking   A previewing method that involves making a list of terms and definitions from the reading and then dividing the terms into smaller clusters of five, seven, or nine to learn the material more effectively.

citation   A source or author of certain material. When browsing the Internet for sources, use only material that has citations crediting the author, where it came from, and who posted it.

cloud computing   A term that describes using the Internet as a storage device and sharing files and folders with others.

co-curricular experience   Learning that occurs outside the classroom through on-campus clubs and groups, co-op programs, internships, or other means.

cognitive restructuring   A technique of applying positive thinking and giving oneself encouraging messages rather than self-defeating, negative ones.

collaborative assignment   A learning activity in which you work and solve problems with your classmates (a high-impact practice).

common intellectual experience   A program in which students take required "common-core" courses, participate in a required learning community, or engage in other shared experiences such as a "common reading" (a high-impact practice).

computer literacy   Facility with electronic tools, both for conducting searches and for presenting to others what you have found and analyzed.

computerized test   A test that is often taken in a computer lab or testing center and is usually not administered online.

content skills   Cognitive, intellectual, or "hard" skills acquired as one gains mastery in an academic field. They include writing proficiency, computer literacy, and foreign language skills.

co-op (cooperative) education   Academic programs in which students alternate a term of classes with a term of employment, allowing them to apply what they are learning in class to the workplace.

corequisites   Courses that must be taken in conjunction with other courses during the same term.

Cornell format   A method for organizing notes in which one side of the notebook page is designated for note taking during class, and the other serves as a "recall" column where main ideas and important details for tests are jotted down as soon as possible after class.

create   The sixth level of Bloom's Taxonomy; involves combining concepts and theories to form new, unique ideas.

credit hours   A representation of the number of clock hours you spend in each class every week during a term, and the number of credits you will earn if you satisfactorily complete a course. A one-credit course generally meets for 50 to 60 minutes once a week.

credit score   A numerical representation of your level of fiscal responsibility, derived from a credit report that contains information about all the accounts in your name. This score can determine your ability to qualify for loans, the interest rates and insurance rates you pay, and can sometimes affect your employability.

critical thinking   Thoughtful consideration of the information, ideas, observations, and arguments that you encounter; in essence, a search for truth.

cultural literacy   The ability to understand and participate in a particular culture.

culture   The aspects of a group of people that are passed on or learned. Traditions, food, language, clothing styles, artistic expression, and beliefs are all part of culture.

cyberbullying   Any behavior performed through electronic or digital media by individuals or groups who repeatedly communicate hostile or aggressive messages intended to inflict harm or discomfort on others.

database   An organized and searchable set of information. Like a special search engine, a database is often classified by a certain subject area, such as chemistry or U.S. history.

deep learning   Understanding the "why" and "how" behind the details.

degree   Official certification that students have completed a course of study in a college or university (e.g., associates, bachelor's, master's, doctoral).

delayed gratification   The ability to resist the temptation for an immediate reward and wait for a later reward.

digital footprint   How you represent yourself—and how others represent you—online on Facebook, Instagram, Twitter, and other social media sites.

digital persona/profile   The version of yourself that you present online on Facebook, Instagram, Twitter, and other social media sites.

discipline   An area of academic study, such as sociology, anthropology, or engineering.

discrimination   The act of treating people differently because of their race, ethnicity, gender, socioeconomic class, or other identifying characteristics, rather than on their merits.

diversity   Variations in social and cultural identities among people living together.

drafting   Step two of the writing process, during which a writer organizes information and ideas into sentences and paragraphs.

dyslexia A widespread developmental learning disorder that can affect the ability to read, spell, or write.

e-book A book in electronic format that can be read on a computer or other digital device.

emotional intelligence (EI) The ability to recognize, understand, use, and manage moods, feelings, and attitudes.

emotional self-awareness Knowing how and why you feel the way you do.

empathy Recognition and understanding of another person's feelings, situation, or point of view.

episodic memory An aspect of long-term memory that deals with particular events, their time, and their place.

essay exam An exam made up of questions that require students to write a few paragraphs or a short essay in response to each question.

ethnicity The identity that is assigned to a specific group of people historically connected by a common national origin or language.

evaluate The fifth level of Bloom's Taxonomy; involves making judgments and decisions about the value of new information.

evidence Facts supporting an argument.

experiential learning Learning by doing and from experience.

extrinsic motivation Motivation that comes from the hope of an external reward or the fear of an undesirable outcome or punishment.

fill-in-the-blank question A test question that consists of a phrase, sentence, or paragraph with a blank space indicating where the student should provide the missing word or words.

financial aid Monetary sources to help pay for college. Financial aid can come in the form of scholarships, grants, loans, work study, and cooperative education.

first-year seminars The course in which you find yourself now, designed to prepare you for your college experience (a high-impact practice).

fixed expense An expense that will cost you the same amount every time you pay it, such as rent.

flash cards A card with words or numbers that is displayed or reviewed as part of a study routine.

flexibility Adapting and adjusting your emotions, viewpoints, and actions as situations change.

forgetting curve The decline of memory over time.

freewriting Writing that is temporarily unencumbered by attention to mechanical processes, such as punctuation, grammar, spelling, context, and so forth.

ganas Spanish word for desire or determination.

gender The range of characteristics pertaining to masculinity and femininity.

general education Introductory courses—such as English, math, history, or psychology—that almost every student must take in order to earn a degree.

global learning or diversity experience Courses and programs in which students explore cultures, life experiences, and worldviews different from their own (a high-impact practice).

grants A form of financial aid awarded by the federal government, state governments, and institutions themselves. Students meet academic qualifications for grants by being admitted to the college and maintaining grades that are acceptable to the grant provider.

grit A combination of perseverance, passion, and resilience.

happiness Being satisfied with yourself, with others, and with your situation in general.

hate crime A crime motivated by prejudice, which occurs when a perpetrator targets a victim because of their membership (or perceived membership) in a certain group.

high-impact practice (HIP) Experiences in college that seem to make the biggest positive differences for students in terms of their learning and success. Examples include first-year seminars and writing-intensive courses.

humanities Branches of knowledge that investigate human beings, their culture, and their self-expression. They include the study of philosophy, religion, literature, music, and art.

identity theft A crime that occurs when someone uses another person's personal information.

impulse control Thinking carefully about potential consequences before acting and delaying gratification for the sake of achieving long-term goals.

inclusive curriculum A curriculum offering courses that introduce students to diverse people, worldviews, and approaches.

independence Making important decisions on your own without having to get everyone's opinion.

information age Our current times, characterized by the primary role of information in our economy and our lives, the need for information retrieval and information-management skills, and the explosion of available information.

informational interview A meeting used to gather information on a field or company and expand one's professional network.

information literacy The ability to find, interpret, and use information to meet your needs.

intellectual property Ownership over nonphysical creative works such as slogans, artwork, and inventions. Copyright, trademarks, and patents are kinds of intellectual property.

interdisciplinary Linking two or more academic fields of study, such as history and religion. Encouraging an interdisciplinary approach to teaching can offer a better understanding of modern society.

interlibrary loan A service that allows you to request an item at no charge from another library at a different college or university.

internship Direct experience in a work setting often related to your career interests.

interpersonal Relating to the interaction between yourself and other individuals. Friendships, professional networks, and family connections are interpersonal relationships that can be mutually beneficial.

intrapersonal Relating to how well you know and like yourself, as well as how effectively you can do the things you need to do to stay happy. Knowing yourself is necessary in order to understand others.

intrinsic motivation Motivation that comes from an internal desire.

keyword A term used to tell a search engine what you're looking for. Keywords are synonyms, related terms, or subtopics of your search topic.

Kolb Inventory of Learning Styles A widely used and referenced learning model that focuses on the abilities that people need to develop in order to learn; based on a four-stage cycle of learning. According to Kolb, effective learners need four kinds of abilities: concrete experience, reflective observation, abstract conceptualization, and active experimentation.

laboratory test Given in many science courses, a test that requires you to move from one lab station to the next to solve problems, identify parts of models or specimens, or explain chemical reactions.

learning community A program in which students take two or more "linked" courses with a group of other students, allowing them to work closely with each other and with instructors (a high-impact practice).

learning disability A disorder such as dyslexia that affects people's ability to either interpret what they see and hear or connect information across different areas of the brain.

learning management system (LMS) A website managed by your college or university that helps you connect with the material you're studying—as well as with your instructors and classmates.

learning objectives The main ideas or skills that students are expected to learn from a particular course, from an entire program of study, or from reading a particular article, chapter, or book.

LGBTQIA An abbreviation that describes gender identities and stands for "lesbian, gay, bisexual, transgender, queer, intersex, asexual."

list format A method for organizing notes that is most effective for taking notes on terms and definitions, facts, or sequences. This format is effective when combined with the Cornell format, with key terms in the left column and their definitions and explanations in the right column.

logical fallacy A false belief or misconception resulting from incorrect reasoning.

long-term memory The type of memory that is used to retain information and can be described in three ways: procedural, semantic, and episodic.

major An area of study such as psychology, engineering, education, or nursing, in which you can earn a degree.

mapping A previewing strategy of drawing a wheel or branching structure to show relationships between main ideas and secondary ideas. This strategy also helps you see how different concepts and terms fit together and helps you make connections between the material at hand and what you already know about the subject.

marking An active reading strategy of underlining, highlighting, or writing margin notes or annotations in your text.

matching question A test question that is set up with terms in one column and descriptions or definitions in the other. The student must match the proper term with its definition.

media literacy The ability to think critically about material distributed to a wide audience through television, film, advertising, radio, magazines, books, and the Internet.

mentor An instructor, professional staff member, or upper-level student on campus who has agreed to serve as a guide and source of support for new students.

merit scholarships Scholarships based on talent, which do not require students to demonstrate financial need. Most merit scholarships are granted by colleges and are part of the admissions and financial aid processes.

microaggression Subtle but offensive comment that reinforces stereotypes of minority populations.

mind map A review sheet with words and visual elements that jog the memory to help you recall information more easily.

mindset What you believe about yourself and about your most basic qualities, such as your personality, intelligence, or talents.

mnemonics Various methods or tricks to aid memory, including acronyms, acrostics, rhymes or songs, and visualization.

motivation The process that initiates, guides, and maintains goal-oriented behaviors; the desire to do things.

multiculturalism The active process of acknowledging, understanding, and respecting the diverse social groups, cultures, religions, races, ethnicities, attitudes, and opinions within a community.

multiple-choice question   A test question that provides a number of possible answers, often between three and five. The answer choices are usually numbered (1, 2, 3, 4, . . .) or lettered (a, b, c, d, . . .), and the test taker selects the correct or best one.

multiple intelligences   A theory developed by Howard Gardner based on the premise that the traditional notion of human intelligence is very limited. According to Gardner, all human beings have at least eight different types of intelligence, including verbal/linguistic, logical/mathematical, visual/spatial, bodily/kinesthetic, musical/rhythmic, interpersonal, intrapersonal, and naturalistic.

multitasking   Doing more than one thing at a time, requiring that you divide your time and attention among tasks.

Myers-Briggs Type Indicator (MBTI)   One of the best-known and most widely used personality inventories that is also used to describe learning preferences. It examines basic personality characteristics and how those relate to human interaction and learning.

need-based scholarship   A scholarship based on both talent and financial need.

nontraditional student   Someone who is not an eighteen-year-old recent high school graduate and may have a family and a job.

office hours   The posted hours when instructors are in their office and available to students.

open-book or open-note test   A test during which students are permitted to refer to their book or notes.

optimism   Looking for the "bright side" of any problem or difficulty and being confident that things will work out for the best.

outline format   A method for organizing notes that uses Roman numerals to represent key ideas and then transitions to using uppercase letters, then Arabic numbers, and then lowercase letters to represent other ideas relating to each key idea.

paragraph format   A method for organizing notes that consists of writing summary paragraphs on what you are reading or hearing.

peer leader   An upper-level student with a record of academic success, knowledge, experience, and willingness to help new students, who serves as a coteacher, informal adviser, mentor, and friend in a college success course.

peer review   A process by which experts in a field read and evaluate the articles in a journal before they are published.

periodical   A resource that is published multiple times a year, such as a magazine.

plagiarism   The act of taking another person's idea or work and presenting it as your own. This gross academic misconduct can result in suspension or expulsion, and even the revocation of the violator's college degree.

prejudice   A preconceived judgment or opinion of someone that is not based on facts or knowledge, such as prejudging someone based entirely on their skin color.

prerequisites   The basic core courses students need to take before they can enroll in upper-level classes in their major.

previewing   Taking a first look at your assigned reading before you really tackle the content.

prewriting   The first stage of the writing process, during which you write things down as they come to mind—based on both the information you found through your research and your own ideas—without consciously trying to organize your thoughts, find exactly the right words, or think about structure.

primary sources   The original research or documentation on a topic, usually referenced either at the end of a chapter or at the back of a book.

problem solving   Approaching challenges step by step and not giving up in the face of obstacles.

procedural memory   An aspect of long-term memory that refers to knowing how to do something, such as solving a mathematical problem or playing a musical instrument.

procrastination   The habit of delaying something that needs your immediate attention.

punctuality   Being on time.

race   A term that refers to biological characteristics shared by groups of people, including skin tone, hair texture and color, and facial features.

reality testing   Ensuring that your feelings are appropriate by checking against external, objective criteria.

religion   A specific set of beliefs and practices generally agreed on by a number of persons or sects.

remember   The first level of Bloom's taxonomy; involves being able to recall ideas and information.

research   A process of steps used to collect and analyze information to increase understanding of a topic or issue. Those steps include asking questions, collecting and analyzing data related to those questions, and presenting one or more answers.

resilience   The ability to adapt to and bounce back from life's hardships and difficulties.

returning student   A student returning to formal education after being out of the educational system for some period of time.

reviewing   The final step in active textbook reading. Reviewing involves looking through your assigned reading again.

review sheet   A list of key terms and ideas developed from your notes. It is valuable as a study aid.

revision   The third and final stage of the writing process, which involves polishing your work until it clearly explains what you want to communicate and is ready for your audience.

scholarly articles   Articles written by experts in their fields, such as researchers, librarians, or professors, and then assessed and edited by other experts in a process called peer review.

scholarly journals   Published collections of original, peer-reviewed research articles written by experts or researchers in a particular academic discipline.

self-actualization   Being satisfied and comfortable with what you have achieved in school, work, and your personal life.

semantic memory   An aspect of long-term memory that involves remembering facts and meanings without regard to where and when you learned those things.

service-learning   Unpaid volunteer service that is embedded in courses across the curriculum (a high-impact practice).

sex   One's biological makeup; typically categorized as male or female but includes individuals who identify as nonbinary, transgender, or intersex.

sexual assault   Any type of sexual contact or behavior that occurs without the explicit consent of the recipient.

sexual harassment   Any kind of unwanted sexual advances or remarks.

short-term memory   How many items you are able to perceive at one time. Memory that disappears in less than 30 seconds (sometimes faster) unless the items are moved to long-term memory.

sisu   A term from Finnish culture that means going beyond one's mental or physical ability, taking action even when things are difficult, and displaying courage and determination in the face of challenge and repeated failures.

social capital   The value of social networks (who people know) and the tendencies that arise for people in these networks to do things for each other.

social responsibility   The establishment of a personal link with a group or community and cooperation with other members toward shared goals.

social sciences   Academic disciplines that examine human aspects of the world, such as sociology, psychology, anthropology, economics, political science, and history.

spirituality   A broad term that includes not only religion but also an exploration of questions about life's meaning and ultimate values.

stacks   The areas in libraries containing shelves that are full of books available for checkout.

stereotype   A generalization—usually exaggerated or oversimplified, and often offensive—that is used to describe or distinguish a group.

stress tolerance   Recognizing the causes of stress and responding in appropriate ways; staying strong under pressure.

student loan   A form of financial aid that must be paid back with interest.

summary   A section at the end of a textbook chapter that sums up a larger section of material and highlights the most important ideas.

Supplemental Instruction (SI)   Scheduled sessions that provide further opportunity to discuss the information presented in classes.

syllabus   A formal statement of course requirements and procedures or a course outline that an instructor provides to all students on the first day of class.

take-home test   Tests taken outside class, for which students can refer to their textbook, notes, and other resources.

thesis statement   A short statement that clearly defines the purpose of a paper.

thriving   Achieving your highest possible level of performance, satisfaction, and self-esteem.

transcript   Your official academic record; it shows your major, when you took particular courses, your grades for each course, and your overall GPA.

transferable skills   General skills that apply to or transfer to a variety of settings. Examples include solid oral and listening abilities, leadership skills, critical-thinking skills, and problem-solving skills.

true/false question   A test question that asks students to determine whether a statement is correct or incorrect.

undergraduate research   A program that gives you the opportunity to participate in systematic investigation and research working one-on-one with a faculty member.

understand   The second level of Bloom's taxonomy; involves being able to restate in your own words what the ideas mean.

values   Those things you feel most strongly about that are formed through your life experiences.

variable expense   An expense that may change over time.

VARK inventory   A sixteen-item questionnaire that focuses on how learners prefer to use their senses (seeing, hearing, reading and writing, or experiencing) to learn. The acronym VARK stands for the four different types of learners: "Visual," "Aural," "Read/Write," and "Kinesthetic."

visualization   A memory technique used to associate words, concepts, or stories with visual images.

wellness   A catchall term for taking care of your mind, body, and spirit that includes keeping fit, making healthy choices, achieving balance, and reducing stress in positive ways.

work-study award   A form of federal financial aid that covers a portion of college costs in return for on-campus employment.

writing-intensive courses   Courses across the curriculum that engage students in multiple forms of writing for different audiences. This textbook offers various writing activities that make your first-year seminar a writing-intensive course (a high-impact practice).

index

disciplines, 133
discrimination
   biases, 292–295
   hate crimes, 296
   overcoming, 296–299
   in pyramid of hate, 294f
discuss, in essay question, 196
Disney, Walt, 38
distractions, 62–63, 178
divergers, 84–85
diversity
   age, 290
   and Bloom's taxonomy, 115
   college curriculum, 299–300
   culture, ethnicity, race, and religion, 288–289
   defined, 287
   economic status, 291
   experiences as high-impact practice, 24
   exploring, 287–295
   fighting hate on campus, 297
   gender and sex, 290–291
   learning challenges, 291–292
   microaggressions, 293
   office of diversity as resource, 306
   physical challenges, 291
   raising awareness, 297
   resources for, 306
   seeking in college, 299–302
   special-interest groups, 302
   stereotyping, 292–295
   in the workplace, 302–303
diversity center, 28
Diversityedu.com, 306
drafting, 224–225
drafts, of online communications, 279
Dropbox, 172
drug abuse, 45, 310
Duckworth, Angela, 36
dyslexia, 94, 95

E

earning potential, 14–15
Ebbinghaus, Hermann, 169
Ebbinghaus forgetting curve, 160, 170
e-cigarettes, 322
Economic Policy Institute, 14
economic status, 291
economy
   characteristics of current, 239–242
   constant change in labor market expectations, 242
   disruptive, 241
   global, 240
   innovation, demand for, 241
   pace of economic activity, 240
   social media and networking, 242
EI. *See* emotional intelligence
e-journals, 218
electronic books, 139, 219
electronic calendar, 53, 55, 59, 95
electronic devices, 128
e-mail, 26
emergency contraceptive pills, 276
emotional health, 310, 317–320
emotional intelligence (EI), 317–318
   counseling to improve, 45
   defined, 39
   in everyday life, 40–42
   identifying skills and competencies, 43, 44
   improving, 42–43
   managing priorities, 42
   questionnaire, 42
   research on, 44–45
   tests, scores, 44
emotional self-awareness, 43

emotions
   anger management, 40, 41
   naming and labeling, 41
   perceiving and managing, 40
   preparing emotionally for tests, 190
   self-awareness, 43
   skills and competencies, 43
   success and well-being, 44–45
empathy, 43
employers
   marketing yourself to, 257–260
   skills and qualities important to, 252
encyclopedias, 214
energy level, 63–65
English as a second language (ESL), 10
   diversity in college, 293
   and reading textbooks, 140, 142
enterprising category, 253f, 254t
episodic memory, 170
eportfolios, 25
Equifax, 343
essay questions, 195–196
ethnicity, 288–289
evaluate, in essay question, 196
Evernote, 158
evidence, examining, 111–112
exam plan, 186
Excel, 158
exercise
   physically preparing for exams, 189
   and wellness, 310, 315–316
Experian, 343
experiential learning opportunities, 257
explain, in essay question, 196
expressive language disorder, 96
extraversion (E) vs. introversion (I) preference, 86–87
extraverts, 87
extrinsic motivation, 32
Eyes on the Prize video series, 299

F

Facebook
   awareness and being proactive, 46
   communicating, 277
   groups for students with learning disabilities, 98
faculty members, 11
   resource for career planning, 262
   services offered by administrators, advisers and staff members, 12–13
"fad" diets, 313
Fair Credit Reporting Act (FCRA), 343
faith communities, on campus, 289
false authorities, appealing to, 113
family relationships, 268–271
fast thinking, 102, 105–106
FastWeb, 346
faulty reasoning, 112–113
feedback, 232
feeling (F) vs. thinking (T) preference, 87
feeling types, personality characteristics, 87
fill-in-the-blank questions, 198
filter bubble, Internet, 304
financial aid
   adviser, 10
   criteria based, 337
   Free Application for Federal Student Aid, 335–336
   keeping your funding, 337
   navigating, 334–335
   part-time students, 10
   qualifying for, 335–336
   and scholarship offices, 28, 346
   for studying abroad, 24
   types of, 333–334
   understanding, 333–337
   working vs. loans, 337–340

Financial Basics: A Money-Management Guide for Students (Knox), 346
first-generation students, 9
first-year seminar, 7
   as a high-impact practice, 24
   resources for learning support services, 98
fixed expense, 331
fixed mindset, 34–36
flash cards
   mobile applications, 174
   previewing strategy, 125
   tool to improve memory, 174
flexibility, 43, 57
Flickr, 242
Florida Atlantic University, 208
focus, 67–68
FocusON, 59
foreword, 133
forgetting curve, 160, 170
four-stage cycle of learning, 84–85
fraternities, 281
Free Application for Federal Student Aid (FAFSA), 335–336, 339, 346
freewriting, 224
friendships, 303

G

gambling, 346
Gardasil, 275
Gardner, Howard, 88–91
gender, 290–291
generalizations, hasty, 113
genital warts, 275
genocide, 294f
global economy, 240
global learning, 24
glossary, 131, 135
Go Ask Alice website, 326
goals
   making choices to achieve, 22
   motivation and, 33
   personal strengths, 19
   reexamining, 206
   resilience and, 37
   setting, 17, 18–20
   short-term vs. long term, 19–20
   SMART, 20–21
   strategies to achieve goals, 37
   time management and study time, 56
Golden Rule, 294
Google, 158, 213–214, 218
Google Drive, 172
Google Scholar, 219
government websites, 218
grades
   downsides of choosing easy courses, 246
   overcoming a poor grade, 204
graduate school
   and grades, 246
   preparing for, 15
grants, 333
gratification, delayed, 44
Greek organizations, 281
grit, 36
growth mindset, 34–36
guided pathways, 22–23

H

Hamilton, 107
hands-on learning method, 83, 92
happiness, 43
hate, pyramid of, 294f
hate crimes
   defined, 296
   fighting, 297

positive prediction of success, 6
purposeful students, 19
reading and employment goals, 121
researching college student success, 213
sexually transmitted infections and campus
    resources, 275
sexually transmitted infections (STIs), 275
sleep scheduling, 63
student learning styles vs. faculty learning styles, 83
study skills required for college, 167
success rate of students who seek assistance, 180
supplemental instruction (SI) activities, 157, 186
supportive learning styles, 77, 78
time spent on reading assignments, 132–133
time-management strategies, 57
working on campus vs. off campus, 257
writing skills, 223
review sheets, 174
reviewing
    drafts, 176
    test preparation, 186
    textbook reading, 129–130
revising, 226
rhymes/songs, 177
risks, 243
risky behaviors, 45
Rolling Stone, 219
romantic relationships, 273–274
roommates, 272
Rose, Reginald, 118
routine, 64–65
Rowling, J. K., 38
rumors, 266

S

safe sex, 274–275
scantron answer sheet, 192
Schlossberg, Nancy, 78
scholarly articles, 215, 216–219
scholarly journals, 216–219
scholarship, 334
scholarship offices, 28
science
    exams, preparing for, 188
    taking notes in class, 157, 159
    textbooks, 135–137
searches, effective, 218
self-actualization, 43
self-awareness, 43
self-discovery, 37
self-motivation, 266
self-regard, 43
self-talk, 190
semantic memory, 170
sensing (S) vs. intuition (N) preference, 87
sensing types, personality characteristics, 87
service learning
    gaining professional experience, 257
    as high-impact practice, 24
sex
    diversity, 290–291
    safe, 274–275
sexual assault, 276–277
Sexual Assault and Relationship Violence Activists, 301
sexual assault and violence, 276–277
sexual health, 274–277
    communicating about, 274–275
    safe sex, 274–275
    sexual assault and violence, protecting yourself
        from, 276–277
    sexually transmitted infections (STIs), 274–275
    using birth control, 276
    wellness, 310
sexual orientation, 290–291
sexually transmitted infections (STIs), 274, 275

short-term goals, 19–20
short-term memory, 169–170
sisu, 36–37
skills, career, 250–253
sleep
    mobile devices and, 324
    physically preparing for exams, 188–189
    and wellness, 310, 316–317
slippery slope, 113
slow thinking, 102, 105–106
SMART goals, 20–21
SnapChat
    being proactive and aware, 46
    communicating, 277
social capital, 242, 248
social category, 253f, 254t
social learning, theory of, 77
social media
    communicating, 277–280
    healthy use of, 282
    old accounts, 46
    outlets of, 242
    professionally structured, 248
    resource for learning support services, 98
    value of social capital, 242
social rejection, 41
social responsibility, 43
social sciences textbooks, 137–138
social smoking, 322
songs, 177
sororities, 281
sources
    authority of, 221
    bias, 221–222
    books, 215
    citation, 227
    in college libraries, 215–219
    common research sources, 215
    evaluating, 220–222
    newspapers, 215
    online databases, 217
    paraphrasing and citation, 218
    periodicals, 219
    questions to help evaluate, 222
    relevance of, 220
    scholarly articles and journals, 215, 216–219
    Wikipedia, 214
Southern Poverty Law Center, 306
speaking
    clarifying your objective, 229
    guidelines for successful speaking, 229–232
    practice your delivery, 231
    prepare your notes, 231
    request feedback, 232
    understanding your audience, 230
    word choice and pronunciation, 232
special-interest groups, 302
Speechnotes, 158
spirituality, 317
Splitwise, 341
stacks
    defined, 215
    library books, 219
standardized tests, 200
Stanford University, 297
State University of New York, 208
Steel, Piers, 58
Steele, Claude, 200
stereotypes
    test anxiety and stereotype threat, 200
    used as mascots, 297
stereotyping, 292
STIs (sexually transmitted infections), 274–275
Stopbullying.gov, 279
stress management
    and caffeine, 313

to maintain wellness, 310, 311–312
    reducing daily stress to improve academic
        performance, 179
    risky coping mechanisms, 45
    test anxiety, 199–204
stress management skills, 43, 44
stress tolerance, 43, 44
student activity
    career interest groups, 302
    Greek organizations, 281
    major affiliated clubs, 302
    organizations that encourage diversity, 302–303
    professional organizations, 262
    special-interest groups, 302
    student organizations, 284
student affairs, 28
student competitions, 257
"Student Counseling Virtual Pamphlet Collection," 284
student loans, 339, 339–340
student organizations, professional, 262
student-run organizations, 300–301
students. *See also* peer leaders
    commuter, 74
    diversity among, 115, 287–306
    first-generation, 9
    importance of relationships with, 8–11
    international, 9–10
    nontraditional, 8
    online learners, 10
    part-time, 10
    traditional, 8
    veterans, 8–9, 28, 262
study abroad, 24
    motivation and benefits of, 32
    multiculturalism, experiencing, 300
    professional experience, 257
study groups
    falling behind in assigned reading, 133
    group collaboration, 180
    for online tests, 194
    preparing for tests, 187
study strategies
    for aural learners, 83
    collaboration with study groups, 180
    explain material to others, 178
    flashcards, 174
    kinesthetic learners, 83
    learning management systems, 92
    by learning style, 83
    mind maps, 174
    mnemonics, 176–177
    organization, 179
    overlearn material, 178
    quiet, 127–128
    for read/write learners, 83
    review sheets, 174
    setting goals for study period, 128
    short, physical breaks, 128
    stress reduction, 179
    test preparation, 185–190
    with tutor, 179
    using an organizer while reading textbooks,
        128–129
    VARK results to improve, 83t
    for visual learners, 83
    writing summaries, 175–176
StudyBlue, flash card app, 158, 174
studying
    avoid distractions, 178
    collaboration, groups, 180
    college vs. high school, 166–167
    comprehending and remembering, 167
    concentration, 168–169
    memorizing words vs. understanding concepts, 170,
        178–179
    overlearn material, 178